CRITICAL DOCUMENTS OF JEWISH HISTORY

CRITICAL
DOCUMENTS OF
JEWISH HISTORY

A Sourcebook

edited by
Ronald H. Isaacs and Kerry M. Olitzky

JASON ARONSON INC.
Northvale, New Jersey
London

The editors gratefully acknowledge permission from the following sources to reprint documents included in this volume:

American Jewish Archives; Central Conference of American Rabbis; Consulate General of Israel in New York, Information Department; the Rabbinical Assembly of America; and The Jewish Theological Seminary of America.

"Some Comments on Centrist Orthodoxy" by Norman Lamm. Coypright © 1986 Rabbinical Council of America. Published in *Tradition* 22:3 (Fall 1986). Used by permission of Norman Lamm and *Tradition* magazine.

"A New Era in Jewish History" by Irving (Yitz) Greenberg. Copyright © 1980 National Center for Jewish Learning and Leadership (CLAL). Used by permission of the author.

This book was set in 11 pt. Electra by Alpha Graphics in Pittsfield, New Hampshire, and printed by Haddon Craftsmen in Scranton, Pennsylvania.

Library of Congress Cataloging-in-Publication Data
Critical documents of Jewish history: a sourcebook / edited by Ronald H. Isaacs and Kerry
    M. Olitzky.
        p. cm.
    Includes index.
    ISBN 1-56821-392-1
        1. Judaism—United States—History—Sources.   2. Jews—History—
    Sources.   3. Israel—History—Sources.   I. Isaacs, Ronald H.
    II. Olitzky, Kerry M.
    BM205.C75   1995   94-44933
    296'.0973—dc20

Manufactured in the United States of America. Jason Aronson Inc. offers books and cassettes. For information and catalog write to Jason Aronson Inc., 230 Livingston Street, Northvale, New Jersey 07647.

Contents

Introduction

The selections included in this volume are not by any means intended to be exhaustive. There is plenty of other material that could almost as easily have found its way into this collection. Even before we started the project, we recognized the risk that there would be critics eager to criticize our efforts and disgree with our selections. Nevertheless, we chose the documents in this volume over hundreds of other possible selections because we believe that these documents in particular (and the people who felt their impact) helped to shape the development of Jewish history as we know it. As a result, in one way or another, they are formative with respect both to the Jewish community in which we live and to our lives as active participants in it. In order to evaluate who we are, where we came from, and where we want to go, individually and collectively, we have to be able to access the sources of our development. As educators, we believe it is crucial for students of all ages to be able to read source documents—as much as we want them to be able to read sacred texts—so that they can draw their own conclusions from them. Unfortunately, due to the length of some of the documents—and our desire to place this material in one publication of manageable length—we were forced to abbreviate slightly in certain places.

While some may recognize many of these documents and the ideas they represent, they may not have ever had the opportunity to read and study them. Needless to say, for many, finding them is often a task in itself. As students of a rich historical tradition, we have learned that there is nothing comparable to the experience of reading the words as they were written. Although, in the interests of the whole, some very long documents have been slightly abbreviated, for the most part, the selections have been reproduced in full. Included are documents that chronicle the history of the Jewish people. Feeling that it was important to understand the Judaism of our neighbors as fully as possible, we have incorporated documents that we believe are foundational to the four major Jewish movements in North America. The third major category of documents refers to Israel, with regard to which we too often rely on

the interpretation of others—even as we try to understand the variety of attitudes in the press and among politicians. Thus, it is our hope that the documents regarding Israel will provide the reader with readily accessible material from which to form his or her own opinion about our homeland.

Every word in this book—from the dismal documents dripping with the
spilled blood of our people in the Holocaust to the incredible pride and passion expressed in every brave word written in the Declaration of Independence of the State of Israel—is part of our legacy as Jews. As the editors of
this collection, our goal is simple: to help you claim what you already own.

I

AMERICAN JEWISH HISTORY

In 1654, twenty-three refugee Jews arrived in Dutch New Amsterdam from Recife, Brazil, just conquered by the Portuguese. Seeking freedom, they began what has been deemed the greatest period of Jewish civilization in the history of Judaism. The journey in America was not easy. Somehow we survived and triumphed. The many waves of immigration that eventually followed this modest beginning contributed to the building of a diversified—and later indigenous—community replete with its own autonomous organizations, movements, and institutions. As a result, while we have occcasionally come together in various times for various reasons, there is no one unified voice that speaks for the American Jewish community. Today, the American Jewish population numbers over six million. From shore to shore, Jews have made their way to America's small towns and large urban centers, making their impact felt in every walk of American life. This section presents significant documents that helped to shape the course of Jewish history in North America.

1

Washington's Letter to the Hebrew Congregation in Newport, Rhode Island 1790

Because it is one of the earliest examples of an official communication between the new United States government and the young Jewish community in a new country, this famous letter from President George Washington to the Jewish settlement in Newport, Rhode Island, is very significant and provides us with a great source of pride.

TO THE HEBREW CONGREGATION IN NEWPORT, RHODE ISLAND

August 21, 1790

Gentlemen:

The reflection on the days of difficulty and danger which are passed is rendered the more sweet from a consciousness that they are succeeded by days of uncommon prosperity and security. If we have wisdom to make the best use of the advantages with which we are now favored, we cannot fail, under the just administration of a good Government, to become a great and happy people.

The Citizens of the United States of America have a right to applaud themselves for having given to Mankind examples of an enlarged and liberal policy: a policy worthy of imitation. All possess alike the liberty of conscience and immunities of citizenship. It is now no more that toleration is spoken of, as if it was by the indulgence of one class of people, that another enjoyed the exercise of their inherent natural rights. For happily the government of the United States, which gives to bigotry no sanction, to persecution no assistance, requires only that they who live under its protection, should demean themselves as good citizens, in giving it on all occasions their effectual support.

It would be inconsistent with the frankness of my character not to avow that I am pleased with your favorable opinion of my administration, and your fervent wishes for my felicity. May you—the Children of the Stock of Abraham, who dwell in this land, continue to merit and enjoy the good-will of the other Inhabitants; while every one shall sit in safety under his own vine and fig-tree, and there shall be none to make them afraid. May the Father of all mercies scatter light and not darkness in our paths, and make us all in our several vocations useful here, and, in His own due time and way, everlastingly happy.

Your servant,
G. Washington

2

Maryland's "Jew Bill" 1818

During the years from 1797 to 1826, one of the fiercest battles for the equality of Jews in the United States took place in Maryland. This bill, which came to be called the "Jew Bill," was introduced in 1818. It was intended to alter the state constitution in order to stop the practice of requiring a religious test of all those holding civil office and in order that a Jewish person might take the oath of office "on the five books of Moses."

AN ACT To extend to the sect of people professing the Jewish religion, the same rights and privileges that are enjoyed by Christians.
WHEREAS, it is the acknowledged right of all men to worship God according to the dictates of their own conscience. And whereas, it is declared by the 36th Section of the bill of rights of this state, "That the manner of administering an oath to any person ought to be such as those of the religious persuasion, profession, or denomination of which such person is one, generally esteem the most effectual confirmation by the attestation of the divine Being." And whereas, religious tests for civil employment, though intended as a barrier against the depraved, frequently operate as a restraint upon the conscientious, and as a qualification for civil office, therefore,

Sec. 1. Be it enacted, By the General Assembly of Maryland, that no religious test, declaration or subscription of opinion as to religion, shall be required from any person of the sect called Jews, as a qualification to hold or exercise any office or employment of profit or trust in this state.

Sec. 2. And be it enacted, That every oath to be administered to any person of the sect called Jews, shall be administered on the five books of Moses, agreeably to the religious education of that people, and not otherwise.

Sec. 3. And be it enacted, That if this act shall be confirmed by the General Assembly, after the next election, of delegates, in the first session after such new election, as the constitution and form of government direct; that in such case this act and the alteration and amendments of the constitution and form of government therein contained, shall be taken and considered, and shall constitute and be valid as part of said constitution and form of government, to all intents and purposes, any thing in the declaration of rights, constitution, and form of government contained, to the contrary notwithstanding.

Sec. 4. And be it enacted, That the several clauses and sections of the declaration of rights, constitution and form of government, and every part of any law of this state, contrary to the provisions of this act, so far as respects the sect of people aforesaid, shall be, and the same is hereby declared to be repealed and annulled on the confirmation hereof.

3

Judah Touro's Will
1854

Judah Touro (1775–1854) is one of the best-known names in American Jewish philanthropy. Often we don't think of a will as a significant document. Yet Judah Touro's philanthropy helped stabilize an incipient Jewish community. While he bequeathed his funds to numerous institutions, this will established the foundation for building numerous early American synagogues.

Judah Touro
United States of America
State of Louisiana, City of New Orleans

Be it Known that on this Sixth day of January in the year of our Lord One Thousand, Eight Hundred and Fifty Four, and of the Independence of the United States of America the Seventy Eighth at a quarter before Ten O'Clock A.M.

Before me, Thomas Layton, a notary Public, in and for the city of New Orleans, aforesaid duly commissioned and sworn, and in Presence of Messieurs, Jonathan Montgomery, Henry Sheperd Jr. and George Washington Lee competent witnesses residing in said city ad hereto expressly required.

Personally appeared Mr Judah Touro of this City, Merchant, whom I the said Notary and said witnesses found setting in a room at his residence No 128, Canal Street, Sick of body, but sound of mind, memory and Judgment as did appear to me, the said Notary and to said witnesses. And the said Judah Touro requested me, the notary to receive his last will or Testament, which he dictated to me, Notary, as follows, to wit & in presence of said witnesses.

1st I declare that I have no forced heirs.

2nd I desire that my mortal remains be buried in the Jewish cemetery in New Port Rhode Island, as soon as practicable after my decease.

3rd I nominate and appoint my trusty and esteemed friends Rezin Davis Sheperd of Virginia, Aaron Keppel Josephs of New Orleans, Gershom Kursheedt of New Orleans, and Pierre Andre Destrac Cazenave of New Orleans, my Testamentary Executors and the detainers of my Estate, making, however, the following distinction between my said Executors, to wit: to the said Aaron Keppel Josephs, Gershom Kursheedt and Pierre Andre Destrac Cazenave, I give and bequeath to each one separately the sum of Ten Thousand dollars, which those esteemed friends, but also as in consideration of all Services they may have hitherto rendered me, and in lieu of the commissions to which they would be entitled hereafter in the capacity of Testamentary Executors, say my dear old and devoted friend the said Rezin Davis Sheperd, after the payment of my particular legacies and the debts of my succession, the Universal Legatee of the rest and residue of my estate, moveable, and immoveable.

In case of the death, absence, or inhability [sic] to act of one or more of my said Executors, I hereby empower the remaining Executor or Executors to act in carrying out the provisions of this my last Will; and in the event or default of any one or more of my said Executors before my own demise, then and in that case, it is my intention that the heirs or legal representatives of those who may depart this life before my own death, Shall inherit in their Stead the legacies hereinabove respectively made to them.

4th I desire that all leases of my property and which may be in force at the time of my demise, Shall be faithfully executed until the Same Shall have expired.

5th I desire that all the Estate Real, Personal and mixed, of which I may die possessed, Shall be disposed of in the manner directed by this my last will or Testament.

6th I give and bequeath to the Hebrew Congregation the "Dispersed of Judah" of the City of New Orleans, all that certain property situated in Bourbon Street immediately adjoining their Synagogue, being the present School house and the residence of said Mr Gershom Kursheedt, the same purchased by me from the Bank of Louisiana; and also to the said Hebrew Congregation, the Two adjoining brick Houses purchased from the Heirs of David Urquhart, the revenue of said property to be applied to the founding and support of the Hebrew School connected, with Said congregation, as well to the defraying of the Salary of their Reader or Minister, Said Property to be conveyed accordingly by my said Executors to said congregation, with all necessary restrictions.

7th I give and bequeath to found the "Hebrew Hospital of New Orleans" The entire property purchased for me, at the succession sale of the late

C. Paulding upon which the Building now Known as the "Touro Infirmary" is situated: The said contemplated Hospital to be organized according to law, as a charitable Institution for the relief of the Indigent Sick, by my Executors and such other persons as they may associate with them conformably with the laws of Louisiana.

8th I give and bequeath to the Hebrew Benevolent Association of New Orleans Five Thousand Dollars.

9th I give and bequeath to the Hebrew Congregation "Shangarar Chased" of New Orleans Five Thousand Dollars.

10th I give and bequeath to the Ladies Benevolent Society of New Orleans, the Sum of Five Thousand Dollars.

11th I give and bequeath to the Hebrew Foreign Mission Society of New Orleans, Five Thousand Dollars.

12th I give and bequeath to the Orphans Homes asylum of New Orleans, the sum of Five Thousand Dollars.

13th I give and bequeath to the Society for relief of Destitute Orphan Boys in the Fourth District, Five Thousand Dollars.

14th I give and bequeath to the St Anna's Asylum for the relief of destitute females and children, the sum of Five Thousand Dollars.

15th I give and bequeath to the New Orleans Female Orphan asylum at the corner of Camp & Prytania Streets, Five Thousand Dollars.

16th I give and bequeath to the St Mary's Catholic Boys Asylum of which my old and esteemed friend Mr Anthony Rasch is chairman of its Executive Committee, the sum of Five Thousand Dollars.

17th I give and bequeath to the Milne Asylum of New Orleans, Five Thousand Dollars.

18th I give and bequeath to the Fireman's charitable Association of New Orleans, Four Thousand Dollars.

19th I give and bequeath to the Seaman's Home in the First District of New Orleans Five Thousand Dollars.

20th I give and bequeath for the purpose of establishing an Alms House, in the City of New Orleans, and with the view of contributing as far as possible for the prevention of mendicity in said city, the sum of Eighty Thousand Dollars (say $80,000); and I desire that The Alms House, thus contemplated, shall be organized according to law; and further it is my desire that after my Executors Shall have legally appointed proper persons to administer and control the direction of its affairs, then such persons legally so appointed and their successors in office, conjointly with the Mayor of the City of New Orleans and his successors in office shall have the perpetual direction and control thereof.

21st I give and bequeath to the City of New Port in the State of Rhode Island, the Sum of Ten Thousand Dollars, on condition that the said sum be expended in the purchase and improvement of the property in Said City, Known as the "Old Stone Mill" to be Kept as a public Park or Promenade ground.

22d I give and bequeath to the Red Wood library of New Port aforesaid, for Books & Repairs Three Thousand Dollars.

23. I give and bequeath to the Hebrew Congregation Oharbay Shalome of Boston Massachusetts Five Thousand Dollars.

24. I give and bequeath to the Hebrew Congregation of Hartford Connecticut Five Thousand Dollars.

25. I give and bequeath to the Hebrew Congregation of New Haven Connecticut Five Thousand Dollars.

26. I give and bequeath to the North American Relief Society for the Indigent Jews of Jerusalem Palestine of the City and State of New York (Sir Moses Montefiore of London, their agent) Ten Thousand Dollars, Say ($10,000).

27. It being my earnest wish to co-operate with the said Sir Moses Montefiore of London, Great Britain, in endevouring [sic] to ameliorate the condition of our unfortunate Jewish brethern [sic] in the Holy Land, and to secure to them the inestimable privilege of worshipping the Almighty according to our Religion, without molestation, I therefore give and bequeath the sum of Fifty Thousand Dollars to be paid by my Executors for said object through the said Sir Moses Montefiore, in such manner as he may advise as best calculated to promote the aforesaid objects, and in case of any legal or other difficulty or impediment in the way of carrying said bequest into effect, according to my intentions, then and in that case, I desire that the said sum of Fifty Thousand Dollars be invested by my Executors in the foundation of a Society in the City of New Orleans Similar in its object to the North American Relief Society for the Indigent Jews of Jerusalem, Palestine, of the City of New York, to which I have referred in this my last Will.

28. It is my wish and desire that the Institutions to which I have already alluded in making this Will, as well as those to which in the further course of making this Will, I shall refer, Shall not be disqualified from inheriting my legacies to them respectively made for reason of not being Incorporated & thereby qualified to inherit by law, but on the contrary, I desire that the parties interested in such Institutions and my Executors Shall facilitate their Organization as soon after my decease as possible, & thus render them duly qualified by law to inherit in the premises according to my wishes.

29. I give and bequeath to the Jews Hospital Society of the City and State of New York Twenty Thousand Dollars.

30. I give and bequeath to the Hebrew Benevolent Society Mashebat Nafesh of New York, Five Thousand dollars.

31. I give and bequeath to the Hebrew Benevolent Society Gimelet Chased of New York Five Thousand Dollars.

32. I give and bequeath to the Talmueh [sic] Torah School fund attached to the Hebrew Congregation Sheareth Israel of the City of New York and to said Congregation Thirteen Thousand Dollars.

33. I give and bequeath to the Educational Institute of the Hebrew Congregation Briai Jeshurum [sic] of the City of New York the sum of Three Thousand Dollars.

34. I give and bequeath to the Hebrew Congregation Shangarai Tefila of New York, Three Thousand Dollars.

35. I give and bequeath to the Ladies Benevolent Society of the City of New York, the same of which Mrs Richey Levy was a directress at the time of her death, and of which Mistress I. B. Kursheedt was first Directress in 1850, Three Thousand Dollars.

36. I give and bequeath to the Female Hebrew Benevolent [Society] of Philadelphia (Miss Gratz Secretary) Three Thousand Dollars.

37. I give and bequeath to the Hebrew Education Society of Philadelphia (Pennsylvania) Twenty Thousand Dollars.

38. I give to the United Hebrew Benevolent Society of Philadelphia aforesaid Three Thousand Dollars.

39. I give and bequeath to the Hebrew Congregation Ashabat Israel of Fells Point Baltimore, Three Thousand Dollars.

40. I give and bequeath to the Hebrew Congregation Beth Shalome of Richmond, Virginia, Five Thousand dollars.

41. I give and bequeath to the Hebrew Congregation Sheareth Israel of Charleston South Carolina the sum of Five Thousand Dollars.

42. I give and bequeath to the Hebrew Congregation Shangarai Shamoyen of Mobile Alabama Two Thousand Dollars.

43. I give and bequeath to the Hebrew Congregation Mikve Israel of Savannah Georgia Five Thousand Dollars.

44. I give and bequeath to the Hebrew Congregation of Montgomery Alabama Two Thousand dollars say ($2000).

45. I give and bequeath to the Hebrew Congregation of Memphis Tennessee Two Thousand dollars.

46. I give and bequeath to the Hebrew Congregation Adas Israel of Louisville Kentucky Three Thousand Dollars.

47. I give and bequeath to the Hebrew Congregation Briai Israel [sic] of Cincinnati Ohio Three Thousand Dollars.

48. I give and bequeath to the Hebrew School Talmud Jeladin of Cincinnati Ohio Five Thousand Dollars.

49. I give and bequeath to the Jews Hospital of Cincinnati Ohio Five Thousand dollars.

50. I give and bequeath to the Hebrew Congregation Tifareth Israel of Cleveland Ohio, Three Thousand Dollars.

51. I give and bequeath to the Hebrew Congregation Briai El [sic] of St Louis Missouri Three Thousand dollars.

52. I give and bequeath to the Hebrew Congregation of Beth El of Buffalo New York Three Thousand (say Three Thousand Dollars).

53. I give and bequeath to the Hebrew Congregation Beth El of Albany New York Three Thousand Dollars.

54. I give and bequeath to the three following Institutions named in the Will of my greatly beloved brother the late Abraham Touro of Boston, the following Sums.

First, To the Asylum for Orphan Boys in Boston Massachusetts, Five Thousand dollars.

Second, To the Female Orphan Asylum of Boston aforesaid, Five Thousand Dollars.

Third, And to the Massachusetts General Hospital Ten Thousand Dollars.

55. I give and bequeath Ten Thousand dollars for the purpose of paying the salary of a Reader or Minister to officiate at the Jewish Synagogue of New Port Rhode Island and to endow the Ministry of the same as well as to keep in repair and embellish the Jewish Cemetary [sic] in New Port aforesaid; the said amount to be appropriated and paid or invested for that purpose in such manner, as my Executors may determine Concurrently with the Corporation of New Port aforesaid, if necessary; And it is my wish and desire that David Gould and Nathan H. Gould sons of my Esteemed friend the late Isaac Gould Esq of New Port aforesaid, should continue to oversee the Improvements in said Cemetary and direct the same, and as a testimony of my regard and in consideration of Services rendered by their Said Father, I give and bequeath the Sum of Two Thousand Dollars to be equally divided between them, the said David and said Nathan H. Gould.

56. I give and bequeath Five Thousand Dollars to Miss Catherine Hays now of Richmond Virginia, as an expression of the Kind remembrance in which that esteemed friend is held by me.

57. I give and bequeath to the Misses Catherine, Harriet and Julia

Myers, the three daughters of Mr Moses M. Myers of Richmond Virginia the Sum of Seven Thousand Dollars to be equally divided between them.

58. I give and bequeath the Sum of Seven Thousand dollars to the Surviving Children of the late Samuel Myers of Richmond, Virginia, to be equally divided between them in token of my remembrance.

59. I give and bequeath to my Friend Mr. Supply Clapp Thwing of Boston Massachusetts, the sum of Five Thousand Dollars as a token of my esteem and Kind remembrance.

60. I give and bequeath the sum of Three Thousand Dollars to my respected friend the Revd Isaac Leeser of Philadelphia as a token of my regard.

61. I give and bequeath the Sum of Three Thousand Dollars to my friends the Revd Moses N Nathan, now of London and his wife to be equally divided between them.

62. I give and bequeath the Sum of Three Thousand dollars to my friend the Revd Theodore Clapp of New Orleans, in token of my remembrance.

63. To Mistress Ellen Brooks, Wife of Gorham Brooks Esquire of Boston Massachusetts and daughter of my friend and Executor Rezin Davis Sheperd, I give the sum of Five Thousand dollars, the same to be employed by my Executor in the purchase of a suitable Memorial to be presented to her as an earnest of my very Kind regard.

64. I give and bequeath the sum of Twenty Five Hundred dollars to be employed by my executors in the purchase of a suitable Memorial of my esteem to be presented to Mrs M. D. Josephs wife of my friend Aaron K. Josephs Esquire of this City.

65. I give and bequeath the Sum of Twenty Five Hundred dollars to be employed by my Executors in the purchase of a suitable Memorial of my esteem for Mistress Rebecca Kursheedt wife of Mr Benjamin Florance of New Orleans.

66. I revoke all other Wills or Testaments which I have made previously to these presents.

Thus it was that this Testament or last Will was dictated to me, the notary, by the said Testator in presence of the witnesses herein-above named and undersigned and I have written the same such as it was dictated to me, by the Testator, in my own proper hand in presence of Said Witnesses; and having read this Testament in a loud and audible voice to the Said Testator, in presence of Said Witnesses, he, the Said Testator, declared in the same presence that he well understood the Same and persisted therein.

All of which was done at one time, without interruption or turning aside to other acts.

Thus Done and passed at the said City of New Orleans at the Said residence of the said Mr Judah Touro, the day, month and year first before written in the presence of Messieurs Jonathan Montgomery, Henry Sheperd Jr and George Washington Lee, all three being the Witnessed as aforesaid, who with the Said Testator, and me, the Said Notary have hereunto Signed their names.

"Signed" J. Touro—J. Montgomery—Henry Sheperd—Geo. W. Lee—Thos Layton, Not: Pub:

I Certify the foregoing to be a true copy of the original act, on file and of Record in my office.

In faith whereof I grant these presents, under my signature, and the impress of my Seal of office, at the City of New Orleans, this Twenty First day of January 1854.

Signed
Thos Layton Not: Pub:

4

Cleveland Conference
1855

A conference of rabbis was held in Cleveland in 1855, where it was resolved to convene a synod and call upon all American Jewish congregations to send their ministers and delegates to attend it. They also unanimously agreed that the following resolutions should be the leading principles of the future synods.

1. The Bible as delivered to us by our fathers and as now in our possession is of immediate divine origin and the standard of our religion.

2. The Talmud contains the traditional legal and logical exposition of the biblical laws which must be expounded and practiced according to the comments of the Talmud.

3. The Resolutions of a Synod in accordance with the above principles are legally valid.

5

Order No. 11
1862

General Ulysses S. Grant

Order No. 11 from General Ulysses S. Grant was telegraphed from the military headquarters of the Department of the Tennessee located in Holly Springs, Mississippi, to all post commanders in the department. It was rescinded by President Abraham Lincoln following (but not necessarily as a result of) a meeting with a small contingent of Jews from Paducah, Kentucky, who had traveled to Washington to discuss this matter with the president.

The Jews, as a class violating every regulation of trade established by the Treasury Department and also department orders, also hereby expelled from the department within twenty-four hours from the receipt of this order.

Post commanders will see that all of this class of people be furnished passes and required to leave, and anyone returning after such notification will be arrested and held in confinement until an opportunity occurs of sending them out as prisoners, unless furnished with permit from headquarters.

No passes will be given these people to visit headquarters for the purpose of making personal application for trade permits.

By order of Maj. Gen. U. S. Grant

6

The New Colossus
1883

Emma Lazarus

This sonnet, written by Emma Lazarus, was purchased for fifteen hundred dollars as a contribution to the fund being raised to provide a pedestal on Bedloe's Island for the Statue of Liberty, the colossal figure of "Liberty Enlightening the World." These lines were inscribed on a bronze tablet and placed inside the pedestal. Since the statue reminded Lazarus of the Colossus of Rhodes, one of the seven wonders of the ancient world, she called her sonnet *The New Colossus*.

Not like the brazen giant of Greek fame,
With conquering limbs astride from land to land,
Here at our sea-washed sunset gates shall stand,
A mighty woman with a torch, whose flame
Is the imprisoned lightning, and her name
Mother of Exiles. From her beacon hand
Glows world-wide welcome; her mild eyes command
The air-bridged harbor that twin cities frame.
"Keep, ancient lands, your storied pomp!" cries she,
With silent lips. "Give me your tired, your poor,
Your huddled masses yearning to breathe free,
The wretched refuse of your teeming shore,
Send these, the homeless tempest-tost to me.
I lift my lamp beside the golden door!"

7

American Council for Judaism —
A Statement of Policy
1944

Growing out of the early anti-Zionist position of the Reform movement, the American Council for Judaism maintained — and still maintains (among its tiny remnant of members) — a position on Judaism as religion only. Once Israel declared its independence in 1948, and particularly after the Six Day War of 1967, its position became relatively moot. While it gained some popularity in its early years, its current supporters are few.

The American Council for Judaism, Inc., was organized to present the views of Americans of Jewish faith on problems affecting the future of their own lives and the lives of world Jewry in the present hour of world confusion.

The Council reaffirms the historic truth that the Jews of the world share common traditions and ethical concepts, which find their derivation in the same religious sources. . . .

As Americans of Jewish faith we believe implicitly in the fundamentals of democracy, rooted, as they are, in moralities that transcend race and state, and endow the individual with rights for which he is answerable only to God. We are thankful to be citizens of a country and to have shared in the building of a nation conceived in a spirit which knows neither special privilege nor inferior status for any man.

For centuries Jews have considered themselves nationals of those countries in which they have lived. Whenever free to do so, they have assumed, and will again assume, full responsibilities of citizenship in accordance with the ancient Jewish command, "The law of the land is the law." Those countries in which Jews have lived have been their homes; those lands their homelands. In those nations where political action was expressed through minority groups, the Jew, following the law of his land, accepted minority status, thereby frequently gaining an improvement over previous conditions of inferior citizenship. Such East European concepts, however, have resulted in a misunderstanding, shared by Jews and non-Jews, a misunderstanding which we seek to dispel. American Jews hope that in the peace for which all of us pray, the old principle of minority rights will be supplanted by the more modern principle of equality and freedom for the individual. The interest of American Jews in the individual Jew in countries where the minority right principle prevailed is not to be confused with acceptance of this East European political principle.

As a result of the bigotry, sadism, and ambitions for world conquest of the Axis powers, millions of our co-religionists who made homes in and were nationals of other lands have been violently deported and made victims of indescribable barbarism. No other group has been so brutishly attacked and for one reason only—on the false claims that there are racial barriers or nationalistic impulses that separate Jews from other men.

The plight of those Jews together with millions of oppressed fellow men of all faiths, calls for the profoundest sympathy and the unbounded moral indignation of all freemen. . . .

We believe that wherever possible the forced emigres should be repatriated in their original homelands under conditions which will enable them to live as free, upstanding individuals.

For our fellow Jews we ask only this: Equality of rights and obligations with their fellow nationals. In our endeavors to bring relief to our stricken fellow Jews, and to help rebuild their lives on a more stable basis, we rely wholly on both democracy and religion, and which have been declared as the principles which shall prevail in the better world for which the United Nations are fighting. . . .

Palestine has contributed in a tangible way to the alleviation of the present catastrophe in Jewish life by providing a refuge for a part of Europe's persecuted Jews. We hope it will continue as one of the places for such resettlement, for it has been clearly demonstrated that practical colonizing can be done, schools and universities built, scientific agriculture extended, commerce intensified, and culture developed. This is the record of achievement of eager, hard-working settlers who have been aided in their endeavors by Jews all over the world, in every walk of life and thought.

We oppose the effort to establish a National Jewish State in Palestine or anywhere else as a philosophy of defeatism, and one which does not offer a practical solution of the Jewish problem. We dissent from all those related doctrines that stress the racialism, the nationalism, and the theoretical homelessness of the Jews. We oppose such doctrines as inimical to the welfare of

Jews in Palestine, in America, or wherever Jews may dwell. We believe that the intrusion of Jewish national statehood has been a deterrent in Palestine's ability to play even a greater role in offering a haven for the oppressed, and that without the insistence upon such statehood, Palestine would today be harboring more refugees from Nazi terror. The very insistence upon a Jewish Army has led to the raising of barriers against our unfortunate brethren. There never was a need for such an army. There has always been ample opportunity for Jews to fight side by side with those of other faiths in the armies of the United Nations.

Palestine is part of Israel's religious heritage, as it is a part of the heritage of two other religions of the world. We look forward to the ultimate establishment of a democratic, autonomous government in Palestine, wherein Jews, Moslems and Christians shall be justly represented; every man enjoying equal rights and sharing equal responsibilities; a democratic government in which our fellow Jews shall be free Palestinians whose religion is Judaism, even as we are Americans whose religion is Judaism.

8

American Jewish
Tercentenary Proclamation
1954

As the Jewish community celebrated the tercentenary of its arrival on American shores, its major organizational leaders felt moved to issue a proclamation. This proclamation celebrates America, its freedom, and the unique Jewish community its democratic ideals has helped to nurture.

To Our Jewish Brethren in the United States of America
PEACE BE WITH YOU AND YOUR NEIGHBORS

BE IT KNOWN TO YOU that in Elul 5714 (September 1954) the Jewish community of the United States will commemorate the 300th anniversary of Jewish settlement in this country.

BY THE GRACE OF GOD and under the protection of the Constitution of the United States, we have lived and prospered in this land. We have been an integral part of American life. We have worked with all other Americans in the never-ending search for the democratic way of life and for the light of faith. Our ancient prophetic ideals and the teachings of the sages have been foundation stones of this nation. Our work, our hopes, and, above all, our living religion, have been among our proudest offerings to the American community.

IN SOME LANDS ACROSS THE SEAS our brethren have felt the searing flame of prejudice, persecution, and death. We in America have had the sad yet inspiring opportunity to save the lives of scores of thousands—to bring comfort to the oppressed, to help in the making of a new and honored nation on the ancient soil of Israel, and to acquire a new recognition of our responsibility for human welfare in keeping with the ancient teachings of our faith. In some lands across the seas our brethren have been pressed to give up their religious beliefs and practices and to disappear in a well of

namelessness. BUT WITHIN THE HOME OF AMERICA we have succeeded in preserving the unique identity of the Jewish religion, worshipping
in keeping with our historic tradition; and we have preserved our ancient
teachings, our ethics, and our religious ideals in the free climate of our nation. Our religion is strong, as our American loyalty is strong.

MINDFUL OF THESE BLESSINGS and with deep gratitude in our hearts
to the God of Israel, who, in 1654, led our fathers to the shores of this great
new land,

WE HEREBY PROCLAIM the period from Elul 5714 (September 1954)
to the end of Sivan 5715 (May 1955) as one of thanksgiving, prayer, study,
and celebration of the American Jewish Tercentenary.

WE CALL ON ALL OUR BRETHREN throughout the nation to participate in the observance of this anniversary; to offer thanks unto the Lord for
the blessings bestowed on us in America; to pray for the continued peace
and prosperity of our country and all its inhabitants and to rededicate ourselves to the ideals of our faith within the freedom of American democracy.

Barnett R. Brickner
Central Conference of American Rabbis

Simon G. Kramer
American Jewish Tercentenary

Theodore L. Adams
Rabbinical Council of America

Harry Halpern
Rabbinical Assembly of America

Max J. Etra
Union of Orthodox Jewish Congregations of America

Charles Rosengarten
United Synagogue of America

Maurice N. Eisendrath
Union of American Hebrew Congregations

Norman Salit
Synagogue Council of America

9

Bicentennial Letter to the President from the Rabbis of the Six Colonial Jewish Congregations 1976

When the United States celebrated its bicentennial, the Jewish community wanted to participate in the spirit of celebration in its own way. Thus, the rabbis of the six congregations that were active during the colonial period and remain as viable institutions joined together to write the president and offer congratulations.

The President
The White House
Washington, D.C.

Dear Mr. President:

We, the spiritual leaders of the six Colonial Jewish Congregations, commend to you and our Nation congratulations and divine benediction as the Bicentennial celebration climaxes.

As our forefathers tendered President Washington felicitations on the occasion of his Inauguration, expressing in those documents love of America and dedication on the part of its Jewish citizens to the majestic precepts and freedoms for which it was established, we, in this generation, would affirm their sentiments. May the blessing of liberty, justice and compassion be forthcoming unto our more than two hundred million citizens, to them and their progeny after them. May Washington's promise "to bigotry no sanction, to persecution no assistance" continue to be the bedrock of public policy.

As the founding fathers so clearly understood, love and loyalty to country increase in proportion to the freedoms secured, the privileges extended, and the egalitarian principles promoted. The commitment of the stock of

Abraham is ever to vouchsafe these American values for all people, whether descendants of the first settlers, or more recently removed to these shores.

Be assured, Sir, of the steadfast loyalty of the American Jewish community to the American dream and the American territory. We will defend it against its enemies, foreign and domestic. We will give of our energies, wisdom and skill for the common weal. We will promote the cause of other democracies of this world, including the land of Israel, sacred to all generations of our people. We do so on the conviction that democratic governments need the unique strength which sister democracies can provide, especially in a world where many nations are hostile to elemental human freedoms.

May the "wonder-working Deity" Who has revealed to His children their common origin and destiny and has commanded them to be brethren one to the other, excite the will of all American races and stocks to observe this 200th Birthday in benevolent spirit. May we remember that which is most inspiring in the past. May we reclaim the conviction of Presidents Washington, Jefferson and Madison that in this nation men will forever govern themselves.

Your humble and obedient servants,
Rabbi Louis C. Gerstein
The Congregation Shearith Israel, New York, New York

Rabbi Theodore Lewis
Congregation Jeshuat Israel (Touro Synagogue), Newport, Rhode Island

Rabbi Saul J. Rubin
Congregation Mickve Israel, Savannah, Georgia

Rabbi Ezekiel N. Musliah
The Congregation Mikveh Israel, Philadelphia, Pennsylvania

Rabbi Edward L. Cohn
Kahal Kadosh Beth Elohim, Charleston, South Carolina

Rabbi Jack D. Spiro
Congregation Beth Ahabah-Beth Shalome, Richmond, Virginia

II

WORLD JEWISH HISTORY

Following the destruction of the First Temple in 586 B.C.E., when the Jewish community was exiled to Babylonia, Jews began their journey into the world. While many Jews returned to the land of Israel at the conclusion of the exile in 538 B.C.E., others stayed in Babylonia and eventually traveled elsewhere. Following patterns of economic development, recession, and anti-Jewish actions, Jews have moved from country to country seeking refuge and security. In these countries, Jews have interacted with the national cultures, contributing to and absorbing some of their salient elements, reshaping them and making them their own. As a result, Jews can be found in nearly every country in the world. Hence the sage advice of American Jewish historian Jacob Rader Marcus: there is never a first Jew. Someone always preceded him. This section presents the reader with some of the documents that helped to shape the life of the world's Jewish community.

10

Edict of Ferdinand and Isabella for the Expulsion of the Jews 1492

By issuing this edict, King Ferdinand and Queen Isabella expelled the Jews from Spain in 1492. Of the estimated 150,000 exiles, most found refuge in North Africa and the Turkish Empire, where their descendants (*Sephardim*) continue to preserve the Spanish traditions and language.

Whereas, having been informed that in these kingdoms, there were some bad Christians who judaized and apostatized from our holy Catholic faith, the chief cause of which was the communication of Jews with Christians; at the Cortes we held in the city of Toledo in the year 1480, we ordered the said Jews in all the cities, towns, and places in our kingdoms and dominions, to separate into Jewries and place apart, where they should live and reside, hoping by their separation alone to remedy the evil. Furthermore, we have sought and given orders, that inquisition should be made in our said kingdoms, which, as is known, for upwards of twelve years has been, and is done, whereby many guilty persons have been discovered, as is notorious. And as we are informed by the inquisitors, and many other religious, ecclesiastical, and secular persons, that great injury has resulted and does result, and it is stated, and appears to be, from the participation, society, and communication they held and do hold with Jews, who it appears always endeavor in every way they can to subvert our holy Catholic faith, and to make faithful Christians withdraw and separate themselves therefrom, and attract and pervert them to their injurious opinions and belief, instructing them in the ceremonies and observances of their religion, holding meetings where they read and teach them what they are to believe and observe according to their religion; seeking to circumcise them and their children; giving them books from which they may read their prayers; and explaining to them the fasts they are to observe; assembling with them to read and to teach them the histories of their law; notifying to them the festivals previous to their occurring, and instructing them what they are to do and observe thereon; giving and carrying to them from their houses unleavened bread and meat slaughtered with ceremonies; instructing them what they are to refrain from, as well as in food as in other matters, for the due observance of their religion, and persuading them all they can to profess and keep the law of Moses; giving them to understand, that except that, there is no other law or truth, which is proved by many declarations and confessions, as well of Jews themselves as of those who have been perverted and deceived by them, which has greatly redounded to the injury, detriment, and opprobrium of our holy Catholic faith.

Notwithstanding we were informed of the major part of this before, and we knew the certain remedy for all these injuries and inconveniences was to separate the said Jews from all communication with Christians, and banish them from all our kingdoms, yet we were desirous to content ourselves by ordering them to quit all the cities, towns, and places of Andalusia, where, it appears, they had done the greatest mischief, considering that would suffice, and that those of other cities, towns and places would cease to do and commit the same.

But as we are informed that neither that, nor the execution of some of the said Jews, who have been guilty of the said crimes and offenses against our holy Catholic faith, has been sufficient for a complete remedy to obviate and arrest so great an opprobrium and offence to the Catholic faith and religion.

And as it is found and appears, that the said Jews, wherever they live and congregate, daily increase in continuing their wicked and injurious purposes; to afford them no further opportunity for insulting our holy Catholic faith, and those whom until now God has been pleased to preserve, as well as those who had fallen, but have amended and are brought back to our Holy Mother Church, which, according to the weakness of our human nature and the diabolical suggestion that continually wages war with us, may easily occur, unless the principal cause of it be removed, which is to banish the said Jews from our kingdoms.

And when any serious and detestable crime is committed by some persons of a college or university, it is right that such college or university should be dissolved and annihilated, and the lesser suffer for the greater, and one be punished for the other; and those that disturb the welfare and proper living of cities and towns, that by contagion may injure others, should be expelled therefrom, and even for lighter causes that might be injurious to the state, how much more then for the greatest, most dangerous, and contagious crimes like this.

Therefore we, by and with counsel and advice from some prelates and high noblemen of our kingdoms, and other learned persons of our council, having maturely deliberated thereon, resolve to order all the said Jews and Jewesses to quit our kingdoms, and never to return or come back to them, or any of them. Therefore we command this our edict to be issued, whereby we command all Jews and Jewesses, of whatever age they may be, that live, reside, and dwell in our said kingdoms and dominions, as well natives as those who are not, who in any manner or for any cause may have come to dwell therein, that by the end of the month of July next, of the present year 1492, they depart from all our said kingdoms and dominions, with their sons, daughters, man-servants, maid-servants, and Jewish attendants, both great and small, of whatever age they may be; and they shall not presume to return to, nor reside therein, or in any part of them, either as residents, travellers, or in any other manner whatever, under pain that if they do not perform and execute the same, and are found to reside in our kingdoms and dominions, or should in any manner live therein, they incur the penalty of death, and confiscation of all their property to our treasury, which penalty they incur by the act itself, without further process, declaration, or sentence.

And we command and forbid any person or persons of our said kingdoms, of whatsoever rank, station, or condition they may be, that they do not presume publicly or secretly to receive, shelter, protect, or defend any Jew or Jewess, after the said term of the end of July, in their lands or houses, or in any other part of our said kingdoms and dominions, henceforward for ever and ever, under pain of losing all their property, vassals, castles, and other possessions; and furthermore forfeit to our treasury any sums they have, or receive from us.

And that the said Jews and Jewesses during the said time, until the end of the said month of July, may be the better able to dispose of themselves, their property, and estates, we hereby take and receive them under our security, protection, and royal safeguard; and insure to them and their properties, that during the said period, until the said day, the end of the said month of July, they may travel in safety, and may enter, sell, barter, and alienate all their moveable and immoveable property, and freely dispose thereof at their pleasure.

And that during the said time, no harm, injury, or wrong whatever shall be done to their persons or properties contrary to justice, under the pains those persons incur and are liable to, that violate our royal safeguard.

We likewise grant permission and authority to the said Jews and Jewesses, to export their wealth and property, by sea or land, from our said kingdoms and dominions, provided they do not take away gold, silver, money, or other articles prohibited by the laws of our kingdoms, but in merchandise and goods that are not prohibited.

And we command all the justices of our kingdoms, that they cause the whole of the above herein contained to be observed and fulfilled, and that they do not act contrary hereto; and they afford all necessary favor, under pain of being deprived of office, and the confiscation of all their property to our exchequer.

11

Edict of Toleration
1782

This document reflects a two-sided approach to limited emancipation, which gave Jews certain freedoms, such as access to schools, the ability to live where they wanted and enter a variety of occupations in Austria. However, they were also excluded from government offices, limited in the number of marriages, and heavily taxed. In exchange for these "freedoms," Jews were expected to abandon Hebrew and Yiddish.

We, Joseph the Second, by the Grace of God, elected Roman Emperor, at all times the Enlarger of the Empire, King in Germany, Hungary, Bohemia, etc., Archduke in Austria, Duke in Burgandy and Lorraine, send Our Grace to all and graciously make known the following:

From the ascension to Our reign We have directed Our most preeminent attention to the end that all Our subjects without distinction of nationality and religion, once they have been admitted and tolerated in Our States, shall participate in common in public welfare, the increase of which is Our care, shall enjoy legal freedom and not find any obstacles in any honest ways of gaining their livelihood and of increasing general industriousness.

Since however the laws and the so-called Jewish Regulations [Judenordnungen] pertaining to the Jewish nation prevailing in Our hereditary countries in general and particularly in Vienna and Lower Austria are not always compatible with these Our most gracious intentions, We hereby will amend them by the virtue of this present edict in so far as the difference in times and conditions necessitates it.

The favors granted to the Jewish nation by this present amendment, whereby the latest Jewish Regulation of May 5, 1764, is fully repealed consist of the following:

As it is Our goal to make the Jewish nation useful and serviceable to the State, mainly through better education and enlightenment of its youth as well as by directing them to the sciences, the arts and the crafts, We hereby grant and order: . . .

8. Graciously, that the tolerated Jews may send their children in such places where they have no German schools of their own, to the Christian primary and secondary schools so that they have at least the opportunity to learn reading, writing and counting. And although they do not have a proper synagogue in Our residence, still We hereby permit them to establish for their children at their own expense their own school organized in the standard way with teachers appointed from amongst their co-religionists. . . .

9. With regard to schools of higher degrees which were never forbidden to Jewish co-religionists, We hereby merely renew and confirm their permission.

10. In order to facilitate their future means of support and to prepare the necessary ways of gaining a livelihood, We hereby most graciously permit them from now to learn all kinds of crafts or trades here as well as elsewhere from Christian masters, certainly also amongst themselves, and to this end to apprentice themselves to Christian masters or to work as their journeymen, and the latter (the Christian craftsmen) may accept them without hesitation. This, however, should not be interpreted as if We wish to exercise any compulsion on the Jews and Christians, We merely grant both sides full freedom to come to an understanding about this amongst themselves to their satisfaction.

11. We hereby further grant to the Jewish nation the general license to carry on all kinds of trade, without however the right of citizenship and mastership from which they remain excluded, to be carried on by them freely, only consequently as it is usual here and even then not before having obtained permission, same as Christians do, from the *Magistrate* in this city and from the government of Lower Austria in the country. . . . Painting, sculpture and the exercise of other liberal arts are equally permitted to them as they are to Christians, —and We further

12. Grant to the Jewish co-religionists the completely free choice of all non-civic branches of commerce and authorize them to apply for the right of wholesale trade under the same conditions and with the same liberties as are obtained and carried on by Our Christian subjects. . . .

15. Considering the numerous openings in trades and the manifold contacts with Christians resulting therefrom, the care for maintaining common confidence requires that the Hebrew and so-called Jewish language and writing of Hebrew intermixed with German, as well as these shall be abolished.

16. In order to facilitate the tolerated Jews in their trades also with regard to the question of servants, it shall be permitted to them from now on to employ as many Jewish as well as Christian servants as their business requires. . . .

18. By this present Decree We hereby permit the existing restrictions with regard to definite Jewish houses to lapse and allow tolerated Jews to lease at their choice their own residences in the city as well as in the suburbs.

19. No less do We hereby completely abolish the head-toll hitherto levied on foreign Jews and permit them to enter Our residence from time to time in order to carry on their business. . . .

23. Besides, We hereby completely remove the double court and chancellery fees hitherto in force only for Jews, and [We remove]

24. In general all hitherto customary distinctive marks and distinctions, such as the wearing of beards, the prohibition against leaving their homes before twelve o'clock on Sundays and holidays, the frequenting of places of public amusement and the like; on the contrary, it shall be permitted to wholesale merchants and their sons as well as to people of rank to carry swords.

25. Since by these favors We almost place the Jewish nation on an equal level with adherents of other religious associations in respect to trade and enjoyment of civil and domestic facilities, We hereby earnestly advise them to observe scrupulously all political, civil and judicial laws of the country to which they are bound same as all other inhabitants, just as they remain subject with respect to all political and legal matters to the provincial and municipal authorities within their jurisdiction and pertinent activities.

Done in Our City of Residence Vienna, the second day of January, 1782, in the eighteenth year of Our reign in the Roman Empire and in the second year of reign in Our hereditary lands.

Commission Sac^{ae} Caes. reg.^{ae} m. tis in consilio

12

May Laws
1882

In 1882, the Russian minister of the interior issued a set of temporary rules that were called the May Laws because they were issued in the month of May. These laws curtailed Jewish residences in villages and started quotas in universities so that students were forced to travel abroad for their education. The May Laws were proposed by Count Ignatiev and sanctioned by the czar on May 3, 1882. They read as follows:

1. As a temporary measure, and until a general revision is made of their legal status, it is decreed that Jews be forbidden to settle anew outside of towns and boroughs, exceptions being admitted only in the case of existing Jewish agricultural colonies.

2. Temporarily forbidden are the issuing of mortgages and other deeds to Jews, as well as the registration of Jews and lessees of real property situated outside of towns and boroughs; and also the issuing to Jews of powers of attorney to manage and dispose of such real property.

3. Jews are forbidden to transact business on Sundays and on the principal Christian holy days; the existing regulations concerning the closing of places of business belonging to Christians on such days to apply to Jews also.

4. The measures laid down in paragraphs 1, 2, and 3 shall apply only to the governments within the Pale of Jewish Settlement [that is, they shall not apply to the ten governments of Poland].

13

The Zionist Programme
(from the First Zionist Congress)
1897

Theodor Herzl established the Zionist Congress, the highest authority in the Zionist Organization. His aim was ostensibly very simple: to convene a congress to bring about an understanding among all Zionists and to thereby unify their endeavors. We have learned that such a task is not so easy. The First Zionist Congress was held in Basel in August of 1897.

The Programme is as follows: —

The aim of Zionism is to create for the Jewish people a legally assured home in Palestine. [The phrase was subsequently altered to read "a publicly, legally assured home."]

In order to attain this object, the Congress adopts the following means:

1. To promote the settlement in Palestine of Jewish agriculturalists, handicraftsmen, industrialists, and men following professions.

2. The centralization of the entire Jewish people by means of general institutions agreeably to the laws of the land.

3. To strengthen Jewish sentiments and national self-conscience.

4. To obtain the sanction of Governments to the carrying out of the objects of Zionism.

14

Nuremberg Laws on Reich Citizenship
1935

The Holocaust did not happen overnight. It was a result of a coordinated effort to destroy Judaism. The Nazis enacted a variety of laws that quickly undermined the entire Jewish community. The citizenship laws were pivotal in this regard.

Reich Citizenship Law
Sept. 15, 1935

The Reichstag has unanimously enacted the following law, which is promulgated herewith:

1

1. A subject of the State is a person who enjoys the protection of the German Reich and who in consequence has specified obligations towards it.
2. The status of subject of the State is acquired in accordance with the provisions of the Reich and State Citizenship Law.

2

1. A Reich citizen is a subject of the State who is of German or related blood, who proves by his conduct that he is willing and fit faithfully to serve the German people and Reich.
2. Reich citizenship is acquired through the granting of a Reich Citizenship Certificate.
3. The Reich citizen is the sole bearer of full political rights in accordance with the Law.

3

The Reich Minister of the Interior, in coordination with the Deputy of the Führer, will issue the Legal and Administrative orders required to implement and complete this Law.

Nuremberg, September 15, 1935
at the Reich Party Congress of Freedom
The Führer and Reich Chancellor
Adolf Hitler
The Reich Minister of the Interior
Frick

15

The Final Solution
1941

While this unfortunate term, which refers to the Nazi attempt to annihilate the Jewish people, is manifest in a variety of documents, we have chosen several that reflect the essential evil of the Nazi plan of genocide. Each time you read these words, they get worse as the faces of those who lost their lives flash into memory. Make no mistake: this was a concerted effort, carefully planned to destroy the entire Jewish community as Hitler attempted to move his war machine through Europe and beyond.

A memo to Adolf Eichmann from an SS major in Poland

L Hö/S
to
Reich Security Main Office
Office IV B4
Attention SS-Lt. Col. Eichmann
Berlin
July 16, 1941

Dear Comrade Eichmann,
    Enclosed is a memorandum on the results of various discussions held locally in the office of the Reich Governor. I would be grateful to have your reactions sometime. These things sound in part fantastic, but in my view are thoroughly feasible.
1 enclosure
L Hö/s   Poznan July 16, 1941
                             Memorandum
Subject: Solution of the Jewish question

During discussions in the office of the Reich Governor various groups broached the solution of the Jewish question in Warthe province. The following solution is being proposed.

1. All the Jews of the Warthe province will be taken to a camp for 300,000 Jews which will be erected in barracks form as close as possible to the coal precincts and which will contain barracks-like installations for economic enterprises, tailor shops, shoe manufacturing plants, etc.

2. All Jews of Warthe province will be brought into this camp. Jews capable of labor may be constituted into labor columns as needed and drawn from the camp.

3. In my view, a camp of this type may be guarded by SS-Brig. Gen. Albert with substantially fewer police forces than are required now. Furthermore, the danger of epidemics, which always exists in the Lodz and other ghettos for the surrounding population, will be minimized.

4. This winter there is a danger that not all of the Jews can be fed anymore. One should weigh honestly, if the most humane solution might not be to finish off those of the Jews who are not employable by means of some quick-working device. At any rate, that would be more pleasant than to let them starve to death.

5. For the rest, the proposal was made that in this camp all the Jewish women, from whom one could still expect children, should be sterilized so that the Jewish problem may actually be solved completely with this generation.

6. The Reich Governor has not yet expressed an opinion in this matter. There is an impression that Government President Übelhör does not wish to see the ghetto in Lodz disappear since he [his office] seems to profit quite well with it. As an example of how one can profit from the Jews, I was told that the Reich Labor Ministry pays 6 Reichsmark from a special fund for each employed Jew, but that the Jew costs only 80 Pfennige.

Nuremberg document PS-710

Reich Marshal of Greater German Reich Göring to
Chief of Security Police and Security Service Heydrich
Berlin, July [31], 1941

Complementing the task already assigned to you in the decree of January 24, 1939, to undertake, by emigration or evacuation, a solution of the Jewish question as advantageous as possible under the conditions at the time, I hereby charge you with making all necessary organizational, functional, and material preparations for a complete solution of the Jewish question in the German sphere of influence in Europe.

In so far as the jurisdiction of other central agencies may be touched thereby, they are so to be involved.

I charge you furthermore with submitting to me in the near future an overall plan of the organizational, functional, and material measures to be taken in preparing for the implementation of the aspired final solution of the Jewish question.

Nuremberg document NG-2586

Secret Reich Matter
Conference Protocol
30 copies
16th copy

I. The following participated in the conference of January 20, 1942, in Berlin, Am Grossen Wannsee 56–58, on the final solution of the Jewish question:

Gauleiter Dr. Meyer and Reich Office Director Dr. Leibrandt, Reich Ministry for the Occupied Eastern Territories

Undersecretary Dr. Stuckart, Reich Ministry of the Interior

Undersecretary Dr. Neumann, [Office of] Plenipotentiary of the Four Year Plan

Undersecretary Dr. Freisler, Reich Justice Ministry

Undersecretary Dr. Buhler, Office of Governor General [of Poland]

Assistant Secretary Luther, Foreign Office

SS [Senior]-Colonel Klopfer, Party Chancellery

Ministerial Director Kritzinger, Reich Chancellery

SS-Major General Hoffman, Race and Resettlement Main Office

SS-Major General Müller, Reich Security Main Office

SS-Lt. Colonel Eichmann, Reich Security Main Office

SS [Senior]-Colonel Dr. Schoengarth, Commanding Officer Security Police and Security Service in General Government (Poland), Security Police and Security Service

SS-Major Dr. Lange, Commander of Security Police and Security Service for General Commissariat Latvia, as deputy of Commanding Officer of Security Police and Security Service for Reich Commissariat [Baltic States and White Russia].

II. Chief of Security Police and Security Service, SS-Lieutenant General Heydrich, opened the meeting by informing everyone that the Reich Marshal [Göring] had placed him in charge of preparations for the final solution of the Jewish question, and that the invitations to this conference had been issued to obtain clarity in fundamental questions. The Reich Marshal's wish to have a draft submitted to him on the organizational, functional, and material considerations aimed at a final solution of the European Jewish question requires that all of the central agencies, which are directly concerned with these problems, first join together with a view to parallelizing their lines of action.

The implementation of the final solution of the Jewish question is to be guided centrally without regard to geographic boundaries from the office of the Reichsführer-SS and Chief of the German Police (Chief of Security Police and Security Service).

The Chief of Security Police and Security Service then reviewed briefly the battle fought thus far against these opponents. The principal stages constituted

    a. Forcing the Jews out of individual sectors of life [*Lebensgebiete*] of the German people

    b. Forcing the Jews out of the living space [*Lebensraum*] of the German people

In pursuance of this endeavor, a systematic and concentrated effort was made to accelerate Jewish emigration from Reich territory as the only temporary solution possibility.

On instructions of the Reich Marshal, a Reich Central Office for Jewish Emigration was established in January, 1939, and its direction was entrusted to the Chief of Security Police and Security Service. In particular the office had the task of

    a. taking every step to *prepare* for a larger volume of Jewish emigration,

    b. *steering* the flow of emigration,

    c. expediting emigration in *individual* cases.

The goal of the task was to cleanse the German living space of Jews in a legal manner.

The disadvantages brought forth by such forcing of emigration were clear to every agency. In the meantime, however, they had to be accepted for the lack of any other solution possibility.

The migration work in the ensuing period was not only a German problem, but also one that concerned the offices of the countries of destination and immigration. Financial difficulties, such as increasingly demanding regulations on the part of various foreign governments for money to be shown by the immigrant or to be paid by him on landing, insufficient berths on ships, constantly increasing immigration restrictions and suspensions—all this placed extraordinary burdens on emigration efforts. In spite of all these difficulties, some 537,000 Jews were moved out from the day of the seizure of power to October 31, 1941. Of this total

from January 30, 1933 out of the Old Reich . . . . ca. 360,000
from March 15, 1938 out of Austria . . . . ca. 147,000
from March 15, 1939 out of the Protectorate
    Bohemia and Moravia . . . . ca. 30,000

The emigration was financed by the Jews (or Jewish political organizations) themselves. In order to avoid having a residue of proletarianized Jews, the Jews with means had to finance the departure of the Jews without means; an appropriate assessment and emigration tax were used to finance the payments of debts owed by the poor Jews in the course of their emigration.

In addition to this levy in Reichsmark, foreign currencies were required for showing or payment on landing. In order to spare German foreign currency reserves, the Jewish financial institutions abroad were called upon by Jewish organizations at home to take care of the collection of an appropriate foreign currency pile. In this manner about $9,500,000 were made available through these foreign Jews as gifts to October 30, 1941.

Meanwhile, in view of the dangers of emigration in time of war and in view of the possibilities in the east, the Reichsführer-SS and Chief of the German Police [Himmler] has forbidden the emigration of Jews.

III. In lieu of emigration, the evacuation of the Jews to the east has emerged, after an appropriate prior authorization by the Führer [Hitler], as a further solution possibility.

While these actions are to be regarded solely as temporary measures, practical experiences are already being gathered here which will be of great importance during the coming final solution of the Jewish question.

Around 11 million Jews are involved in the final solution of the Jewish question. They are distributed as follows among individual countries:

	Country	Number
A.	Old Reich	131,800
	Austria	43,700
	Eastern Territories [Poland]	420,000
	General Government [Poland]	2,284,000
	Bialystok [Poland]	400,000
	Protectorate of Bohemia and Moravia	74,200
	Estonia—free of Jews	
	Latvia	3,500
	Lithuania	34,000
	Belgium	43,000
	Denmark	5,600
	France/occupied territory	165,000
	unoccupied territory	700,000
	Greece	69,000
	Netherlands	160,000
	Norway	1,300
B.	Bulgaria	48,000
	England	330,000
	Finland	2,300
	Ireland	4,000
	Italy, including Sardinia	58,000
	Albania	200
	Croatia	40,000
	Portugal	3,000
	Romania, including Bessarabia	342,000
	Sweden	8,000
	Switzerland	18,000
	Serbia	10,000
	Slovakia	88,000
	Spain	6,000
	Turkey (European portion)	55,500
	Hungary	742,800
	USSR	5,000,000
	Ukraine	2,994,684
	White Russia, excluding Bialystok	446,484

Total: over 11,000,000

So far as the number of Jews of the various foreign countries are concerned, the numbers listed include only Jews by religion, since definitions of Jews according to racial principles are in part still lacking there. Given prevailing attitudes and conceptions, the treatment of the problem in individual countries will encounter certain difficulties, especially in Hungary and Romania. For example, even today a Jew in Romania can buy for cash appropriate documents officially certifying him in a foreign nationality.

The pervasive influence of Jewry in the USSR is known. The European area contains some 5 million, the Asian barely a half million Jews.

The occupational distribution of Jewry in the European area of the USSR was approximately as follows:

agriculture	9.1%
urban workers	14.8%
trade	20.0%
state employees	23.4%
private professions—medical, press, theater, and so forth	32.7%

In the course of the final solution, the Jews should be brought under appropriate direction in a suitable manner to the east for labor utilization. Separated by sex, the Jews capable of work will be led into these areas in large labor columns to build roads, whereby doubtless a large part will fall away through natural reduction.

The inevitable final remainder which doubtless constitutes the toughest element will have to be dealt with appropriately, since it represents a natural selection which upon liberation is to be regarded as a germ cell of a new Jewish development.

In the course of the practical implementation of the final solution, Europe will be combed from west to east. If only because of the apartment shortage and other socio-political necessities, the Reich area—including the Protectorate of Bohemia and Moravia—will have to be placed ahead of the line.

For the moment, the evacuated Jews will be brought bit by bit to so-called transit ghettos from where they will be transported further to the east.

SS-Lieutenant General Heydrich pointed out further that an important prerequisite for the evacuation in general was the exact specification of the category of persons liable to be involved.

It is intended not to evacuate Jews over 65, but to transfer them to an old people's ghetto.

In addition to these age groups—some 30% of the 280,000 Jews lived in the Old Reich and Austria on October 11, 1941, are over 65—the old people's ghetto will receive badly invalid Jewish war veterans and Jews with war decorations. Many intersessions will be eliminated in one blow by means of this purposeful solution.

The start of major individual evacuation operations will depend in large measure on military developments. With regard to the treatment of the final solution in European areas occupied or influenced by us, it was proposed that the appropriate specialists of the Foreign Office get together with the experts having jurisdiction in these matters within the Security Police and Security Service.

In Slovakia and Croatia the situation is no longer all that difficult, since the essential key questions there have already been resolved. Meanwhile, the Romanian government has already appointed a plenipotentiary for Jewish affairs. To settle the matter in Hungary, it will be necessary before long to impose upon the Hungarian government an adviser on Jewish questions.

Regarding a start of preparations in Italy, SS-Lieutenant General Heydrich considers it appropriate to contact Police Chief [Himmler].

In occupied and unoccupied France, the seizure of Jews for evacuation should in all probability proceed without major difficulty.

Assistant Secretary [Foreign Office] then pointed out that with a deeply penetrating treatment of these problems in some countries, such as the nordic states, difficulties would emerge and that meanwhile it would therefore be best to hold these countries in abeyance. In view of the insignificant number of Jews involved there, the postponement would not amount to a substantial restriction. On the other hand, the Foreign Office sees no difficulties in southeastern and western Europe.

SS-Major General Hoffman intends to dispatch a specialist of the Race and Resettlement Office for general orientation to Hungary as soon as the Chief of Security Police and Security Service is about to tackle the situation over there. It was decided that temporarily the specialist of the Race and Resettlement Office—who is not to become active—should be officially attached as an assistant to the Police Attache.

IV. The Nuremberg laws should constitute the basis, so to speak, of the final solution project, while a solution of the mixed marriage and mixed parentage questions is a prerequisite for the complete purification of the problem.

The Chief of the Security Police and Security Service addressed himself to a letter of the Chief of the Reich Chancellery, and speaking theoretically for the moment, dealt with the following points:

1. Treatment of *Mischlinge* ["half-breed"] of the 1st degree

In view of the final solution of the Jewish question *Mischlinge* of the first degree are placed into the same position as Jews.

To be exempted from this treatment will be
> a. *Mischlinge* of the 1st degree married to Germans, if this marriage produced offspring (*Mischlinge* of the 2nd degree).
> These *Mischlinge* of the 2nd degree are in the main placed into the same position as Germans.
> b. *Mischlinge* of the 1st degree who are in some (vital) area have been accorded higher authorities of the party or state. Each individual case has to be examined anew, whereby one must not exclude an unfavorable decision for the *Mischlinge*.

Prerequisite for an exemption must always be basic merits of the *Mischlinge* himself (not merits of the German parent or marital partner).

To avoid any progeny and to clean up the *Mischling* problem once and for all, the *Mischlinge* of the 1st degree who are to be exempted from evacuation must be sterilized. Sterilization is voluntary, but it is a prerequisite for remaining in the Reich. The sterilized "*Mischling*" is then liberated from all the constricting ordinances to which he has heretofore been subjected.

2. Treatment of the *Mischlinge* of the 2nd degree

In principle, the *Mischlinge* of the 2nd degree will be treated as Germans, with the exception of the following cases in which *Mischlinge* of the 2nd degree will be placed into the same position as Jews:
> a. The descent of the *Mischling* of the 2nd degree from a bastard marriage (both parts *Mischlinge*).
> b. Racially exceptionally poor appearance of the *Mischling* of the 2nd degree, so that for external reasons alone he has to be considered a Jew.
> c. A particularly unfavorable appraisal from a police and political viewpoint which indicates that the *Mischling* of the 2nd degree feels and behaves like a Jew.

Even these considerations, however, should not apply if the *Mischling* of the 2nd degree is married to a German.

3. Marriages between full Jews and Germans.

In individual cases, it must be decided whether the Jewish partner is to be evacuated or whether, considering the effect of such a measure on the German relatives, he is to be transferred to an old people's ghetto.

4. Marriages between *Mischlinge* of the 1st degree and Germans
> a. Without children:
> If there are no children, the *Mischling* of the 1st degree is to be evacuated, or transferred to an old people's ghetto.
> b. With children:
> If there are children (*Mischlinge* of the 2nd degree) and they are placed into the same position as Jews, they will be evacuated along with the

[parent who is a] *Mischling* of the 1st degree, or transferred to a ghetto. Insofar as these children are placed into the same position as Germans they are to be exempted from evacuation, and so will [the parent who is a] *Mischling* of the 1st degree.

5. Marriages between *Mischlinge* of the 1st degree and *Mischlinge* of the 2nd degree or Jews

In the case of these marriages, all the elements (including the children) are to be treated as Jews and hence evacuated, or transferred to an old people's ghetto.

6. Marriages between *Mischlinge* of the 1st degree and *Mischlinge* of the 2nd degree.

Both partners, without regard to children, are to be evacuated, or placed into an old people's ghetto, since racially the children, if any, regularly reveal a stronger Jewish blood component than do *Mischlinge* of the 2nd degree.

SS-Major General Hoffman is of the view that one will have to make widespread use of sterilization, especially since the *Mischlinge*, faced with the choice of being evacuated or sterilized, would rather submit to sterilization.

Undersecretary Dr. Stuckart [interior ministry] stated that in this form the practical implementation of the possibilities just mentioned for cleaning up the mixed marriage and mixed parentage problem would entail an endless administrative task. In order to be sure, however, of taking into account also the biological facts, Undersecretary Dr. Stuckart proposed to proceed with compulsory sterilization.

To simplify the *Mischling* problem, one should further think about the possibility of enabling the lawmaker to say in so many words: "These marriages are dissolved."

As for the effect of the evacuation of the Jews on economic life, Undersecretary Newmann [Four Year Plan] declared that at the moment Jews employed in important war work could not be evacuated until replacements become available.

SS-Lieutenant General Heydrich pointed to the fact that in accordance with directives authorized by him for current evacuations, these Jews were not being evacuated anyhow.

Undersecretary Dr. Bühler stated that the General Government [of Poland] would welcome the start of the final solution of this question in its territory, since the transport problem was no overriding factor there and the course of the action would not be hindered by considerations of work utilization. Jews should be removed from the domain of the General Government as soon as possible, because it is precisely here that the Jew constitutes a substantial danger as carrier of epidemics and also because his continued black market activities create constant disorder in the economic structure of the country. Moreover, the majority of the 2½ million Jews involved were not capable of work.

Undersecretary Dr. Bühler stated further that the Chief of the Security Police and Security Service was in charge of the final solution of the Jewish question in the General Government and that his work was being supported by the offices of the General Government. He only had one favor to ask: that the Jewish question in this territory be solved as rapidly as possible.

Finally, there was a discussion of the various types of solution possibilities, with both Gauleiter Dr. Meyer and Undersecretary Dr. Bühler expressing the view that they could carry out certain preparatory measures in their territories on their own, provided, however, that any disturbance of the [non-Jewish] population had to be avoided.

The conference was closed with a plea of the Chief of Security Police and Security Service for the cooperation of all the participants in the implementation of the solution tasks.

16

Prayer for Eating *Hametz* 1944

During Passover of 1944, there was no *matzah* (unleavened bread) available at the Bergen-Belsen concentration camp. Since the rabbis would not permit the inmates to endanger their lives by fasting, they decreed that *hametz* (leaven) could be eaten, provided that the following prayer be recited before each meal.

Our Father in Heaven, behold it is evident and known to Thee that it is our desire to do Thy will and to celebrate the festival of Passover by eating matzah and by observing the prohibition of leavened food. But our heart is pained that the enslavement prevents us and we are in danger of our lives. Behold, we are prepared and ready to fulfill Thy commandment: "And you shall live by my commandments and not die by them."

We pray to Thee that Thou mayest keep us alive and preserve us and redeem us speedily so that we may observe Thy statutes and do Thy will and serve Thee with a perfect heart. Amen.

III

REFORM JUDAISM

While the Reform movement can be traced to nineteenth-century Europe, what we know as Reform Judaism in the United States and Canada is certainly a North American phenomenon. Introduced to the United States by a variety of ideologues and organized into a movement by Isaac Mayer Wise, it quickly took on a life of its own. The Reform movement is represented primarily in the form of those organizations that Wise built: the Union of American Hebrew Congregations (the national organization of congregations), Hebrew Union College-Jewish Institute of Religion (the academic arm and leadership training center with campuses in New York, Cincinnati, Los Angeles, and Jerusalem), and the Central Conference of American Rabbis (a professional body of over fifteen hundred rabbis).

Personal autonomy and the freedom of choice are the hallmarks of Reform Judaism. Thus, it finds its ideological meaning in its diversity. While some may find such variety difficult to understand, it is this sense of pluralism that has allowed the movement to grow so strong, representing over 850 congregations in North America. In a Reform Judaism that is dynamic, these documents best represent the course it has taken through history.

17

The Charleston Creed
1824

The Reformed Society of Israelites in Charleston, South Carolina, represented the first organized efforts of Reform Judaism in North America. This was their established creedal statement.

I believe, with a perfect faith, that God Almighty (blessed be His Name!) is the Creator and Governor of all creation; and that He alone has made, does make, and will make, all things.

I believe, with a perfect faith, that the Creator (blessed be His Name!) is only One in Unity; to which there is no resemblance; and that He alone has been, is, and will be God.

I believe, with a perfect faith, that the Creator (blessed be His name!) is not corporeal, nor to be comprehended by any understanding capable of comprehending only what is corporeal; and that there is nothing like Him in the universe.

I believe, with a perfect faith, that the Creator (blessed be His name!) is the only true object of adoration, and that no other being whatsoever ought to be worshiped.

I believe, with a perfect faith, that the soul of man is breathed into him by God, and is therefore immortal.

I believe, with a perfect faith, that the Creator (blessed be His name!) knows all things, and that He will reward those who observe His commands, and punish those who transgress them.

I believe, with a perfect faith, that the laws of God, as delivered by Moses in the Ten Commandments, are the only true foundations of piety towards the Almighty and of morality among men.

I believe, with a perfect faith, that morality is essentially connected with religion, and that good faith towards all mankind is among the most acceptable offerings to Deity.

I believe, with a perfect faith, that the love of God is the highest duty of His creatures, and that the pure and upright heart is the chosen temple of Jehovah.

I believe, with a perfect faith, that the Creator (blessed be His name!) is the only true Redeemer of all His children, and that He will spread the worship of His name over the whole earth.

18

The Philadelphia Conference 1869

In 1869 a group of German-born Reform rabbis met in Philadelphia in an effort to continue the German Rabbinical Conferences of the 1840s. While they came to terms with a variety of difficult issues, they were unable to reach a lasting agreement.

The Conference adopted the following principles:

1. The Messianic aim of Israel is not the restoration of the old Jewish state under a descendant of David, involving a second separation from the nations of the earth, but the union of all men as children of God in the confession of the unity of God, so as to realize the unity of all rational creatures and their call to moral sanctification.

2. We look upon the destruction of the second Jewish commonwealth not as a punishment for the sinfulness of Israel, but as a result of the divine purpose revealed to Abraham, which, as has become ever clearer in the course of the world's history, consists in the dispersion of the Jews to all parts of the earth, for the realization of their high priestly mission, to lead the nations to the true knowledge and worship of God.

3. The Aaronic priesthood and the Mosaic sacrificial cult were preparatory steps to the real priesthood of the whole people, which began with the dispersion of the Jews, and to the sacrifices of sincere devotion and moral sanctification, which alone are pleasing and acceptable to the Most Holy. These institutions, preparatory to higher religiosity, were consigned to the past, once and for all, with the destruction of the second temple, and only in this sense—as educational influences in the past—are they to be mentioned in our prayers.

4. Every distinction between Aaronides and non-Aaronides, as far as religious rites and duties are concerned, is consequently inadmissible, both in the religious cult and in life.

5. The selection of Israel as the people of religion, as the bearer of the highest idea of humanity, is still, as ever, to be strongly emphasized, and for this very reason, whenever this is mentioned, it shall only be done with full emphasis laid upon the world-embracing mission of Israel and the love of God for all his children.

6. The belief in bodily resurrection has no religious foundation, and the doctrine of immortality refers to the after-existence of the soul only.

7. Urgently as the cultivation of the Hebrew language, in which the treasures of divine revelation are given and the immortal remains of a literature that influences all civilized nations are preserved, must be always desired by us in fulfillment of a sacred duty, yet has it become unintelligible to the vast majority of our co-religionists; therefore, must it make way, as is advisable under existing circumstances, for intelligible language in prayer, which, if not understood, is a soulless form.

Marriage Laws
(a) Marriage

1. The bride shall no longer be a passive party to the marriage ceremony, but a mutual consecration by both bridegroom and bride shall take place by their speaking the same formula of marriage and by the exchange of rings.

2. The following is the formula of marriage: "Be consecrated to me as wife (as husband) according to the law of God."

3. For the traditional benedictions ברכת אירוסין there shall be substituted such a benediction as sets forth the full moral grandeur of marriage, emphasizes the Biblical idea of the union of husband and wife into one personality (והיו לבשר אחד) and designates purity in wedlock as a divine command.

4. Polygamy contradicts the idea of marriage. The marriage of a married man to another woman is as little possible as the marriage of a married woman to another man and must be considered null and void.

5. The priestly marriage laws which presupposed the greater holiness of the Aaronides have lost all significance since the destruction of the Temple and the disappearance of the old sacrificial cult and therefore hold no longer.

(b) Divorce

6. From the Mosaic and rabbinical standpoint divorce is a purely civil act, which never received religious consecration; it is therefore valid only when it proceeds from the civil court. The so-called ritual *Get* is invalid in all cases.

7. A divorce given by the civil court is valid in the eyes of Judaism, if it appears from the judicial documents that both parties have consented to the

divorce, but when the court has decreed a divorce against the wish of one or the other of the couple, Judaism for its part can consider the divorce valid only when the judicial reason for granting the divorce has been investigated and found of sufficient weight in the spirit of Judaism. It is recommended that before deciding the rabbi can obtain the opinion of experts.

8. The decision of the question as to whether, in doubtful cases, the husband or wife is to be declared dead after lengthy disappearance, is to be left to the law of the land.

(c) Levitical Marriage
The command to marry the brother-in-law, and in case of his refusal to take off the shoe, etc., has lost for us all sense, all importance and all binding force.

Circumcision
The male child of a Jewish mother is no less than her female child—in accordance with a never-disputed principle of Judaism—to be considered a Jew by descent even though he be uncircumcised.

19

The Pittsburgh Platform
1885

Prepared in Pittsburgh by a group of fifteen Reform rabbis, this document became the guiding principles of Reform Judaism for fifty years in what has come to be known as its classical period, and is considered to be the pivotal document for American Reform Judaism.

In view of the wide divergence of opinion and of the conflicting ideas prevailing in Judaism today, we, as representatives of Reform Judaism in America, in continuation of the work begun in Philadelphia in 1869, unite upon the following principles:—

First—We recognize in every religion an attempt to grasp the Infinite One, and in every mode, source or book of revelation held sacred in any religious system the consciousness of the indwelling of God in man. We hold that Judaism presents the highest conception of the God-idea as taught in our holy Scriptures and developed and spiritualized by the Jewish teachers in accordance with the moral and philosophical progress of their respective ages. We maintain that Judaism preserved and defended amid continual struggles and trials and under enforced isolation this God-idea as the central religious truth for the human race.

Second—We recognize in the Bible the record of the consecration of the Jewish people to its mission as priest of the One God, and value it as the most potent instrument of religious and moral instruction. We hold that the modern discoveries of scientific researches in the domains of nature and history are not antagonistic to the doctrines of Judaism, the Bible reflecting the primitive ideas of its own age and at times clothing its conception of divine providence and justice dealing with man in miraculous narratives.

Third—We recognize in the Mosaic legislation a system of training the Jewish people for its mission during its national life in Palestine, and to-day we accept as binding only the moral laws and maintain only such ceremonies as elevate and sanctify our lives, but reject all such as are not adapted to the views and habits of modern civilization.

Fourth—We hold that all such Mosaic and rabbinical laws as regulate diet, priestly purity and dress originated in ages and under the influence of ideas altogether foreign to our present mental and spiritual state. They fail to impress the modern Jew with a spirit of priestly holiness; their observance in our days is apt rather to obstruct than to further modern spiritual elevation.

Fifth—We recognize in the modern era of universal culture of heart and intellect the approach of the realization of Israel's great Messianic hope for the establishment of the kingdom of truth, justice and peace among men. We consider ourselves no longer a nation but a religious community, and therefore expect neither a return to Palestine, nor a sacrificial worship under the administration of the sons of Aaron, nor the restoration of any of the laws concerning the Jewish state.

Sixth—We recognize in Judaism a progressive religion, ever striving to be in accord with the postulates of reason. We are convinced of the utmost necessity of preserving the historical identity with our great past. Christianity and Islam being daughter-religions of Judaism, we appreciate their mission to aid in the spreading of monotheistic and moral truth. We acknowledge that the spirit of broad humanity of our age is our ally in the fulfillment of our mission, and therefore we extend the hand of fellowship to all who co-operate with us in the establishment of the reign of truth and righteousness among men.

Seventh—We reassert the doctrine of Judaism, that the soul of men is immortal, grounding this belief on the divine nature of the human spirit, which forever finds bliss in righteousness and misery in wickedness. We reject as ideas not rooted in Judaism the belief both in bodily resurrection and in Gehenna and Eden (hell and paradise), as abodes for everlasting punishment or reward.

Eighth—In full accordance with the spirit of Mosaic legislation which strives to regulate the relation between rich and poor, we deem it our duty to participate in the great task of modern times, to solve on the basis of justice and righteousness the problems presented by the contrasts and evils of the present organization of society.

20

Menu of the *Trefah* Banquet
1883

In 1875, Hebrew Union College was founded for the training of American rabbis. In 1883 the first class of rabbis was set to graduate, and a banquet was planned at an exclusive Cincinnati restaurant. In order not to offend the more traditional members of the group, the meal was supposed to be kosher. However, when clams, a food forbidden by traditional Jewish dietary laws, were served, the traditionalists immediately stood up and stormed out of the room. Some historians believe that this was a deliberate attempt by Isaac Mayer Wise, champion of Reform Judaism, to drive the more traditional members out of the Reform camp. Others believe that it was simply a catering error.

Here is the menu from that banquet (with translations of some of the French terms) as it appeared in the *Cincinnati Enquirer* for July 12, 1883, and which ultimately led to the birth of Conservative Judaism.

Little Neck Clams (half shell)

Amontillado Sherry

Potages (soup)

Consomme (soup) Royal

Sauternes (wines)

Poissons (fish)

Fillet de Boef, aux Champignons (beef with mushrooms)

Soft-shell Crabs

Salade de Shrimps (shrimp salad)

St. Julien (a brand of liquor)

Entree [*Main course*]

Sweet Breads a la Monglas

Petit Pois (peas) a la Francais

Diedescheimer (liquor)

Revelee [*To reawaken the appetite*]

Poulets (chicken) a la Viennoise

Asperges Sauce
Vinaigrette Pommes Pate (potatoe pie)
Roman Punch
Grenouiles (frogs' legs) a la Creme
and Cauliflower Roti (roast)
Vol aux Vents de Pigeons a la Tryolienne
Salade de Laitue
G.H. Mumm Extra Dry
Hors D'Oeuvres
Bouchies de Volaille a la Regeurs
Olives Caviv
Sardeiles (sardines) de Hollands
Brissotins au Supreme Tomatoe
Mayonaise
[*Dessert*]
Sucres (candies)
Ice Cream
Assorted and Ornamented Cakes
Entrements (during the entertainment)
Fromages Varies (various cheeses)
Fruits Varies (various fruits)
Cafe Noir (black coffee)
Martell Cognac

21

The Columbus Platform
1937

Recognizing that the Reform movement had grown beyond the Pittsburgh Platform, whose principles were no longer reflective of the sentiment of its rabbis or laypersons, a group of rabbis prepared a new set of statements that reflected their sentiments at the time. America had become the center of the Diaspora. Zionism was a major political and social force. And Hitler had already moved into power.

Guiding Principles of Reform Judaism
In view of the changes that have taken place in the modern world and the consequent need of stating anew the teachings of Reform Judaism, the Central Conference of American Rabbis makes the following declaration of principles. It presents them not as a fixed creed but as a guide for the progressive elements of Jewry.

A. Judaism and Its Foundations

1. Nature of Judaism. Judaism is the historical religious experience of the Jewish people. Though growing out of Jewish life, its message is universal, aiming at the union and perfection of mankind under the sovereignty of God. Reform Judaism recognizes the principle of progressive development in religion and consciously applies this principle to spiritual as well as to cultural and social life.

Judaism welcomes all truth, whether written in the pages of scripture or deciphered from the records of nature. The new discoveries of science, while replacing the older scientific views underlying our sacred literature, do not conflict with the essential spirit of religion as manifested in the consecration of man's will, heart and mind to the service of God and of humanity.

2. God. The heart of Judaism and its chief contribution to religion is the doctrine of the One, living God, who rules the world through law and love. In Him all existence has its creative source and mankind its ideal of conduct. Through transcending time and space, He is the indwelling Presence of the world. We worship Him as the Lord of the universe and as our merciful Father.

3. Man. Judaism affirms that man is created in the Divine image. His spirit is immortal. He is an active co-worker with God. As a child of God, he is endowed with moral freedom, and is charged with the responsibility of overcoming evil and striving after ideal ends.

4. Torah. God reveals Himself not only in the majesty, beauty and orderliness of nature, but also in the vision and moral strivings of the human spirit. Revelation is a continuous process, confined to no one group and to no one age. Yet the people of Israel, through its prophets and sages, achieved unique insight in the realm of religious truth. The Torah, both written and oral, enshrines Israel's ever-growing consciousness of God and of the moral law. It preserves the historical precedents, sanctions and norms of Jewish life, and seeks to mold it in the patterns of goodness and of holiness. Being products of historical processes, certain of its laws have lost their binding force with the passing of the conditions that called them forth. But as a depository of permanent spiritual ideals, the Torah remains the dynamic source of the life of Israel. Each age has the obligation to adapt the teachings of the Torah to its basic needs in consonance with the genius of Judaism.

5. Israel. Judaism is the soul of which Israel is the body. Living in all parts of the world, Israel has been held together by the ties of a common history, and above all, by the heritage of faith. Though we recognize in the group loyalty of Jews who have become estranged from our religious tradition, a bond which still unites them with us, we maintain that it is by its religion and for its religion that the Jewish people has lived. The non-Jew who accepts our faith is welcomed as a full member of the Jewish community.

In all lands where our people live, they assume and seek to share loyally the full duties and responsibilities of citizenship and to create seats of Jewish knowledge and religion. In the rehabilitation of Palestine, the land hallowed by memories and hopes, we behold the promise of renewed life for many of our brethren. We affirm the obligation of all Jewry to aid in its upbuilding as a Jewish homeland by endeavoring to make it not only a haven of refuge for the oppressed but also a center of Jewish culture and spiritual life.

Throughout the ages it has been Israel's mission to witness to the Divine in the face of every form of paganism and materialism. We regard it as our historic task to cooperate with all men in the establishment of the kingdom of God, of universal brotherhood, justice, truth, and peace on earth. This is our Messianic goal.

B. Ethics

6. Ethics and Religion. In Judaism religion and morality blend into an insoluble unity. Seeking God means to strive after holiness, righteousness and goodness. The love of God is incomplete without the love of one's fellowmen. Judaism emphasizes the kinship of the human race, the sanctity and worth of human life and personality and the right of the individual to freedom and to the pursuit of his chosen vocation. Justice to all, irrespective of race, sect or class is the inalienable right and the inescapable obligation of all. The state and organized government exist in order to further these ends.

7. Social Justice. Judaism seeks the attainment of a just society by the application of its teachings to the economic order, to industry and commerce, and to national and international affairs. It aims at the elimination of man-made misery and suffering, of poverty and degradation, of tyranny and slavery, of social inequality and prejudice, of ill-will and strife. It advocates the promotion of harmonious relations between warring classes on the basis of equity and justice, and the creation of conditions under which human personality may flourish. It pleads for the safeguarding of childhood against exploitation. It champions the cause of all who work and of their right to an adequate standard of living, as prior to the rights of property. Judaism emphasizes the duty of charity, and strives for a social order which will protect men against the material disabilities of old age, sickness, and unemployment.

8. Peace. Judaism, from the days of the prophets, has proclaimed to mankind the ideal of universal peace. The spiritual and physical disarmament of all nations has been one of its essential teachings. It abhors all violence and relies upon moral education, love and sympathy to secure human progress. It regards justice as the foundation of the well-being of nations and the condition of enduring peace. It urges organized international action for disarmament, collective security and world peace.

C. Religious Practice

9. The Religious Life. Jewish life is marked by consecration to these ideals of Judaism. It calls for faithful participation in the life of the Jewish community as it finds expression in home, synagog and school and in all other agencies that enrich Jewish life and promote its welfare.

The Home has been and must continue to be a stronghold of Jewish life, hallowed by the spirit of love and reverence, by moral discipline and religious observance and worship.

The Synagog is the oldest and most democratic institution in Jewish life. It is the prime communal agency by which Judaism is fostered and preserved. It links the Jews of each community and unites them with all Israel.

The perpetuation of Judaism as a living force depends upon religious knowledge and upon the Education of each new generation in our rich cultural and spiritual heritage.

Prayer is the voice of religion, the language of faith and aspiration. It directs man's heart and mind Godward, voices the needs and hopes of the community, and reaches out after goals which invest life with supreme value. To deepen the spiritual life of our people, we must cultivate the traditional habit of communion with God through prayer in both home and synagog.

Judaism as a way of life requires in addition to its moral and spiritual demands, the preservation of the Sabbath, festivals and Holy Days, the retention and development of such customs, symbols and ceremonies as possess inspirational value, the cultivation of distinctive forms of religious art and music and the use of Hebrew, together with the vernacular, in our worship and instruction.

These timeless aims and ideals of our faith we present anew to a confused and troubled world. We call upon our fellow Jews to rededicate themselves to them, and, in harmony with all men, hopefully and courageously to continue Israel's eternal quest after God and His kingdom.

22

Basic Principles of Congregation Beth Israel, Houston, Texas 1943

In 1943 Congregation Beth Israel of Houston, Texas, was swept into what came to be known as the Basic Principles controversy, which led to the second major schism in the congregation's history. Following Rabbi Hyman Judah Schachtel's election to the pulpit, a committee prepared a set of basic principles that were to guide the congregation and its members upon application for membership. These were considered a restatement of the principles established at the Philadelphia Conference (1869) and the Pittsburgh Platform (1885), including a rejection of Jewish nationalism. Rabbi Robert Kahn, serving as assistant rabbi and on leave as an army chaplain, resigned his position with the temple. He was asked to lead Temple Emanu-El of Houston, which emerged out of this controversy over these basic principles. With the eventual establishment of the modern state of Israel, these basic principles were discarded and the controversy was consigned to the past.

Principle No. 1

We believe in the mission of Israel which is witness to the Unity of God throughout the world and to pray and work for the establishment of the kingdom of truth, justice, and peace among all men. Our watchword is "Hear, O Israel. The Lord our God, the Lord is One." We accept it as our sacred duty to worship and to serve Him through prayer, righteous conduct and the study of our Holy Scriptures and glorious history.

Principle No. 2

We are Jews by virtue of our acceptance of Judaism. We consider ourselves no longer a nation. We are a religious community, and neither pray for nor anticipate a return to Palestine nor a restoration of any of the laws concerning the Jewish state. We stand unequivocally for the separation of Church and State. Our religion is Judaism. Our nation is the United States of America. Our nationality is American. Our flag is the "Stars and Stripes." Our race is Caucasian. With regard to the Jewish settlement in Palestine, we consider it our sacred privilege to promote the spiritual, cultural and social welfare of our co-religionists there.

Principle No. 3

We believe in the coming of a Messianic Age and not in a personal Messiah. We recognize that it is our hallowed duty to speed the coming of the Brotherhood of Man under the Fatherhood of God, which is the Messianic ideal for which the righteous of all people work and pray.

Principle No. 4

We accept as binding only the moral laws of Mosaic legislation and prophetic teaching. While respecting the convictions of our Orthodox and Conservative brethren concerning the rabbinical and Mosaic laws, we, however, as an American Reform Congregation reject the religious obligatory nature of the same, as having originated in ages and under influences of ideas and conditions which today are entirely unsuited, unnecessary and foreign to the beliefs and observances of progressive Judaism in modern America. We shall maintain and use in connection with our religious services only such ritual and ceremonies as may be approved by the congregation from time to time and which may symbolize, in effective and beautiful form, the principles of our faith, and which are adapted to the progressive and liberal spirit of our times.

Principle No. 5

We recognize the complete religious equality of woman with man.

Principle No. 6

The treasures of Divine revelation were given in the Hebrew language and in such language are preserved the immortal remains of a literature that influences all civilized nations. As the fulfillment of a sacred duty, therefore, the cultivation of the Hebrew language must always be urgently desired by us. However, the Hebrew language has become unintelligible to the vast majority of our co-religionists; therefore, while a measurable content of Hebrew is essential and desirable in our ritual and services, it must be used wisely as is advisable under existing circumstances.

Principle No. 7

The basis of brotherhood among the Jews throughout the world is religion. Hence, it is our duty to help our co-religionists whenever and wherever the need may arise, even as we must help all mankind that may be in need, in accordance with the principles of our faith.

23

Report on the Ordination of Women
1956

While women had attended Hebrew Union College since its early days, none had been ordained. Throughout its history, the faculty of Hebrew Union College-Jewish Institute of Religion and the members of the Central Conference of American Rabbis debated the issue at various times—reflecting the reality of the status of its female students or simply reviewing the academic nature of the question. While there was one woman who was ordained as a rabbi in Europe prior to World War II—only to perish several months later in one of Hitler's death camps—HUC-JIR ordained Rabbi Sally Priesand in 1972. This decision changed the face of the rabbinate and consequently American Judaism.

To the Central Conference of American Rabbis
Colleagues:

This report for which you asked covers an issue which was long ago explored and resolved by this Conference. All we bring is reinforcement of the same arguments which convinced this body in 1922, or contemporary enlightenment regarding them.

The CCAR was brought into being by Isaac M. Wise in 1889. At one of the early meetings of this Conference, just three years after its creation, on July 10, 1892, the following resolution was adopted: "Whereas we have progressed beyond the idea of a secondary position of women in Jewish congregations, we recognize the importance of their hearty cooperation and active participation in congregational affairs; therefore be it resolved that women be eligible to full membership with all the privileges of voting and holding office in our congregations." This early resolution demonstrates that the CCAR began its history with the determination that men and women shall have equal status in Reform Jewish affairs.

In submitting this report on the ordination of women on an equal basis with men, sixty-four years after the aforementioned resolution was approved, this Committee is simply meeting its assignment from the 1955 Conference to reexamine the already settled subject of the religious equality of the sexes in Reform Judaism, with special reference to the unqualified acceptance of women as our colleagues in the rabbinate.

Since that 1892 resolution was passed, this question was subjected to another critical review by the Conference, a review that preceded what we present today by thirty-four years. The issue arose in the 1922 meeting of the Conference when Dr. Jacob Z. Lauterbach wrote a responsum on the question, "Shall Women be Ordained Rabbis?" Dr. Lauterbach argued the traditional orthodox position against their ordination. Among other arguments, his opinion that ordination of women might jeopardize the authoritative character of our traditional ordination ranked highly. Dr. David Neumark, rejecting Dr. Lauterbach's position, argued at this same Conference, "You cannot treat the Reform rabbinate from the Orthodox point of view. Orthodoxy is Orthodoxy and Reform is Reform. Our good relations with our Orthodox brethren may still be improved upon by a clear and decided stand on this question. They want us either to be Reform or to return to the fold of real genuine Orthodox Judaism from whence we came."

After lengthy debate, the following statement was submitted and was overwhelmingly adopted by the convention: "The ordination of woman as rabbi is a modern issue; due to the evolution in her status in our day. The Central Conference of American Rabbis has repeatedly made pronouncement urging the fullest measure of self-expression for woman, as well as the fullest utilization of her gifts to the service of the Most High, and gratefully acknowledges the enrichment and enlargement of congregational life which has resulted therefrom.

"Whatever may have been the specific legal status of Jewish woman regarding certain religious functions, her general position in Jewish religious life has ever been an exalted one. She has been the priestess in the home, and our sages have always recognized her as the preserver of Israel. In view of these Jewish teachings and in keeping with the spirit of our age and the traditions of our Conference, we declare that woman cannot justly be denied the privilege of ordination." Dr. Lauterbach, flexible and pliant in his thinking, along with young Rabbi Brickner, now President of our Conference, were among the seven men who officially signed this document as it was submitted to the 1922 convention.

In his presidential message in June 1955, Dr. Brickner wrote, "I am taking the liberty of bringing back for your consideration a question answered long ago. The Reform movement pioneered in granting equality to women. Why should we grant women degrees only in religious education, qualifying them to be educational directors, yet denying them the prerogative to be preachers as well as teachers? They have a special spiritual and emotional fitness to be rabbis, and I believe that many women would be attracted to this calling."

Our President continued with the recommendation, subsequently accepted by last year's Conference, that a Committee be appointed to reevaluate this subject, and to present a report to this 1956 Convention. The Committee, consisting of the rabbis whose names are signed below, did indeed give this subject resolute scrutiny and study. We examined the issue in the light of the age-old traditions of our faith and in the light of the sixty-four year old traditions of this Conference. These are the facts we reviewed.

The recognition of women as of equal status with men goes back to the very beginning of the liberal movement in Judaism in Germany long before it spread to America. At the "Conference of the Rabbis of Germany" which took place in Frankfort on the Main in July, 1845, it was stated that, "one of the marked achievements of the Reform movement has been the change in the status of women. According to the Talmud and the Rabbinic Code, woman can take no part in public religious functions but," the rabbis of this convention added, "this Conference declares that woman has the same obligation as man to participate from youth up in the instruction in Judaism and in the public services, and that the custom not to include women in the number of individuals necessary for the conducting of a public service (a *minyan*) is only a custom and has no religious basis." This opinion was expressed to the Frankfort Conference by Rabbi Samuel Adler.

At the Breslau Rabbinical Conference held in July, 1846, the Conference agreed, "that woman be entitled to the same religious rights and subject to the same religious duties as man." In accordance with this principle, the rabbinic body made the following pronouncements: "That women are obliged to perform religious acts as depend upon a fixed time שהזמן גרמא בה מצוה in so far as such acts have significance for our religious consciousness. That the benediction שלא עשני אישה which owed its origin to the belief in the inferiority of woman be abolished. That the female sex is obligated from youth up to participate in religious services and be counted for *minyan*."

It was at this Breslau Conference that Einhorn said, "It is our sacred duty to declare with all emphasis the complete religious equality of woman with man in view of the religious standpoint that we represent, according to which an equal degree of natural holiness inheres in all people the distinctions in sacred writ having therefore only relative and momentary significance. Life, which is stronger than all theory, has already accomplished something in this respect, but much is still wanting for complete equality, and even the little that has been achieved lacks still legal sanction. It is therefore our mission to make legal declaration of the equal religious obligation and justification of woman in as far as this is possible. We have the same right to do this as had the synod under Rabbenu Gershom eight hundred years ago, which passed new religious decrees in favor of the female sex."

The denial to women of equal status with man in the performance of religious duties, obligations, and functions is clearly a survival of the oriental conception of woman's inferiority. To condemn woman to the role of a silent spectator, an auditor, in the synagogue while granting her an important voice in the home is illogical and unnatural in an occidental society; it is incongruous with the customs, standards and ideals of our age. It is true that in Orthodox Judaism the oriental conception of woman's inferiority is codified in the *Shulhan Aruch*, but Reform Judaism has long maintained that these paragraphs do not express its liberal view. The emancipation of woman applies to life within the synagogue as well as to life outside the synagogue.

In view of woman's parity with man, we believe that the unwarranted and outmoded tradition of reducing woman to an inferior status with regard to ordination for the rabbinate be abandoned. Specifically, we believe that she should be given the right to study for the rabbinate, that she should be ordained if and when she has properly completed the course of study, and that she should then be admitted into the CCAR upon application for membership.

The question before us is purely academic at this time. We have no particular case in point. We are drawing a general pattern, not a specific tracing. We are establishing a principle which may be applied as the need arises in the future. We believe that the time has long since passed when a person's sex should constitute a bar to self-expression in any area of human endeavor. The only proper passport to participation in any profession is adequate training and proven capability, regardless of sex. During the last few centuries, the position of women has undergone an enormous revolution. At long last, we must remove the final barrier in her way to becoming a teacher in Israel, a rabbi, of an equal status with men.

This attitude reflects the unaltered conviction of this Conference. It has been the consistent judgement of this body, with each reopening of the subject, for it is in harmony with the high esteem and respect in which women of virtue and valor have always been held in Israel. The opposing viewpoint that would limit woman's activity to a separate and segregated area of expression was refuted and rejected by rabbis generations ago. Furthermore, the religious equality of women with men can be assumed as universally confessed in all liberal denominations. A number of Protestant Christian denominations such as the Unitarians, the Universalists, the Presbyterians and others have already taken the step to ordain qualified women as ministers. We are not among the first liberal religionists to take this step.

As members of the CCAR, we are in two areas, that of traditional attachment and that of liberal influence. We hear the hour strike on both clocks. We know both arguments. But assuming that we wish to extend the horizons of our faith, we should proceed to remove from woman the degradation of segregation. As liberal rabbis who are concerned with the refinement of Jewish practices, and who are sensitive to the currents of today's thinking, we can reach no other decision about the ordination of women. A modern rabbi with discerning eyes and sensitive conscience must, we believe, support these contentions.

Therefore, this Committee recommends to this Conference that it endorse the admission into the HUC-JIR of educationally and spiritually qualified female rabbinical students. We further recommend that, when a woman shall have satisfactorily completed the course of study leading to ordination as rabbi, as prescribed by the faculty, the CCAR shall endorse her ordination as a rabbi in Israel. Lastly, we recommend that the CCAR welcome into its ranks any woman who has been ordained as a rabbi, who may apply for membership into this professional association.

Respectfully submitted,
Joseph L. Fink, *Chairman*
Louis Binstock
Beryl D. Cohon
Maurice N. Eisendrath
Alfred L. Friedman
Nelson Glueck
James G. Heller
Ferdinand Isserman

The report was discussed and a motion was passed to table action so that those who have an opposite point of view may have an opportunity to present a report.

24

The Centenary Perspective
1976

Led by leading liberal theologian Eugene B. Borowitz, a group of Reform rabbis prepared this document, which reflected the pluralistic nature of the Reform movement in the latter part of the twentieth century to mark the occasion of the centennial of the movement in America. It reflects what is considered mainstream Reform Judaism in North America today.

The Central Conference of American Rabbis has on special occasions described the spiritual state of Reform Judaism. The centenaries of the founding of the Union of American Hebrew Congregations and the Hebrew Union College-Jewish Institute of Religion seem an appropriate time for another such effort. We therefore record our sense of the unity of our movement today.

One Hundred Years: What We Have Taught
We celebrate the role of Reform Judaism in North America, the growth of our movement on this free ground, the great contributions of our membership to the dreams and achievements of this society. We also feel great satisfaction at how much of our pioneering conception of Judaism has been accepted by the Household of Israel. It now seems self-evident to most Jews: that our tradition should interact with modern culture; that its forms ought to reflect a contemporary esthetic; that its scholarship needs to be conducted by modern, critical methods; and that change has been and must continue to be a fundamental reality in Jewish life. Moreover, though some still disagree, substantial numbers have also accepted our teachings: that the ethics of universalism implicit in traditional Judaism must be an explicit part of our Jewish duty; that women should have full rights to practice Judaism; and that Jewish obligation begins with the informed will of every individual. Most modern Jews, within their various religious movements, are embracing Re-

form Jewish perspectives. We see this past century as having confirmed the essential wisdom of our movement.

One Hundred Years: What We Have Learned
Obviously, much else has changed this past century. We continue to probe the extraordinary events of the past generation, seeking to understand their meaning and to incorporate their significance in our lives. The Holocaust shattered our easy optimism about humanity and its inevitable progress. The State of Israel, through its many accomplishments, raised our sense of the Jews as a people to new heights of aspiration and devotion. The widespread threats to freedom, the problems inherent in the explosion of new knowledge and of ever more powerful technologies, and the spiritual emptiness of much of Western culture have taught us to be less dependent on the values of our society and to reassert what remains perennially valid in Judaism's teaching. We have learned again that the survival of the Jewish people is of highest priority and that in carrying out our Jewish responsibilities we help move humanity toward messianic fulfillment.

Diversity within Unity, the Hallmark of Reform
Reform Jews respond to change in various ways according to the Reform principle of the autonomy of the individual. However, Reform Judaism does more than tolerate diversity; it engenders it. In our uncertain historical situation we must expect to have far greater diversity than previous generations knew. How we shall live with diversity without stifling dissent and without paralyzing our ability to take positive action will test our character and our principles. We stand open to any position thoughtfully and conscientiously advocated in the spirit of Reform Jewish belief. While we may differ in our interpretation and application of the ideas enunciated here, we accept such differences as precious and see in them Judaism's best hope for confronting whatever the future holds for us. Yet in all our diversity we perceive a certain unity and we shall not allow our differences in some particulars to obscure what binds us together.

I. God
The affirmation of God has always been essential to our people's will to survive. In our struggle through the centuries to preserve our faith we have experienced and conceived of God in many ways. The trials of our own time and the challenges of modern culture have made steady belief and clear understanding difficult for some. Nevertheless, we ground our lives, personally and communally, on God's reality and remain open to new experiences

and conceptions of the Divine. Amid the mystery we call life, we affirm that human beings, created in God's image, share in God's eternality despite the mystery we call death.

II. The People Israel

The Jewish people and Judaism defy precise definition because both are in the process of becoming. Jews, by birth or conversion, constitute an uncommon union of faith and peoplehood. Born as Hebrews of the ancient Near East, we are bound together like all ethnic groups by language, land, history, culture, and institutions. But the people of Israel is unique because of its involvement with God and its resulting perception of the human condition. Throughout our long history our people has been inseparable from its religion with its messianic hope that humanity will be redeemed.

III. Torah

Torah results from the relationship between God and the Jewish people. The records of our earliest confrontations are uniquely important to us. Lawgivers and prophets, historians and poets gave us a heritage whose study is a religious imperative and whose practice is our chief means to holiness. Rabbis and teachers, philosophers and mystics, gifted Jews in every age amplified the Torah tradition. For millennia, the creation of Torah has not ceased and Jewish creativity in our time is adding to the chain of tradition.

IV. Our Obligations: Religious Practice

Judaism emphasizes action rather than creed as the primary expression of a religious life, the means by which we strive to achieve universal justice and peace. Reform Judaism shares this emphasis on duty and obligation. Our founders stressed that the Jew's ethical responsibilities, personal and social, are enjoined by God. The past century has taught us that the claims made upon us may begin with our ethical obligations, but they extend to many other aspects of Jewish living, including: creating a Jewish home centered on family devotion; lifelong study; private prayer and public worship; daily religious observance; keeping the Sabbath and the holy days; celebrating the major events of life; involvement with the synagogue and community; and other activities which promote the survival of the Jewish people and enhance its existence. Within each area of Jewish observance Reform Jews are called upon to confront the claims of Jewish tradition, however differently perceived, and to exercise their individual autonomy, choosing and creating on the basis of commitment and knowledge.

V. Our Obligations: The State of Israel and the Diaspora

We are privileged to live in an extraordinary time, one in which a third Jewish commonwealth has been established in our people's ancient homeland. We are bound to that land and to the newly reborn State of Israel by innumerable religious and ethnic ties. We have been enriched by its culture and ennobled by its indomitable spirit. We see it providing unique opportunities for Jewish self-expression. We have both a stake and a responsibility in building the State of Israel, assuring its security, and defining its Jewish character. We encourage *aliyah* for those who wish to find maximum personal fulfillment in the cause of Zion. We demand that Reform Judaism be unconditionally legitimized in the State of Israel.

At the same time that we consider the State of Israel vital to the welfare of Judaism everywhere, we reaffirm the mandate of our tradition to create strong Jewish communities wherever we live. A genuine Jewish life is possible in any land, each community developing its own particular character and determining its Jewish responsibilities. The foundation of Jewish community life is the synagogue. It leads us beyond itself to cooperate with other Jews, to share their concerns, and to assume leadership in communal affairs. We are therefore committed to the full democratization of the Jewish community and to its hallowing in terms of Jewish values.

The State of Israel and the Diaspora, in fruitful dialogue, can show how a people transcends nationalism even as it affirms it, thereby setting an example for humanity which remains largely concerned with dangerously parochial goals.

VI. Our Obligations: Survival and Service

Early Reform Jews, newly admitted to general society and seeing in this the evidence of a growing universalism, regularly spoke of Jewish purpose in terms of Jewry's service to humanity. In recent years we have become freshly conscious of the virtues of pluralism and the values of particularism. The Jewish people in its unique way of life validates its own worth while working toward the fulfillment of its messianic expectations.

Until the recent past our obligations to the Jewish people and to all humanity seemed congruent. At times now these two imperatives seemed congruent. We know of no simple way to resolve such tensions. We must, however, confront them without abandoning either of our commitments. A universal concern for humanity unaccompanied by a devotion to our particular people is self-destructive; a passion for our people without involvement in humankind contradicts what the prophets have meant to us. Judaism calls us simultaneously to universal and particular obligations.

Hope: Our Jewish Obligation

Previous generations of Reform Jews had unbounded confidence in humanity's potential for good. We have lived through terrible tragedy and been compelled to reappropriate our tradition's realism about the human capacity for evil. Yet our people has always refused to despair. The survivors of the Holocaust, on being granted life, seized it, nurtured it, and, rising above catastrophe, showed humankind that the human spirit is indomitable. The State of Israel, established and maintained by the Jewish will to live, demonstrates what a united people can accomplish in history. The existence of the Jew is an argument against despair; Jewish survival is warrant for human hope.

We remain God's witness that history is not meaningless. We affirm that with God's help people are not powerless to affect their destiny. We dedicate ourselves, as did the generations of Jews who went before us, to work and wait for that day when "They shall not hurt or destroy in all My holy mountain for the earth shall be full of the knowledge of the Lord as the waters cover the sea."

25

Report of the Committee on Patrilineal Descent on the Status of Children of Mixed Marriages as Adopted by the Central Conference of American Rabbis 1983

While patrilineal descent was de facto for most Reform rabbis since the 1950s, in the 1980s, following a challenge by Rabbi Alexander Schindler, president of the Union of American Hebrew Congregations, the Reform rabbinate sought to make the practice de jure. This document served as the beginning of what has resulted in significant discord between the traditional and liberal elements of the Jewish community.

The purpose of this document is to establish the Jewish status of the children of mixed marriages in the Reform Jewish community of North America.

One of the most pressing human issues for the North American Jewish community is mixed marriage, with all its attendant implications. For our purpose, mixed marriage is defined as a union between a Jew and a non-Jew. A non-Jew who joins the Jewish people through conversion is recognized as a Jew in every respect. We deal here only with the Jewish identity of children born of a union in which one parent is Jewish and the other parent is non-Jewish.

This issue arises from the social forces set in motion by the Enlighten-ment and the Emancipation. They are the roots of our current struggle with mixed marriage. "Social change so drastic and far reaching could not but affect on several levels the psychology of being Jewish. . . . The result of Emancipation was to make Jewish identity a private commitment rather than a legal status, leaving it a complex mix of destiny and choice" (Robert Selt-zer, *Jewish People, Jewish Thought*, p. 544). Since the Napoleonic Assembly of Notables of 1806, the Jewish community has struggled with the tension between modernity and tradition. This tension is now a major challenge, and it is within this specific context that the Reform movement chooses to respond. Wherever there is ground to do so, our response seeks to establish Jewish identity of the children of mixed marriages.

According to the Halacha as interpreted by traditional Jews over many centuries, the offspring of a Jewish mother and a non-Jewish father is recognized as a Jew, while the offspring of a non-Jewish mother and a Jewish father is considered a non-Jew. To become a Jew, the child of a non-Jewish mother and a Jewish father must undergo conversion.

As a Reform community, the process of determining an appropriate response has taken us to an examination of the tradition, our own earlier responses, and the most current considerations. In doing so, we seek to be sensitive to the human dimensions of this issue.

Both the Biblical and the Rabbinic traditions take for granted that ordinarily the paternal line is decisive in the tracing of descent within the Jewish people. The Biblical genealogies in Genesis and elsewhere in the Bible attest to this point. In intertribal marriage in ancient Israel, paternal descent was decisive. Numbers 1:2, etc., says: "By their families, by their fathers' houses" (*lemishpechotam leveit avotam*), which for the Rabbis means "The line [literally: 'family'] of the father is recognized; the line of the mother is not" (*Mishpachat av keruya mishpacha; mishpachat em einah keruya mishpacha*; Bava Batra 109b, Yevamot 54b; cf. *Yad*, Nachalot 1.6).

In the Rabbinic tradition, this tradition remains in force. The offspring of a male *Kohen* who marries a Levite or Israelite is considered a *Kohen*, and the child of an Israelite who marries a *Kohenet* is an Israelite. Thus: *yichus*, lineage, regards the male line as absolutely dominant. This ruling is stated succinctly in Mishna Kiddushin 3.12 when *kiddushin* (marriage) is licit and no transgression (*ein avera*) is involved, the line follows the father. Furthermore, the most important *parental* responsibility to teach Torah rested with the father (Kiddushin 29a; cf. *Shulchan Aruch*, Yoreh De-a 245.1).

When, in the tradition, the marriage was considered not to be licit, the child of that marriage followed the status of the mother (Mishna Kiddushin 3.12, *havalad kemotah*). The decision of our ancestors thus to link the child inseparably to the mother, which makes the child of a Jewish mother Jewish and the child of a non-Jewish mother non-Jewish regardless of the father, was based upon the fact that the woman with her child had no recourse but to return to her own people. A Jewish woman could not marry a non-Jewish man (cf. *Shulchan Aruch*, Even Ha-ezer 4.19, *la tafsei kiddushin*). A Jewish man could not marry a non-Jewish woman. The only resource in Rabbinic law for the woman in either case was to return to her own community and people.

Since Emancipation, Jews have faced the problem of mixed marriage and the status of the offspring of mixed marriage. The Reform Movement responded to the issue. In 1947 the CCAR adopted a proposal made by the Committee on Mixed Marriage and Intermarriage:

> With regard to infants, the declaration of the parents to raise them as Jews shall be deemed sufficient for conversion. This could apply, for example, to adopted children. This decision is in line with the traditional procedure in which, according to the Talmud, the parents bring young children (the Talmud speaks of children earlier than the age of three) to be converted, and the Talmud comments that although an infant cannot give its consent, it is permissible to benefit somebody without his consent (or presence). On the same page the Talmud also speaks of a father bringing his children for conversion, and says that the children will be satisfied with the action of their father. If the parents therefore will make a declaration to the rabbi that it is their intention to raise the child as a Jew, the child may, for the sake of impressive formality, be recorded in the Cradle-Roll of the religious school and thus be considered converted.
>
> Children of religious school age should likewise not be required to undergo a special ceremony of conversion but should receive instruction as regular students in the school. The ceremony of Confirmation at the end of the school course shall be considered in lieu of a conversion ceremony.
>
> Children older than confirmation age should not be converted without their own consent. The Talmudic law likewise gives the child who is converted in infancy by the court the right to reject the conversion when it becomes of religious age. Therefore the child above religious school age, if he or she consents sincerely to conversion, should receive regular instruction for that purpose and be converted in the regular conversion ceremony. [CCAR *Yearbook*, Vol. 57]

This issue was again addressed in the 1961 edition of the *Rabbi's Manual*:

> Jewish law recognizes a person as Jewish if his mother was Jewish, even though the father was not a Jew. One born of such mixed parentage may be admitted to membership in the synagogue and enter into marital relationship with a Jew, provided he has not been reared in or formally admitted into some other faith. The child of a Jewish father and a non-Jewish mother, according to traditional law, is a Gentile; such a person would have to be formally converted in order to marry a Jew or become a synagogue member.
>
> Reform Judaism, however, accepts such a child as Jewish without a for-

mal conversion, if he attends a Jewish school and follows a course of studies leading to Confirmation. Such procedure is regarded as sufficient evidence that the parents and the child himself intend that he shall live as a Jew. [*Rabbi's Manual*, p. 112]

We face today an unprecedented situation due to the changed conditions in which decisions concerning the status of the child of a mixed marriage are to be made.

There are tens of thousands of mixed marriages. In a vast majority of these cases the non-Jewish extended family is a functioning part of the child's world, and may be decisive in shaping the life of the child. It can no longer be assumed *a priori*, therefore, that the child of a Jewish mother will be Jewish any more than that the child of a non-Jewish mother will not be.

This leads us to the conclusion that the same requirements must be applied to establish the status of a child of a mixed marriage, regardless of whether the mother or the father is Jewish.

Therefore:

The Central Conference of American Rabbis declares that the child of one Jewish parent is under the presumption of Jewish descent. This presumption of the Jewish status of the offspring of any mixed marriage is to be established through appropriate and timely public and formal acts of identification with the Jewish faith and people. The performance of these *mitzvot* serves to commit those who participate in them, both parent and child, to Jewish life.

Depending on circumstances,[1] *mitzvot* leading toward a positive and exclusive Jewish identity will include entry into the covenant, acquisition of a Hebrew name, Torah study, Bar/Bat Mitzvah, and *Kabbalat Torah* (Confirmation).[2] For those beyond childhood claiming Jewish identity, other public acts or declarations may be added or substituted after consultation with their rabbi.

1. According to the age or setting, parents should consult a rabbi to determine the specific *mitzvot* which are necessary.
2. A full description of these and other *mitzvot* can be found in *Shaarei Mitzvah*.

26

Report of the Ad Hoc Committee on Homosexuality and the Rabbinate Adopted by the Convention of the Central Conference of American Rabbis 1990

The issue of homosexuality will undoubtedly be the most significant social issue that the Jewish community faces during the end of the twentieth century. Unafraid to go against the status quo, the Reform movement boldly accepted gay and lesbian Jews into their synagogues and decided to accept them for ordination as rabbis, as this document suggests.

Composition of the Committee

Chair: Selig Salkowitz; Norman J. Cohen, A. Stanley Dreyfus (RPC), Joseph B. Glaser (CCAR), Walter Jacob, Yoel H. Kahn, Samuel E. Karff, Peter S. Knobel, Joseph Levine, Jack Stern, Richard S. Sternberger (UAHC), Ronald B. Sobel (RPC), Elliot L. Stevens (CCAR), Harvey M. Tattelbaum, Albert Vorspan (UAHC), Margaret M. Wenig, Gary Zola (HUC-JIR).

Origin of the Committee

The Committee was formed in response to a resolution proposed by Margaret Holub (then student rabbi) and Margaret Wenig for the June 1986 Convention of the Central Conference of American Rabbis in Snowmass, Colorado. The proposed resolution dealt with the admissions policies of the Hebrew Union College — Jewish Institute of Religion and of the CCAR and with placement policy of the Rabbinical Placement Commission. The matter was referred for further study.

Given the seriousness of the issues and the broad implications for the Reform rabbinate and for the entire movement, President Jack Stern appointed a broadly-representative ad hoc committee and named Selig Salkowitz as its chair. The committee's first meeting took place in the autumn of 1986. Following that meeting, in order to ensure adequate institutional participation, the committee invited the Union of American Hebrew Congregations, the HUC-JIR, and the Rabbinical Placement Commission to appoint official representatives. The committee has met regularly during the past four years. Through extensive study and discussion, the committee has sought to arrive at a unified position on homosexuality and the rabbinate. From the outset, the committee was keenly aware of both the controversial nature and the complexity of the issues. The committee's deliberations have been characterized by vigorous debate carried on in a spirit of warm collegiality. All members found themselves profoundly moved. However, the committee did not achieve consensus on every issue, and recognized that there are legitimate differences of opinion. The committee calls upon members of the Conference to be sensitive to and accepting of those whose positions differ from their own.

The committee undertook a comprehensive investigation of the subject. Its members read studies on the origin and nature of sexual identity, and of homosexuality specifically, and reviewed some of the contemporary legal literature, and studied documents prepared by Christian groups grappling with the status of homosexuals and homosexuality within their own denominations with a specific focus on the question of ordination. Yoel H. Kahn prepared an extensive anthology of articles on Judaism and homosexuality which cut across denominational lines. The committee commissioned Eugene B. Borowitz, Yoel H. Kahn, Robert S. Kirschner, and Peter S. Knobel to prepare working papers.[1] Consultations were held with leaders of other

1. *Homosexuality, the Rabbinate, and Liberal Judaism: Papers prepared for the Committee on Homosexuality and the Rabbinate*, Selig Salkowitz, Chair. "Halakhah and Homosexuality: A Reappraisal," by Robert Kirschner. "On Homosexuality and the Rabbinate, a Covenantal Response," by Eugene B. Borowitz. "Judaism and Homosexuality," by Yoel H. Kahn. "Homosexuality: A Liberal Jewish Theological and Ethical Reflection," by Peter S. Knobel.

Copies of these were distributed to the entire membership of the CCAR prior to the June 1989 convention in Cincinnati. These papers should be consulted for a description of the range of positions considered by the committee.

Jewish streams. The committee solicited and received anonymous personal testimony from gay and lesbian rabbis and rabbinic students. It reviewed the admissions policies of the HUC-JIR and the CCAR as well as the placement policy of the Rabbinical Placement Commission. It read previous resolutions of the UAHC biennial conventions and the CCAR conventions, and related Reform Responsa. The work of previous committees was also reviewed. It convened a late night information session at the Tarpon Springs Convention of 1987; submitted a draft resolution to the CCAR Executive Board in 1988 (which was sent back to the committee for further consideration); sponsored a plenary session at the Centennial Convention in Cincinnati in 1989 at which Leonard S. Kravitz and Yoel H. Kahn presented papers[2] followed by workshops; held consultations at each of the regional CCAR Kallot and with MaRaM; and requested that the UAHC sponsor workshops at upcoming regional biennials.

This document is meant to summarize the results of our deliberations, to indicate areas of agreement and disagreement, and to encourage further discussion and understanding. It represents four years of struggle and growth. We hope that it will serve as a model for those who take up these matters upon which we have diligently and painstakingly deliberated.

Concern for Gay and Lesbian Colleagues

The committee is acutely aware that the inability of most gay and lesbian rabbis to live openly as homosexuals is deeply painful. Therefore, the committee wishes to avoid any action that will cause greater distress to our colleagues. As a result, the committee has determined that a comprehensive report is in the best interest of our Conference and the Reform movement as a whole.

Publicly acknowledging one's homosexuality is a personal decision that can have grave professional consequences. Therefore, in the light of the limited ability of the Placement Commission or the CCAR to guarantee the tenure of the gay or lesbian rabbis who "come out of the closet," the committee does not want to encourage colleagues to put their careers at risk. Regrettably, a decision to declare oneself publicly can have potentially nega-

2. Yoel H. Kahn, "The Kedusha of Homosexual Relationships," and Leonard S. Kravitz, "Address." The papers were distributed to the members of the Conference through the regional presidents as material for discussion at the regional kallot. They should be consulted for an understanding of the two different approaches to the subject of the religious status of homosexual relationships.

tive effects on a person's ability to serve a given community effectively. In addition, the committee is anxious to avoid a situation in which pulpit selection committees will request information on the sexual orientation of candidates. The committee urges that all rabbis, regardless of sexual orientation, be accorded the opportunity to fulfill the sacred vocation that they have chosen.

Civil Rights for Gays and Lesbians

All human beings are created *betselem Elohim* ("in the divine image"). Their personhood must therefore be accorded full dignity. Sexual orientation is irrelevant to the human worth of a person. Therefore, the Reform movement has supported vigorously all efforts to eliminate discrimination in housing and employment.[3] The committee unequivocally condemns verbal and physical abuse against gay men and lesbian women or those perceived to be gay or lesbian. We reject any implication that AIDS can be understood as God's punishment of homosexuals. We applaud the fine work of gay and lesbian outreach synagogues, and we, along with the UAHC, call upon rabbis and congregations to treat with respect and to integrate fully all Jews into the life of the community regardless of sexual orientation.

Origin and Nature of Sexual Identity

The committee's task was made particularly difficult because the specific origin of sexual identity and its etiology are still imperfectly understood.

Scholars are not likely to come to an agreement anytime soon about the causes of sexual orientation, or its nature. Various disciplines look at sexuality in different ways and rarely confront each other's ideas. . . . Short of definitive evidence, which no theory has thus far received, the disagreement is likely to continue. Cognitive and normative pluralism will persist for the indefinite future.[4]

The lack of unanimity in the scientific community and the unanimous condemnation of homosexual behavior by Jewish tradition adds to the com-

3. CCAR resolution 1977. UAHC resolutions 1975, 1985, 1987, and 1989.
4. David Greenberg, *The Construction of Homosexuality* (Chicago, 1988), pp. 480–481.

plexity of the question. It is clear, however, that for many people sexual orientation is not a matter of conscious choice but is constitutional and therefore not subject to change. It is also true that for some, sexual orientation may be a matter of conscious choice. The committee devoted considerable time in its discussion to the significance of conscious choice as a criterion for formulating a position on the religious status of homosexuality. The majority of the committee believes that the issue of choice is crucial. For some on the committee the issue of choice is not significant.

In Jewish tradition heterosexual, monogamous, procreative marriage is the ideal human relationship for the perpetuation of societies, covenantal fulfillment, and the preservation of the Jewish people. While acknowledging that there are other human relationships which possess ethical and spiritual value and that there are some people for whom heterosexual, monogamous, procreative marriage is not a viable option or possibility,[5] the majority of the committee reaffirms unequivocally the centrality of this ideal and its special status as *kiddushin*. To the extent that sexual orientation is a matter of choice, the majority of the committee affirms that heterosexuality is the only appropriate Jewish choice for fulfilling one's covenantal obligations.

A minority of the committee dissents, affirming the equal possibility of covenantal fulfillment in homosexual and heterosexual relationships. The relationship, not the gender, should determine its Jewish value — *kiddushin*.

The committee strongly endorses the view that all Jews are religiously equal regardless of their sexual orientation. We are aware of loving and committed relationships between people of the same sex. Issues such as the religious status of these relationships as well as the creation of special ceremonies are matters of continuing discussion and differences of opinion.

Sexual Morality and the Rabbi

The general subject of sexual morality is important. The committee, in various stages of its deliberations, sought to discuss homosexuality within that larger framework. However, it concluded that while a comprehensive statement of sexuality and sexual morality was a desideratum, it was beyond the mandate of the committee.

Nevertheless, rabbis are both role models and exemplars. Therefore, the committee calls upon all rabbis — without regard to sexual orientation — to conduct their private lives with discretion and with full regard for the mores

5. Cf. *Gates of Mitzvah*, p. 11, note at bottom of page.

and sensibilities of their communities, and in consonance with the preamble to the CCAR's *Code of Ethics*:

> As teachers of Judaism, rabbis are expected to abide by the highest moral values of our religion: the virtues of family life, integrity, and honorable social relationships. In their personal lives they are called upon to set an example of the ideals they proclaim.

Our Relationship to *Kelal Yisrael* and the Non-Jewish Community

The committee devoted considerable discussion to the effect of any statement on our relationship to *Kelal Yisrael*. The committee expressed deep concern about the reactions of the other Jewish movements and strongly urges that the dialogue continue with them on this issue. Nevertheless, it concluded that our decision should be governed by the principles and practices of Reform Judaism. Similarly, the committee considered and discussed with the members of MaRaM the possible effects of a statement on Reform Judaism in Israel. Again, it concluded that while sensitivity was in order, the committee could address only the North American situation. In addition, the committee attempted to assess how various stands would affect our relationship with non-Jewish groups. Again, the committee was concerned but felt that it had to make its decision independent of that consideration.

Congregational Issues

The acceptance by our congregations of gay and lesbian Jews as rabbis was a topic of discussion. We know that the majority of Reform Jews strongly support civil rights for gays and lesbians, but the unique position of the rabbi as spiritual leader and Judaic role model make the acceptance of gay or lesbian rabbis an intensely emotional and potentially divisive issue. While we acknowledge that there are gay and lesbian rabbis who are serving their communities effectively, with dignity, compassion, and integrity, we believe that there is a great need for education and dialogue in our congregations.

Admissions Policy of the College-Institute

One of the original issues that brought the committee into existence was a concern about the admissions policy of the College-Institute. President Alfred Gottschalk has recently set forth the admissions policy of HUC-JIR. The written guidelines state that HUC-JIR considers sexual orientation of an applicant only within the context of a candidate's overall suitability for the rabbinate, his or her qualifications to serve the Jewish community effectively, and his or her capacity to find personal fulfillment within the rabbinate. The committee agrees with this admissions policy of our College-Institute.

Membership in the CCAR

The CCAR has always accepted into membership, upon application, all rabbinic graduates of the HUC-JIR.

The committee reaffirms this policy to admit upon application rabbinic graduates of the HUC-JIR.

Placement

Since its inception, the Rabbinical Placement Commission has provided placement services to all members of the CCAR in good standing, in accordance with its rules.

The committee agrees with this policy of the Rabbinical Placement Commission which provides placement services to all members of the CCAR in good standing, in accordance with the Commission's established rules.

Respectfully submitted,

Chair: Selig Salkowitz; Norman J. Cohen,
A. Stanley Dreyfus (RPC), Joseph B. Glaser (CCAR),
Walter Jacob, Yoel H. Kahn, Samuel E. Karff, Peter S. Knobel,
Joseph Levine, Jack Stern, Richard S. Sternberger (UAHC),
Ronald B. Sobel (RPC), Elliot L. Stevens (CCAR),
Harvey M. Tattelbaum, Albert Vorspan (UAHC),
Margaret M. Wenig, Gary Zola (HUC-JIR).

Committee Endorsement

The committee expresses its sincere appreciation to the many members of the CCAR who communicated with it in writing and orally. We urge all rabbis to study and reflect on these critical issues in order to lead their congregations and other members of the Jewish community toward greater awareness and sensitivity through education and dialogue. The committee unanimously endorses this report as a fair reflection of four years of deliberation and urges its adoption.

IV

CONSERVATIVE JUDAISM

The Conservative movement represents what is called the Historical School, or "Breslau School," identified with Zecharias Frankel. Rabbi Frankel argued for the development of a historic conservative conception of Judaism sensitive to contemporary needs through organic reform. Beginning in 1887 as a rabbinical school with an enrollment of eight, the Conservative movement now includes an academic center with five distinct degree-granting programs, a rabbinic body with a membership of over 1,300, and a congregational arm composed of more than 800 congregations representing well over 255,000 member families in the United States, Canada, Israel, Europe, and South America. The movement has also spawned a host of affiliated schools, youth programs, summer camping programs, men's and women's organizations, and publications. This section presents several salient documents that helped to shape the movement that is known as Conservative Judaism.

27

Constitution and Bylaws of the Jewish Theological Seminary Association 1886

The Jewish Theological Seminary, founded on January 31, 1886, is the rabbinical seminary and academic arm of the Conservative movement. Founded by Sabato Morais, it was firmly established in 1902 under the presidency of Solomon Schechter, who gave it direction. Sabato Morais served as rabbi of Congregation Mikve Israel in Philadelphia. He sought to establish a school to train rabbis and teachers who would preserve traditional Jewish values and practice against the onslaught of the so-called radical Reform group. Its headquarters are now in New York, with branches in Los Angeles and Jerusalem.

Preamble

The necessity having been made manifest for associated and organized effort on the part of Jews of America faithful to Mosaic Law and ancestral traditions, for the purpose of keeping alive the true Judaic spirit; in particular by the establishment of a Seminary where the Bible shall be impartially taught, and Rabbinical literature faithfully expounded, and more especially where youths, desirous of entering the ministry, may be thoroughly grounded in Jewish knowledge and inspired by the precept and the example of their instructors with the love of the Hebrew language, and a spirit of fidelity and devotion to the Jewish law, the subscribers have, in accordance with a resolution adopted at a meeting of ministers held Shebat 25, 5646 (January 31, 1886), at the Synagogue Shearith Israel, New York, agreed to organize The Jewish Theological Seminary Association, and to adopt for its government the following Constitution and By-Laws:

CONSTITUTION
Article I
Name

The Association shall be known as The Jewish Theological Seminary Association.

Article II
Object

The purpose of this Association being the preservation in America of the knowledge and practice of historical Judaism, as ordained in the Law of Moses [תורת משה: Torat Moshe], and expounded by the prophets [נביאים: Nev'iim) and sages (חכמים: chachamim) of Israel in Biblical and Talmudical writings, it proposes in furtherance of its general aim, the following specific objects:

1. The establishment and maintenance of a Jewish Theological Seminary for the training of rabbis and teachers.

2. The attainment of such cognate purposes as may upon occasion be deemed appropriate.

Article III
Membership

Sec. 1.—The Membership of this Association shall consist of four classes, namely:
1. Subscribers; 2. Patrons; 3. Congregational Members; 4. Honorary Patrons.

Sec. 2.—Any person may become a subscriber to the Association by the payment of such dues as defined in the By-Laws. Subscribers shall be entitled to be present at all meetings of the Association, and to receive copies of all official reports published by the Association or its Committees.

Sec. 3.—Any Jew or Jewess may become a Patron of this Association upon election by the Trustees, by the payment of such dues as are defined in the By-Laws. Patrons shall have all the privileges of subscribers, and shall be eligible to appointment upon Committees and to election to the Board of Trustees.

Sec. 4.—Any Jewish Congregation or cognate association, may become a member of this Association if duly elected by a vote of two-thirds of the Trustees, as provided in the By-Laws. Congregational members shall be entitled to representation at meetings by delegates appointed according to the provisions set forth in the By-Laws. Delegates shall have all the privileges of patrons, and shall be entitled to hold office and to cast one vote each at all meetings of the Association.

Sec. 5.—Any person eligible as a patron, who may establish a scholarship or a fellowship according to the provisions of the By-Laws, or who may donate to the Seminary or to the Association the sum of five hundred dollars or more, shall be an Honorary Patron, and as such entitled to all the privileges set forth in Section 3 of this article.

Article IV
Meetings

Sec. 1—This Association shall meet in Biennial Convention in the month of Adar (in leap-year, Adar Shenee); the place of meeting to be decided upon at the previous convention, and the day to be selected by the Board of Trustees.

Sec. 2—Special meetings of the Association, of which at least thirty days' notice must be given, may at any time be called by the Board of Trustees.

Sec. 3—Until the number of congregational members of this Association shall exceed thirteen, delegates from a majority of said congregational members shall form a quorum for the transaction of business at any meeting or convention of the Association; except for the amendment of the constitution, when delegates from two-thirds of the congregational members shall be necessary to form a quorum. When the number of congregational members of the Association shall exceed thirteen, delegates from several congregational members shall constitute a quorum for the transaction of all business except the amendment of the constitution, which shall require a two-thirds quorum as provided in the preceding paragraph.

Article V
Officers of Conventions

Sec. 1.—Each Convention shall elect its own officers as follows:—A. President, two Vice-Presidents and two Secretaries. The President of the Board of Trustees shall call the Convention to order, and appoint a committee upon credentials, and the nomination and election of officers shall be the first business after the reception of the report of said committee.

Sec. 2.—The President of the Board of Trustees shall preside at special meetings of the Association; and the meeting shall elect vice-presidents and secretaries.

Article VI
Board of Trustees

Sec. 1.—As soon as possible after the adoption of this constitution, there shall be elected by ballot, by a majority vote of the delegates present, a Board of Trustees consisting of fifteen members, five of whom shall be elected to serve for two years, five for four years, and five for six years; and at the Convention of the year 5648, and biennially at each Convention thereafter, five trustees shall be elected to serve for six years each. In case of failure to elect, the incumbents shall hold over until their successors are chosen.

Sec. 2.—Vacancies occurring in the Board of Trustees shall be filled by the Board for the unexpired terms.

Article VII
Power of Trustees

Sec. 1.—The management of the affairs of the Association and of the Seminary shall be vested in the Board of Trustees. They shall have power to collect the revenue of the Association and to expend the same in furtherance of its objects. They shall elect the professors and other teachers of the Seminary and fix the salaries to be paid the professors and teachers. They shall have power to employ and pay such other officers, agents and servants as may from time to time be deemed necessary. They shall, with the advice and consent of the Faculty, establish, and from time to time alter or enlarge, the curriculum. They shall have full power over the admission, rejection, suspension, expulsion, and graduation of students, provided that no student shall be graduated except upon recommendation of the Faculty. They shall procure a charter for the Seminary, granting the right to confer the degrees of Rabbi and Teacher; and they shall be empowered to confer said degrees upon such graduates of the Seminary, and such eminent persons as the Faculty may recommend. They shall have power to adopt rules and regulations for their own government, and for the government of the Seminary, not inconsistent with the Constitution and By-Laws of the Association, and shall exercise such other appropriate powers as may be necessary to well conduct the affairs of an institution of learning.

Sec. 2.—The Board of Trustees shall meet monthly, and as often as may be necessary. The meetings shall be held in the City of New York, or from time to time at such other place as may be determined at a preceding meeting of the Board. Eight trustees shall constitute a quorum for the transaction of business.

Sec. 3.—The Board of Trustees shall at their first meeting following their election, within three weeks thereof, and biennially thereafter at the first meeting following the Convention, choose from among their own number a President, a Vice-President, a Secretary and a Treasurer who shall perform the duties usual to their respective offices as set forth in the By-Laws.

Sec. 4.—Special meetings of the Board of Trustees may be called by the President at his own option, and must be called by him when requested in writing by the three Trustees. Five days' notice setting forth the occasion of the call shall be given of such special meeting, and no business shall be transacted other than that for which the meeting shall have been called.

Article VIII
Seminary

Sec. 1.—The Seminary shall be known as the Jewish Theological Seminary of America.

Sec. 2.—It shall be located in the City of New York.

Sec. 3.—Any person may be admitted into the Seminary as a student, who possesses such qualifications and complies with such regulations as may be established by the Board of Trustees.

Sec. 4.—The Trustees shall have power to rent or purchase a suitable building for the Seminary, or to buy ground and erect a building thereon. They shall not contract any mortgage or bonded indebtedness except by direction of the Association.

Article IX
Adoption of By-Laws

The Association shall have power to adopt By-Laws for its government, not inconsistent with this Constitution or with the Constitution and laws of the United States, or with the Constitution and laws of the State of New York.

Article X
Amendments

This Constitution may be altered or amended by a vote of three-fourths of the persons entitled to vote, present at any meeting of the Association; provided that the necessary quorum of delegates from two-thirds of all the congregational members of the Association be present at said meeting; and provided further that the proposition for amendment shall have been submitted in writing, signed by at least three delegates, at a Biennial Convention held at least six months previously, and that the notice for the meeting shall have set forth in full the article or articles to be amended and the amendments or alterations proposed. And no further amendment to the Constitution or to the proposition for amendment which shall not have been so submitted and set forth in the notice for the meeting shall be entertained.

BY-LAWS
Article I
Dues

Sec. 1. — The dues of subscribers shall be five dollars per annum, payable in advance in the month of Shebat in each year. Subscribers may become life subscribers by one payment of one hundred dollars in lieu of annual payments.

Sec. 2. — The dues of patrons shall be ten dollars per annum, payable in advance in the month of Shebat each year. Patrons may become life patrons by the payment of two hundred dollars in lieu of annual payments.

Sec. 3. — Clause a. — The dues of congregations payable in advance in the month of Shebat in each year shall be twenty-five dollars per annum of congregations of twenty-five members or more, and fifteen dollars per annum for congregations of less than twenty-five members. Each congregation shall, upon such payment, be entitled to one delegate.

Clause b. — Congregations may become entitled to additional delegates, as follows: For each sum not less than twenty-five dollars, one additional delegate; and for each sum of fifty dollars, two additional delegates, provided that no congregation shall be entitled to more than ten delegates. Contributions by congregations in excess of the amount necessary for the maximum number of delegates shall be credited to such congregations in the list of donations. The number of delegates to which each congregation may be entitled shall be fixed by the Board of Trustees in accordance with the average of dues and assessments contributed by said congregation during the period elapsing between Convention and Convention. At special meetings each Congregation may be represented by the number of delegates to which it was entitled at the preceding Convention.

Clause c.—Any Jewish Association becoming a "congregational member" shall pay dues as set forth in clauses a and b, and shall be entitled to delegate representation as therein provided.

Clause d.—The Board of Trustees shall have power to accept semi-annual or quarterly payments, at their discretion, from congregational members unable to pay the full amount in one sum; provided that the dues established in clause a must be paid in one amount as therein declared.

Article II
Congregational Members

Sec. 1.—The congregations and associations represented at the organization meetings of the Association shall assume the duties and be entitled to the rights of members upon the signing of the Constitution by their accredited representatives.

Sec. 2.—Congregations and other Jewish Associations desirous of becoming members of this Association shall signify said desire in a written communication from their authorized officials to the Board of Trustees. Said communication shall set forth the adherence of the applicant to the objects of this Association and of the Seminary as embodied in the preamble to the Constitution, and in Articles II and VIII of the Constitution. It shall state the number of members and seat-holders, and the amount proposed to be contributed during the first year. The Trustees shall prepare a blank form of application in accordance with the above provisions.

Sec. 3.—Any congregation or other Jewish association making application as above, may be elected a member of this Association at any meeting of the Board, subsequent to that at which its application shall be been presented, provided that the notice for said meeting shall have set forth the principal facts contained in said application, and shall have stated that the election would take place. The affirmative vote of ten Trustees shall be necessary to an election.

Article III
Scholarships and Fellowships

Sec. 1.—Any person contributing two thousand five hundred dollars or more to the treasury of the Association shall be entitled to establish a Scholarship to be known by the name of the donor or any person whom the donor may designate.

Sec. 2.—Any person contributing five thousand dollars or more to the Treasury of the Association shall be entitled to establish a Fellowship to be known by the name of the donor, or any person whom the donor may designate. The donor may nominate the incumbent of said Fellowship, subject to the approval of the Board of Trustees.

Article IV
Business

The Order of Business at the Conventions of this Association shall be as follows:—
1. Prayer.
2. Presenting Credentials.
3. Report of Committee on Credentials.
4. Nomination and Election of Officers.
5. Report of President.
6. Report of Trustees.
7. Reports of Committees {Standing Committees
                                          Special Committees}.
8. Unfinished Business.
9. Communications from Congregations.
10. New Business, giving precedence to any subject made a special order.

Article V
Suspension and Expulsion of Congregations

Sec. 1.—The delegates of any congregational member one year in arrears for dues shall not be permitted to vote at any meetings of the Association.

Sec. 2.—Congregations in arrears for dues for two years or longer may be suspended by a majority vote of the Board of Trustees. Congregational members in suspension shall not be entitled to representation at the meetings or conventions of the Association.

Sec. 3.—Congregational members in arrears for three years shall forfeit all privileges of membership.

Sec. 4.—Suspended congregational members shall be reinstated by the Trustees on payment of arrearages, or may be reinstated without payment of arrearages by a unanimous vote of the delegates at any Biennial Convention.

Sec. 5.—Congregational members that have been dropped shall be subject to the conditions for re-admission prescribed in Article II, but shall not be eligible for application until arrearages have been paid, except said arrearages be remitted by unanimous vote at a Biennial Convention.

Sec. 6.—Congregational members may be dropped or suspended for cause by a two-thirds vote of the delegates present at any Biennial Convention, provided said action be recommended to the Convention by a vote of two-thirds of the Board of Trustees at a meeting of which due notice (not less than thirty days) shall have been given said members, and it shall have the right to be heard by the Trustees at such meeting. The resolution of the Board of Trustees recommending the expulsion of any congregational member for cause, shall be set forth in full upon the notices for the Convention, and its discussion shall be made a special order for a stated time. The Trustees shall have the right to open and close said discussion.

Article VI
Duties of Officers and Trustees

Sec. 1.—It shall be the duty of the President to preside at all meetings of the Board, and to perform the usual functions of the chair. He shall appoint all committees unless otherwise ordered, and shall be ex-officio a member of all committees. He shall be entitled to a vote upon a tie, upon a call of the yeas and nays, upon the questions of election, suspension or expulsion of members of the Association, or of the Board, of professors, teachers, or other officials at the Seminary or of the Board, or of students and candidates for degrees. He shall countersign the warrants upon the Treasurer, ordered by the Board and drawn by the Secretary. He shall be the Chief Executive Officer of the Association and shall have such other powers appropriate to his office as may be conferred by resolution of the Board or of the Association. He shall report annually to the Board at its meeting in the month of Shebat, and biennially to the Association at its conventions.

Sec. 2.—The Vice-President shall act as President in case of the absence or inability of the former officer; or in case of his resignation until a successor shall be elected by the Board.

Sec. 3.—The Secretary shall keep full and correct minutes of the Board. He shall issue notices for all meetings of the Board and of the Association. He shall be the medium of communication between the Board and the members of the Association, the press, and the public generally. He shall, when directed by the Board, issue warrants upon the Treasurer. He shall sign all receipts for dues, and deliver the same to the Treasurer. He shall keep a correct account between the Association and its members and the Association and the Treasurer. He shall have the custody of the seal of the Association, and of all books and papers not otherwise provided for. He shall perform such other duties appropriate to his office as may be from time to time required by the Board. He shall within thirty days after the election of his successor deliver to the latter all property of the Association in his possession.

Sec. 4.—The Treasurer shall, collect the revenues of the Association upon bills drawn and signed by the Secretary, and shall be the custodian of the moneys, deeds, and other valuables of the Association, which he shall deposit in the name of the Association in a Bank or Safe Deposit Institution approved by the Board. He shall give bonds for the faithful performance of his duties in such sum as may be required by the Board. He shall pay out no money except upon a warrant ordered by the President and Secretary. He shall keep a correct account of all moneys and valuables received and expended by him, and shall preserve all warrants and vouchers. He shall report to the Board monthly, and submit his accounts for audit annually, or as often as may be required by the Board. He shall report to the Association biennially at its Conventions, setting forth in full all assets and liabilities. Within thirty days after the election of his successor, the bond of the latter being approved, he shall transfer to the new Treasurer, upon an order of the Board, signed by the President and Secretary, all property of the Association in his possession.

Sec. 5.—Clause a.—At the first meeting of the Board following his election, and thereafter annually in the month of Nisan or Iyar as may be, the President shall appoint the following Standing Committees:—

1. Committee on Finance, consisting of five members, inclusive of Secretary and Treasurer.

2. Committee on Membership, consisting of five members inclusive of the Secretary.

3. Committee on Library, consisting of five members inclusive of the Treasurer.

4. Committee on Seminary, consisting of five members, three of whom shall be residents of the City of New York.

Clause b.—The duties of the Committees shall be defined by the Board. The Committees shall report annually to the Board in the month of Shebat.

Sec. 6.—The Board of Trustees shall report to the Association, through the Secretary, biennially at each Convention.

Article VII
Amendments

Sec. 1.—Until the Convention of the year 5648, amendments to the By-Laws may be made by the Board of Trustees, and shall have force until the next regular meeting of the Jewish Theological Seminary Association.

Sec. 2.—These By-Laws may be altered or amended by a vote of two-thirds of the delegates present at any meeting of the Association, under the same provisions as to proposition and notice as are set forth in the article of the Constitution relating to amendments of that instrument; except that propositions may be likewise made at any meeting of the Board of Trustees sixty days prior to a convention, and if duly set forth on the notices for the convention may be then acted upon.

28

The Lieberman *Ketubah*
1955

The *ketubah* is the Jewish marriage contract. It came into existence two thousand years ago, and its earliest formulation was created by Rabbi Shimon ben Shetach, president of the ancient rabbinic court. As an important innovation, the *ketubah* recognizes that—in addition to love—legal commitment is necessary to consummate a marriage. The traditional *ketubah* specified the husband's primary obligations to his wife, including honoring her, providing her with food and clothing, and fulfilling all conjugal obligations.

In the Conservative movement, the *ketubah* was given a new function when Rabbi Saul Lieberman, professor of Talmud at the Jewish Theological Seminary of America, added a revolutionary clause that transformed the *ketubah* into a private agreement between the bride and groom. With this clause, Rabbi Lieberman wanted to open up the possibility of bringing a civil action against a recalcitrant husband who refused to comply with the terms of his wife's *ketubah*. It is still uncertain whether today's courts will enforce the agreement, since civil courts tend to avoid cases that involve religious obligations.

In the name of the Lord, the Eternal God, Amen.
This Ketubah witnesseth before God and man, that on the _____ day of the week, the _____ of the month _____, in the year _____, corresponding to the _____ day of _____, 19____, the holy covenant of marriage was entered into between _____ bridegroom, and _____ his bride, at _____. Duly conscious of the solemn obligations of marriage, the bridegroom made the following declaration to his bride: "Be thou consecrated unto me as my wife according to the laws and traditions of Moses and Israel. I will love, honor and cherish thee; I will protect and support thee, and I will faithfully care for thy needs, as prescribed by Jewish law and tradition." And the bride made the following declaration to the groom: "In accepting the marriage ring, I pledge you all my love and devotion, and I take upon myself the fulfillment of all the duties incumbent

upon a Jewish wife." And both together agreed that if this marriage shall ever be dissolved under civil law, then either husband or wife may invoke the authority of the Beth Din of the Rabbinical Assembly and the Jewish Theological Seminary of America or its duly authorized representatives, to decide what action by either spouse is then appropriate under Jewish matrimonial law; and if either spouse shall fail to honor the demand of the other or to carry out the decision of the Beth Din or its representatives, then the other spouse may invoke any and all remedies available in civil law and equity to enforce compliance with the Beth Din's decision and this solemn obligation.

Bride and groom then together declared before God and man that they have signed their names to this Ketubah of their own free will without reservation or restraint, and that they intend to be bound by this holy covenant so long as they shall live.

_____ Bridegroom _____ Bride
_____ Rabbi _____ Witness _____ Witness

29

Final Report of the Commission for the Study of the Ordination of Women as Rabbis 1979

Beginning in the 1970s, the Conservative movement took decisive steps in a variety of areas to confront the internal problems that led many Conservative leaders to question whether Conservative Judaism had a promising future in American Jewish life. Among the most important issues was certainly the official position of the seminary on the ordination of women. Probably no other single issue could have more effectively forced the Conservative movement to come to terms with its own identity. In 1977–1978 a commission to study the issue of women's ordination was created, composed of seminary faculty, rabbis, academicians from other schools, and representative laypersons from Conservative synagogues. The commission's final report, signed by eleven of its fourteen members, concluded by recommending that the Jewish Theological Seminary of America allow applications from female candidates. The final report was presented at the Rabbinical Assembly convention in 1979, and in 1985 Amy Eilberg became the first woman ordained by the Jewish Theological Seminary.

January 30, 1979

I. PREAMBLE

The deliberative body issuing this report was formed at the behest of the Rabbinical Assembly, which, at its annual convention held in May 1977 in Liberty, New York, passed the following resolution:

Be it resolved that the Rabbinical Assembly respectfully petitions the Chancellor of the Jewish Theological Seminary of America to establish an interdisciplinary commission to study all aspects of the role of women as spiritual leaders in the Conservative Movement.

Be it further resolved that this study commission, whose membership shall reflect the pluralism and diversity of the Conservative Movement, shall be responsible for a progress report on its findings to be presented to the Executive Council of the Rabbinical Assembly in the spring of 1978, and for a final report and recommendation at the 1979 Convention of the Rabbinical Assembly.

The formation of the Commission was announced in October 1977 by Gerson D. Cohen, Chancellor of the Jewish Theological Seminary of America, and Chairman of the Commission. Shortly thereafter, the Commission convened a series of meetings which continued throughout 1978, and which will be described below. With the submission of this final report to the 1979 Convention of the Rabbinical Assembly, the Commission terminates its career.

The fourteen men and women who accepted invitations to serve on the Commission represented a wide array of disciplines, backgrounds, and geographical regions. Their names follow:

1. Gerson D. Cohen (Chairman), Chancellor, the Jewish Theological Seminary of America.

2. Haim Z. Dimitrovsky, Professor of Talmudic Exegesis, The Jewish Theological Seminary of America.

3. Victor Goodhill, Professor of Otologic Research, University of California at Los Angeles.

4. Marion Siner Gordon, Attorney, Royal Palm Beach, Florida, and Lenox, Massachusetts.

5. Rivka Harris, Assyriologist, Chicago, Illinois.

6. Milton Himmelfarb, Editor, American Jewish Year Book, and Director of Information, American Jewish Committee, New York, New York.

7. Francine Klagsbrun, Author, New York, New York.

8. Fishel A. Pearlmutter, Rabbi, Congregation B'nai Israel, Toledo, Ohio.

9. Harry M. Plotkin, Attorney, Washington, D.C.

10. Norman Redlich, Dean, New York University School of Law.

11. Elijah J. Schochet, Rabbi, Congregation Beth Kodesh, Canoga Park, California.

12. Wilfred Shuchat, Rabbi, Congregation Shaar Hashomayim, Westmount Quebec.

13. Seymour Siegel, Professor of Theology, The Jewish Theological Seminary of America.

14. Gordon Tucker (Executive Director), Assistant to the Chancellor, The Jewish Theological Seminary of America.

The first task which the Commission faced was the definition of the problem it was to consider, and an interpretation of its mandate. Although the resolution of the Rabbinical Assembly was intentionally broad, referring as it did to "all aspects of the role of women as spiritual leaders in the Conservative Movement," it was decided at the outset that this Commission would deal specifically with the question of whether qualified women may and should be ordained as rabbis by the Rabbinical School of the Jewish Theological Seminary of America. Ruled outside of the scope of the Commission's deliberations were such issues as the investiture of women as cantors, and more general forms of ritual participation and leadership. The question of whether women already ordained by a recognized rabbinical assembly ought to be considered for membership in the Rabbinical Assembly, although related to the main question, was considered by the Commission to be subordinate to it. In any event, it was the Commission's understanding that the sense of the 1977 Rabbinical Assembly Convention was that any action by the Rabbinical Assembly on membership procedures for women should and would be deferred until the Commission reported its findings on the question of ordination at the Seminary, and until the Seminary's faculty took action on the basis of the report. Thus, the Commission's inquiry focused on the posture it would recommend to the Seminary with respect to female applicants to its Rabbinical School.

This final report on the Commission's activities will have the following form: first, the procedures which were followed will be described. Then, the specific areas of inquiry will be treated, and a summary of the evidence gathered and the subsequent discussion will be provided. Following that, the recommendation of the majority of the Commission on the main question will be presented and elaborated, along with some additional recommendations which the Commission felt a responsibility to offer at this time. Finally, a separate section will contain those opinions and recommendations of members of the Commission which diverged from the majority view.

II. PROCEDURES

Several operating principles were established at once at the Commission's initial meeting on December 12, 1977.

1. Each member of the Commission had been invited to serve by dint of personal experience and expertise, and not as a representative of any organization or institution to which he or she belonged.

2. The Commission would actively consult as wide a sampling of the constituency of the Conservative Movement as possible: rabbis, organizational leadership, synagogue leadership, and to the extent that it was possible, individuals as well.

3. The Commission would approach the main question from the perspectives of the many disciplines which impinged upon it. Those included *halakhah*, ethics, economics, sociology, psychology, and education. Pragmatic and symbolic considerations were also deemed to be important objects of deliberation.

4. Most important, despite the acknowledgment of the many facets considered relevant to the inquiry, the Commission was unanimous in its commitment to the following guideline: *no recommendation would be made which, in the opinion of members of the Commission, after having heard the testimony of experts, would contravene or be incompatible with the requirements of* halakhah *as the latter had been theretofore observed and developed by the Conservative Movement.* Thus, the Commission not only committed itself to recognizing the primacy of the role played by the *halakhah* in Conservative Judaism but in effect decided that in matters which profoundly affect the future course of the Movement, halakhic considerations and constraints must be of primary significance.

The specifics of procedure for the life of the Commission were as follows:

(a) The meeting of December 12, 1977, in New York determined operating guidelines and was otherwise devoted to a general discussion of the issues to be considered.

(b) A second meeting took place over a three-day period in New York, from March 12 to March 14, 1978. During that time, invited testimony was heard from the leadership of the Rabbinical Assembly, the United Synagogue of America, and the Women's League for Conservative Judaism. Those who presented testimony were thoroughly questioned by the Commission members. The first extensive discussion of the halakhic dimensions of the issue took place at this meeting, and several members undertook to research that particular aspect thoroughly in the ensuing months, in keeping with the Commission's insistence on conformity with Jewish legal norms. Plans were made for establishing lines of communication with the general constituency of the Movement, the implementation of which will be described in the paragraphs immediately following.

(c) Public meetings were arranged for various locals in North America, at which all persons affiliated with the Conservative Movement were invited to present testimony before several members of the Commission. These meetings were not for the purpose of counting "votes" pro or con, but rather for the purpose of gathering information on the problems which concerned the rank and file of the Movement, and the arguments which were being formulated by the laity. It was felt to be a fundamental principle of Jewish practice that any decision concerning Jewish usage, even an halakhically based decision, must take account of what will be reasonably acceptable to the community. Accordingly, meetings were set up as follows:

(a) Vancouver, British Columbia, on July 20, 1978.

(b) Los Angeles, California, on September 5–6, 1978.

(c) Minneapolis, Minnesota, on September 13, 1978.

(d) Chicago, Illinois, on September 14, 1978.

(e) Washington, D.C., on September 17, 1978.

(f) New York, New York, on November 1–2, 1978.

(g) Toronto, Ontario, on November 22, 1978.

(h) New York, New York (for members of the faculty and student body of the Jewish Theological Seminary of America), on December 3, 1978.

All of the above mentioned public meetings were taped, and the transcripts have been made available to the public upon request. Arguments which were heard in the course of these meeting will be incorporated in the discussion of the substantive issues below. Nevertheless, some general, qualitative observations on these meetings should be made at this point:

(i) Although no tally was made, or indeed ever contemplated, it was manifest that the overwhelming majority of those who chose to testify at these meeting strongly favored the ordination of women.

(ii) It became equally clear that women are very much interested in continuing their drive toward full religious equalization with men; moreover, many young women are seriously interested in the rabbinate as a career.

iii) By and large, those women who aspire to become Conservative rabbis have a strong commitment to traditional values and law. In fact, many of those women could probably be characterized as having a pattern of religious observance lying near the more traditional end of the spectrum of Conservative Jewish practice.

(iv) The Conservative communities, as they were represented at these public meetings, seem to be prepared to accept, even if gradually, rabbinic leadership by women.

Needless to say, these observations must be considered in light of the uncertainty concerning just how representative a sampling of the community were those who took the trouble to testify at the hearings. In spite of the fact that there was fairly wide and general publicity in advance of each meeting, there was evidence that, for whatever reason, some persons who would oppose the ordination of women did not take the trouble to attend the hearings. On the other hand, those who did make the effort to testify probably constituted a better sampling of those Conservative Jews who have strong feelings on the subject, and that in itself is significant. In that connection, the following should be noted: the Commission took great satisfaction and pride in the fact that in community after community across North America, Conservative Jews were motivated by this issue to seriously contemplate their own personal stances not only with respect to the issue at hand, but also with respect to Jewish commitment generally. In many cases, people took the initiative in reading and studying about the issue, and in that sense, the Commission's enterprise was an educative force in the community.

The Commission met again in New York on December 6–7, 1978. During those two days members shared and discussed the results of their own researches and investigations, considered new evidence from various sources (e.g., the regional hearings, and the unsolicited communications which were addressed to the Commission fairly steadily throughout its lifetime), and eventually arrived at tentative conclusions. Subsequently, Commission members communicated via the mails and the telephone in order to arrive at the final version of this report.

Thus, the Commission was active for slightly less than fourteen months, during which time it met as a complete body for six full days, convened six public hearings plus one hearing for the Seminary community, received considerable testimony, both solicited and unsolicited, and itself commissioned a scientific survey of the Conservative laity on the issue being confronted.

III. THE ISSUE

There are certain aspects to the question at hand regarding which it was at once established that there was unanimity among members of the Commission. These are some of the more obvious considerations which come to mind: the ability and willingness of women to perform rabbinic duties as well as men, the right to equal job opportunities, the right to pursue a career of one's choice. Indeed, it could be said that with respect to the context in which general feminist issues are discussed, there was never any serious dispute among Commission members, nor apparently within the community either. There were and are, for example, many men who fully accept the fact that their wives are pursuing careers, as well as women actually pursuing careers, who nevertheless oppose the ordination of women.

It was therefore determined at the outset that this could not be treated solely as a feminist issue. From that point of view, there was plainly very little to discuss. The complexity of the issue at hand stemmed from the fact that, although there is general agreement concerning the questions which characterize general feminist debates, there is still a wide range of other considerations of which account must be taken. Those considerations include some peculiar to the rabbinate, to Jewish practice in general, and to Conservative Judaism in particular. It was about these special considerations that discussion and debate revolved.

A. Halakhic Considerations

As indicated above, the demands of *halakhah* led the list of matters to be resolved. Even though the Commission was not charged with developing an halakhic stance or approach for the Conservative Movement, its commitment to the notion that legitimacy within Conservative Judaism must be measured first and foremost by an halakhic standard made theoretical discussions concerning the processes of *halakhah* indispensable.

The Commission eventually adopted the classical position which had been embraced by the religious leadership of the Conservative Movement since its founding. That stance maintains that the body of Jewish law is not uniform in texture, but is rather composed of materials which fall into two main categories, usually referred to as *de-oraita* (biblically ordained) and *de-rabbanan* (rabbinically developed). That which is *de-oraita* is tantamount to destroying the core of the Jewish pattern of life as it has existed for millennia. There is positive precedent for doing so only in the most dire of circumstances, and even then with extreme caution and conservatism.

The much greater (that is, in terms of volume) overlay which is *de-rabbanan*, on the other hand, comes with procedures for change and development. What is *de-rabbanan* can develop, is in fact meant to develop, as the conditions of the Jewish community change. That is what ensures the vibrancy and the continuity of the *halakhah* as the coordinate system which roots all Jewish communities.

It is commonplace among Conservative Jews that the recognition of the flexibility and fluidity of the *halakhah* is one of the hallmarks of Conservative Judaism, and this is certainly true. It is equally the case that this recognition constitutes in many ways a major distinction between Conservatism and Orthodoxy. Yet it ought not be forgotten that there are important similarities between Conservatism and Orthodoxy which need reemphasis. In particular, it cannot be stressed too strongly that the strength of Conservative Judaism depends as much on its continuation as a movement devoted to tradition as it does on its continued devotion to halakhic development. The two are inseparable in classical terms, and the centrality of tradition expresses itself in the conditions under which development becomes acceptable. These conditions include:

1. The core which is *de-oraita* may not be altered or displaced. The general principles of, for example, *kashrut* or *Shabbat* could never be displaced as central pillars of Conservative Judaism.

2. Development in the domain of *de-rabbanan* must not be abrupt or discontinuous, must be rooted in traditional exegetical methodologies, and above all, must be ratified by the community of the committed and the informed.

3. The impetus for development in what is *de-rabbanan* must come from *within* the community of the committed and the informed, and not be an external influence originating outside the concerned Jewish community.

When the Commission determined that it would not recommend anything which would contravene the *halakhah*, it was to this view of the halakhic process that it was appealing. Faithfulness to this process constitutes, in the opinion of the Commission, a *sine qua non* for legitimacy within the Conservative Movement. Of course, the view outlined above is not univocal or free of ambiguities. Indeed, there is a certain amount of inherent ambiguity attending all three of the conditions lately listed. There is, in fact, no clear-cut demarcation line between *de-oraita* and *de-rabbanan*. Nevertheless, the existence of gray areas does not negate the fact that the areas which are clearly black or white are well distinguished, and it certainly does not preclude the use of criteria which give rise to those gray areas. Given the obvious fact that some ambiguities will be unavoidable, the alternative would be paralysis, which could not possibly serve the cause of *halakhah*.

Once agreement was reached on the philosophical and theoretical level, the specific halakhic problems which arise were addressed. As is well known from the recent literature on this issue, there are a variety of halakhic criteria which have traditionally distinguished between men and women. Primary among these are the following:

1. According to some sources, women may be ineligible to be appointed to any office of communal responsibility in the Jewish community.

2. Women are exempted from the obligation to study Torah (except for the acquisition of knowledge concerning obligations they do have), although there is no problem presented by their voluntarily assuming that obligation.

3. Women are exempted from positive time-depended commandments, with a few notable exceptions. The most relevant commandments under this category for purposes of this Commission are those relating to public worship,

for exemption from performance raises problems concerning eligibility to discharge the obligation of another person who cannot claim exemption.

4. Women are traditionally ineligible to serve as witnesses in judicial proceedings, including the execution of documents determining personal and familial status.

5. Women are, by virtue of (4) above, considered by most traditional authorities to be ineligible to serve as judges.

All of these sex-role distinctions of the *halakhah* were discussed and researched by members of the Commission. The results of those deliberations will now be summarized:

The role of the rabbi as we know it today is not one which is established in classical Jewish texts, but rather is one which has evolved through social need and custom. Consequently, there is no specifiable halakhic category which can be identified with the modern rabbinate, nor with the currently accepted mode of ordination. Ordination at the Jewish Theological Seminary of America is done in a way which is nearly indistinguishable from the granting of an academic degree at the successful completion of a course of study. Of course, it still has a profound religious and symbolic significance not shared by any academic degree. In other words, issues relating to ordination are not halakhic issues per se, though it is certainly true that there may be serious ramifications of decisions concerning ordination which can lead to a confrontation with certain halakhic principles. Strictly speaking, point (1) above is general enough to present an halakhic problem concerning ordination. That point has its origin in a passage in the halakhic midrash on the Book of Deuteronomy, the *Sifre*. On the verse in Deuteronomy 17:15, "You shall be free to set a king over yourself," the *Sifre* comments, "A king and not a queen." Extrapolating from this comment, Maimonides in *Laws Relating to Kings 1:5* says, "Only men may be appointed to positions of authority in Israel."

Insufficient as Halakhic Barrier.

After considering the opinion of Maimonides on this matter, the Commission decided that it was beset by numerous ambiguities and uncertainties and should not be accounted as an immutable provision of the *halakhah*. The modern rabbinate cannot be analogized to an appointment on the order of magnitude of the ancient monarchy. The many obvious high level appointments of women in modern Jewish life indicate the passing of this principle from general Jewish usage. The Commission therefore determined that this *halakhah* as formulated by Maimonides was insufficient to pose an halakhic barrier to the ordination of women.

With respect to point (2) above, the Conservative Movement has already taken the strongest possible stand in favor of obligating women to study Torah on a basis equal to that of men. The Movement's introduction of *Bat Mitzvah* half a century ago, its educational programs in Camp Ramah, United Synagogue Youth, Leaders Training Fellowship and last but not least, the schools of the Jewish Theological Seminary, all bear witness to that stand. Indeed, the history of the Conservative Movement on the issue of the religious education of women not only vitiates the force of point (2), but actually constitutes a consideration in favor of ordaining women, as will be noted below.

Points (3), (4), and (5) are a group in several respects. First, they have all been dealt with to some extent by a constituent arm of the Conservative Movement. Second, they are all halakhic sex-role distinctions which are secondary to the issue of ordination, as will be explained. Third, although they are secondary to the ordination issue *logically*, they are closely connected to the rabbinic role *practically*. These points accounted for most of the halakhically based discussion during the Commission's proceedings.

Matters of halakhic import in the Conservative Movement have always been channeled through the Rabbinical Assembly Committee on Jewish Law and Standards (henceforth: the Law Committee). That Committee's composition and rules of procedure have varied considerably over the years, but it has consistently defined itself as a panel which primarily makes recommendations on the basis of legal scholarship; its decisions have binding power on Movement leaders only when a very strong consensus condition is met. For the past several years, the operating rule has been that only a position held by all but two or fewer members of the Committee is binding; a minority position with three adherents on the Committee becomes a legitimate option for Conservative congregations and rabbis. Despite inevitable disagreements concerning one or another of the Law Committee's decisions, nearly universal respect has been accorded to the principle of legitimate option. Accordingly, in considering the proper course for the entire Conservative Movement on a matter such as the one under scrutiny, the history of the Law Committee's treatment of some of the related questions must be looked into.

The Law Committee published a majority decision in 1955 which allowed women the privilege of an *aliyah* at Torah reading services. Although this practice is far from universal in Conservative congregations, it is a practice which is growing and which was legitimated by the 1955 decision. In 1973, the same committee issued a majority responsum which permitted congregations to count women as part of the *minyan* for public worship. This practice has likewise not nearly become universal, but the number of congregations which have been accepting it is steadily growing. Finally, a *mi-*

nority report in 1974 declared that women should be permitted to serve as witnesses in legal proceedings, including the signing of *ketubot* and *gittin*. Since that minority report was issued by six committee members, the rules of the Law Committee imply that it is a legitimate option for rabbis and congregations in the Conservative Movement. Thus, the Commission established that the practices referred to in points (3), (4), and (5) had already been declared by the Committee on Jewish Law and Standards of the Rabbinical Assembly to be halakhically acceptable options within the Conservative Movement. Hence the Commission determined that its resolution of the ordination issue could not lead to a possible contravention of a binding standard for the Conservative Movement.

More important than the foregoing observations was the fact that irrespective of what one's halakhic view is on the matter of a woman performing these practices, they are strictly secondary to the issue of ordination. A wide variety of functions are viewed as part of the role of the rabbi today. Among these are teaching, preaching, counselling, officiating at religious ceremonies, representing the Jewish community, etc. Leading a prayer service as the *shaliah tzibur*, receiving an *aliyah*, or even signing a *ketubah* or *get* as a witness are not among the essential functions. A rabbi supervising divorce proceedings might be entitled to sign the *get* as a witness, and may on occasion do so as a matter of convenience, but surely it is not the rabbi's role qua rabbi to do so. Similar observations would apply to other forms of testimony and to the various roles associated with public worship which have been mentioned. The simple fact is that the rabbinate, as noted above, is not defined or circumscribed by halakhic strictures. Hence there can be no direct halakhic objection to the conferral of the title of "rabbi" upon a woman, together with all the rights and responsibilities to perform the functions essentially connected to the office. In connection with this, the Commission noted that it is a commonplace to ordain *Kohanim*, even though officiating at a funeral, which can pose halakhic problems for a *Kohen*, is popularly viewed as a rabbinic function.

One objection raised against this analysis was given very serious consideration by the Commission. It was as follows: granted that the religious functions in question are logically distinct from the role of the rabbi, they are certainly connected closely enough in practice to be a serious cause for concern. Specifically, it is unreasonable, according to this objection, to ordain a woman, place her in a pulpit in a small community, and expect that she will not lead prayer services, sign legal documents affecting personal status, etc. The very inevitability of one event following on the heels of the other might make the two inseparable for the purposes of this discussion.

In the course of lengthy consideration of this objection, the Commission noted several things: (a) As indicated above, previous Law Committee decisions have resolved the problems concerning the practices in question for many members of the Conservative Movement. Indeed, there are already many congregations giving *aliyot* to women and counting them in a *minyan*, and there are Conservative rabbis who, in accordance with the minority responsum of the Law Committee, allow knowledgeable women to sign *ketubot* and *gittin*. (b) Even for those who do not accept the lenient positions on these issues (and this group is largest on the question of testimony, where a good number believe that a female serving as a witness is contrary to biblical law), the objection is still not connected to ordination itself, but rather to an assessment of what is quite likely to happen given a certain job situation in a certain place. The Commission decided that there was little point in speculating on such matters, particularly given the fact that with the increased education and activism of women in the Conservative Movement, the act of ordination itself would not be likely to significantly affect the prevalence of practices which are not universally accepted. Excessive concern over possible objectionable effects of an unobjectionable action (i.e., ordination), where those effects are objectionable to only part of the community, and are not caused solely by that action, can easily degenerate into an *ad infinitum* list of potential objections. (c) Observations (a) and (b) taken together make it clear that there is no cogent argument on halakhic grounds for denying a sincere, committed woman the opportunity to study for and achieve the office of rabbi.

In closing this section on *halakhah*, the Commission notes that in the medieval period, the spiritual leadership of women was not unknown. One bit of evidence for this is to be found in the fourteenth-century work of a Spanish rabbi, known as *Sefer Hahinukh*, which assumes that a woman is eligible to perform the most basic of the classical rabbinic functions, viz., deciding specific matters of law. Section 152 of that treatise, which deals with the prohibition of deciding matters of ritual law while intoxicated, notes that the prohibition "applies to males, as well as to a knowledgeable woman who is eligible to give such instruction."

To summarize, then: The halakhic objections to the ordination of women center around disapproval of the performance by a woman of certain functions. Those functions, however, are not essentially rabbinic, nor are they universally disapproved, by the accepted rules governing the discussion of *halakhah* in the Conservative Movement. *There is no direct halakhic objection to the acts of training and ordaining a woman to be a rabbi, preacher, and teacher in Israel.*

The problems associated with ancillary functions were deemed by the Commission to be insufficient grounds for denying a considerable and growing group of highly talented and committed Jewish women the access they desire to the roles of spiritual and community leaders.

B. Ethical Considerations

Although there was some discussion on the subject, there was not agreement among Commission members concerning precisely what the relationship is or ought to be between *halakhah* and ethics. One general observation was, however, agreed upon. In many areas of Jewish law, the developmental history of the *halakhah* exhibits a strong tendency to approach ever more closely an ideal ethical state within the parameters and constraints of the *halakhah*. Indeed, echoing the opinion of Rav that the *mitzvot* were given us in order to "refine us," the Commission accepted the view that the commandments have among their chief purposes the ethical perfection of the individual and of society. The basic ethical principle underlying the democratic society in which we live—a principle that has deep roots in our biblical-rabbinic tradition—is that each person should have at least a legally equal opportunity to pursue a chosen career. This principle should be followed within the Jewish community more especially where no specific *halakhic* violation is involved. Since there is no specific *halakhic* argument against ordaining women, denying a Jewish woman the opportunity to serve the Jewish community and the cause of Torah as a rabbi merely because she is a woman would be ethically indefensible.

One ethical objection considered by the Commission was actually rooted in sociology and economics. That objection invoked the possibility, or even the likelihood, considering the initial experiences of other movements which have ordained women, that female Conservative rabbis might at first face great difficulty in finding congregational positions. This argument then maintained that it is unethical to train people for a profession with the knowledge that they will find it extremely difficult to practice that profession and thereby fulfill their aspirations and earn a livelihood. The Commission dealt with this objection in several ways. First, it was noted that the results of the public hearings which were held in the fall of 1978 did not indicate that most congregations would be unreasonably reluctant to hire a female rabbi. On the contrary, there was growing evidence, gathered at the Commission's hearings and through the United Synagogue of America, that the receptivity to female rabbis in the communities was much higher now than it had been several years ago. Apparently, familiarity with the issues, as well as the presence and visibility of some ordained women over the last six years had taken effect. At any rate, the assumption of a bleak future in the job market seemed quite unjustified, particularly given the fact that the Conservative Movement is experiencing a shortage of rabbis to serve its congregations.

In addition, the Commission questioned whether job placement was a legitimate ethical issue. Many graduate and professional schools in all fields train students year after year despite wide fluctuations in the job market. While the size of an entering class should certainly not be excessively out of line with what the market can absorb, there is nothing unethical about providing an opportunity for a person to train for his or her chosen profession despite possible difficulties in locating a suitable job situation. What could be improper is withholding information about the realities of the job market, but that is certainly not a serious possibility.

A more serious ethical concern was voiced many times by many interested parties. This objection concerned the right of a minority to have its commitment to conscience respected. Specifically, it was argued as follows: when the Law Committee decided certain halakhic issues by means of majority and minority reports, those whose consciences directed them to the more traditional position would still feel comfortable and legitimate, while respecting their colleagues' right to choose the position which they felt was mandated by the relevant factors. Were the Seminary to begin ordaining women, however, it would be the first time that the central academic institution of the Movement would have entered the arena to take a public stance on an issue of *halakhah*, a stance which could *ipso facto* become the standard of the Movement. Those who opposed the ordination of women on religious grounds would then have no legitimate option but to silently acquiesce in the decision, or to leave the Movement.

The sincerity and frequency with which this argument was raised led the Commission to consider it very carefully. Having done so, the Commission recognized that there would indeed be some unavoidable uneasiness whatever its recommendation would be. Nevertheless, there were three points which were found to mitigate some of the strength of the objection:

(1) This objection partially hinges on the assumption that there are serious matters of halakhic import connected with a decision by the Seminary to ordain women, and that these are serious enough to create difficult crises of conscience. Because of the analysis given in the previous section of this report, it was felt that this objection was overstated.

(2) The objection apparently is intended to argue that the Seminary faculty should not be taking a stance, so as to avoid foreclosing the legitimacy of the opposing view. It fails to take into account the fact that at this point, for the Seminary faculty not to vote to change the status quo would *in*

itself be a stance on the issue. Moreover, it has been the observation of the Commission that there are commitments to conscience among those who favor the ordination of women which are as strong as those among opponents of that decision. The reality is that the Seminary faculty, irrespective of what it does, is going to give rise to some uneasiness in some quarters. This is not to say that one position is obviously better than another, but it does obviate the force of this objection to action on the part of the Seminary faculty. The important issue which does arise out of this is the need to assuage the uneasiness and ensure that it is only a temporary reaction to a decision of great import.

(3) Finally, this objection reveals a bias, which has often been expressed to the Commission, against the Seminary faculty taking a stand on halakhic matters affecting the Conservative Movement. This bias was of particular concern to the Commission, and was discussed on several occasions. It was ultimately the consensus of the Commission that on an issue such as the present one, one which will affect the very nature of the American rabbinate, and which manifestly will not go away if ignored, it is rather the unavoidable responsibility of the Seminary faculty to get involved and take a stand. The Commission assumes that the stand which the faculty will find it necessary to take on any halakhic issue will be a thoroughly informed stand, and that the decision which it now must of necessity make on the issue of ordaining women will be based not only on the careful study of this report, but on the examination of all other data available to it which relate to this issue.

The most compelling ethical argument heard by the Commission was one in favor of ordaining women, and it was heard from members of the Conservative laity in many different parts of North America. As noted in the previous section, the Conservative Movement has a proud history of educating Jewish females in Jewish Studies from the earliest ages on a perfect par with males. In fact, it is worth considering for a moment what it is like today for boys and girls to grow up in a committed Jewish home identified and affiliated with the Conservative Movement. Such a boy and girl would both be given the very same Hebrew or Day School education from the outset. Both would prepare for *Bar* or *Bat Mitzvah* ceremonies and in most cases perform the same functions in the service. Both would likely receive intense Judaic training at Camp Ramah. They would proceed to Hebrew High School, join LTF and/or United Synagogue Youth. In many congregations, they would participate in public worship equally through adolescence, building on their acquired Jewish skills. They would seek out the same reinforcement of their Jewish values while away at college, and form a more sophisticated intellectual commitment to Judaism. That commitment would in some cases be strong enough to generate a desire to study for the rabbinate at the Seminary of the Conservative Movement. Suddenly, discontinuously, at this point, the female is differentiated from the male in being unable to fulfill the education she was given and encouraged to pursue in the way she chose to fulfill it.

This scenario was not an abstract creation, but rather was the actual testimony of many parents who, confronted by the problem, were unable to explain the sudden differentiation to their daughters. In considering this increasingly common phenomenon, the Commission felt that it was morally wrong to maintain an educational structure that treats males and females equally up to the final stage, but distinguishes between them at that stage, *without a firm and clearly identifiable halakhic reason for doing so.* In such a case, the Commission felt that the secondary halakhically related issues dealt with in the previous section paled even further in significance. On balance, the ethical arguments *coupled with the absence of halakhic counter-argument* were considered by the Commission to constitute a strong case for the training and ordination of women as rabbis at the Jewish Theological Seminary of America.

C. Other Considerations

A good deal of other evidence came to the attention of the Commission and was discussed by it. Most of it tended to support a decision to recommend the training and ordination of women as Conservative rabbis. These blocks of evidence fall under a variety of rubrics and will be summarized in this section.

(1) Preliminary data from the survey commissioned by this body indicated that, in absolute numbers, a majority of the laity of the Conservative Movement was ready to accept women in the role of congregational spiritual leader.

(2) Those persons who testified at the regional hearings convened by the Commission represented an extraordinary range of backgrounds, talents, professions, and ages. In all, a considerable majority of these strongly favored the ordination of women in the Conservative Movement. Another fact which came to light as a result of the hearings was that there are more women interested in pursuing this career out of genuine commitment to the traditional Jewish community than had been assumed.

(3) Although the opinions of members of the psychological profession previously reported in the literature were mixed, those professionals in the

field who made contact voluntarily with the Commission were overwhelmingly positive and encouraging on the issue of ordination.

(4) Two United Synagogue congregations are currently being served in some rabbinic or quasi-rabbinic role by a woman, and both communicated, through official leadership as well as through individual congregants, their satisfaction with that situation.

(5) The student body of the Seminary's Rabbinical School, when surveyed by the Student Government, expressed support for the admission of women to the Rabbinical School by an affirmative vote of 74 percent.

(6) It became clear as well that a decision not to ordain women would mean the neglect if not the rejection of a pool of talented, committed, and energetic women who could eventually represent 50 percent of the potential spiritual leaders, and who could play a major role in revitalizing Jewish tradition and values in the Conservative Movement. Indications are that the Movement cannot afford the cost of refusing to take advantage of that leadership talent at the present time.

There was one other major consideration which was voiced many times, and could best be classified under the category of "symbolism." The point was raised by many persons who believed on substantive grounds that the ordination of women was both correct and defensible, but who feared what they termed the symbolic break with tradition that such a move would represent. For exponents of this argument, the symbolic result of admitting women to the rabbinate would be a blurring of the ideological lines which have divided Conservatism from more liberal Jewish movements. That, it is claimed, would destroy the main attraction of the Conservative Movement, to wit, the coexistence of authenticity of tradition with a critical view aimed at developing that tradition within the framework of halakhic norms.

The Commission took this argument most seriously, but concluded that it was insufficient to militate against ordaining women. The reason for this conclusion was that, by the Commission's own commitments and chosen procedures, a recommendation in favor of ordination would be based on a thorough and predominant commitment to *halakhah*. In a case such as this, where a recommended development is consistent with *halakhah*, and manifestly to the advantage of the community, symbolic considerations must not be allowed to block that development. To be sure, the symbolic considerations must be taken very seriously, but rather as a challenge to educate the community to the extent that it is evident to all that the development is in consonance with the historical ideological commitments of Conservative Judaism, and does not represent an ideological shift. It is hoped that this report will constitute a first step in that process of education.

IV. Recommendations

Based on its overall commitment to halakhic authority, and all of the evidence and reasoning which have been summarized or alluded to in this report, the signatories to this majority opinion recommend that qualified women be ordained as rabbis in the Conservative Movement. Specifically, the recommendations are:

A. That the Rabbinical School of the Jewish Theological Seminary of America revise its admission procedures to allow for applications from female candidates and the processing thereof for the purpose of admission to the ordination program on a basis equal to that maintained heretofore for males.

B. That this revision of policy be accomplished as quickly as possible, preferably so as to allow applications from women for the academic year beginning in September 1979.

C. That the Jewish Theological Seminary of America take steps to set up appropriate apparatuses for the recruitment, orientation, and eventually, career placement of female rabbinical students.

D. That the major arms of the Conservative Movement immediately begin discussion of procedures to be followed to educate the community concerning issues raised in this report so as to ensure as smooth and as harmonious an adjustment to the new policy as possible.

In making these recommendations, the Commission is making no recommendation in regard to traditional practices relating to testimony, and no implications concerning such practices should be drawn on the basis of this report.

The following members of the Commission join in supporting the above majority report:

Gerson D. Cohen	Fishel A. Pearlmutter
Victor Goodhill	Harry M. Plotkin
Marion Siner Gordon	Norman Redlich
Rivkah Harris	Seymour Siegel
Milton Himmelfarb	Gordon Tucker
Francine Klagsbrun	

Minority Opinion

Although the signatories to this section are in sympathy with the many arguments and sentiments expressed by our colleagues on the Commission, and embodied in the majority opinion given above, we remain opposed to the ordination of women as rabbis in the Conservative Movement. Since many of the reasons for this conclusion have already been discussed or at least mentioned earlier in this report, we shall simply briefly list our motivations for arriving at this recommendation.

A. Our main thrust has to do with certain halakhic problems which cannot in our opinion be separated from the question of ordination but flow from it almost inexorably. Not all congregations accept the view that women may be counted in a *minyan*, receive *aliyot*, or lead the service in liturgical prayer as a surrogate for others. Many more congregations and many Jews outside our Movement may be affected by practices in connection with testimony relating to marriage and divorce, where the laws are restrictive in the case of women. You cannot, within the present climate of the Conservative Movement, ordain women and expect that they will not at some point infringe on these halakhic restrictions in the performance of their rabbinical duties.

B. We fear the possible disruption of the unity of the Movement. One of the consequences of a decision to ordain women might very well be the violations of halakhic principles adhered to by others in the Movement, which in turn would result in the untenable position of individual rabbis being unable in good conscience to recognize the validity of marriages, divorces, and conversions supervised by one of their colleagues.

C. A decision to ordain women would mark the first time in recent history that the Seminary had entered the arena of halakhic decision-making. The centrality and authority of the Seminary would perforce be a uniformizing influence which could have the unfortunate effect of foreclosing the options of minorities wishing to remain with the movement.

D. Finally, we are concerned that at a time when American Jewish youth seem to be turning more toward traditional values, and to an authentic halakhic life-style, this would seriously compromise the traditional image of the Conservative Movement, and the Jewish Theological Seminary of America as an authentic halakhic institution. We feel strongly that such matters of symbolism must be taken as seriously as possible, for a wrong decision on an issue of this magnitude will, in our opinion, alienate many more halakhically committed people than it will attract.

For these reasons, we recommend to the leaders of the Conservative Movement that appropriate roles be created for Jewish women short of ordination so that their commitment and talents may be a source of blessing and not of unnecessary controversy.

The following members of the Commission join in supporting the above minority opinion:
Haim Z. Dimitrovsky, Elijah J. Schochet, Wilfred Shuchat

30

Emet Ve-Emunah Statement of Principles of Conservative Judaism 1985

In 1985 a commission of laypersons and rabbis was established in the Conservative movement to begin work on a statement of principles for Conservative Judaism. This commission consisted of members of the United Synagogue for Conservative Judaism, the Federation of Jewish Men's Clubs, the Cantors' Assembly, the Rabbinical Assembly, and the Jewish Educator's Assembly. In 1988 *Emet Ve-Emunah Statement of Principles of Conservative Judaism* was published. This was the first time that the movement had published an official statement of the principles for which it stood. The following document is the introductory statement to Emet Ve-Emunah written by the late Robert Gordis, chairman of the Commission on the Philosophy of Conservative Judaism.

INTRODUCTION: THE COMMISSION, THE STATEMENT, THE MOVEMENT

The centennial of the Jewish Theological Seminary of America celebrated in 1986–87 has focused attention on the first hundred years of the history of Conservative Judaism on this continent. Actually the movement had its inception in Germany a half century earlier. In 1845 a meeting of modern rabbis convened in Frankfurt. On the third day Rabbi Zechariah Frankel left the meeting in protest against a proposed resolution that declared that the Hebrew language was not "objectively necessary" for worship, but should be retained "in deference to the older generation." When in 1857 the Jewish Theological Seminary, the first modern institution for the training of rabbis, was founded in Breslau, Frankel was appointed its Rector. Within a few years the institution became the dominant intellectual force in the religious life of central and western European Jewry and beyond. Basically, the movement which Frankel founded was a reaction against Reform on the one hand, and Orthodoxy on the other. The Breslau Seminary was the inspiration and model for similar institutions founded in Vienna, Budapest, London and Berlin, as well as overseas on the American continent.

The Breslau Seminary became the center of the most distinguished modern research scholarship in the fields of Jewish literature, history and institutions, in a word, the meticulous study of the past. But there was little concern for Jewish theology, law and the philosophy of Judaism in the present.

Frankel himself called his outlook "positive-historical Judaism." By this term he meant that Judaism is the result of a historical process and that its adherents are called upon to take a positive attitude toward the product of this development as we encounter it today. While his opponents, both to the left and the right, challenged him to explicate his philosophy of Judaism more concretely, Frankel was rarely drawn into polemics. Having evidently little taste for theology, he concentrated upon building up Jewish learning through the medium of his own research and that of his colleagues on the Breslau faculty and by training rabbis to serve Jewish communities in central Europe and beyond.

In the congregations served by these rabbis, minor innovations were introduced in the ritual. They were designed to accommodate Jewish tradition to the new conditions and insights of the modern age, while preserving intact the structure and content of traditional Jewish observance.

This pattern was largely repeated on American soil. The Jewish Theological Seminary, founded in 1886, had a difficult existence for a decade and a half. In 1902, Solomon Schechter was invited to these shores to serve as its president. He assembled a constellation of scholars of the greatest eminence. In addition to himself, it included Louis Ginzberg, Alexander Marx, Israel Friedlaender, Israel Davidson and Mordecai Kaplan, as well as a galaxy of other scholars, perhaps less well known, but highly gifted and creative. The Seminary faculty and many of its early alumni produced valuable works in the field of historical and literary scholarship.

A growing number of American Jews joined the ranks of Conservative Judaism, demonstrating that the movement met a felt need in the burgeoning American Jewish community. This numerical success strengthened the conviction among many leaders of the movement that there was little need for spelling out in detail the guiding principles and subtler nuances of the movement on such fundamentals as God and man, Israel and the world, ethics and ritual.

The practical considerations that seemed to support the wisdom of avoiding, or at least minimizing the discussion of theological, philosophical and legal issues were reinforced by significant inner factors. The first lay in the character of Conservative Judaism. It had emerged as a reactive movement called into being to stem the tide of Reform, a task in which it has proved highly successful by demonstrating that the Jewish tradition was eminently compatible with loyalty to American life. The thousands of men and women who joined its ranks were generally emphatic in declaring what they were not. They were far less concerned with exploring the implications of what they were for.

The second motive was the desire to preserve, and if possible, enhance, Jewish unity, and certainly not to increase division in Israel. In founding the United Synagogue, Schechter had hoped to unite all congregations respectful of tradition in any degree, right, left and center, under one banner, as the name of the organization indicates. To be sure most Orthodox congregations soon began to look elsewhere for leadership, but the hope lingered among many leaders of Conservative Judaism that by avoiding clear-cut delineation of the principles of the movement, divisions could be avoided, at least within the ranks of Conservative Judaism.

Moreover Judaism had rarely sought to formulate a system of beliefs; even Maimonides had not succeeded in winning universal acceptance for his Thirteen Principles, the *Ani Ma'amin.* Judaism, perhaps unconsciously, had long acted on the principle: far better the blurring of differences than the burning of dissidents.

Finally, a third factor entered into the picture—the sheer intellectual and spiritual difficulty involved in articulating a religious outlook for Conservative Judaism as a whole. Individual Jewish scholars and thinkers, both in the academic world and in the congregational rabbinate, had written works which contained valuable insights for such a project, but they were views of individuals, often influential, but not normative for the movement as a whole.

One can understand and appreciate these factors which militated against formulating statements of ideology until now. In our own time, however, the growing self-awareness of each school of thought in Judaism and latterly, the deeper concern with religious issues among the most genuinely dedicated members of the community, demand answers to questions it earlier seemed easier to avoid.

The formulation of basic doctrine is a particularly difficult task for Conservative Judaism, far more than for its sister movements. Reform Judaism has denied the authority of Jewish law, so that each rabbi and each congregant is free to choose whatever elements of the tradition seem appealing in the name of "individual autonomy."

American Orthodoxy, divided into a dozen groups and factions, is theoretically united under the dogma that both the Written and Oral Law were given by God to Moses on Sinai, and have remained unchanged and un-

changeable through the ages. In fact, this promise of a safe harbor of absolute certainty in a world where everything may be questioned has been the
source of the attraction that Orthodoxy has possessed for many of our contemporaries. This comes at a high price, however. The results of modern
scholarship that reveal a long history of development in Judaism are ignored,
and the challenges presented by modern life are disregarded when possible
or minimized when it is not.

It is Conservative Judaism that most directly confronts the challenge to
integrate tradition with modernity. By retaining most of the tradition while
yet being hospitable to the valuable aspects of modernity, it articulates a vital,
meaningful vision of Judaism for our day. Difficult as this task is, there is
comfort in the observation of our Sages that "lefum tzaara agra," according
to the pain involved is the reward (Avot 5:24).

The twentieth century, the most eventful in Jewish history, had made
this task especially important. The establishment of the State of Israel, the
horror of the Holocaust, and the extraordinary growth and creativity of the
North American Jewish community all demand new synthesis and applications of the new and the old in both thought and action. Jews must also respond to several major developments affecting the human species as a whole,
including especially the feminist movement, the staggering advances in technology and biomedical research, and the awesome threat of nuclear annihi-
lation. As these pages will make clear, the Conservative community has its
own distinctive view of many of these issues, one which is coherent and yet
pluralistic, thoughtful and yet oriented to action, traditional and yet responsive to the present.

The Conservative philosophy has been expressed in the lives of Conservative Jews for decades. A number of Conservative rabbis and lay leaders
have also articulated it, in whole or in part, in written or oral form. As the
Conservative community matured however, it increasingly felt the need to
have an official statement of its principles. A decisive step was taken in 1985.
The official heads of two arms of the movement, Doctor Gerson D. Cohen,
then Chancellor of the Jewish Theological Seminary, and Rabbi Alexander
Shapiro, then President of the Rabbinical Assembly, agreed to set up a Commission on the Ideology (now the Philosophy) of Conservative Judaism, consisting of seven members appointed from the faculty of the Seminary and
seven members from the Rabbinical Assembly. The writer, who had been a
member of the Seminary faculty for thirty-seven years and also President of
the Rabbinical Assembly, was invited to become Chairman of the Commission since he represented both agencies of the movement. Its membership
was subsequently enlarged to include representatives of the United Syna-

gogue of America, the Women's League for Conservative Judaism, the Federation of Jewish Men's Clubs, the Cantors' Assembly and the Jewish Educators' Assembly, and a rabbinic colleague from Israel so that the Commission could speak for all segments of the Conservative community.

The following rabbis and laypersons were members of the Commission:

Robert Gordis, Chairman
Rabbi Kassel Abelson
Rabbi Howard Addison
Rabbi Jacob B. Agus z"l
Rabbi Elliot N. Dorff
Rabbi Neil Gillman
Mr. Max Goldberg
Rabbi Simon Greenberg
Ms. Evelyn Henkind
Judge Norman Krivosha
Dr. Anne Lapidus Lerner
Rabbi David Lieber
Mr. Francis Mintz
Rabbi Ludwig Nadelmann z"l
Rabbi David Novak
Rabbi Stanley Rabinowitz
Rabbi Gilbert S. Rosenthal
Rabbi Benjamin Segal
Rabbi Alexander Shapiro
Dr. Miriam Klein Shapiro
Rabbi Seymour Siegel
Mr. Jacob Stein
Rabbi Gordon Tucker

The following were ex-officio members of the Commission:

Dr. Gerson Cohen, Chancellor, Jewish Theological Seminary (1972–86)
Dr. Ismar Schorsch, Chancellor, Jewish Theological Seminary (1986–)
Rabbi Alexander Shapiro, President, Rabbinical Assembly (1984–86)
Rabbi Kassel Abelson, President, Rabbinical Assembly (1986–)
Mr. Marshall Wolke, President, United Synagogue of America (1981–85)
Mr. Franklin Kreutzer, President, United Synagogue of America (1985–)
Ms. Selma Weintraub, President, Women's League for Conservative Judaism (1982–86)
Ms. Evelyn Auerbach, President, Women's League for Conservative Judaism (1986–)
Cantor Saul Z. Hammerman, President, Cantors' Assembly (1985–87)

Cantor Solomon Mendelson, President, Cantor's Assembly (1987–)
Dr. Michael Korman, President, Jewish Educators' Assembly (1985–87)
Rabbi Marim Charry, President, Jewish Educators' Assembly (1987–)

During the period from 1985–86 Rabbi Akiba Lubow was Secretary of the Commission. In 1987 Ms. Rebecca Jacobs served in the same capacity.

The Editorial committee consisted of Elliot Dorff, Robert Gordis, Rebecca Jacobs, David Lieber, and Gilbert S. Rosenthal.

During the course of its history the Commission sustained grievous losses in the passing of two of its most dedicated members, Rabbi Jacob B. Agus and Rabbi Ludwig Nadelmann, who were called to the Academy on High. Their presence was sorely missed, *yehi zikhram barukh.*

There were ten meetings of the full Commission, each lasting two days, from May 25–26, 1985 to November 9–10, 1987.

It is safe to say that as the Commission began its work there was considerable doubt as to the possibility of its success. First and foremost, there was the inherent difficulty of formulating in words the outlook of a movement numbering some two million men and women with hundreds of leaders. Second, there was the omnipresent danger of its producing a document that would exacerbate differences within the movement by seeking to define its position on controversial questions. On the other hand, the attempt to avoid this result might produce a bland statement that would paper over the differences by issuing an anthology of platitudes. In other words, Conservative Judaism would stand revealed as a coalition rather than a movement, the fate that seems to pervade so many areas of contemporary society.

Whatever judgment will ultimately be passed upon the results of our labors, the members of the Commission were later profoundly gratified to find that they were achieving a far greater consensus than they had dared hope.

Our method of procedure was as follows: In order to orient the members of the Commission to the issues before them and lay the basis for a free yet friendly discussion of the points at issue, the Chairman at the opening meeting proposed that each member be invited to prepare a personal *Ani Ma'amin,* a credo of his or her fundamental beliefs and approaches to the major problems of life as a Jew and as a human being. Each paper was the subject of a detailed analysis and critique at the early meetings of the Commission. These papers, as revised on the basis of this process, will be published in a volume together with the *Statement of Principles of Conservative Judaism.* Over and beyond the intrinsic value of their contents, these *Ani Ma'amin* presentations will afford an insight into the individual world-views of the members of the Commission and thus add a personal and pluralistic dimension to the collective Statement. It should be added that the preparation of these individual statements was optional and not all members availed themselves of this invitation.

Following the preparation of these individual papers, the Commission decided upon the specific topics to be included in the *Statement of Principles*. Each member of the Commission was asked to prepare a preliminary draft of one or several of these sections. In some instances the same theme was presented in preliminary drafts by more than one member of the Commission. Each section was then studied by the entire membership, line by line, and discussed at succeeding meetings. The texts were revised, supplemented or contracted as a result of these detailed discussions. Virtually every section bears the marks of contributions by the entire membership. Most drafts were revised two or three times, some even more. The cooperative spirit between authors of the original drafts and their colleagues made these discussions a warm, friendly experience as well as a stimulating intellectual encounter for the participants.

The Commission, acting as a Committee of the Whole, then formally adopted the definitive version for inclusion in the Statement. Finally, the Editorial Committee read the text and introduced stylistic revisions that did not affect the substance.

While we believe that this Statement of Principles presents a consensus of the views of the movement, it should not be necessary to point out that the *Statement of Principles of Conservative Judaism* is not a catechism or a test of faith. While more than one position falls within the parameters of Conservative Judaism, that fact is reflected in the Statement. Pluralism is a characteristic not only of Judaism as a whole, but of every Jewish school of thought that is nurtured by the spirit of freedom. Acceptance of the Statement of Principles as a whole or in detail is not obligatory upon every Conservative Jew, lay or rabbinic. Nor is each member of the Commission necessarily in agreement with every position embodied in the Statement.

As our work progressed there were two major lessons we learned of far-reaching consequence for the movement. First, it is frequently proclaimed that Conservative Judaism is in decline, in danger of degenerating into a small coterie of survivors or of splitting into a number of hostile groups. During these two years of working together we have learned that, like the announcement of Mark Twain's death, the report of the imminent demise of Conservative Judaism is vastly exaggerated.

Second, we found what some might have doubted at the outset; that while there are differences regarding attitudes and procedures on some issues, there is a far greater area of agreement within our ranks. All groups within the movement accept the fundamentals of the philosophy of Conservative Judaism which find frequent expression in our Statement of Principles. These may summarily be set down as follows:

"In the beginning God . . ." — Though we differ in our perceptions and experiences of reality, we affirm our faith in God as the Creator and Governor of the universe. His power called the world into being; His wisdom and goodness guide its destiny. Of all the living creatures we know, humanity alone, created in His image and endowed with free will, has been singled out to be the recipient and bearer of Revelation. The product of this human-divine encounter is the Torah, the embodiment of God's will revealed and pre-eminently to the Jewish people through Moses, the Prophets and the Sages, as well as to the righteous and wise of all nations. Hence, by descent and destiny, each Jew stands under the divine command to obey God's will.

Second, we recognize the authority of Halakhah which has never been monolithic or immovable. On the contrary, as modern scholarship has abundantly demonstrated, the Halakhah has grown and developed through changing times and diverse circumstances. This life-giving attribute is doubly needed today in a world of dizzying change.

Third, though the term was unknown, pluralism has characterized Jewish life and thought through the ages. This is reflected in the variety of views and attitudes of the biblical legislators, priests, prophets, historians, psalmists and Wisdom teachers, the hundreds of controversies among the rabbis of the Talmud and in the codes and responsa of their successors. The latter-day attempt to suppress freedom of inquiry and the right to dissent is basically a foreign importation into Jewish life.

Fourth, the rich body of Halakhah and Aggadah and the later philosophic and mystical literature, all seeking to come closer to God's presence, are a precious resource for deepening the spiritual life of Israel and humankind.

Fifth, all the aspects of Jewish law and practice are designed to underscore the centrality of ethics in the life of the Jews.

Sixth, Israel is not only the Holy Land where our faith was born and developed but it plays an essential role in our present and future. Israel is a symbol of the unity of the Jewish people the world over, the homeland for millions of Jews and a unique arena for Jewish creativity. Together with our responsibility to Israel is our obligation to strengthen and enrich the life of Jewish communities throughout the world — including, it need hardly be said, our own.

Seventh, Jewish law and tradition, properly understood and interpreted, will enrich Jewish life and help mold the world closer to the prophetic vision of the Kingdom of God.

We hope this Statement will serve as a description of the state of belief in Conservative Judaism as a whole. We trust it will indicate to all individual Jews what is expected of them by the movement to which they give their allegiance. Above all, we pray that it will help teach each of our brothers and sisters what we must ask of ourselves as human beings and as Jews.

We also cherish the hope that many who are not affiliated with Conservative Judaism may find that this Statement of Principles expresses their innermost convictions and ideals. We know that there are untold numbers of men and women in North America, in Israel and throughout the world who have been adherents of Conservative Judaism without being conscious of where they belong. We hope that they will be stimulated to join our movement and thus strengthen its influence for good.

May our brothers and sisters everywhere become more concerned not merely with survival but with a Judaism worthy of survival, so that the Divine promise made to Abraham may be fulfilled for his descendants: "Be thou a blessing."

For the privilege of sitting together and pondering God's ways with Israel and Israel's covenant with God, we humbly bless and hallow His name.
Robert Gordis, Chairman
Commission on the Philosophy of Conservative Judaism
February 3, 1988
Tu Bishevat 5748
The fortieth year of Israel's independence

31

Union for Traditional Judaism, Declaration of Principles 1993

The Union for Traditional Judaism and its rabbinical seminary (the Institute for Traditional Judaism) were founded by those faculty members of the Jewish Theological Seminary of America (JTS) and their constituents in the Conservative movement who rejected what was considered the liberalization of JTS and the movement. The establishment of both the union and the institute immediately followed the decision of the Jewish Theological Seminary of America to ordain women as rabbis.

The Jewish tradition teaches that:

1. *One God created the universe and endowed the humans in it with intelligence and the ability to choose good or evil,*
2. *God revealed Torah to Israel (torah min hashamayim), and*
3. *Torah—both written and oral—as transmitted and interpreted by our sages, from Sinai down through the generations, authoritatively expresses the will of God for the Jewish People*[1]

Building on the Foundation of these Beliefs, the Union for Traditional Judaism is Committed to the Following:

A. The Authority of Halakhah (Jewish Law)—(*Derekh haHalakhah veSamkhutah*)
     Study and observance of Torah is the means whereby Jews draw closer to God and become His partners in creation, sanctifying the world under

---

1. *Cf. Maimonides, Introduction to Commentary on the Mishnah, tr. Kafih, (Mosad HaRav Kook: Jerusalem, 1963), pp. 4–16.*

His dominion. Torah is the yardstick by which we determine right from wrong and the permitted from the forbidden; we concretize it in our daily lives through adherence to Halakhah. Both as it pertains to our relationship with God and our relationship with others, Halakhah is binding upon us even when it conflicts with popular trends in contemporary society.

Torah must also guide our actions when we face new situations in which the law is not clear. Such matters must be decided by scholars who are distinguished by their depth of Torah knowledge and piety. In making these decisions, these scholars use their judgment in applying Torah values and Halakhic principles to the cases before them. Though new discoveries in other fields of human knowledge are relevant factors in Halakhic decision making, Jewish law alone is the final arbiter of Jewish practice. Response to today's challenges should be compassionate and may be creative but must always take place within the parameters of the Halakhic system. This process functions effectively only in the context of a community which is committed to observing Halakhah and which abides by the decisions of its recognized Halakhic authorities.

B. Free and Open Inquiry with Intellectual Honesty—(*Yosher Da'at*)

It is a sacred imperative to apply our God-given intellect and abilities to any and all fields of human endeavor in order to better understand and appreciate our universe. Our quest for all forms of knowledge, when carried out with a sense of awe at the wisdom of God's creation,[2] is a religious act.[3]

Since the universe and Torah issue from the same Source, they must each be understood in light of the other. We must therefore strive to deepen our understanding of Torah in the context of God's creation. Thus we utilize all available methods and all potentially relevant disciplines in interpreting the sacred texts of our tradition. Intellectual honesty requires that we seriously consider new discoveries in any field of knowledge in our search for new meanings *(hiddushim)* in Torah[4]; but intellectual honesty also requires that we recognize the fallibility of our human perceptions and the limitations of our methodologies. This recognition keeps us from drawing conclusions which contradict any of the three beliefs stated above.[5]

2. *Mah rabu ma'asekha hashem, Psalm 104:24.*
3. *Cf. Maimonides, Mishneh Torah, Hilkhot Yesodei ha Torah 2:2.*
4. *Cf. RaSHBaM on Genesis 37:2.*
5. *This relationship between intellectual honesty and these beliefs is implicit in the motto of the Institute for Traditional Judaism: emunah tzerufah veyosher da'at (genuine faith and intellectual honesty).*

C. Love and Respect for Our Fellow Jews — (*Ahavat Yisrael*)

The *mitzvah* of *ahavat yisrael* directs us to relate lovingly and respectfully to all Jews regardless of their level of commitment to traditional Jewish beliefs and observance of Halakhah. We must cooperate, to the fullest extent possible within the parameters of Halakhah, with other Jewish groups and their leaders, without regard to the political boundaries of denominational affiliation. Shared history and common destiny are sufficient reason for making far-reaching efforts to preserve the unity of *kelal yisrael* (the entire Jewish people).

In addition to demanding mutual respect, *ahavat yisrael* requires that we champion adherence to halakhic norms.[6] Bringing Jews closer to Torah is one of the most important challenges we face today, and we believe that this goal can most readily be achieved through an approach which encourages, educates and persuades. In taking such an approach, we are emulating God's display of love and concern for the Jewish people even when they were not fulfilling their religious commitments.[7] God expects us to continually strive to reach our collective potential as a community. We must therefore create synagogue and communal settings where all Jews are made to feel at home, yet are constantly stimulated to bring Jewish observance and study into their homes and their daily lives by rabbis and laymen whose own shared striving and commitment are evident.

D. Love and Respect for Humanity and Creation — (*Kevod haberiyot*)

God's covenant of Torah with the Jewish people does not annul His relationship with the world or with humankind; rather, it enhances it. God continually cares for the world He has created (*hashgahah*) and for every person in it. Since the Jewish people are commanded to imitate God's loving care, we must be concerned with creation in general and with humanity in particular. In the case of creation, we must respect the integrity of nature and oppose its degradation. In the case of humanity, we must respect the dignity of all human beings and oppose their oppression. God's covenant of Torah assumes universal morality then raises us to a higher spiritual level (*kedushah*) as we approach universal redemption (*ge'ulah*).

E. Redemption — (*Ge'ulah*)

We share the age-old dreams for messianic deliverance and trust that ultimate redemption will come when God sees fit. We see in history the

6. *Leviticus 19:17–18.*
7. *Nehemiah 9.*

unfolding of this divine promise and regard the establishment and development of the State of Israel as a step toward its fulfillment *(reishit tzmihat ge'ulateinu)*. We are fortunate to live in a time when we can actively participate as partners in this process.

These are the beliefs and principles for which the Union of Traditional Judaism stands. We call upon all who support these ideals to help us in implementing them throughout the Jewish world. We pray that the work of the U.T.J. will heighten the place of Torah in this world *(lehagdil torah ulehaadirah)* and bring us closer to God.

V

RECONSTRUCTIONISM

While he was a professor at the Jewish Theological Seminary of America, Mordecai Kaplan developed the ideology and organizational structure for the Reconstructionist movement, the only Jewish religious movement indigenous to North America. Focusing on the notion that Judaism is more than just religion, Kaplan claimed that it is, in fact, a civilization. His approach was so appealing that it was absorbed, to a large extent, into prevailing philosophies of the other major Jewish movements. Following his death, the movement underwent many significant changes. Kaplan was a naturalist, but current Reconstructionist ideologues argue for a more theistic approach to God. Much of the current interest in the Jewish Renewal movement emanates from the movement's Reconstructionist Rabbinical College. In this section, some of the earliest Reconstructionist documents are reproduced.

32

Thirteen Wants
1922

Mordecai Kaplan

In the Society for the Advancement of Judaism, Mordecai Kaplan proposed an organization that would incorporate his religious and community philosophy. In this document, Kaplan outlines the basic operating principles for the organization. The Society for the Advancement of Judaism is currently the movement's flagship synagogue in Manhattan.

In view of the changed conditions in Jewish life, the criterion of loyalty to Judaism can no longer be the acceptance of a creed, but the experience of the need to have one's life enriched as a modern religious civilization, we subscribe to the following thirteen wants:

1. We want Judaism to help us overcome temptation, doubt, and discouragement.

2. We want Judaism to imbue us with a sense of responsibility for the righteous use of the blessings wherewith God endows us.

3. We want the Jew so to be trusted that his yea will be taken as yea, and his nay as nay.

4. We want to learn how to utilize our leisure to best advantage physically, intellectually, and spiritually.

5. We want the Jewish home to live up to its traditional standards of virtue and piety.

6. We want the Jewish upbringing of our children to further their moral and spiritual growth and to accept with joy their heritage as Jews.

7. We want the synagogue to enable us to worship God in sincerity and truth.

8. We want our religious traditions to be interpreted in terms of under-standable experience and to be made relevant to our present-day needs.

9. We want to participate in the upbuilding of Eretz Yisrael as a means to the renaissance of the Jewish spirit.

10. We want Judaism to find rich, manifold, and ever new expression in philosophy, in letters, and in the arts.

11. We want all forms of Jewish organization to make for spiritual pur-pose and ethical endeavor.

12. We want the unity of Israel throughout the world to be fostered through mutual help in time of need, and through cooperation in the fur-therance of Judaism at all times.

13. We want Judaism to function as a potent influence for justice, free-dom, and peace in the life of men and nations.

33

Why "Reconstructionist"?
1928

In response to critics who questioned the need for another Jewish movement, Mordecai Kaplan sought to defend his choice of the term "Reconstructionist."

Nowadays, when people do not read but run, the choosing of a name for any new movement or idea is important. There may be nothing in a name until you put something into it. But once a name becomes identified with certain specific purposes, it is wisdom, when you have grown to new purposes, to find a new name rather than torture new meanings out of the old name.

The movement in American Jewish life known as Conservative Judaism has committed itself to dealing with the problem of Judaism as a problem of religion only. This is an error, and it is the same error which is responsible for the failure of the Reform movement. It is a fundamental error, because it is an approach to the problem which, while seeking to bring order out of chaos, actually multiplies the division. The moment you propose one mode of worship or one attitude toward observance for another, you automatically divide. These very things depend on taste, habit, and pressure of necessity. Hence, it is about them that our differences are most deeply rooted and therefore most irreconcilable. A religious party, by its very nature, declares itself against rapprochement in respect to such differences. A religious party is, by its very nature, interested in these differences only. The Conservatives are a religious party. How, then, can a Conservative movement be a unifying movement?

It will not be gainsaid that the problem of Jewish life is just this problem of unity. A solution to the problem of Jewish life depends upon finding, or making, a positive ideology which will enable both Orthodox and Reform, both believers and nonbelievers, to meet in common and to work together. It is only by conceiving Judaism as a civilization, and not as a general religious movement embracing many sects, that we will be able to construct such an ideology and *reconstruct the Jewish civilization*. To interpret Judaism as a civilization is to open the way for unity, because such interpretation enables us to seek the neutral factors of unity in language, the rebuilding of Palestine, and social relationships among Jews. In Judaism as a civilization, religion, the most important element in it, will flourish the better because it will not then be the subject of so much negative controversy.

The Society for the Advancement of Judaism, therefore, prefers to be considered a branch of the *Reconstructionist* movement in Jewish life, rather than of the Conservative. We are religiously allied with the Conservative party, but our interest is not in the organization of a religious party as such. In the Reconstructionist party, any Jewish group of any shade or quality of belief may find enough positive content to develop Jewish consciousness. Develop this Jewish consciousness, and you have Jewish unity.

34

The Reconstructionist Position
1935

In the *Reconstructionist*, the journal he founded in 1935, Mordecai Kaplan was able to introduce his philosophy into the dialogue about current issues of Jewish life. This vehicle allowed him to engage the Jewish community on a regular basis.

However welcome any new Jewish periodical must be as a sign of its Jewish awakening, it should justify its coming into existence on the ground of some distinctive policy or platform. Accordingly, in presenting this first issue of the *Reconstructionist*, the editors wish to state what is to be the philosophy of Jewish life by which they will be guided in their editorial comment and in their selection of articles and book reviews.

The uncertainty as to the meaning of Judaism, and the doubt as to its power to contribute to the enrichment of the life of the individual or to the promotion of human welfare generally, are ominous symptoms of the disintegration of Jewish life. The persistence and ubiquity of anti-Semitism have discredited for most Jews the policy of deliberate flight from Judaism, and have exposed the futility of assimilation. But pressure from without can result at best only in the continuance of Jews as a separate group. Such continuance, unillumined by the hope of a worthwhile future, can have no meaning or value for the Jews and can be nothing but a burden. The Jews should find joy in being Jews. Their Jewishness should be to them a source of enrichment and a means to the realization of what is best in them. To help bring this about is the task to which we apply ourselves.

We approach this task from the point of view of Judaism as a religious civilization. Other religious interpretations of Judaism, such as Reformism, Orthodoxy, Conservatism, are in their very nature divisive and thus afford no basis for cooperation with Jews who hold contrary opinions. We envisage

Judaism as the proper concern of all Jews, religious and unreligious, conservative and radical, and we recognize the fact that all who take an affirmative attitude toward Judaism contribute to Jewish civilization, even if they deny that Judaism *is* a civilization, and by denying weaken the value of their contribution.

In affirming that Judaism is a civilization we give emphasis to the fact that it includes many more interests than are commonly associated with the term religion, that it includes communal organization, language, law, art, mores, customs, as well as religion. Moreover, all of these elements are organically related to each other; to omit any of them is to distort Judaism. All of them are functions of the group life of Israel, and cannot be maintained unless we maintain the unity and integrity of the Jewish people and the continuity of its spiritual efforts.

We believe that the material and spiritual welfare of the Jews can be achieved only through Jewish communal organization which answers the vital needs of the Jews, and which is rendered articulate through a plastic and creative ideology. In pursuance of these objectives we favor the establishment of Jewish communal life in America, democratically administered and organized in such a manner as to include all Jews who wish to identify themselves with the Jewish people, regardless of what their personal philosophy may be.

In affirming that Judaism is a *religious* civilization, we recognize first, the historic fact that the God idea has dominated the entire pattern of Jewish life in the past, and that continuity with our past is impossible without giving to religion a position, if not of primacy, at least of *primus inter pares*; and secondly, the social fact that a mature and complete civilization is bound to find expression in the idea of God and in forms of religious worship in which the hopes and ideals of human life are rendered articulate. It is that very sense of need for religion that impels us to reinterpret the traditional beliefs in keeping with what for us must be a tenable world outlook, and to revise and develop the traditional usages in keeping with spiritual needs which we can genuinely experience.

We consider the establishment of Palestine indispensable to the life of Judaism in the diaspora. We seek to enable Jewish civilization so to root itself in the soil of Palestine as to make of that land the cultural center for Israel's intellectual and spiritual rebirth. We oppose any attempt to render Palestine the object of imperialist aims or the victim of private profit seeking. We endorse every effort toward the establishment of a cooperative commonwealth in Palestine based upon social justice and social cooperation.

Realizing that Jewish life in the modern world cannot be self-sufficient, Jews are not exempt from the suffering and frustration incidental to the social crisis, nor are they free from the responsibility of sharing in the creative task of bringing order out of the present chaos. The proved inadequacy of ancient sanctions to prevent injustice, oppression and war is reflected in attitudes of cynicism, despair and ruthless self-seeking. We need a renewal of faith and a vision of new possibilities. We have need again to conceive of a Messianic age, a utopia toward which to direct all our strivings, something worthwhile to which we might look forward. Nothing less than a movement for a thoroughgoing change in our social and economic order can satisfy this need.

We are opposed to Fascism in every form. We object to any philosophy of government which seeks to curtail the rights of individuals to the free pursuit of personal salvation through participation in any religious or cultural activity, or through affiliation with any national or ethnic group. We see in economic imperialism and the competitive scramble for foreign markets the dominant cause of war in modern times, and we shall support all efforts looking to the establishment of such economic and social conditions and such international relationships as shall eliminate the known causes of war and increase the scope of mutual cooperation for human welfare. In the meantime, recognizing the horror and irrationality of war as a means of adjusting conflicting interests, we shall support every effort looking to the perfection of machinery for the peaceful adjudication of such conflicts and to the utilization of such machinery as exists, wherever possible. Under no circumstances shall we give countenance or support to an imperialistic war that is designed to advance the interests of exploiting and oppressing classes.

We dare not be reconciled to an economic system that crushes the laboring masses and permits the existence of want in an economy of potential plenty. Social righteousness is possible only upon the establishment of a cooperative society, the elimination of the profit system, and the public ownership of all natural resources and basic industries. Until these objectives are achieved our sympathies and our support go to labor in its struggle with its employers for a more equitable distribution of the income of industry, and in the assertion of its right to organize for the protection of its interests without interference from its employers.

These are our principles. We pledge our best efforts to their advancement.

35

The Reconstructionist Foundation
1940

When Mordecai Kaplan established the Reconstructionist Foundation in 1940, he did not see it as a fourth movement. Instead, he thought that it would provide a catalyst for progress and unity in American Judaism, especially in regard to his conceptualization of Judaism as a civilization.

The Jewish Reconstructionist movement seeks to foster the physical and spiritual survival of the Jewish people by means of a new approach to Jewish life and tradition. It proposes ways and means of living a maximum Jewish life within the setting of a modern democratic state. Though its program is directed specifically to American Jews, its philosophy applies to Jewish life everywhere.

Reconstructionism views Judaism as a dynamic religious civilization. It addresses itself to the most urgent Jewish needs of our day, which are the following: (1) to restore the spiritual unity of the Jewish people, (2) to reorganize the communal life of the American Jews, (3) to aid the development of Israel, (4) to revitalize Jewish religion, (5) to encourage Jewish cultural creativity in education, literature, and the arts, (6) to intensify participation by Jews in all activities that further the ideals of American democracy. These are the objectives which Reconstructionism strives to attain.

The Spiritual Unity of the Jewish People

Every Jew depends upon every other Jew for the energy, resources, and courage with which to live as a Jew and to achieve complete self-fulfillment as a human being. This interdependence constitutes that spiritual unity which makes of the Jews a people. This status as a people is in need of being given formal recognition, so that there be no misunderstanding as to what it is that unites Jews, nor any misgivings as to their professing dual allegiance or conflicting loyalties.

The Reorganization of Jewish Communal Life

American Jews have formed all kinds of organizations and federations for specific purposes. These purposes, growing out of the circumstances of Jewish life, are in their very nature interdependent. They are treated, however, as though they had nothing to do with one another. The result is that though each purpose may singly be achieved, it does not further Jewish life as a whole. That is true not only of fraternal organization, social service, overseas relief and Zionist activity but even of the synagogue and the religious school.

The only way to overcome the fragmentation of Jewish life is to have Jews form themselves into organic communities that would function as the instruments of Jewish life as a whole, and that would meet all its needs in the order of their urgency and importance. Such a community would have to be democratically organized and represent all Jews who wish to be identified with it. Those who at present serve the various organizations and federations would then serve the entire community.

Such reorganized communal life would not only coordinate our activities efficiently. It would also integrate the Jew into the living body of the Jewish people, and give him that inner security which comes from belonging and from being wanted and welcomed.

The Development of Israel

As Americans, our primary civilization is American, and as Jews we share with Jews throughout the world the civilization of the Jewish people. The hub of Jewish civilization is bound to be in Israel, where it is the primary civilization of the land, and where the spiritual and cultural revival provides a reservoir of cultural and ethical values for all Jewry. In Israel, Jewish life can fulfill the historic aspirations of the Jewish people and should, therefore, be built upon firm foundations of social, political and economic justice for all inhabitants of that country. That very expectation, supported by efforts to bring about its fulfillment, is bound to exercise a deep moral and spiritual influence of Jewish life everywhere.

The Revitalization of Jewish Religion

Traditional religions, because they appear to be unrelated to the needs and problems of modern life, seem to be losing their hold on many people. Jewish religion, to be a vital force in the life of the individual Jew, should be relevant to his everyday actions and should have meaning for Jewish living in two civilizations, the American and the Jewish. Indifference to Jewish religion on the part of many Jews stems from the fact that religion, in their minds, is identified with particular doctrines and practices to which they cannot subscribe intellectually. However, religion can be so reinterpreted in every generation as to meet both the intellectual demands and the spiritual needs of that generation. It should always be recognized that the true function of religion is to influence man to live in harmony with the will of God as the Power that makes for the realization of the best in one's life and in one's people. That is the function which Jewish religion will have to fulfill, if it is to be once again the core of Jewish civilization.

Effective Jewish Education

Jewish education to be effective today, should transmit to the child the heritage of the past so that he may be equipped as a Jew to live in the present and to be prepared to meet the problems of the foreseeable future. Jewish education includes every aspect of Jewish culture: religion, Hebrew language, literature, contemporary Jewish problems, and the esthetic expression of the Jewish experience. Because the home is so important an influence in all education, the Jewish home should have a cultural and spiritual atmosphere that is authentically Jewish. Since education is not confined to the home, however, some regular portion of the time of each adult and child should be devoted to acquiring Jewish knowledge.

The Cultivation of the Arts

Art forms such as poetry, drama, music, dance, sculpture, and the graphic arts are no longer viewed as extra-curricular in the life of a people. They have come to be recognized as an integral and indispensable element in man's effort to raise himself above the level of the subhuman. If Judaism is to have a humanizing and spiritualizing influence it must accord to the arts no less significant a position than that which they occupy in all modern civilizations.

Jewish artists should be encouraged and stimulated to express their creativity within the sphere of Jewish life. They should be assisted through every means such as subsidies, scholarships, art exhibits, and promotion of competitive contests. What is needed, above all, is affirmative evaluation of the place of arts in Judaism, on the part of rabbis and teachers through the various means at their command.

Furtherance of American Democracy

The improvement of human relations has always been a major element in Jewish civilization. The concepts of the Fatherhood of God and the Brotherhood of Man are based on the Jewish view that mankind is one, that man must learn to transcend the differences among races, peoples, and religions. The Brotherhood of Man means cooperative effort to make a better life for all men. Jews should strive for the establishment of a social order that combines the maximum of human cooperation with the maximum of personal freedom. Jewish organizations and institutions ought to make Jews sensitive to those social evils that impede the attainment of this goal. Jewish communities and Jews individually should cooperate with the general population in furthering all movements which have as their purpose the eradication of poverty, exploitation, violence and war.

VI

PHILOSOPHY/THEOLOGY

While the foundational ideology of the Jew finds its roots in the Bible, there are a variety of philosophical and theological concepts that developed throughout Jewish history, which extend and transcend these basic ideas essential to Judaism. Each generation has continued to add to the layers of Jewish thinking, bringing its own nuances to ideas central to Judaism. This section presents some of the salient philosophical and theological documents of the Jewish people.

36

The Ten Commandments
(*Aseret Hadibrot*)

The Ten Commandments, more precisely translated from the Hebrew *aseret hadibrot* as the ten statements or ten utterances, appears in two slightly different forms in Exodus 20:1–17 and Deuteronomy 5:1–18.

1. I am Adonai your God, who brought you out of the land of Egypt, out of the house of bondage.
2. You shall have no other gods in place of me, nor make for yourself any idols.
3. You shall not speak God's name for no purpose.
4. Remember the Sabbath day and keep it holy.
5. Honor your father and mother.
6. Do not murder.
7. Do not commit adultery.
8. Do not steal.
9. Do not bear false witness against your neighbor.
10. Do not covet anything that your neighbor owns.

37

The 613 Commandments
12th century

Moses Maimonides

There are a variety of listings of the 613 commandments considered to be the number of *mitzvot* contained in the Torah. This listing, prepared by Moses Maimonides and enumerated in his *Sefer Ha-Mitzvot,* is the version accepted by the majority of Jewish teachers and scholars.

Positive Commandments
The Jew is required to (1) believe that God exists and to (2) acknowledge God's unity; to (3) love, (4) fear, and (5) serve God. The Jew is also instructed to (6) cleave to God (by associating with and imitating the wise) and to (7) swear only by God's name. One must (8) imitate God and (9) sanctify God's name.

The Jew must (10) recite the *Shema* each morning and evening and (11) study the Torah and teach it to others. The Jew should bind *tefillin* on the (12) head and (13) the arm. The Jew should make (14) *tzitzit* for the garments and (15) fix a *mezuzah* on the door. The people are to be (16) assembled every seventh year to hear the Torah read and (17) the king must write a special copy of the Torah for himself. (18) Every Jew should have a Torah scroll. One should (19) praise God after eating.

The Jews should (20) build a Temple and (21) respect it. It must be (22) guarded at all times and the (23) Levites should perform their special duties in it. Before entering the Temple or participating in its service the priests (24) must wash their hands and feet; they must also (25) light the candelabrum daily. The priests are required to (26) bless Israel and to (27) set the shewbread and frankincense before the Ark. Twice daily they must (28) burn the incense on the golden altar. Fire shall be kept burning on the altar (29) continually and the ashes should be (30) removed daily. Ritually unclean persons must be (31) kept out of the Temple. Israel (32) should honor its priests, who must be (33) dressed in special priestly raiment. The priests should (34) carry the Ark on their shoulders, and the holy anointing oil (35) must be prepared according to its special formula. The priestly families should officiate in (36) rotation. In honor of certain dead close relatives the priests should (37) make themselves ritually unclean. The high priest may marry (38) only a virgin.

The (39) *tamid* sacrifice must be offered twice daily and the (40) high priest must also offer a meal-offering twice daily. An additional sacrifice (*musaf*) should be offered (41) every Sabbath, (42) on the first of every month, and (43) on each of the seven days of Passover. On the second day of Passover (44) a meal offering of the first barley must also be brought. On Shavuot a (45) *musaf* must be offered and (46) two loaves of bread as a wave offering. The additional sacrifice must also be made on (47) Rosh Hashanah and (48) on the Day of Atonement when the (49) Avodah must also be performed. On every day of the festival of (50) Sukkot a *musaf* must be brought as well as on the (51) eighth day thereof.

Every male [and female] Jew should make (52) pilgrimage to the Temple three times a year and (53) appear there during the three pilgrim Festivals. One should (54) rejoice on the Festivals.

On the 14th of Nisan one should (55) slaughter the paschal lamb and (56) eat of its roasted flesh on the night of the 15th. Those who were ritually impure in Nisan should slaughter the paschal lamb on the (57) 14th of Iyar and eat it with (58) *matzah* and bitter herbs. Trumpets should be (59) sounded when the festive sacrifices are brought and also in times of tribulation.

Cattle to be sacrificed must be (60) at least eight days old and (61) without blemish. All offerings must be (62) salted. It is a *mitzvah* to perform the ritual of (63) the burnt offering, (64) the sin offering, (65) the guilt offering, (66) the peace offering (67) and the meal offering.

Should the Sanhedrin err in a decision its members (68) must bring a sin offering which offering must also be brought (69) by a person who has unwittingly transgressed a *karet* prohibition (i.e., one which, if done deliberately, should incur *karet*). When in doubt as to whether one has transgressed such a prohibition a (70) "suspensive" guilt offering must be brought.

For (71) stealing or swearing falsely and for other sins of a like nature, a guilt offering must be brought. In special circumstances the sin offering (72) can be according to one's means.

One must (73) confess one's sins before God and repent for them.

A (74) man or (75) woman who has a seminal issue must bring sacrifice; a woman must also bring a sacrifice (76) after childbirth.

A leper must (77) bring a sacrifice after he [or she] has been cleansed.

One must (78) tithe one's cattle. The (79) firstborn of clean (i.e., permitted) cattle are holy and must be sacrificed. Firstborn children must be (80) redeemed. The firstling of the ass must be (81) redeemed; if not (82) its neck has to be broken.

Animals set aside as offerings (83) must be brought to Jerusalem without delay and (84) may be sacrificed only in the Temple. Offerings from outside the land of Israel (85) may also be brought to the Temple.

Sanctified animals (86) which have become blemished must be redeemed. A beast exchanged for an offering (87) is also holy. The priests should eat (88) the remainder of the meal offering and (89) the flesh of sin and guilt offerings; but consecrated flesh which has become (90) ritually unclean or (91) which was not eaten within its appointed time must be burned.

A Nazirite must (92) let his hair grow during the period of his separation. When that period is over he must (93) shave his head and bring his sacrifice.

A person must (94) honor one's vows and one's oaths which a judge can (95) annul only in accordance with the law.

Anyone who touches (96) a carcass or (97) one of the eight species of reptiles becomes ritually unclean; food becomes unclean by (98) coming into contact with a ritually unclean object. Menstruous women (99) and those (100) lying-in after childbirth are ritually impure. A (101) leper, (102) a leprous garment, (103) and a leprous house are all ritually unclean. A man having (104) a running issue is unclean, as is (105) semen. A woman suffering from (106) running issue in also impure. A (107) human corpse is ritually unclean. The purification water (*mei niddah*) purifies (108) the unclean, but it makes the clean ritually impure. It is a *mitzvah* to become ritually clean (109) by ritual immersion. To become cleansed of leprosy one (110) must follow the specified procedure and also (111) shave off all of one's hair. Until cleansed the leper (112) must be bareheaded with clothing in disarray so as to be easily distinguishable.

The ashes of (113) the red heifer are to be used in the process of ritual purification.

If a person (114) undertakes to give one's own value to the Temple, one must do so. Should a person declare (115) an unclean beast, (116) a house, or (117) a field as a donation to the Temple, one must give their value in money as fixed by the priest. If one unwittingly derives benefit from Temple property (118) full restitution plus a fifth must be made.

The fruit of (119) the fourth year's growth of trees is holy and may be eaten only in Jerusalem. When you reap your fields you must leave (120) the corners, (121) the gleanings, (122) the forgotten sheaves, (123) the misformed bunches of grapes and (124) the gleanings of the grapes for the poor.

The first fruits must be (125) separated and brought to the Temple and you must also (126) separate the great heave offering (*terumah*) and give it to the priests. You must give (127) one tithe of your produce to the Levites and separate (128) a second tithe which is to be eaten only in Jerusalem. The Levites (129) must give a tenth of their tithe to the priests.

In the third and sixth years of the seven year cycle you should (130) separate a tithe for the poor instead of a second tithe. A declaration (131) must be recited when separating the various tithes and (132) when bringing the first fruits to the Temple.

The first portion of the (133) dough must be given to the priest.

In the seventh year (*shemittah*) everything that grows is (134) ownerless and available to all; the fields (135) must lie fallow and you may not till the ground. You must (136) sanctify the Jubilee year [50th] and on the Day of Atonement in that year (137) you must sound the *shofar* and set all Hebrew slaves free. In the Jubilee year all land is to be (138) returned to its ancestral owners and, generally, in a walled city (139) the seller has the right to buy back a house within a year of the sale.

Starting from entry into the land of Israel, the years of the Jubilee must be (140) counted and announced yearly and septennially.

In the seventh year (141) all debts are annulled but (142) one may exact a debt owed by a foreigner.

When you slaughter an animal you must (143) give the priest his share as you must also give him (144) the first of the fleece. When a person makes a *cherem* (a special vow) you must (145) distinguish between what belongs to the Temple (i.e., when God's name was mentioned in the vow) and between what goes to the priests. To be fit for consumption, beast and fowl must be (146) slaughtered according to the law and if they are not of a domesticated species (147) their blood must be covered with earth after slaughter.

Set the parent bird (148) free when taking the nest. Examine (149) beast, (150) fowl, (151) locusts and (152) fish to determine whether they are permitted for consumption.

The Sanhedrin should (153) sanctify the first day of every month and reckon the years and the seasons.

You must (154) rest on the Sabbath day and (155) declare it holy at its onset and termination. On the 14th of Nisan (156) remove all leaven from your ownership and on the night of the 15th (157) relate the story of the exodus from Egypt; on that night (158) you must also eat *matzah*. On the (159) first and (160) seventh days of Passover you must rest. Starting from the first day of the first sheaf (16th of Nisan) you shall (161) count 49 days. You must rest on (162) Shavuot and on (163) Rosh Hashanah; on the Day of Atonement you must (164) fast and (165) rest. You must also rest on (166) the first and (167) the eighth day of Sukkot during which festival you shall (168) dwell in booths and (169) take the four species. On Rosh Hashanah (170) you are to hear the sound of the *shofar*.

Every male should (171) give half a shekel to the Temple annually. You must (172) obey a prophet and (173) appoint a king. You must also (174) obey the Sanhedrin; in the case of division, (175) yield to the majority. Judges and officials shall be (176) appointed in every town and they shall judge the people (177) impartially.

Whoever is aware of evidence (178) must come to court to testify.

Witnesses shall be (179) examined thoroughly and, if found to be false, (180) shall have done to them what they intended to do to the accused.

When a person is found murdered and the murderer is unknown the ritual of (181) decapitating the heifer must be performed.

Six cities of refuge should be (182) established. The Levites, who have no ancestral share in the land, shall (183) be given cities to live in.

You must (184) build a fence around your roof and remove potential hazards from your home.

Idolatry and its appurtenances (185) must be destroyed, and a city which has become perverted must be (186) treated according to the law. You are instructed to (187) destroy the seven Canaanite nations, and (188) blot out the memory of Amalek, and (189) to remember what they did to Israel.

The regulations for wars other than those commanded in the Torah (190) are to be observed and a priest should be (191) appointed for special duties in times of war. The military camp must be (192) kept in a sanitary condition. To this end, every soldier must be (193) equipped with the necessary implements.

Stolen property must be (194) restored to its owner. Give (195) charity to the poor. When a Hebrew slave goes free the owner must (196) give him gifts. Lend to (197) the poor without interest; to the foreigner you may (198) lend at interest. Restore (199) a pledge to its owner if he needs it. Pay the worker his wages (200) on time; (201) permit him to eat of the produce with which he is working. You must (202) help unload an animal when necessary, and also (203) help load human or beast [of burden]. Lost property (204) must be restored to its owner. You are required (205) to reprove the sinner but you must (206) love your neighbor as yourself. You are instructed (207) to love the proselyte. Your weights and measures (208) must be accurate.

Respect the (209) wise; (210) honor and (211) revere your parents. You should (212) perpetuate the human species by marrying (213) according to the law. A bridegroom is to (214) rejoice with his bride for one year. Male children must (215) be circumcised. Should a man die childless, his brother must either (216) marry his widow or (217) release her (*chalitza*). He who violates a virgin must (218) marry her and may never divorce her. If a man unjustly accuses his wife of premarital promiscuity (219) he shall be flogged, and may never divorce her. The seducer (220) must be punished according to the law. The female captive must be (221) treated in accordance with her special regulations. Divorce can be executed (222) only by means of a written document. A woman suspected of adultery (223) has to submit to the required test.

When required by the law (224) you must administer the punishment of flogging and you must (225) exile the unwitting homicide. Capital punishment shall be by (226) the sword, (227) strangulation, (228) fire, or (229) stoning, as specified. In some cases the body of the executed (230) shall be hanged, but it (231) must be brought to burial the same day.

Hebrew slaves (232) must be treated according to the special laws for them. The master should (233) marry his Hebrew maidservant or (224) redeem her. The alien slave (235) must be treated according to the regulations applying to him.

The applicable law must be administered in the case of injury caused by (236) a person, (237) an animal or (238) a pit. Thieves (239) must be punished. You must render judgment in cases of (240) trespass by cattle, (241) arson, (242) embezzlement by an unpaid guardian and in claims against (243) a paid guardian, a hirer, or (244) a borrower. Judgment must also be rendered in disputes arising out of (245) sales, (248) inheritance and (246) other matters generally. You are required to (247) rescue the persecuted even if it means killing the oppressor.

Textual Sources for Positive Commandments

1. Exodus 20:2
2. Deuteronomy 6:4
3. Deuteronomy 6:13
4. Deuteronomy 6:13
5. Exodus 23:25; Deuteronomy 11:13; (Deuteronomy 6:13 and 13:5)
6. Deuteronomy 10:20
7. Deuteronomy 19:20
8. Deuteronomy 28:9
9. Leviticus 22:32
10. Deuteronomy 6:7
11. Deuteronomy 6:7
12. Deuteronomy 6:8
13. Deuteronomy 6:8
14. Numbers 15:38
15. Deuteronomy 6:9
16. Deuteronomy 31:12
17. Deuteronomy 17:18
18. Deuteronomy 31:19
19. Deuteronomy 8:10
20. Exodus 25:8
21. Leviticus 19:30
22. Numbers 18:4
23. Numbers 18:23
24. Exodus 30:19
25. Exodus 27:21
26. Numbers 6:23
27. Exodus 25:30
28. Exodus 30:7
29. Leviticus 6:6
30. Leviticus 6:3
31. Numbers 5:4
32. Leviticus 21:8

33. Exodus 28:2
34. Numbers 7:9
35. Exodus 30:31
36. Deuteronomy 18:6–8
37. Leviticus 21:2–3
38. Leviticus 21:13
39. Numbers 28:3
40. Leviticus 6:13
41. Numbers 28:9
42. Numbers 28:11
43. Leviticus 23:26
44. Leviticus 23:10
45. Numbers 28:26–27
46. Leviticus 23:17
47. Numbers 29:1-2
48. Numbers 28:26–27
49. Leviticus 16
50. Numbers 29:13
51. Numbers 29:36
52. Exodus 23:14
53. Exodus 34:23; Deuteronomy 16:16
54. Deuteronomy 16:14
55. Exodus 12:6
56. Exodus 12:8
57. Numbers 9:11
58. Numbers 9:11; Exodus 12:8
59. Numbers 10:10; 10:9
60. Leviticus 22:27
61. Leviticus 22:21
62. Leviticus 2:13
63. Leviticus 1:2
64. Leviticus 6:18

65. Leviticus 7:1
66. Leviticus 3:1
67. Leviticus 2:1; 6:7
68. Leviticus 4:13
69. Leviticus 4:27
70. Leviticus 5:17–18
71. Leviticus 5:15, 21–25;
    19:20–21
72. Leviticus 5:1–11
73.. Numbers 5:6–7
74. Leviticus 15:13–15
75. Leviticus 15:28–29
76. Leviticus 12:6
77. Leviticus 14:10
78. Leviticus 27:32
79. Exodus 13:2
80. Exodus 22:28;
    Numbers 18:15
81. Exodus 34:20
82. Exodus 13:13
83. Deuteronomy 12:5
84. Deuteronomy 12:14
85. Deuteronomy 12:26
86. Deuteronomy 12:15
87. Leviticus 27:33
88. Leviticus 8:9
89. Exodus 29:33
90. Leviticus 7:19
91. Leviticus 7:17
92. Numbers 6:5
93. Numbers 6:18
94. Deuteronomy 23:24
95. Numbers 30:3
96. Leviticus 11:8, 24
97. Leviticus 11:29–31
98. Leviticus 11:34
99. Leviticus 15:19
100. Leviticus 12:2
101. Leviticus 13:3
102. Leviticus 13:51
103. Leviticus 14:44
104. Leviticus 15:2
105. Leviticus 15:16

106. Leviticus 15:19
107. Numbers 19:14
108. Numbers 19:13, 21
109. Leviticus 15:16
110. Leviticus 14:2
111. Leviticus 14:9
112. Leviticus 13:45
113. Numbers 19:2–9
114. Leviticus 27:2–8
115. Leviticus 27:11–12
116. Leviticus 27:14
117. Leviticus 27:16, 22–23
118. Leviticus 5:16
119. Leviticus 19:24
120. Leviticus 19:9
121. Leviticus 19:9
122. Deuteronomy 24:19
123. Leviticus 19:10
124. Leviticus 19:10
125. Exodus 23:19
126. Deuteronomy 18:4
127. Leviticus 27:30;
     Numbers 18:24
128. Deuteronomy 14:22
129. Numbers 18:26
130. Deuteronomy 14:28
131. Deuteronomy 26:13
132. Deuteronomy 26:5
133. Numbers 15:20
134. Exodus 23:11
135. Exodus 34:21
136. Leviticus 25:10
137. Leviticus 25:9
138. Leviticus 25:24
139. Leviticus 25:29–30
140. Leviticus 25:8
141. Deuteronomy 15:3
142. Deuteronomy 15:3
143. Deuteronomy 18:3
144. Deuteronomy 18:4
145. Leviticus 27:21, 28
146. Deuteronomy 12:21
147. Leviticus 17:13

148. Deuteronomy 22:7
149. Leviticus 11:2
150. Deuteronomy 14:11
151. Leviticus 11:21
152. Leviticus 11:9
153. Exodus 12:2;
      Deuteronomy 16:1
154. Exodus 23:12
155. Exodus 20:8
156. Exodus 12:15
157. Exodus 13:8
158. Exodus 12:8
159. Exodus 12:16
160. Exodus 12:16
161. Leviticus 23:35
162. Leviticus 23
163. Leviticus 23:24
164. Leviticus 16:29
165. Leviticus 16:29, 31
166. Leviticus 23:35
167. Leviticus 23:42
168. Leviticus 23:42
169. Leviticus 23:40
170. Numbers 29:1
171. Exodus 30:12–13
172. Deuteronomy 18:15
173. Deuteronomy 17:15
174. Deuteronomy 17:11
175. Exodus 23:2
176. Deuteronomy 16:18
177. Leviticus 19:15
178. Leviticus 5:1
179. Deuteronomy 13:15
180. Deuteronomy 19:19
181. Deuteronomy 21:4
182. Deuteronomy 19:3
183. Numbers 35:2
184. Deuteronomy 22:8
185. Deuteronomy 12:2; 7:5
186. Deuteronomy 13:17
187. Deuteronomy 20:17
188. Deuteronomy 25:19
189. Deuteronomy 25:17

190. Deuteronomy 20:11–12
191. Deuteronomy 20:2
192. Deuteronomy 23:14–15
193. Deuteronomy 23:14
194. Leviticus 5:23
195. Deuteronomy 15:8;
      Leviticus 25:35–36
196. Deuteronomy 15:14
197. Exodus 22:24
198. Deuteronomy 23:21
199. Deuteronomy 24:13;
      Exodus 22:25
200. Deuteronomy 24:15
201. Deuteronomy 23:25–26
202. Exodus 23:5
203. Deuteronomy 22:4
204. Deuteronomy 22:1;
      Exodus 23:4
205. Leviticus 19:17
206. Leviticus 19:18
207. Deuteronomy 10:19
208. Leviticus 19:36
209. Leviticus 19:32
210. Exodus 20:12
211. Leviticus 19:3
212. Genesis 1:28
213. Deuteronomy 24:1
214. Deuteronomy 24:5
215. Genesis 17:10;
      Leviticus 12:3
216. Deuteronomy 25:5
217. Deuteronomy 25:9
218. Deuteronomy 22:29
219. Deuteronomy 22:18–19
220. Exodus 22:15–23
221. Deuteronomy 21:11
222. Deuteronomy 24:1
223. Numbers 5:15–27
224. Deuteronomy 25:2
225. Numbers 35:25
226. Exodus 21:20
227. Exodus 21:16
228. Leviticus 20:14

229. Deuteronomy 22:24
230. Deuteronomy 21:22
231. Deuteronomy 21:23
232. Exodus 21:2
233. Exodus 21:8
234. Exodus 21:8
235. Leviticus 25:46
236. Exodus 21:18
237. Exodus 21:28
238. Exodus 21:33–34

239. Exodus 21:37–22:3
240. Exodus 22:4
241. Exodus 22:5
242. Exodus 22:6–8
243. Exodus 22:9–12
244. Exodus 22:13
245. Leviticus 25:14
246. Exodus 22:8
247. Deuteronomy 25:12
248. Numbers 27:8

Prohibitions

It is (1) forbidden to believe in the existence of any but the One God.

You may not make images (2) for yourself or (3) for others to worship or for (4) any other purpose.

You must not worship anything but God either in (5) the manner prescribed for Divine worship or (6) in its own manner of worship.

Do not (7) sacrifice children to Molech.

You may not (8) practice necromancy or (9) resort to "familiar spirits" neither should you take idolatry or its mythology (10) seriously.

It is forbidden to construct a (11) pillar or (12) dais even for the worship of God or to (13) plant trees in the Temple.

You may not (14) swear by idols or instigate an idolater to do so, nor may you encourage or persuade any (15) non-Jew or (16) Jew to worship idols.

You must not (17) listen to or love anyone who disseminates idolatry nor (18) should you withhold yourself from hating him [or her]. Do not (19) pity such a person. If somebody tries to convert you to idolatry (20) do not defend that person or (21) conceal the fact.

It is forbidden to (22) derive any benefit from the ornaments of idols. You may not (23) rebuild what has been destroyed as a punishment for idolatry nor may you (24) gain any benefit from its wealth. Do not (25) use anything connected with idols or idolatry.

It is forbidden (26) to prophecy in the name of idols or prophecy (27) falsely in the name of God. Do not (28) listen to the one who prophesies for idols and do not (29) fear the false prophet or hinder his execution.

You must not (30) imitate the ways of idolaters or practice their customs; (31) divination, (32) soothsaying, (33) enchanting, (34) sorcery, (35) charming, (36) consulting ghosts or (37) familiar spirits and (38) necromancy are forbidden. Women must not (39) wear male clothing nor men [clothing] (40) of women. Do not (41) tattoo yourself in the manner of the idolaters.

You may not wear (42) garments made of both wool and linen nor may you shave [with a razor] the sides of (43) your head or (44) your beard. Do not (45) lacerate yourself over your dead.

It is forbidden to return to Egypt to (46) dwell there permanently or to (47) indulge in impure thoughts or sights. You may not (48) make a pact with the seven Canaanite nations or (49) save the life of any member of them. Do not (50) show mercy to idolaters, (51) permit them to dwell in the land of Israel or (52) intermarry with them. A Jewish woman may not (53) marry an Ammonite or Moabite even if he converts to Judaism but should refuse [for reasons of genealogy alone] (54) a descendant of Esau or (55) an Egyptian who are proselytes. It is prohibited to make (56) peace with the Ammonite or Moabite nations.

The (57) destruction of fruit trees even in times of war is forbidden as is wanton waste at any time. Do not (58) fear the enemy and do not (59) forget the evil done by Amalek.

You must not (60) blaspheme the Holy Name, (61) break an oath made by it, (62) take it in vain or (63) profane it. Do not (64) test Adonai [who is], God.

You may not (65) erase God's name from the holy texts or destroy institutions devoted to Divine worship. Do not (66) allow the body of one hanged to remain so overnight.

Be not (67) lax in guarding the Temple.

The high priest must not enter the Temple (68) indiscriminately; a priest with a physical blemish may not (69) enter there at all or (70) serve in the sanctuary and even if the blemish is of a temporary nature, he may not (71) participate in the service there until it has passed.

The Levites and the priests must not (72) interchange in their functions. Intoxicated persons may not (73) enter the sanctuary or teach the Law. It is forbidden for (74) non-priests, (75) unclean priests or (76) priests who have performed the necessary ablution but are still within the time limit of their uncleanness to serve in the Temple. No unclean person may enter (77) the Temple or (78) the Temple Mount.

The altar must not be made of (79) hewn stones nor may the ascent to it be by (80) steps. The fire on it may not be (81) extinguished nor may any other but the specified incense be (82) burned on the golden altar. You may not (83) manufacture oil with the same ingredients and in the same proportions as the anointing oil which itself (84) may not be misused. Neither may you (85) compound incense with the same ingredients and in the same proportions as that burnt on the altar. You must not (86) remove the staves from the Ark, (87) remove the breastplate from the ephod or (88) make any incision in the upper garment of the high priest.

It is forbidden to (89) offer sacrifices or (90) slaughter consecrated animals outside the Temple. You may not (91) sanctify, (92) slaughter, (93) sprinkle the blood of or (94) burn the inner parts of a blemished animal even if the blemish is (95) of a temporary nature and even if it is (96) offered by Gentiles. It is forbidden to (97) inflict a blemish on an animal consecrated for sacrifice.

Leaven or honey may not (98) be offered on the altar, neither may (99) anything unsalted. An animal received as the hire of a harlot or as the price of a dog (100) may not be offered.

Do not (101) kill an animal and its young on the same day.

It is forbidden to use (102) olive oil or (103) frankincense in the sin offering or (104), (105), in the jealousy offering (sotah). You may not (106) substitute sacrifices even (107) from one category to the other. You may not (108) redeem the firstborn of permitted animals. It is forbidden to (109) sell the tithe of the herd or (110) sell or (111) redeem a field consecrated by the cherem vow.

When you slaughter a bird for a sin offering you may not (112) split its head.

It is forbidden to (113) work with or (114) shear a consecrated animal. You must not slaughter the paschal lamb (115) while there is still leaven about; nor may you leave overnight (116) those parts that are to be offered up or (117) to be eaten.

You may not leave any part of the festive offering (118) until the third day or any part of (119) the second paschal lamb or (120) the thanksgiving offering until the morning.

It is forbidden to break a bone of (121) the first or (122) second paschal lamb or (123) to carry their flesh out of the house where it is being eaten. You must not (124) allow the remains of the meal offering to become leaven. It is also forbidden to eat the paschal (125) raw or sodden or to allow (126) an alien resident, (127) an uncircumcised person or an (128) apostate to eat of it.

A ritually unclean person (129) must not eat of holy things nor may (130) holy things which have become unclean be eaten. Sacrificial meat (131) which is left after the time-limit or (132) which was slaughtered with wrong intentions must not be eaten. The heave offering must not be eaten by (133) a non-priest, (134) a priest's sojourner or hired worker, (135) an uncircumcised person, or (136) an unclean priest. The daughter of a priest who is married to a non-priest may not (137) eat of holy things.

The meal offering of the priest (138) must not be eaten, neither may (139) the flesh of the sin offerings sacrificed within the sanctuary or (140) consecrated animals which have become blemished. You may not eat the second tithe of (141) corn, (142) wine, or (143) oil or (144) unblemished firstlings outside Jerusalem. The priests may not eat the (145) sin-offerings or the trespass-offerings outside the Temple courts or (146) the flesh of the burnt-offering at all. The lighter sacrifices (147) may not be eaten before the blood has been sprinkled. A non-priest may not (148) eat of the holiest sacrifices and a priest (149) may not eat the first-fruits outside the Temple courts.

One may not eat (150) the second tithe while in a state of impurity or (151) in mourning; its redemption money (152) may not be used for anything other than food and drink.

You must not (153) eat untithed produce or (154) change the order of separating the various tithes.

Do not (155) delay payment of offerings—either freewill or obligatory—and do not (156) come to the Temple on the pilgrim festivals without an offering.

Do not (157) break your word.

A priest may not marry (158) a harlot, (159) a woman who has been profaned from the priesthood, or (160) a divorcee; the high priests must not (161) marry a widow or (162) take one as a concubine. Priests may not enter the sanctuary with (163) overgrown hair of the head or (164) with torn clothing; they must not (165) leave the courtyard during the Temple service. An ordinary priest may not render himself (166) ritually impure except for those relatives specified, and the high priest should not become impure (167) for anybody in (168) any way.

The tribe of Levi shall have no part in (169) the division of the land of Israel or (170) in the spoils of war.

It is forbidden (171) to make oneself bald as a sign of mourning for one's dead.

A Jew may not eat (172) unclean cattle, (173) unclean fish, (174) unclean fowl, (175) creeping things that fly, (176) creatures that creep on the ground, (177) reptiles, (178) worms found in fruit or produce or (179) any detestable creature.

An animal that had died naturally (180) is forbidden for consumption as is (181) a torn or mauled animal. One must not eat (182) any limb taken from a living animal. Also prohibited is (183) the sinew of the thigh (*gid hanefesh*) as is (184) blood and (185) certain types of fat (*chelev*). It is forbidden (186) to cook meat together with milk or (187) eat of such a mixture. It is also forbidden to eat (188) of an ox condemned to stoning (even should it have been properly slaughtered).

One may not eat (189) bread made of new corn or the new corn itself, either (190) roasted or (191) green, before the *omer* offering has been brought on the 16th of Nisan. You may not eat (192) *orlah* or (193) the growth of mixed planting in the vineyard. Any use of (194) wine libations to idols is prohibited, as is (195) gluttony and drunkenness. One may not eat anything on (196) the Day of Atonement. During Passover it is forbidden to eat (197) leaven (*chametz*) or (198) anything containing a mixture of such. This is also forbidden (199) after the middle of the 14th of Nisan [the day before Passover]. During Passover no leaven may be (200) seen or (201) found in your possession.

A Nazirite may not drink (202) wine or any beverage made from grapes; he may not eat (203) grapes, (204) dried grapes, (205) grape seeds or (206) grape peel. He may not render himself (207) ritually impure for his dead nor may he (208) enter a tent in which there is a corpse. He must not (209) shave his hair.

It is forbidden (210) to reap the whole of a field without leaving the corners for the poor; it is also forbidden to (211) gather up the ears of corn that fall during reaping or to harvest (212) the misformed clusters of grapes, or (213) the grapes that fall or to (214) return to take a forgotten sheaf.

You must not (215) sow different species of seed together or (216) corn in a vineyard; it is also forbidden to (217) crossbreed different species of animals or (218) work with two different species yoked together.

You must not (219) muzzle an animal working in a field to prevent it from eating.

It is forbidden to (220) till the earth, (221) to prune trees, (222) to reap [in the usual manner] produce or (223) fruit which has grown without cultivation in the seventh year (*shemittah*). One may also not (224) till the earth or prune trees in the Jubilee year, when it is also forbidden to harvest [in the usual manner] (225) produce or (226) fruit that has grown without cultivation.

One may not (227) sell one's landed inheritance in the land of Israel permanently or (228) change the lands of the Levites or (229) leave the Levites without support.

It is forbidden to (230) demand repayment of a loan after the seventh year; you may not, however, (231) refuse to lend to the poor because that year is approaching. Do not (232) deny charity to the poor or (233) send a Hebrew slave away empty-handed when he finishes his period of service. Do not (234) dun your debtor when you know that he [or she] cannot pay. It is forbidden to (235) lend to or (236) borrow from another Jew at interest or (237) participate in an agreement involving interest either as a guarantor, witness, or writer of the contract.

Do not (238) delay in the payment of wages.

You may not (239) take a pledge from a debtor by violence, (240) keep a poor person's pledge when he [or she] needs it, (241) take any pledge from a widow or (242) from any debtor if he [or she] earns a living from it.

Kidnapping (243) a Jew is forbidden.

Do not (244) steal or (245) rob by violence. Do not (246) remove a land marker or (247) defraud.

It is forbidden (248) to deny receipt of a loan or a deposit or (249) to swear falsely regarding another person's property.

You must not (250) deceive anybody in business. You may not (251) mislead a person even (252) verbally or (253) do him [or her] injury in trade.

You may not (254) return or (255) otherwise take advantage of, a slave who has fled to the land of Israel from his master, even if his master is a Jew.

Do not (256) afflict the widow or the orphan. You may not (257) misuse or (258) sell a Hebrew slave; do not (259) treat him cruelly or (260) allow a heathen to mistreat him. You must not (261) sell your Hebrew maidservant or, if you marry her, (262) withhold food, clothing, and conjugal rights from her. You must not (263) sell a female captive or (264) treat her as a slave.

Do not (265) covet another person's possessions even if you are willing to pay for them. Even (266) the desire alone is forbidden.

A worker must not (267) cut down standing corn during one's work or (268) take more fruit than one can eat.

One must not (269) turn away from a lost article which is to be returned to its owner nor may you (270) refuse to help a person or an animal which is collapsing under its burden.

It is forbidden to (271) defraud with weights and measures even (272) to possess inaccurate weights.

A judge must not (273) perpetrate injustice, (274) accept bribes or be (275) partial or (276) afraid. He [or she] may (277) not favor the poor or (278) discriminate against the wicked; he [or she] should not (279) pity the condemned or (280) pervert the judgment of strangers or orphans.

It is forbidden to (281) hear one litigant without the other being present. A capital case cannot be decided by (282) a majority of one.

A judge should not (283) accept a colleague's opinion unless he [or she] is convinced of its correctness; it is forbidden to (284) appoint as a judge someone who is ignorant of the law.

Do not (285) give false testimony or accept (286) testimony from a wicked person or from (287) relatives of a person involved in the case. It is forbidden to pronounce judgment (288) on the basis of the testimony of one witness.

Do not (289) murder.

You must not convict on (290) circumstantial evidence alone.

A witness (291) must not sit as a judge in capital cases.

You must not (292) execute anybody without due proper trial and conviction.

Do not (293) pity or spare the pursuer.

Punishment is not to be inflicted for (294) an act committed under duress.

Do not accept ransom (295) for a murderer or (296) a manslayer.

Do not (297) hesitate to save another person from danger and do not (298) leave a stumbling block in the way or (299) mislead another person by giving wrong advice.

It is forbidden (300) to administer more than the assigned number of lashes to the guilty.

Do not (301) tell tales or (302) bear hatred in your heart. It is forbidden to (303) shame a Jew, (304) to bear a grudge or (305) to take revenge.

Do not (306) take the dam when you take the young birds.

It is forbidden to (307) shave a leprous scale or (308) remove other signs of that affliction. It is forbidden (309) to cultivate a valley in which a slain body was found and in which subsequently the ritual of breaking the heifer's neck (eglay arufah) was performed.

Do not (310) suffer a witch to live.

Do not (311) force a bridegroom to perform military service during the first year of his marriage. It is forbidden to (312) rebel against the transmitters of the tradition or to (313) add or (314) detract from the precepts of the law.

Do not curse (315) a judge, (316) a ruler or (317) any Jew.

Do not (318) curse or (319) strike a parent.

It is forbidden to (320) work on the Sabbath or (321) walk further than the permitted limits (eruv). You may not (322) inflict punishment on the Sabbath.

It is forbidden to work on (323) the first or (324) the seventh day of Passover, on (325) Shavuot, on (326) Rosh Hashanah, on the (327) first and (328) eighth (*Shemini Atzeret*) days of Sukkot and (329) on the Day of Atonement.

It is forbidden to enter into an incestuous relationship with one's (330) mother, (331) stepmother, (332) sister, (333) half-sister, (334) son's daughter, (335) daughter's daughter, (336) daughter, (337) any woman and her daughter, (338) any woman and her son's daughter, (339) any woman and her daughter's daughter, (340) father's sister, (341) mother's sister, (342) paternal uncle's wife, (343) daughter-in-law, (344) brother's wife and (345) wife's sister.

It is also forbidden to (346) have sexual relations with a menstruous woman.

Do not (347) commit adultery.

It is forbidden for (348) a man or (349) a woman to have sexual intercourse with an animal.

Homosexuality (350) is forbidden, particularly with (351) one's father or (352) uncle.

It is forbidden to have (353) intimate physical contact (even without actual intercourse) with any of the women with whom intercourse is forbidden.

A *mamzer* may not (354) marry a Jewish woman.

Prostitution (355) is forbidden.

A divorcee may not be (356) remarried to her first husband if, in the meanwhile, she had married another.

A childless widow may not (357) marry anybody other than her late husband's brother.

A man may not (358) divorce a wife whom he married after having raped her or (359) after having slandered her.

A eunuch may not (360) marry a Jewish woman.

Castration (361) is forbidden.

You may not (362) elect as king anybody who is not of the seed of Israel.

The king may not accumulate an excessive number of (363) horses, (364) wives, or (365) wealth.

Textual Sources for Prohibitions
1. Exodus 20:3	4. Exodus 20:20
2. Exodus 20:4	5. Exodus 20:5
3. Leviticus 19:4	6. Exodus 20:5

7. Leviticus 18:21
8. Leviticus 19:31
9. Leviticus 19:31
10. Leviticus 19:4
11. Deuteronomy 16:21
12. Leviticus 20:1
13. Deuteronomy 16:21
14. Exodus 23:13
15. Exodus 23:13
16. Deuteronomy 13:12
17. Deuteronomy 13:9
18. Deuteronomy 13:9
19. Deuteronomy 13:9
20. Deuteronomy 13:9
21. Deuteronomy 13:9
22. Deuteronomy 7:25
23. Deuteronomy 13:17
24. Deuteronomy 13:18
25. Deuteronomy 7:26
26. Deuteronomy 18:20
27. Deuteronomy 18:20
28. Deuteronomy 13:3, 4
29. Deuteronomy 18:22
30. Leviticus 20:23
31. Leviticus 19:26;
    Deuteronomy 18:10
32. Deuteronomy 18:10
33. Deuteronomy 18:10–26
34. Deuteronomy 18:10–11
35. Deuteronomy 18:10–11
36. Deuteronomy 18:10–11
37. Deuteronomy 18:10–11
38. Deuteronomy 18:10–11
39. Deuteronomy 22:5
40. Deuteronomy 22:5
41. Leviticus 19:28
42. Deuteronomy 22:11
43. Leviticus 19:27
44. Leviticus 19:27
45. Deuteronomy 16:1, 14:1;
    Leviticus 19:28
46. Deuteronomy 17:16
47. Numbers 15:39
48. Exodus 23:32;
    Deuteronomy 7:2
49. Deuteronomy 20:16
50. Deuteronomy 7:2
51. Exodus 23:33
52. Deuteronomy 7:3
53. Deuteronomy 23:4
54. Deuteronomy 23:8
55. Deuteronomy 23:8
56. Deuteronomy 23:7
57. Deuteronomy 20:19
58. Deuteronomy 7:21
59. Deuteronomy 25:19
60. Leviticus 24:16;
    Exodus 22:27
61. Leviticus 19:12
62. Exodus 20:7
63. Leviticus 22:32
64. Deuteronomy 6:16
65. Deuteronomy 12:4
66. Deuteronomy 21:23
67. Numbers 18:5
68. Leviticus 16:2
69. Leviticus 21:23
70. Leviticus 21:17
71. Leviticus 21:18
72. Numbers 18:3
73. Leviticus 10:9–11
74. Numbers 18:4
75. Leviticus 22:2
76. Leviticus 21:6
77. Numbers 5:3
78. Deuteronomy 23:11
79. Exodus 20:25
80. Exodus 20:26
81. Leviticus 6:6
82. Exodus 30:9
83. Exodus 30:32
84. Exodus 30:32
85. Exodus 30:37
86. Exodus 25:15
87. Exodus 28:28
88. Exodus 28:32

89. Deuteronomy 12:13
90. Leviticus 17:3–4
91. Leviticus 22:20
92. Leviticus 22:22
93. Leviticus 22:24
94. Leviticus 22:22
95. Deuteronomy 17:1
96. Leviticus 22:25
97. Leviticus 22:21
98. Leviticus 2:11
99. Leviticus 2:13
100. Deuteronomy 23:19
101. Leviticus 22:28
102. Leviticus 5:11
103. Leviticus 5:11
104. Numbers 5:15
105. Numbers 5:15
106. Leviticus 27:10
107. Leviticus 27:26
108. Numbers 18:17
109. Leviticus 27:33
110. Leviticus 27:28
111. Leviticus 27:28
112. Leviticus 5:8
113. Deuteronomy 15:19
114. Deuteronomy 15:19
115. Exodus 34:25
116. Exodus 23:10
117. Exodus 12:10
118. Deuteronomy 16:4
119. Numbers 9:13
120. Leviticus 22:30
121. Exodus 12:46
122. Numbers 9:12
123. Exodus 12:46
124. Leviticus 6:10
125. Exodus 12:9
126. Exodus 12:45
127. Exodus 12:48
128. Exodus 12:43
129. Leviticus 12:4
130. Leviticus 7:19
131. Leviticus 19:6–8
132. Leviticus 7:18
133. Leviticus 22:10
134. Leviticus 22:10
135. Leviticus 22:10
136. Leviticus 22:4
137. Leviticus 22:12
138. Leviticus 6:16
139. Leviticus 6:23
140. Deuteronomy 14:3
141. Deuteronomy 12:17
142. Deuteronomy 12:17
143. Deuteronomy 12:17
144. Deuteronomy 12:17
145. Deuteronomy 12:17
146. Deuteronomy 12:17
147. Deuteronomy 12:17
148. Deuteronomy 12:17
149. Exodus 29:33
150. Deuteronomy 26:14
151. Deuteronomy 26:14
152. Deuteronomy 26:14
153. Leviticus 22:15
154. Exodus 22:28
155. Deuteronomy 23:22
156. Exodus 23:15
157. Numbers 30:3
158. Leviticus 21:7
159. Leviticus 21:7
160. Leviticus 21:7
161. Leviticus 21:14
162. Leviticus 21:15
163. Leviticus 10:6
164. Leviticus 10:6
165. Leviticus 10:7
166. Leviticus 21:1
167. Leviticus 21:11
168. Leviticus 21:11
169. Deuteronomy 18:1
170. Deuteronomy 18:1
171. Deuteronomy 14:1
172. Deuteronomy 14:7
173. Leviticus 11:11
174. Leviticus 11:13

175. Deuteronomy 14:19
176. Leviticus 11:41
177. Leviticus 11:44
178. Leviticus 11:42
179. Leviticus 11:43
180. Deuteronomy 14:21
181. Exodus 22:30
182. Deuteronomy 12:23
183. Genesis 32:33
184. Leviticus 7:26
185. Leviticus 7:23
186. Exodus 23:19
187. Exodus 34:26
188. Exodus 21:28
189. Leviticus 23:14
190. Leviticus 23:14
191. Leviticus 23:14
192. Leviticus 19:23
193. Deuteronomy 22:9
194. Deuteronomy 32:38
195. Leviticus 19:26;
     Deuteronomy 21:20
196. Leviticus 23:29
197. Exodus 13:3
198. Exodus 13:20
199. Deuteronomy 16:3
200. Exodus 13:7
201. Exodus 12:19
202. Numbers 6:3
203. Numbers 6:3
204. Numbers 6:3
205. Numbers 6:4
206. Numbers 6:4
207. Numbers 6:7
208. Leviticus 21:11
209. Numbers 6:5
210. Leviticus 23:22
211. Leviticus 19:9
212. Leviticus 19:10
213. Leviticus 19:10
214. Deuteronomy 24:19
215. Leviticus 19:19
216. Deuteronomy 22:9

217. Leviticus 19:19
218. Deuteronomy 22:10
219. Deuteronomy 25:4
220. Leviticus 25:4
221. Leviticus 25:4
222. Leviticus 25:5
223. Leviticus 25:5
224. Leviticus 25:11
225. Leviticus 25:11
226. Leviticus 25:11
227. Leviticus 25:23
228. Leviticus 25:33
229. Deuteronomy 12:19
230. Deuteronomy 15:2
231. Deuteronomy 15:9
232. Deuteronomy 15:7
233. Deuteronomy 15:13
234. Exodus 22:24
235. Leviticus 25:37
236. Deuteronomy 23:20
237. Exodus 22:24
238. Leviticus 19:13
239. Deuteronomy 24:10
240. Deuteronomy 24:12
241. Deuteronomy 24:17
242. Deuteronomy 24:10
243. Exodus 20:13
244. Leviticus 19:11
245. Leviticus 19:13
246. Deuteronomy 19:14
247. Leviticus 19:13
248. Leviticus 19:11
249. Leviticus 19:11
250. Leviticus 25:14
251. Leviticus 25:17
252. Exodus 22:20
253. Exodus 22:20
254. Deuteronomy 23:16
255. Deuteronomy 23:17
256. Exodus 22:21
257. Leviticus 25:39
258. Leviticus 25:42
259. Leviticus 25:43

260. Leviticus 25:53
261. Exodus 21:8
262. Exodus 21:10
263. Deuteronomy 21:14
264. Deuteronomy 21:14
265. Exodus 20:17
266. Deuteronomy 5:18
267. Deuteronomy 23:26
268. Deuteronomy 23:25
269. Deuteronomy 22:3
270. Exodus 23:5
271. Leviticus 19:35
272. Deuteronomy 25:13
273. Leviticus 19:15
274. Exodus 23:8
275. Leviticus 19:15
276. Deuteronomy 1:17
277. Leviticus 19:15:
        Exodus 23:3
278. Exodus 23:6
279. Deuteronomy 19:13
280. Deuteronomy 24:17
281. Exodus 23:1
282. Exodus 23:2
283. Exodus 23:2
284. Deuteronomy 1:17
285. Exodus 20:16
286. Exodus 23:1
287. Deuteronomy 24:16
288. Deuteronomy 19:15
289. Exodus 20:13
290. Exodus 23:7
291. Numbers 35:30
292. Numbers 35:12
293. Deuteronomy 25:12
294. Deuteronomy 22:26
295. Numbers 35:31
296. Numbers 35:32
297. Leviticus 19:16
298. Deuteronomy 22:8
299. Leviticus 19:14
300. Deuteronomy 25:2–3
301. Leviticus 19:16

302. Leviticus 19:17
303. Leviticus 19:17
304. Leviticus 19:18
305. Leviticus 19:18
306. Deuteronomy 22:6
307. Leviticus 13:33
308. Deuteronomy 24:8
309. Deuteronomy 21:4
310. Exodus 22:17
311. Deuteronomy 24:5
312. Deuteronomy 17:11
313. Deuteronomy 13:1
314. Deuteronomy 13:1
315. Exodus 22:27
316. Exodus 22:27
317. Leviticus 19:14
318. Exodus 21:17
319. Exodus 21:15
320. Exodus 20:10
321. Exodus 16:29
322. Exodus 35:3
323. Exodus 12:16
324. Exodus 12:16
325. Leviticus 23:21
326. Leviticus 23:25
327. Leviticus 23:35
328. Leviticus 23:36
329. Leviticus 23:28
330. Leviticus 18:7
331. Leviticus 18:8
332. Leviticus 18:9
333. Leviticus 18:11
334. Leviticus 18:10
335. Leviticus 18:10
336. Leviticus 18:10
337. Leviticus 18:17
338. Leviticus 18:17
339. Leviticus 18:17
340. Leviticus 18:12
341. Leviticus 18:13
342. Leviticus 18:14
343. Leviticus 18:15
344. Leviticus 18:16

345. Leviticus 18:18
346. Leviticus 18:19
347. Leviticus 18:20
348. Leviticus 18:23
349. Leviticus 18:23
350. Leviticus 18:22
351. Leviticus 18:7
352. Leviticus 18:14
353. Leviticus 18:6
354. Deuteronomy 23:3
355. Deuteronomy 23:18

356. Deuteronomy 24:4
357. Deuteronomy 25:5
358. Deuteronomy 22:29
359. Deuteronomy 22:19
360. Deuteronomy 23:2
361. Leviticus 22:24
362. Deuteronomy 17:15
363. Deuteronomy 17:16
364. Deuteronomy 17:17
365. Deuteronomy 17:17

38

Eight Degrees of *Tzedakah*
12th century

Moses Maimonides

Much of the writing done by Moses Maimonides has been popularized and given a central place in Judaism. The account of the levels of *tzedakah*, often represented by a ladder, is among the most popular of these writings.

1. The person who gives reluctantly and with regret.
2. The person who gives graciously, but less than one should.
3. The person who gives what one should, but only after being asked.
4. The person who gives before being asked.
5. The person who gives without knowing to whom one gives, although the recipient knows the identity of the donor.
6. The person who gives without making one's identity known.
7. The person who gives without knowing to whom one gives. The recipient does not know from whom he receives.
8. The person who helps another to support oneself by a gift or a loan or by finding employment for that person, thus helping that person to become self-supporting.

39

Thirteen Principles of Faith
12th century

Moses Maimonides

Many Jewish scholars have attempted to articulate the central belief system of Judaism, while others have eschewed such an attempt. This set of principles is the best known and has found its way into a variety of settings, including the Yigdal hymn. The twelfth principle is associated with those Jews who marched into the gas chambers with these words still on their lips and has been set to a variety of melodies.

1. I believe with perfect faith that the Creator, blessed be Your name, is the Author and Guide of everything that has been created, and that God alone has made, does make, and will make all things.

2. I believe with perfect faith that the Creator, blessed be Your name, is a Unity, and that there is no unity in any manner like unto You, and that You alone are our God, who was, is, and will be.

3. I believe with perfect faith that the Creator, blessed be Your name, is not a body, and that You are free from all the accidents of matter, and that You have not any form whatsoever.

4. I believe with perfect faith that the Creator, blessed be Your name, is the first and the last.

5. I believe with perfect faith that to the Creator, blessed be Your name, and to You alone, it is right to pray, and that it is not right to pray to any being besides You.

6. I believe with perfect faith that all the words of the prophets are true.

7. I believe with perfect faith that the prophecy of Moses our teacher, peace be unto him, was true, and that he was the chief of the prophets, both of those that preceded and of those that followed him.

8. I believe with perfect faith that the whole Torah, now in our possession, is the same that was given to Moses our teacher, peace be unto him.

9. I believe with perfect faith that this Torah will not be changed, and that there will never be any other law from the Creator, blessed be Your name.

10. I believe with perfect faith that the Creator, blessed be Your name, knows every deed of the human race and all of their thoughts, as it is said, "It is You who fashions the hearts of them all, that give heed to all their deeds."

11. I believe with perfect faith that the Creator, blessed be Your name, rewards those that keep Your *mitzvot*, and punishes those who transgress them.

12. I believe with perfect faith in the coming of the Messiah, and, though Messiah tarry, I will wait daily for his coming.

13. I believe with perfect faith that there will be a resurrection of the dead at the time when it shall please the Creator, blessed be Your name, and exalted be the remembrance of You for ever and ever.

40

Daily Prayer of a Physician
12th century

Attributed to Moses Maimonides

While Moses Maimonides probably did not write the text for this prayer, it does contain important moral and ethical standards by which a physician should order his or her professional life. Regardless of its origin, it serves as a Jewish Hippocratic Oath and has become an important part of Jewish folk literature.

Almighty God, You have created the human body with infinite wisdom. You have combined ten thousand times ten thousand organs in it that act in harmony without stopping to preserve the whole body in all its beauty — the body which is the receptacle for the immortal soul. They are always working in perfect order, agreement and accord. Yet, when the fragility of matter or the unleashing of passions obscures this order or interrupts this accord, then forces clash. As a result, the body crumbles into the primal dust from which it came. You send to humankind diseases as beneficent messengers to foretell of approaching danger and urge humans to avert it.

You have blessed Your earth, Your rivers and Your mountains with healing substances. They enable Your creatures to alleviate their suffering and to heal their illnesses. You have endowed humankind with the wisdom to relieve the suffering of one's neighbor, to recognize disorders, extract healing substances, discover their powers, and then to prepare and apply them to suit every ill. In Your Eternal Providence You have chosen me to watch over the life and health of Your creatures. I am now about to apply myself to the duties of my profession. Support me in these great labors, Almighty God, that they may benefit humankind, for without Your help not even the least thing will succeed.

Inspire me with love for my art and for Your creatures. Do not allow a thirst for profit or ambition for renown and admiration to interfere with my profession. These are the enemies of truth and of love for humankind. They can lead astray in the great task of attending to the welfare of Your creatures. Preserve the strength of my body and my soul so that they will always be ready to cheerfully help and support rich and poor, good and bad, enemy as well as friend. In the one who suffers let me see only the human being. Illumine my mind that it recognizes what presents itself and that it may comprehend what is absent or hidden. Let it not fail to see what is visible, but do not permit it to arrogate to itself the power to see what cannot be seen, for delicate and indefinite are the bounds of the great art of caring for the lives and health of Your creatures. Let me never be absent-minded. May no strange thoughts divert my attention at the bedside of the sick, or disturb my mind in its silent labors, for great and sacred are the thoughtful deliberations required to preserve the lives and health of Your creatures.

Grant that my patients have confidence in me and my art and follow my directions and my counsel. Remove from their midst all charlatans and the whole host of officious relatives and know-it-all caregivers, cruel people who arrogantly frustrate the wisest purposes of our art and often lead Your creatures to their death.

Should those who are wiser than I wish to improve and instruct me, let my soul gratefully follow their guidance; for vast is the extent of our art. Should conceited fools, however, censure me, then let love for my profession steel me against them, so that I remain steadfast without regard for age, reputation, or honor, because surrender would bring to Your creatures sickness and death.

Imbue my soul with gentleness and calmness when older colleagues, proud of their age, wish to displace me, scorn me or disdainfully teach me. May even this be of advantage to me, for they know many things of which I am ignorant, but do not let their arrogance give me pain. For they are elderly and in old age they are not masters of their passions. I also hope to attain old age upon this earth, before You, Almighty God!

Let me be content in everything except in the great science of my profession. Never allow the thought to arise in me that I have attained sufficient knowledge, but vouchsafe to me the strength, leisure and ambition to always increase my knowledge. For art is great, but the human mind is ever capable of expanding.

Almighty God! You have chosen me in Your mercy to watch over the life and death of Your creatures. I now apply myself to my profession. Support me in this great task so that it may benefit humankind. Without Your help not even the least thing will succeed.

41

Ikkarim/Basic Principles of Joseph Albo
1485

Joseph Albo, a Spanish philosopher who lived in the fifteenth century, was disturbed by what he saw as an erosion of faith in the Jewish community. Thus, he sought in his *Sefer Ha-ikkarim* to present a reasoned approach to Jewish law with a focus on the basic teachings of Jewish religion. In this way, he hoped to restore the faith of the people.

Dogmas:
1. Existence of God
   Shorashim/Secondary Radicals:
   A. God's unity
   B. God's incorporeality
   C. God's independence of time
2. Divine revelation
   Shorashim/Secondary Radicals:
   A. Appointment of prophets as the mediums of this divine revelation
   B. Belief in the unique greatness of Moses as a prophet
   C. Binding force of the Mosaic law until another shall have been divulged and proclaimed in as public a manner
3. Retributive divine justice
   Shorash/Secondary Radical:
   A. Belief in bodily resurrection

42

Transactions of the Parisian Sanhedrin 1806

In the era of emancipation, Jews were permitted to enter the general society. Concerned about the relevance of rabbinic law, Napoleon convoked an assembly of notables in 1806. If in law the separate Jewish community was abolished and rabbinic authority no longer held sway over the community, then what indeed would be the status of rabbinic law? Thus he articulated the following set of questions, to which the assembly responded. Two years later, a Grand Sanhedrin was convened to enact these decisions.

Questions proposed to the Assembly of the Jews by the Commissioners named by His Majesty the Emperor and King, to transact whatever concerns them.

1. Is it lawful for Jews to marry more than one wife?

It is not lawful for Jews to marry more than one wife: in all European countries they conform to the general practice of marrying only one.

Moses does not command expressly to take several; but he does not forbid it. He seems even to adopt that custom as generally prevailing, since he settles the rights of inheritance between children of different wives. Although this practice still prevails in the East, yet their ancient doctors have enjoined them to restrain from taking more than one wife, except when the man is enabled by his fortune to maintain several.

The case has been different in the West; the wish of adopting the customs of the inhabitants of this part of the world has induced the Jews to renounce Polygamy. But as several individuals still indulged in that practice, a synod was convened at Worms in the eleventh century, composed of one hundred Rabbis, with Gerson at the head. This assembly pronounced an anathema against every Israelite who should, in future, take more than one wife.

184

Although this prohibition was not to last for ever, the influence of European manners has universally prevailed.

2. Is divorce allowed by the Jewish religion? Is divorce valid, although not pronounced by the courts of Justice, and by virtue of laws in contradiction with the French code?

Repudiation is allowed by the law of Moses; but it is not valid if not previously pronounced by the French code.

In the eyes of every Israelite, without exception, submission to the prince is the first of duties. It is a principle generally acknowledged among them, that, in every thing relating to civil or political interests the law of the state is the supreme. Before they were admitted in France to share the rights of all citizens, and when they lived under a particular legislation which set them at liberty to follow their religious customs, they had the facility of repudiating their wives; but it was extremely rare to see it into practice.

Since the revolution, they have acknowledged no other laws on this head but those of the empire. At the epochs when they were admitted to the rank of citizens, the Rabbis and the principal Jews appeared before the municipalities of their respective places of abode, and took an oath to conform in every thing to the laws, and to acknowledge no other rules in all civil matters.

Consequently they can no longer consider as valid the repudiation pronounced by their Rabbis, since, to make it valid, it must have been previously pronounced by competent tribunals; for, in like manner as by an arrete of the Consular Government, the Rabbis could not impart the matrimonial benediction till it appeared to them that the civil contract had been performed before a civil officer, in like manner they cannot pronounce repudiation, until it appears to them that it has already been pronounced by a sentence which gives it validity. Supposing even that the aforesaid "arrete" had been silent on this head, still the rabbinical repudiation could not be valid; for, according to the Rabbis who have written on the civil code of the Jews, such as Joseph Caro in the Abeneser, repudiation is valid only, in case there should be no opposition of any kind. And as the law of the state would form an opposition, in point of civil interests—since one of the parties could avail himself or herself of it against the other—it necessarily follows that, under the influence of the civil code, rabbinical repudiation cannot be valid. Consequently, since the time the Jews have begun to enter into engagement before the civil officer, no one, attached to religious practices, can repudiate his wife but by a double divorce—that pronounced by the law of the state, and that prescribed by the law of Moses; so that under this point of view, it may be justly affirmed, that the Jewish religion agrees on this subject with the civil code.

3. *Can a Jewess marry a Christian, or a Jew a Christian woman? Or has the law ordered that the Jews should only intermarry among themselves?*

The law does not say that a Jewess cannot marry a Christian, nor a Jew a Christian woman; nor does it state that the Jews can only intermarry among themselves.

The only marriages expressly forbidden by the law, are those with the seven Canaanite nations, with Amon and Moab, and with the Egyptians. The prohibition is absolute concerning the seven Canaanite nations; with regard to Amon and Moab, it is limited, according to many Talmudists, to the men of those nations, and does not extend to the women; it is even thought that these last would have embraced the Jewish religion. As to Egyptians, the prohibition is limited to the third generation. The prohibition in general applies only to nations in idolatry. The Talmud declared formally that modern nations are not to be considered as such, since they worship, like us, the God of heaven and earth. And, accordingly, there has been, at several periods, intermarriages between Jews and Christians in France, in Spain, and in Germany: these marriages were sometimes tolerated, and sometimes forbidden by the laws of those sovereigns, who had received Jews in their dominions.

Unions of this kind are still found in France; but we cannot dissemble that the opinion of the Rabbis is against these marriages. According to their doctrine, although the religion of Moses has not forbidden the Jews from intermarrying with nations not of their religion, yet, as marriage, according to the Talmud, requires religious ceremonies called Kiddushin, with the benediction used in such cases, no marriage can be *religiously* valid unless these ceremonies have been performed. This could not be done towards persons who would not both of them consider these ceremonies as sacred; and in that case the married couple could separate without the *religious* divorce; they would then be considered as married *civilly* but not *religiously*.

Such is the opinion of the Rabbis, members of this assembly. In general they would be no more inclined to bless the union of a Jewess with a Christian, or of a Jew with a Christian woman, than Catholic priests themselves would be disposed to sanction unions of this kind. The Rabbis acknowledge, however, that a Jew, who marries a Christian woman, does not cease on that account, to be considered as a Jew by his brethren, any more than had he married a Jewess civilly and not religiously.

4. In the eyes of Jews are Frenchmen considered as brethren or as strangers?

In the eyes of Jews Frenchmen are their brethren, and are not strangers.

The true spirit of the law of Moses is consonant to this mode of considering Frenchmen.

When the Israelites formed a settled and independent nation, their law made it a rule for them to consider strangers as their brethren.

With the most tender care for their welfare, their lawgiver commands to love them. "Therefore, you should love the strangers," says he to the Israelites, "for you were strangers in the land of Egypt."

Respect and benevolence towards strangers are enforced by Moses, not as an exhortation to the practice of social morality only, but as an obligation by God. "When you reap the harvest of your land," says he to them, "you should not make clean riddance of the corners of the field when you reap, neither should you gather any gleaning of your harvest; you should leave them to the poor and to the stranger; I am Adonai your God. When you cut down your harvest in the field, you should not go back again to fetch it: it should be for the stranger, for the fatherless, and the widow: that Adonai your God may bless the work of your hands. You should neither vex a stranger nor oppress him. Adonai your God does execute judgement on behalf of the orphan and widow, and loves the stranger, in giving him food and clothing. Therefore, you should love the stranger; for you were strangers in the land of Egypt."

To these sentiments of benevolence towards the stranger, Moses has added the precept of general love for humankind: "Love your fellow creature as yourself."

David also expresses himself in these terms: "Adonai is good to all: and God's tender mercies are over all God's works." This doctrine is also professed by the Talmud.

"We are bound," says a Talmudist, "to love as our brethren all those who observe the *Noachides*, whatever their religious opinions may otherwise be. We are bound to visit their sick, to bury their dead, to assist their poor, like those of Israel. In short, there is no act of humanity which a true Israelite is not bound to perform towards those who observe the *Noachides*." What are these precepts? To abstain from idolatry, from blasphemy, from adultery, not to kill or hurt our neighbors, neither to rob or to deceive, to eat only the flesh of animals killed; in short, to observe the rules of justice; and therefore all the principles of our religion make it our duty to love Frenchmen as our brethren.

A Pagan having consulted the Rabbi Hillel on the Jewish religion, and wishing to know in a few words, in what it consisted, Hillel thus answered him: "Do not to others what you should not like to have done to you. This," said he, "is all our religion; the rest are only consequences of this principle."

A religion whose fundamental maxims are such—a religion which makes a duty of loving the stranger—which enforces the practice of social virtues, must surely require that its followers should consider their fellow citizens as brethren.

And how could they consider them otherwise when they inhabit the same land, when they are ruled and protected by the same government, and by the same laws? When they enjoy the same rights, and have the same duties to fulfill? There exists even between the Jew and Christian, a tie which abundantly compensates for religion—it is the tie of gratitude. This sentiment was at first excited in us by the mere grant of toleration. It has been increased, these eighteen years, by new favors from government, to such a degree of energy, that now our fate is irrevocably linked with the common fate of all Frenchmen. Yes, France is our country; all Frenchmen are our brethren, and this glorious title, by raising us in our own esteem, becomes a sure pledge that we shall never cease to be worthy of it.

5. In either case what conduct does their law prescribe towards Frenchmen not of their religion?

The line of conduct prescribed towards Frenchmen not of our religion, is the same as that prescribed between Jews themselves; we admit of no difference but that of worshipping the Supreme Being, every one in his own way.

The answer to the preceding question has explained the line of conduct which the law of Moses and the Talmud prescribe towards Frenchmen not of our religion. At the present time, when the Jews no longer form a separate people, but enjoy the advantage of being incorporated with the Great Nation (which privilege they consider as a kind of political redemption), it is impossible that a Jew should treat a Frenchman, not of his religion, in any other manner than he would treat one of his Israelite brethren.

6. Do the Jews born in France, and treated by the law as French citizens, acknowledge France as their country? Are they bound to defend it? Are they bound to obey the laws, and to follow the directions of the civil code?

Men who have adopted a country, who have resided in it these many generations—who, even under the restraint of particular laws which abridged their civil rights, were so attached to it that they preferred being debarred from the advantages common to all other citizens, rather than leave it, cannot but consider themselves as Frenchmen in France; and they consider as equally sacred and honorable the bound duty of defending their country.

Jeremiah (chapter 29) exhorts the Jews to consider Babylon as their country, although they were to remain in it only for seventy years. He exhorts them to till the ground, to build houses, to sow, and to plant. His recommendation was so much attended to, that Ezra (chapter 2) says, that when Cyrus allowed them to return to Jerusalem to rebuild the temple, forty-two thousand three hundred and sixty only, left Babylon; and that this number was mostly composed of the poorer people, the wealthy having remained in that city.

The love of the country is in the heart of Jews a sentiment so natural, so powerful, and so consonant to their religious opinions, that a French Jew considers himself, in England, as among strangers, although he may be among Jews; and the case is the same with English Jews in France.

To such a pitch is this sentiment carried among them, that, during the last war, French Jews have been seen fighting desperately against other Jews, the subjects of countries then at war with France.

Many of them are covered with honorable wounds, and others have obtained, in the field of honor, the noble rewards of bravery.

7. Who names the Rabbis?

Since the revolution, the majority of the chiefs of families names the Rabbi, wherever there is a sufficient number of Jews to maintain one, after previous inquiries as to the morality and learning of the candidate. This mode of election is not, however, uniform; it varies according to place, and, to this day, whatever concerns the election of Rabbis is still in a state of uncertainty.

8. What kind of Police-jurisdiction have the Rabbis among the Jews? What judicial power do they exercise among them?

The Rabbis exercise no manner of Police Jurisdiction among the Jews.

The qualification of Rabbi is nowhere to be found in the law of Moses, neither did it exist in the days of the first Temple; it is only mentioned towards the end of those of the second.

At these epochs the Jews were governed by Sanhedrin or tribunals. A supreme tribunal, called the Grand Sanhedrin, sat in Jerusalem, and was composed of seventy-one Judges.

There were inferior courts, composed of three judges for civil causes and for police; and another composed of twenty-two judges, which sat in the capital to decide matters of less importance, and which was called the "Lesser Sanhedrin."

It is only in the Mishna and in the Talmud that the word Rabbi is found for the first time applied to a doctor in the law; and he was commonly indebted for this qualification to his reputation, and to the opinion generally entertained of his learning.

When the Israelites were totally dispersed, they formed small communities in those places where they were allowed to settle in certain numbers.

Sometimes in these circumstances, a Rabbi and two other doctors formed a kind of tribunal, named Bet Din, that is, House of Justice; the Rabbi fulfilled the functions of Judge, and the other two those of his assessors.

The attributes, and even the existence of these tribunals, have, to this day, always depended on the will of governments under which the Jews have lived, and on the degree of tolerance they have enjoyed. Since the revolution those rabbinical tribunals are totally suppressed in France, and in Italy. The Jews, raised to the rank of citizens, have conformed in everything to the laws of the state; and, accordingly, the functions of Rabbis, wherever any are established are limited to preaching morality in the temples, blessing marriages, and pronouncing divorces.

In places where there are no Rabbis, the Jew who is best instructed in his religion, may, according to the law, impart the marriage benediction without the assistance of a Rabbi; this is attended with an inconvenience, the consequences of which it certainly would be proper to prevent, by extending to all persons, called upon to bless a marriage, the restrictions which the consular Arrete places on functions of Rabbis in this particular.

As to the judicial powers, they possess absolutely none; for there is among them neither a settled ecclesiastical hierarchy, nor any subordination in the exercise of their religious functions.

9. Are the forms of the elections of the Rabbis and their police-jurisdiction, regulated by the law, or are they only sanctioned by custom?

The answer to the preceding questions makes it useless to say much on this, only it may be remarked that, even supposing that Rabbis should have, to this day, preserved some kind of police-judicial-jurisdiction among us, which is not the case, neither such jurisdiction, nor the forms of the elections, could be said to be sanctioned by the law; they should be attributed solely to custom.

10. Are there professions from which the Jews are excluded by their law?

There are none: on the contrary, the Talmud (tractate Kiddushin, chapter 1) expressly declares that "the father who does not teach a profession to his child, rears him up to be a villain."

11. Does the law forbid the Jews from taking usury from their brethren?

Deuteronomy (chapter 23, verse 19) says, "You will not lend with *interest* to your brother, interest of money, interest of food, interest of anything that is lent with interest."

The Hebrew word *nechech* has been improperly translated by the word "usury": in the Hebrew language it means *interest* of any kind, and not *usurious* interest. It cannot be taken in the acceptation now given in the word "usury."

It is even impossible that it could ever have had that acceptation: for usury is an expression relative to, and compared with, another and a lawful interest; and the text contains nothing which alludes to the other term of comparison. What do we understand by usury? Is it not an interest above the legal interest, above the rate fixed by the law? If the law of Moses has not fixed this rate, can it be said that the Hebrew words means an unlawful interest? The word *nechech* in the Hebrew language answers the Latin word *faenus*: to conclude that it means "usury," another word should be found which would mean "interest"; and as such a word does not exist, it follows that all interest is usury, and that all usury is interest.

What was the aim of the lawgiver in forbidding one Hebrew to lend upon interest to another? It was to draw closer between them the bonds of fraternity, to give them a lesson of reciprocal benevolence, and to engage them to help and assist each other with disinterestedness.

The first thought had been to establish among them the equality of property, and the mediocrity of private fortune; hence the institution of the sabbatical year, and of the year of jubilee; the first of which came every seventh year, and the other every fifty years. By the sabbatical year all debtors were released from their obligations: the year of jubilee brought with it the restitution of all estates sold or mortgaged.

It was easy to foresee, that the different qualities of the ground, the greater or lesser industry, the untowardness of the seasons, which might affect both, would necessarily make a difference in the produce of land, and that the more unfortunate Israelite would claim the assistance of him whose fortune should have better favored. Moses did not intend that this last should avail himself of this situation, and that he should require from the other the price of the service he was soliciting; that he should thus aggravate the misery of his brother, and enrich himself by his spoils. It is with a view to this that he says, "You will not lend with interest to your brother." But what want could there exist among the Jews, at a time when they had no trade of any kind? When so little money was in circulation, when the greatest equality prevailed in property? It was, at most a few bushels of corn, some cattle, some agricultural implements; and Moses required that such services should be gratuitous; his intention was to make of his people a nation of husbandmen. For a long time after him, and though Idumaea was at not great distance from the seashores, inhabited by the Tyrians, the Sidonians, and other nations possessing shipping and commerce, we do not see the Hebrew addicted to trade; all the regulation of their lawgiver seemed designed to divert their attention from commerce.

The prohibition of Moses must therefore be considered only as a principle of charity, and not as a commercial regulation. According to the Talmud, the loan alluded to is to be considered almost as a family loan, as a loan made to a man in want; for in case of a loan made to a merchant, even a Jew, profit adequate to risk should be considered as lawful.

Formerly the word "usury" carried no invidious meaning; it simply implied any interest whatever. The word usury can no longer express the meaning of the Hebrew text: and accordingly the Bible of Osterwald and that of the Portuguese Jews, call "interest" that which Sacy, from the Vulgate, has called "usury."

The law of Moses, therefore, forbids all manner of interest on loan, not only between Jews, but between a Jew and his countryman, without distinction of religion. The loan must be gratuitous whenever it is to oblige those who claim our assistance, and when it is not intended for commercial speculation.

We must not forget that these laws, so humane and so admirable at these early periods, were made for a people which then formed a state and held rank among nations.

If the remnants of this people, now scattered among all nations, are attentively considered, it will be seen, that since the Jews have been driven from Palestine, they no longer have had a common country, they no longer have had to maintain among them the primeval equality of property. Although filled with the spirit of their legislation, they have been sensible that the letter of the law could no longer be obeyed when its principle was done away; and they have, therefore, without any scruple, lent money on interest to trading Jews, as well as to men of different persuasions.

12. Does it forbid or does it allow usury towards strangers?

We have seen, in the answer to the foregoing question, that the prohibition of usury, considered as the smallest interest, was a maxim of charity and of benevolence, rather than a commercial regulation. In this point of view it is equally condemned by the law of Moses and by the Talmud; we are generally forbidden, always on the score of charity, to lend upon interest to our fellow-citizens of different persuasions, as well as to our fellow-Jews.

The disposition of the law, which allows to take interest from the stranger, evidently refers only to nations in commercial intercourse with us; otherwise there would be an evident contradiction between this passage and twenty others of the sacred writings.

"Adonai your God loves the stranger, in giving him food and raiment; therefore you should love the stranger for you were strangers in the land of Egypt. One law shall be to the one that is homeborn, and to the stranger. Hear the causes between your brethren and judge righteously between every person and his brother, and the stranger that is with him. If a stranger sojourns with you in your land you should not vex him. You should neither vex a stranger nor oppress him, for you were strangers in the land of Egypt. If your brother is very poor or fallen in decay with you, you should then relieve him, indeed though he is a stranger or a sojourner."

Thus, the prohibition extended to the stranger who dwells in Israel; the Holy Writ places them under the safeguard of God; he is a sacred guest, and God orders us to treat him like the widow and like the orphan.

It is evident that the text of the Vulgate, *Extranei faenaberis et fratri tuo non faenaberis*, can be understood only as meaning foreign nations in commercial intercourse with us; and, even in this case, the Holy Writ, in allowing to take interest from the stranger, does not mean an extraordinary profit, oppressive and odious to the borrower. *Non licuisse Israelitis*, say the doctors, *ururas immoderatas exigere ab extraneis, etiam divitibus, res est per se nota.*

Can Moses be considered as the lawgiver of the universe, because he was the lawgiver of the Jews? Were the laws he gave to the people, which God had entrusted to his care, likely to become the general laws of humankind? "You should not lend with interest to your brother." What security had he, that, in the intercourse which would be naturally established between the Jews and foreign nations, these last would renounce customs generally prevailing in trade, and lend to the Jews without requiring any interest? Was he then bound to sacrifice the interest of his people, and to impoverish the Jews to enrich foreign nations? Is it not absolutely absurd to reproach him with having put a restriction to the precept contained in Deuteronomy? What lawgiver would not have considered such a restriction as a natural principle of reciprocity?

How far superior in simplicity, generosity, justice, and humanity, is the law of Moses, on this head, to those of the Greeks and of the Romans! Can we find, in the history of the ancient Israelites, those scandalous scenes of rebellion excited by the harshness of creditors towards their debtors; those frequent abolitions of debts to prevent the multitude, impoverished by the extortions of lenders, from being driven to despair?

The law of Moses and its interpreters have distinguished, with a praiseworthy humanity, the different uses of borrowed money. Is it to maintain a family? Interest is forbidden. Is it to undertake a commercial speculation, by which the principal is adventured? Interest is allowed, even between Jews. "Lend to the poor," says Moses. Here the tribute of gratitude is the only kind of interest allowed; the satisfaction of obliging is the sole recompense of the conferred benefit. The case is different in regard to capitals employed in extensive commerce: there, Moses allows the lender to come in for a share of the profits of the borrower; and as commerce was scarcely known among the Israelites, who were exclusively addicted to agricultural pursuits, and as it was carried on only with strangers, that is with neighboring nations, it was allowed to share its profits with them.

It is in this view of the subject that M. Clermont-Tonnerre made use of these remarkable words in the first National Assembly: "It is said that usury is permitted to the Jews; this assertion is grounded only on a false interpretation of a principle of benevolence and fraternity which forbade them from lending interest to one another."

This opinion is also that of Puffendorf and of other writers on the law of nations.

The antagonists of the Jews have laid a great stress on a passage of Maimonides, who seems to represent as a precept, the expression "*Anochri tassih* (make profit of the stranger)." But although Maimonides has presumed to maintain this opinion, it is well known that his sentiments have been most completely refuted by the learned rabbi Abarbenel. We find, besides, in the Talmud, a treatise of *Makkot* (Perfection) that one of the ways to arrive at perfection is to lend without interest to the stranger, even to the idolater. Whatever besides might have been the condescension of God to the Jews, if we may be allowed the expression, it cannot be reasonably supposed that the common parent of humankind could, at any time, make usury a precept.

The opinion of Maimonides, which excited all Jewish doctors against him, was principally condemned by the famous Rabbi Moses de Gironda and Solomon Benadaret, upon the grounds, first, that he had relied on the authority of Siffri, a private doctor, whose doctrine has not been sanctioned by the Talmud; for it is a general rule that every rabbinical opinion which is not sanctioned by that work is considered as null and void. Secondly, because, if Maimonides understood that the word *Nachri* (stranger) was applicable to the Cannanite people doomed by God to destruction, he ought not to have confounded a public right, arising from an extraordinary order of God to the Israelites, considered as a nation, with the private right of an individual towards another individual of that same nation.

It is an incontrovertible point, according to the Talmud, that interest, even among Israelites, is lawful in commercial operations, where the lender, running some of the risk of the borrower, becomes a sharer in his profits. This is the opinion of all Jewish doctors.

It is evident that opinions, teeming with absurdities, and contrary to all rules of social morality, although advanced by a Rabbi, can no more be imputed to the general doctrine of the Jews, than similar notions, if advanced by Catholic theologians, could be attributed to the evangelical doctrine. The same may be said of general charge made against the Hebrews, that they are naturally inclined to usury: it cannot be denied that some of them are to be found, though not so many as is generally supposed, who follow that nefarious traffic condemned by their religion.

But if there are some not over-nice in this particular, is it just to accuse one hundred thousand individuals in this vice? Would it not be deemed an injustice to lay the same imputation on all Christians because some of them are guilty of usury?

43

I Am a Jew
late 19th–early 20th century

Edmond Fleg

Edmond Fleg was a French author who was read widely in his day. He had lost Judaism only to find it again in what he called "Palestine and Paris": a union of Jewish particularism and humanity's worldwide concerns.

I am asked why I am a Jew. It is to you, my grandson who are not yet born, that I would make my reply.

When will you be old enough to understand me? My eldest son is nineteen years old. My younger son is fourteen years old. When will you be born? In ten years, perhaps fifteen. . . . When will you read what I here set down? About 1959, 1960? Will people still read in 1960? What form will the world then take? Will the mechanical have suppressed the spiritual? Will the mind have created a new universe for itself? Will the problems that trouble me to-day exist for you? Will there be any Jews left?

I believe there will. They have survived the Pharaohs, Nebuchadnezzar, Constantine, Mohammed; they have survived the inquisition and assimilation; they will survive the automobile.

But you, my child, will you be a Jew? People say to me: You are a Jew because you were born a Jew. You did not will to be one; you cannot change that. Will this explanation suffice for you, if born a Jew, you no longer feel that you are a Jew?

I myself, at the age of twenty, thought I had no further interest in Israel. I was convinced that Israel would disappear, that in twenty years people would no longer speak of it. Twenty years have passed, and twelve more, and I am again become a Jew—so obviously that I am asked why I am a Jew.

That which happened to me may happen to you also, my child. If you believe that the name of Israel is extinguished within you, pay heed and wait; some day it will be rekindled. It is a very old story, which begins anew each century. Israel has had a thousand opportunities to die; a thousand times it has been reborn. I want to tell you how it died and was reborn in me, so that, if it die in you, you in turn may experience its rebirth.

Thus I will have brought Israel to you, and you will bring it to others if you will, if you can. And we two in our way will have treasured and transmitted the divine behest: — "These words which I command thee shall be upon thy heart and upon thy soul; bind them as a sign upon thy hand and let them be as frontlets between thine eyes. Thou shalt teach them to thy children. . . ."

I am a Jew because born of Israel and having lost it, I felt it revive within me more alive than I am myself.

I am a Jew because born of Israel, and having found it again, I would have it live after me more alive than it is within me.

I am a Jew because the faith of Israel demands no abdication of the mind.

I am a Jew because the faith of Israel asks every possible sacrifice of my soul.

I am a Jew because in places where there are tears and suffering the Jew weeps.

I am a Jew because in every age where the cry of despair is heard the Jew hopes.

I am a Jew because the message of Israel is the most ancient and the most modern.

I am a Jew because Israel's promise is a universal promise.

I am a Jew because for Israel the world is not finished; men will complete it.

I am a Jew because for Israel man is not yet created; men are creating him.

I am a Jew because Israel places Man and his Unity above nations and above Israel itself.

I am a Jew because above Man, image of the Divine Unity, Israel places the unity which is divine.

VII

ISRAEL

The land of Israel is the birthplace of the Jewish people. Here the spiritual, political, and religious identity of the people was shaped. Israel was always the focus of the religious attention of the Jews of the Diaspora. The yearning to return one day to Jerusalem has been an integral and vibrant part of both Jewish literature and liturgy. The ingathering of the exiles, the return of the Jewish people to the land of their ancestors from the countries of their dispersion, is one of the fundamental principles on which the State of Israel was founded.

"Next year in Jerusalem"—the imperative that inaugurates the festival of Passover and closes the Day of Atonement—symbolizes the eternal longing of the Jewish people to visit Israel. This section presents some of the salient documents in the history of the State of Israel.

44

"Hatikvah"
1878

Naphtali Herz Imber

While never officially adopted as the national anthem of Israel, the text for "Hatikvah" was written by poet Naphtali Herz Imber, probably in Jassy in 1878, and inspired by the founders of Petach Tikvah (outside of Tel Aviv). The music was prepared by Samuel Cohen and is based on a Romanian folk song.

Kol od ba-levav penimah
Nefesh Yehudi homiyyah
U-le-fa'atei mizrach kadimah
Ayin le-Tziyyon tzofiyah

Od lo avdah tikvatenu
Ha-tikvah bat shenot alpayim
Lihyot am chofshi be-artzenu
Eretz Tziyyon viY-rushalayim

As long as deep in the heart
The soul of a Jew yearns
And towards the East
An eye looks to Zion

Our hope is not yet lost
The hope of two thousand years
To be a free people in our land
The land of Zion and Jerusalem

45

The Balfour Declaration
1917

The Balfour Declaration is a British declaration of sympathy for the Zionist position. It was written by Arthur James Balfour, foreign secretary, to Lord Rothschild. This declaration became British policy when its war department voted its acceptance.

Foreign Office
November 2nd, 1917

Dear Lord Rothschild,

I have much pleasure in conveying to you, on behalf of His Majesty's Government, the following declaration of sympathy with Jewish Zionist aspirations which has been submitted to, and approved by, the Cabinet:

"His Majesty's Government view with favour the establishment in Palestine of a national home for the Jewish people, and will use their best endeavours to facilitate the achievement of this object, it being clearly understood that nothing shall be done which may prejudice the civil and religious rights of existing non-Jewish communities in Palestine, or the rights and political status enjoyed by Jews in any other country."

I should be grateful if you would bring this declaration to the knowledge of the Zionist Federation.

Yours,
Arthur James Balfour

46

White Paper: Text for the Mandate for Palestine 1939

The White Paper was the British government's statement of policy regarding Palestine. It declared Britain's intention of setting up after ten years an independent Palestinian state, in the government of which Jews and Arabs would participate proportionate to their numbers. The document was opposed by those in the Zionist movement, yet it guided British policy throughout the ensuing years.

The Council of the League of Nations:

Whereas the Principal of Allied Powers have agreed, for the purpose of giving effect to the provisions of article 22 of the Covenant of the League of Nations, to entrust to a Mandate selected by the said Powers the administration of the territory of Palestine, which formerly belonged to the Turkish Empire, within such boundaries as may be fixed by them; and

Whereas the Principal Allied Powers have also agreed that the Mandatory should be responsible for putting into effect the declaration originally made on the 2nd November, 1917, by the Government of his Britannic Majesty, and adopted by the said Powers, in favour of the establishment in Palestine of a national home for the Jewish people, it being clearly understood that nothing should be done which might prejudice the civil and religious rights of existing non-Jewish communities in Palestine or the rights and political status enjoyed by Jews in any other country; and

Whereas recognition has thereby been given to the historical connection of the Jewish people with Palestine and to the grounds for reconstituting their national home in that country; and

Whereas the Principal Allied Powers have selected His Britannic Majesty as the Mandatory for Palestine; and

Whereas the mandate in respect of Palestine has been formulated in the following terms and submitted to the Council of the League for approval; and

Whereas His Britannic Majesty has accepted the mandate in respect of

Palestine and undertaken to exercise it on behalf of the League of Nations in conformity with the following provisions; and

Whereas by the aforementioned article 22 (paragraph 8), it is provided that the degree of authority, control or administration to be exercised by the Mandatory, not having been previously agreed upon by the members of the League, shall be explicitly defined by the Council of the League of Nations:

Confirming the said mandate, defines its terms as follows:

Article 1

The Mandatory shall have full powers of legislation and of administration, save as they may be limited by the terms of this mandate.

Article 2

The Mandatory shall be responsible for placing the country under such political, administrative and economic condition as will secure the establishment of the Jewish national home, as laid down in the preamble, and the development of self-governing institutions, and also for safeguarding the civil and religious rights of all the inhabitants of Palestine, irrespective of race and religion.

Article 3

The Mandatory shall, so far as circumstances permit, encourage local autonomy.

Article 4

An appropriate Jewish agency shall be recognized as a public body for the purpose of advising and co-operating with the Administration of Palestine in such economic, social and other matters as may affect the establishment of the Jewish national home and the interests of the Jewish population in Palestine and, subject always to the control of the Administration, to assist and take part in the development of the country.

The Zionist organisation, so long as its organisation and constitution are in the opinion of the Mandatory appropriate, shall be recognized as such agency. It shall take steps in consultation with His Britannic Majesty's Government to secure the co-operation of all Jews who are willing to assist in the establishment of the Jewish national home.

Article 5

The Mandatory shall be responsible for seeing that no Palestine territory shall be ceded or leased to, or in any way placed under the control of, the Government of any foreign Power.

Article 6

The Administration of Palestine, while ensuring that the rights and position of other sections of the population are not prejudiced, shall facilitate Jewish immigration under suitable conditions and shall encourage, in co-operation with the Jewish agency referred to in Article 4, close settlement by Jews on the land, including State lands and waste lands not required for public purposes.

Article 7

The Administration of Palestine shall be responsible for enacting a nationality law. There shall be included in this law provisions framed so as to facilitate the acquisition of Palestinian citizenship by Jews who take up their permanent residence in Palestine.

Article 8

The privileges and immunities of foreigners, including the benefits of consular jurisdiction and protection as formerly enjoyed by Capitulation or usage in the Ottoman Empire, shall not be applicable in Palestine.

Unless the Powers whose nationals enjoyed the aforementioned privileges and immunities on the 1st August, 1914, shall have previously renounced the right to their re-establishment, or shall have agreed to their non-application for a specified period, these privileges and immunities, shall, at the expiration of the mandate, be immediately re-established in their entirety or with such modifications as may have been agreed upon between the Powers concerned.

Article 9

The Mandatory shall be responsible for seeing that the judicial system established in Palestine shall assure to foreigners, as well as to natives, a complete guarantee of their rights.

Respect for the personal status of the various peoples and communities and for their religious interests shall be fully guaranteed. In particular, the control and administration of Wakfs shall be exercised in accordance with religious law and the dispositions of the founders.

Article 10

Pending the making of special extradition agreements relating to Palestine, the extradition treaties in force between the Mandatory and other foreign Powers shall apply to Palestine.

Article 11

The Administration of Palestine shall take all necessary measures to safeguard the interests of the community in connection with the development of the country, and, subject to any international obligations accepted by the Mandatory, shall have full power to provide for public ownership or control of any of the natural resources of the country or of the public works, services and utilities established or to be established therein. It shall introduce a land system appropriate to the needs of the country, having regard, among other things, to the desirability of promoting the close settlement and intensive cultivation of the land.

The Administration may arrange with the Jewish agency mentioned in article 4 to construct or operate, upon fair and equitable terms, any public works, services and utilities, and to develop any of the natural resources of the country, in so far as these matters are not directly undertaken by the Administration. Any such arrangements shall provide that no profits distributed by such agency, directly or indirectly, shall exceed a reasonable rate of interest on the capital, and any further profits shall be utilised by it for the benefit of the country in a manner approved by the Administration.

Article 12

The Mandatory shall be entrusted with the control of the foreign relations of Palestine and the rights to issue exequaturs to consuls appointed by foreign Powers. He also shall be entitled to afford diplomatic and consular protection to citizens of Palestine when outside its territorial limits.

Article 13

All responsibility in connection with the Holy Places and religious buildings or sites in Palestine, including that of preserving existing rights and of securing free access to the Holy Places, religious buildings and sites and the free exercise of worship, while ensuring the requirements of public order and decorum, is assumed by the Mandatory, who shall be responsible solely to the League of Nations in all matters connected herewith, provided that nothing in this article shall prevent the Mandatory from entering into such arrangements as he may deem reasonable with the Administration for the purpose of carrying the provisions of this article into effect; and provided also that nothing in this mandate shall be construed as conferring upon the Mandatory authority to interfere with the fabric of the management of purely Moslem sacred shrines, the immunities of which are guaranteed.

Article 14

A special Commission shall be appointed by the Mandatory to study, define and determine the rights and claims in connection with the Holy Places and the rights and claims relating to the different religious communities in Palestine. The method of nomination, the composition and the functions of this Commission shall be submitted to the Council of the League for its approval, and the Commission shall not be appointed or enter upon its functions without the approval of the Council.

Article 15

The Mandatory shall see that complete freedom of conscience and the free exercise of all forms of worship, subject only to the maintenance of public order and morals, are ensured to all. No discrimination of any kind shall be made between the inhabitants of Palestine on the ground of race, religion or language. No person shall be excluded from Palestine on the sole ground of his religious belief.

The right of each community to maintain its own schools for the education of its own members in its own language, while conforming to such educational requirements of a general nature as the Administration may impose, shall not be denied or impaired.

Article 16

The Mandatory shall be responsible for exercising such supervision over religious or eleemosynary bodies of all faiths in Palestine as may be required for the maintenance of public order and good government. Subject to such supervision, no measure shall be taken in Palestine to obstruct or interfere with the enterprise of such bodies, or to discriminate against any representative or member of them on the ground of his religion or nationality.

Article 17

The Administration of Palestine may organise on a voluntary basis the forces necessary for the preservation of peace and order, and also for the defence of the country, subject, however, to the supervision of the Mandatory, but shall not use them for purposes other than those above specified save with the consent of the Mandatory. Except for such purposes, no military, naval or air forces shall be raised or maintained by the Administration of Palestine.

Nothing in this article shall preclude the Administration of Palestine from contributing to the cost of the maintenance of the forces of the Mandatory in Palestine.

The Mandatory shall be entitled at all times to use the roads, railways and ports of Palestine for the movement of armed forces and the carriage of fuel and supplies.

Article 18

The Mandatory shall see that there is no discrimination in Palestine against the nationals of any State member of the League of Nations (including companies incorporated under its laws) as compared with those of the Mandatory or of any foreign State in matters concerning taxation, commerce or navigation, the exercise of industries or professions, or in the treatment of merchant vessels or civil aircraft. Similarly, there shall be no discrimination in Palestine against goods originating in or destined for any of the said States, and there shall be freedom of transit under equitable conditions across the mandated area.

Subject as aforesaid and to the other provisions of this mandate the Administration of Palestine, may on the advice of the Mandatory, impose such taxes and customs duties as it may consider necessary, and take such steps as it may think best to promote the development of the natural resources of the country and to safeguard the interests of the population. It may also, on the advice of the Mandatory, conclude a special customs agreement with any State the territory of which in 1914 was wholly included in Asiatic Turkey or Arabia.

Article 19

The Mandatory shall adhere on behalf of the Administration of Palestine to any general international conventions already existing, or which may be concluded hereafter with the approval of the League of Nations, respecting the slave traffic, the traffic in arms and ammunition, or the traffic in drugs, or relating to commercial equality, freedom of transit and navigation, aerial navigation and postal, telegraphic and wireless communication or literary, artistic or industrial property.

Article 20

The Mandatory shall co-operate on behalf of the Administration of Palestine, so far as religious, social and other conditions may permit, in the execution of any common policy adopted by the League of Nations for preventing and combating disease, including diseases of plants and animals.

Article 21

The Mandatory shall secure the enactment within twelve months from this date, and shall ensure the execution of a Law of Antiquities based on the following rules. This law shall ensure equality of treatment in the matter of excavations and archaeological research to the nationals of all States members of the League of Nations.

(1)

"Antiquity" means any construction or any product of human activity earlier than the year A.D. 1700.

(2)

The law for the protection of antiquities shall proceed by encouragement rather than by threat.

Any person who, having discovered an antiquity without being furnished with the authorisation referred to in paragraph 5, reports the same to an official of the competent Department, shall be rewarded according to the value of the discovery.

(3)

No antiquity may be disposed of except to the competent Department, unless this Department renounces the acquisition of any such antiquity.

No antiquity may leave the country without an export licence from the said Department.

(4)

Any person who maliciously or negligently destroys or damages an antiquity shall be liable to a penalty to be fixed.

(5)

No clearing of ground or digging with the object of finding antiquities shall be permitted, under penalty of fine, except to persons authorised by the Department.

(6)

Equitable terms shall be fixed for expropriation, temporary or permanent, of lands which might be of historical or archaeological interest.

(7)

Authorisation to excavate shall only be granted to persons who show sufficient guarantees of archaeological experience. The Administration of Palestine shall not, in granting these authorisations, act in such a way as to exclude scholars of any nation without good grounds.

(8)

The proceeds of excavations may be divided between the excavator and the competent Department in a proportion fixed by that Department. If division seems impossible for scientific reasons, the excavator shall receive a fair indemnity in lieu of a part of the find.

Article 22

English, Arabic and Hebrew shall be the official languages of Palestine. Any statement or inscription in Arabic on stamps or money in Palestine shall be repeated in Hebrew, and any statement or inscription in Hebrew shall be repeated in Arabic.

Article 23

The Administration of Palestine shall recognize the holy days of the respective communities in Palestine as legal days of rest for the members of such communities.

Article 24

The Mandatory shall make to the Council of the League of Nations an annual report to the satisfaction of the Council as to the measures taken during the year to carry out the provisions of the mandate. Copies of all laws and regulations promulgated or issued during the year shall be communicated with the report.

Article 25

In the territories lying between the Jordan and the eastern boundary of Palestine as ultimately determined, the Mandatory shall be entitled, with the consent of the Council of the League of Nations, to postpone or withhold application of such provisions of this mandate as he may consider inapplicable to the existing local conditions, and to make such provision for the administration of the territories as he may consider suitable to those conditions, provided that no action shall be taken which is inconsistent with the provisions of articles 15, 16 and 18.

Article 26

The Mandatory agrees that if any dispute whatever should arise between the Mandatory and another member of the League of Nations relating to the interpretation or the application of the provisions of the mandate, such dispute, if it cannot be settled by negotiation, shall be submitted to the Permanent Court of International Justice provided for by article 14 of the Covenant of the League of Nations.

Article 27

The consent of the Council of the League of Nations is required for any modifications of the terms of this mandate.

Article 28

In the event of the termination of the mandate hereby conferred upon the Mandatory, the Council of the League of Nations shall make such arrangements as may be deemed necessary for safeguarding in perpetuity, under guarantee of the League, the rights secured by articles 13 and 14, and shall use its influence for securing, under the guarantee of the League, that the Government of Palestine will fully honour the financial obligations legitimately incurred by the Administration of Palestine during the period of the mandate, including the rights of public servants to pensions and gratuities.

The present instrument shall be deposited in original archives of the League of Nations, and certified copies shall be forwarded by the Secretary-General of the League of Nations to all members of the League.

Done at London, the 24th day of July, 1922.

47

The Declaration of the Establishment
of the State of Israel
1948

For five months following the distribution of the United Nations Partition Plan, the United States State Department attempted to prevent Israel from declaring its independence, suggesting that it might instead become a U.S. trusteeship. Under Ben-Gurion's leadership, such a position was rejected and Israel declared its independence.

IN THE LAND OF ISRAEL the Jewish people came into being. In this Land was shaped their spiritual, religious, and national character. Here they lived in sovereign independence. Here they created a culture of national and universal import, and gave to the world the eternal Book of Books.

Exiled by force, still the Jewish people kept faith with their Land in all the countries of their dispersion, steadfast in their prayer and hope to return and here revive their political freedom.

Fired by this attachment of history and tradition, the Jews in every generation strove to renew their roots in their ancient homeland, and in recent generations they came home in their multitudes.

Veteran pioneers and defenders, and newcomers braving blockade, they made the wilderness bloom, revived their Hebrew tongue, and built villages and towns. They founded a thriving society, master of its own economy and culture, pursuing peace but able to defend itself, bringing the blessing of progress to all the inhabitants of the Land, dedicated to the attainment of sovereign independence.

In 1897 the First Zionist Congress met at the call of Theodor Herzl, seer of the vision of the Jewish State, and gave public voice to the right of the Jewish people to national restoration in their Land.

This right was acknowledged in the Balfour Declaration on 2 November 1917, and confirmed in the Mandate of the League of Nations, which accorded international validity to the historical connection between the Jewish people and the Land of Israel, and to their right to re-establish their National Home.

The holocaust that in our time destroyed millions of Jews in Europe again proved beyond doubt the compelling need to solve the problem of Jewish homelessness and dependence by the renewal of the Jewish State in the Land of Israel, which would open wide the gates of the Homeland to every Jew and endow the Jewish people with a status of a nation with equality of rights within the family of nations.

Despite every hardship, hindrance and peril, the remnant that survived the grim Nazi slaughter in Europe, together with Jews from other countries, pressed on with their exodus to the Land of Israel and continued to assert their right to a life of dignity, freedom and honest toil in the Homeland of their people.

In the Second World War, the Jewish community in the Land of Israel played its full part in the struggle of nations championing freedom and peace against the Nazi forces of evil. Its war effort and the lives of its soldiers won it the right to be numbered among the founding peoples of the United Nations.

On 29 November 1947, the General Assembly of the United Nations adopted a resolution calling for the establishment of a Jewish State in the Land of Israel, and required the inhabitants themselves to take all measures necessary on their part to carry out the resolution. This recognition by the United Nations of the right of the Jewish people to establish their own State is irrevocable.

It is the natural right of the Jewish people, like any other people, to control their own destiny in their sovereign State.

ACCORDINGLY WE, the members of the National Council, representing the Jewish people in the Land of Israel and the Zionist Movement, have assembled on the day of the termination of the British Mandate for Palestine, and, by virtue of our natural and historic right and of the resolution of the General Assembly of the United Nations, do hereby proclaim the establishment of a Jewish State in the Land of Israel—the State of Israel.

WE RESOLVE that, from the moment the Mandate ends, at midnight on the Sabbath, the sixth of Iyar 5708, the fifteenth day of May 1948, until the establishment of the duly elected authorities of the State in accordance with a Constitution to be adopted by the Elected Constituent Assembly not later than 1 October 1948, the National Council shall act as the Provisional

Council of State, and its executive arm, the National Administration, shall constitute the Provisional Government of the Jewish State, and the name of that State shall be Israel.

THE STATE OF ISRAEL will be open to Jewish immigration and the ingathering of exiles. It will devote itself to developing the Land for the good of all its inhabitants.

It will rest upon the foundations of liberty, justice and peace as envisioned by the Prophets of Israel. It will maintain complete equality of social and political rights for all its citizens, without distinction of creed, race or sex. It will guarantee freedom of religion and conscience, of language, education and culture. It will safeguard the Holy Places of all religions. It will be loyal to the principles of the United Nations Charter.

THE STATE OF ISRAEL will be prepared to cooperate with the organs and representatives of the United Nations in carrying out the General Assembly resolution of 29 November 1947, and will work for the establishment of the economic union of the whole Land of Israel.

WE APPEAL to the United Nations to assist the Jewish people in the building of their State, and to admit the State of Israel into the family of nations.

EVEN AMIDST the violent attacks launched against us for months past, we call upon the sons of the Arab people dwelling in Israel to keep the peace and to play their part in building the State on the basis of full and equal citizenship and due representation in all its institutions, provisional and permanent.

WE EXTEND the hand of peace and good-neighbourliness to all the States around us and to their peoples, and we call upon them to cooperate in mutual helpfulness with the independent Jewish nation in its Land. The State of Israel is prepared to make its contribution in a concerned effort for the advancement of the entire Middle East.

WE CALL upon the Jewish people throughout the Diaspora to join forces with us in immigration and construction, and to be at our right hand in the great endeavour to fulfil the age-old longing for the redemption of Israel.

WITH TRUST IN THE ROCK OF ISRAEL, we set our hands in witness to this Proclamation, at this session of the Provisional Council of State, on the soil of the Homeland, in the city of Tel Aviv, this Sabbath eve, the fifth day of Iyar, 5708, the fourteenth day of May, nineteen hundred and forty-eight.

48

Law of Return
1950

Every Jew has the right to return home to Israel. This was established by law early in the history of the modern State of Israel. However, the interpretation of this law has been the subject of controversy almost since it was passed by the Knesset in 1950.

1. Every Jew has the right to come to this country as an *oleh*.

2. (a) *Aliyah* shall be by *oleh*'s visa.

(b) An *oleh*'s visa shall be granted to every Jew who has expressed his desire to settle in Israel, unless the Minister of Immigration is satisfied that the applicant—

(1) is engaged in an activity directed against the Jewish people; or

(2) is likely to endanger public health or the security of the State.

3. (a) A Jew who has come to Israel and subsequent to his arrival has expressed his desire to settle in Israel may, while still in Israel, receive an *oleh*'s certificate.

(b) The restrictions specified in section 2(b) shall apply to the grant of an *oleh*'s certificate, but a person shall not be regarded as endangering public health on account of an illness contracted after his arrival in Israel.

4. Every Jew who has immigrated to this country before the coming into force of this Law, and every Jew who was born in this country, whether before or after the coming into force of this Law, shall be deemed to be a person who has come to this country as an *oleh* under this law.

5. The Minister of Immigration is charged with the implementation of this Law and may make regulations as to any matter relating to such implementation and also as to the grant of *oleh*'s visas and *oleh*'s certificates to minors up to the age of 18 years.

DAVID BEN-GURION   MOSHE SHAPIRA
Prime Minister   Minister of Immigration

YOSEF SPRINZAK
Acting President of the State
Chairman of the Knesset

AMENDMENT—1954

1. In section 2(b) of the Law of Return, 5710—1950—
    (1) the full stop at the end of paragraph (2) shall be replaced by a
        semi-colon, and the word "or" shall be inserted thereafter;
    (2) the following paragraph shall be inserted after paragraph (2): "(3)
        is a person with a criminal past, likely to endanger public welfare."
2. In sections 2 and 5 of the Law, the words "the Minister of Immigration" shall be replaced by the words "the Minister of the Interior."

MOSHE SHARETT   YOSEF SERLIN
Prime Minister   Minister of Health

YITZCHAK BEN-ZVI
President of the State

AMENDMENT NO. 2—1970

1. In the Law of Return, 5710—1950, the following sections shall be
inserted after section 4:

> 4A. (a) The rights of a Jew under this Law and the rights of an
> *oleh* under the Nationality Law 5712—1952, as well as the rights
> of an *oleh* under any other enactment, are also vested in a child
> and a grandchild of a Jew, the spouse of a Jew, the spouse of a child
> of a Jew and the spouse of a grandchild of a Jew, except for a per-
> son who has been a Jew and has voluntarily changed his religion.
> (b) It shall be immaterial whether or not a Jew by whose right a
> right under subsection (a) is claimed is still alive and whether or
> not he has immigrated to Israel.
> (c) The restrictions and conditions prescribed in respect of a Jew
> or an *oleh* by or under this Law or by the enactments referred to in
> subsection (a) shall also apply to a person who claims a right under
> subsection (a).
> 4B. For the purposes of this Law, "Jew" means a person who was
> born of a Jewish mother or has become converted to Judaism and
> who is not a member of another religion.

2. In section 5 of the Law of Return, 5710—1950, the following shall be added at the end: "Regulations for the purposes of sections 4A and 4B require the approval of the Constitution, Legislation and Juridical Committee of the Knesset."

3. In the Population Registry Law, 5725—1965, the following section shall be inserted after section 3:

3A. (a) A person shall not be registered as a Jew by ethnic affiliation or religion if a notification under this Law or another entry in the Registry or a public document indicates that he is not a Jew, so long as the said notification, entry or document has not been controverted to the satisfaction of the Chief Registration Officer or so long as declaratory judgment of a competent court or tribunal has not otherwise determined.

(b) For the purposes of this Law and of any registration or document thereunder, "Jew" has the same meaning as in section 4B of the Law of Return 5710—1950.

(c) This section shall not derogate from a registration effected before its coming into force.

GOLDA MEIR	GOLDA MEIR
Prime Minister	Prime Minister
	Acting Minister of
	the Interior

SHNEUR ZALMAN SHAZAR
President of the State

49

Nationality Law
1952

For those who do not fall under the Law of Return or choose to go through the process of naturalization, this law determines the eligibility of the individual and the process through which the individual is naturalized.

Part One: Acquisition of Nationality

1. Israel nationality is acquired—
   by return (section 2),
   by residence (section 3),
   by birth (section 4),
   by naturalization (sections 5 to 9).
   There shall be no Israel nationality save under this Law.

2. (a) Every *oleh* under the Law of Return, 5710—1950, shall become an Israel national.

   (b) Israel nationality by return is acquired—
   (1) by a person who came as an *oleh* into, or was born in, the country before the establishment of the State—with effect from the day of the establishment of the State;
   (2) by a person having come to Israel as an *oleh* after the establishment of the State—with effect from the day of his *aliyah*;
   (3) by a person born in Israel after the establishment of the State with effect from the day of his birth:
   (4) by a person who has received an *oleh*'s certificate under section 3 of the Law of Return, 5710—with effect from the day of the issue of the certificate.

   (c) This section does not apply—
   (1) to a person having ceased to be an inhabitant of Israel before the coming into force of this Law:
   (2) to a person of full age who, immediately before the day of

the coming into force of this Law or, if he comes to Israel as an *oleh* thereafter, immediately before the day of his *aliyah* or the day of the issue of his *oleh's* certificate is a foreign national who, on or before such day, declares that he does not desire to become an Israel national;

(3) to a minor whose parents have made a declaration under paragraph (2) and included him therein.

3. (a) A person who, immediately before the establishment of the State, was a Palestinian citizen and who does not become an Israel national under section 2, shall become an Israel national with effect from the day of the establishment of the State if—

(1) he was registered on the 4th Adar, 5712 (1st March 1952) as an inhabitant under the Registration of Inhabitants Ordinance, 5709—1949; and

(2) he is an inhabitant of Israel on the day of the coming into force of this Law; and

(3) he was in Israel, or in an area which become Israel territory after the establishment of the State, from the day of the establishment of the State to the day of the coming into force of this Law, or entered Israel legally during that period.

(b) A person born after the establishment of the State who is an inhabitant of Israel on the day of the coming into force of this Law, and whose father or mother becomes an Israel national under subsection (a), shall become an Israel national with effect from the day of his birth.

4. A person born while his father or mother is an Israel national shall be an Israel national from birth; where a person is born after his father's death, it shall be sufficient that his father was an Israel national at the time of his death.

5. (a) A person of full age, not being an Israel national, may obtain Israel nationality by naturalization if—

(1) he is in Israel; and

(2) he had been in Israel for three years out of five years preceding the day of the submission of his application; and

(3) he is entitled to reside in Israel permanently; and

(4) he has settled, or intends to settle, in Israel; and

(5) he has some knowledge of the Hebrew language; and

(6) he has renounced his prior nationality or has proved that he will cease to be a foreign national upon becoming an Israel national.

(b)Where a person has applied for naturalization, and he meets the requirements of subsection (a), the Minister of the Interior, if he thinks fit to do so, shall grant him Israel nationality by the issue of a certificate of naturalisation.

(c) Prior to the grant of nationality, the applicant shall make the following declaration:

"I declare that I will be a loyal national of the State of Israel."

(d) Nationality is acquired on the day of the declaration.

6. (a) (1) A person who has served in the regular service of the Defence Army of Israel or who, after the 16th Kislev, 5708 (29th November, 1947) has served in some other service which the Minister of Defence, by declaration published in *Reshumot*, has declared to be military service for the purpose of this section, and who has been duly discharged from this service; and

(2) a person who has lost a son or daughter in such service, are exempt from the requirements of section 5 (a), except the requirement of section 5 (a) (4).

(b)A person applying for naturalisation after having made a declaration under section 2 (c) (2) is exempt from the requirement of section 5 (a) (2).

(c)A person who immediately before the establishment of the State was a Palestinian citizen is exempt from the requirement of section 5 (a) (5).

(d)The Minister of the Interior may exempt an applicant from all or any of the requirements of section 5(a) (1), (2), (5) and (6) if there exists in his opinion a special reason justifying such exemption.

7. The spouse of a person who is an Israel national or who has applied for Israel nationality and meets or is exempt from the requirements of section 5 (a) may obtain Israel nationality by naturalisation even if she or he is a minor or does not meet the requirements of section (5) (a).

8. Naturalisation confers Israel nationality also upon the minor children of the naturalized person.

9. (a) Where a minor, not being an Israel national, is an inhabitant of Israel, and his parents are not in Israel or have died or are unknown, the Minster of the Interior, on such conditions and with effect from such day as he may think fit, may grant him Israel nationality by the issue of a certificate of naturalisation.

(b) Nationality may be granted as aforesaid upon the application of the father or mother of the minor or, if they have died or are unable to apply, upon the application of the guardian or person in charge of the minor.

Part Two: Loss of Nationality

10. (a) An Israel national of full age, not being an inhabitant of Israel, may declare that he desires to renounce his Israel nationality; such renun-

ciation is subject to the consent of the Minister of the Interior; the declarant's Israel nationality terminates on the day fixed by the Minister.

(b) The Israel nationality of a minor, not being an inhabitant of Israel, terminates upon his parents' renouncing their Israel nationality; it does not terminate as long as one of his parents remains an Israel national.

11. (a) Where a person, having acquired Israel nationality by naturali-sation —

(1) has done so on the basis of false particulars; or

(2) has been abroad for seven consecutive years and has no effective connection with Israel, and has failed to prove that his effective connection with Israel was severed otherwise than by his own volition; or

(3) has committed an act of disloyalty towards the State of Israel, a District Court may, upon the application of the Minister of the Interior, revoke such person's naturalisation.

(b) The Court may, upon such application, rule that revocation shall apply also to such children of the naturalized person as acquired Israel nationality by virtue of his naturalisation and are inhabitants of a foreign country.

(c) Israel nationality terminates on the day on which the judgment revoking naturalisation ceases to be appealable or on such later day as the Court may fix.

12. Loss of Israel nationality does not relieve from a liability arising out of such nationality and created before its loss.

Part Three: Further Provisions

13. In this Law—"of full age" means the age of eighteen years or over;
"minor" means a person under eighteen years of age;
"child" includes an adopted child, and "parents" includes adoptive parents;
"foreign nationality" includes foreign citizenship, and
"foreign national" includes a foreign citizen, but does not include a Palestinian citizen.

14. (a) Save for the purposes of naturalisation, acquisition of Israel nationality is not conditional upon renunciation of a prior nationality.

(b) An Israel national who is also a foreign national shall, for the purposes of Israel law, be considered an Israel national.

(c) An inhabitant of Israel residing abroad shall, for the purposes of this Law, be considered an inhabitant of Israel so long as he has not settled abroad.

15. An Israel national may obtain from the Minister of the Interior a certificate attesting his Israel nationality.

16. A person who knowingly gives false particulars as to a matter affecting his own or another person's acquisition or loss of Israel nationality is liable to imprisonment for a term not exceeding six months or to a fine not exceeding five hundred pounds, or to both such penalties.

17. (a) The Minister of the Interior is charged with the implementation of this Law and may make regulations as to any matter relating to its implementation, including the payment of fees and exemption from the payment thereof.

(b) The Minister of Justice may make regulations as to proceedings in District Courts under this Law, including appeals from decisions of such Courts.

18. (a) The Palestinian Citizenship Orders, 1925–1942 are repealed with effect from the day of the establishment of the State.

(b) Any reference in any provision of law to Palestinian citizenship or Palestinian citizens shall henceforth be read as a reference to Israel nationality or Israel nationals.

(c) Any act done in the period between the establishment of the State and the day of the coming into force of this Law shall be deemed to be valid if it were valid had this Law been in force at the time it was done.

19. (a) This Law shall come into force on the 21st Tammuz, 5712 (14th July, 1952).

(b) Even before that day, the Minister of the Interior may make regulations as to declarations under section 2 (c) (2).

MOSHE SHARETT   MOSHE SHAPIRA
Minister of Foreign Affairs   Minister of the Interior

YOSEF SPRINZAK
Chairman of the Knesset
Acting President of the State

AMENDMENT—1958

1. Section 10 of the Nationality Law, 5712—1952, shall be replaced by the following section:

"10. (a) An Israel national of full age, not being an inhabitant of Israel, may declare that he desires to renounce his Israel nationality.

(b) An Israel national of full age who declares that he desires to cease being an inhabitant of Israel may, if the Minister of the Interior considers that there is a special reason justifying it declare that he desires to renounce his Israel nationality.

(c) Every remuneration of Israel nationality is subject to the consent of the Minister of the Interior.

(d) Where the Minister of the Interior has consented to the renunciation, Israel nationality shall terminate on the day fixed by the Minister.

(e) The Israel nationality of a minor terminates upon his parents' renouncing their Israel nationality, but where the parents have renounced their Israel nationality under subsection (b), the Minister of the Interior may, if he considers that there is a special reason justifying it, refuse to consent to the renunciation in so far as it concerns the termination of the minor's Israel nationality.

(f) The Israel nationality of a minor shall not terminate by virtue of this section so long as one of his parents remains an Israel national."

DAVID BEN-GURION   ISRAEL BAR-YEHUDA
Prime Minister   Minister of the Interior

YITZCHAK BEN-ZVI
President of the State

AMENDMENT NO. 2 — 1968

1. In section 1 of the Nationality Law, 5712 — 1952, (hereafter referred to as "the principal Law"), the line "or by naturalisation (sections 5 to 9)" shall be replaced by the lines:

"by birth and residence in Israel (section 4A)
by naturalisation (sections 5 to 8) or
by grant (section 9)."

2. In section 2 of the principal Law —

(1) paragraphs (2) and (3) of subsection (c) shall be replaced by the following paragraphs:

"(2) to a person of full age who immediately before the day of his *aliyah* or immediately before the day of the issue of his *oleh's* certificate was a foreign national who, on or before that day or within three months thereafter and while still a foreign national declares that he does not wish to become an Israel national; a person as aforesaid may, by written notice to the Minister of the Interior, waive his right to make a declaration under this paragraph;

(3) to a minor of foreign nationality born outside Israel whose parents have made a declaration under paragraph (2) and included him

therein; for this purpose, a declaration by one parent shall be sufficient if the written consent of the other parent has been attached
thereto or if the declarant is entitled to have sole possession of the
minor;

(4) to a person born in Israel after the establishment of the State to
a diplomatic or consular representative of a foreign state, other than
an honorary representative";

(2) the following subsection shall be inserted after subsection (c);

"(d) An Israel resident on whom Israel nationality has not been conferred by reason of a declaration under subsection (c) (3) may, in
the period between his eighteenth birthday and his twenty-first birthday, declare that he wishes to become an Israel national, and from
the day of his declaration he shall be an Israel national by virtue of
return."

AMENDMENT NO. 3—1971

1. In the Nationality Law, 5712—1952, the following subsection shall
be added at the end of section 2:

"(e) Where a person has expressed his desire to settle in Israel, being a
person who has received, or is entitled to receive an *oleh's* visa under the Law
of Return, 5710—1950, the Minister of the Interior may at his discretion,
grant him, upon his application, nationality by virtue of return even before
his *aliya*."

GOLDA MEIR   YOSEF BURG
Prime Minister   Minister of
the Interior

SHNEUR ZALMAN SHAZAR
President of the State

50

Rabbinical Courts Jurisdiction (Marriage and Divorce) Law 1953

Because there is no civil marriage in Israel, the laws regarding marriage and divorce are very important in Israel — especially as they affect liberal and secular Jews.

1. Matters of marriage and divorce of Jews in Israel, being nationals or residents of the State, shall be under the exclusive jurisdiction of rabbinical courts.

2. Marriages and divorces of Jews shall be performed in Israel in accordance with Jewish religious law.

3. Where a suit for divorce between Jews has been filed in a rabbinical court, whether by the wife or by the husband, a rabbinical court shall have exclusive jurisdiction in any matter connected with such suit, including maintenance for the wife and for the children of the couple.

4. Where a Jewish wife sues her Jewish husband or his estate for maintenance in a rabbinical court, otherwise than in connection with divorce, the plea of the defendant that a rabbinical court has no jurisdiction in the matter shall not be heard.

5. Where a woman sues her deceased husband's brother for *chalitza* in a rabbinical court, the rabbinical court shall have exclusive jurisdiction in the matter, also as regards maintenance for the woman until the day on which *chalitza* is given.

6. Where a rabbinical court, by final judgment, has ordered that a husband be compelled to grant his wife a letter of divorce or that a wife be compelled to accept a letter of divorce from her husband, a district court may, upon expiration of six months from the day of the making of the order,

on the application of the Attorney General, compel compliance with the order by imprisonment.

7. Where a rabbinical court, by final judgment, has ordered that a man be compelled to give her brother's widow *chalitza*, a district court may, upon expiration of three months from the day of the making of the order, on application of the Attorney General, compel compliance with the order by imprisonment.

8. For the purpose of sections 6 and 7, a judgment shall be regarded as final when it is no longer appealable.

9. In matters of personal status of Jews, as specified in article 51 of the Palestine Orders in Council 1922 to 1947, or in the Succession Ordinance, in which a rabbinical court has not exclusive jurisdiction under this Law, a rabbinical court shall have jurisdiction after all parties concerned have expressed their consent thereto.

10. A judgment given by a rabbinical court after the establishment of the State and before the coming into force of this Law, after the case had been heard in the presence of the litigants, and which would have been validly given had this Law been in force at the time, shall be deemed to have been validly given.

11. The Minister of Religious Affairs is charged with the implementation of this Law.

MOSHE SHARETT   MOSHE SHAPIRA
Minister of Foreign Affairs   Minister of the Religious Affairs
Acting Prime Minister

YITZCHAK BEN-ZVI
President of the State

51

United Nations Security Council Resolution 242 1967

In November 1967, the United Nations Security Council passed Resolution 242, asking Israel to remove its troops from areas conquered in the Six Day War and to work for a just and lasting peace. This resolution asked the Arab states to give up all claims to the land of the State of Israel and for all peoples in the area to live in peace.

Adopted Unanimously at the 1382nd Meeting
The Security Council NOVEMBER 22, 1967

Expressing its continuing concern with the grave situation in the Middle East, Emphasizing the inadmissibility of the acquisition of territory by war and the need to work for a just and lasting peace in which every state in the area can live in security, emphasizing further that all member states in their acceptance of the Charter of the United Nations have undertaken a commitment to act in accordance with Article 2 of the Charter,

1. Affirms that the fulfillment of Charter principles requires the establishment of a just and lasting peace in the Middle East which should include the application of both the following principles:

(I) Withdrawal of Israeli armed forces from territories occupied in the recent conflict,

(II) Termination of all claims or states of belligerency and respect for and acknowledgement of the sovereignty, territorial integrity and political independence of every state in the area and their right to live in peace within secure and recognized boundaries free from threats or acts of force,

2. Affirms further the necessity

(A) For guaranteeing freedom of navigation through international waterways in the area,

(B) For achieving a just settlement of the refugee problem,

(C) For guaranteeing the territorial inviolability and political independence of every state in the area, through measures including the establishment of demilitarized zones,

3. Requests the secretary-general to designate a special representative to proceed to the Middle East to establish and maintain contacts with the states concerned in order to promote agreement and assist efforts to achieve a peaceful and accepted settlement in accordance with the provisions and principles of this resolution.

4. Requests the secretary-general to report to the Security Council on the progress of the efforts of the special representative as soon as possible.

52

Matters of Dissolution of Marriage (Jurisdiction in Special Cases) Law 1969

Since matters of divorce historically were handled by the rabbinical court, the state of Israel needed to develop laws which would govern those divorces between Jews and non-Jews, as well as those divorces which have been granted by different countries.

1. (a) Matters of dissolution of marriage which are not within the exclusive jurisdiction of a religious court shall be within the jurisdiction of the District Court or a religious court, as the President of the Supreme Court may determine.

(b) This Law shall not apply where both spouses are Jews, Muslims, Druze or members of one of the Christian communities which maintain a religious court in Israel.

2. (a) Where one of the spouses is a Jew, a Muslim, a Druze, or a member of one of the Christian communities which maintain a religious court in Israel, the President of the Supreme Court shall not exercise his power under section 1 until he has received an opinion from a religious court as provided in this section.

(b) The Attorney-General or his representative shall apply in writing to the religious court concerned or to each of the two religious courts concerned, describing the circumstances of the case and requesting a written opinion as to whether, in the circumstances described, the religious court would perform or grant a divorce, or annul the marriage or declare it void *ab initio*, and the religious court shall give the opinion as requested.

(c) When the requested opinion has been given, the Attorney-General shall submit it to the President of the Supreme Court, who, after perusing the opinion, shall at his discretion decide whether to refer the matter to a religious court or to the District Court.

3. The President of the Supreme Court may refrain from determining jurisdiction under this Law if he is of the opinion that in the circumstances of the case the applicant should not be granted relief.

4. (a) Article 55 of the Palestine Order in Council, 1922–1947, shall not apply to a matter dealt with by this Law.

(b) The provisos in article 64(1) and in the second sentence of article 65 of the said Order in Council shall not apply to a matter in respect of which jurisdiction is determined under this Law.

5. (a) The District Court vested with jurisdiction under this Law shall apply one of the undermentioned to the matter, in the following order of preference:

    (1) the domestic law of the common domicile of the spouses;

    (2) the domestic law of the last common domicile of the spouses;

    (3) the domestic law of the country of which both spouses are nationals;

    (4) the domestic law of the place where the marriage was contracted: Provided that the Court shall not deal with the matter in accordance with any such law as aforesaid if different rules would apply thereunder to the two spouses.

(b) In the absence of any law applicable under subsection (a), the Court may apply the domestic law of the domicile of one of the spouses, as it may deem just in the circumstances of the case.

(c) Consent of the spouses shall always be a ground for divorce.

6. In this Law—

"dissolution of marriage" includes divorce, annulment of marriage and the declaration of a marriage as void *ab initio*;

"religious court" means a rabbinical court, a Sharia court, a religious court of a Christian community and a Druze religious court, all within the respective meanings assigned to these terms by law;

"domicile" has the meaning assigned to this term by section 80 of the Capacity and Guardianship Law, 5722–1962.

7. The Minister of Justice may make regulations as to the proceedings before the President of the Supreme Court and as to the request of the Attorney-General or his representative for an opinion of a religious court under this Law.

8. The provisions of this Law shall not derogate from section 9 of the Rabbinical Courts Jurisdiction (Marriage and Divorce) Law, 5713–1953, or from section 18 of the Courts Law, 5717–1957.

GOLDA MEIR
Prime Minister

GOLDA MEIR
Prime Minister
Acting Minister
of Justice

SHNEUR ZALMAN SHAZAR
President of the State

53

United Nations Resolution 338
1973

Following the Yom Kippur War of 1973, when Israel was attacked and — amidst significant casualties — was eventually victorious, Israel and Egypt determined to maintain a peaceful coexistence. While it was initiated through this United Nations resolution, it was eventually worked out in the Camp David Accords (which follow).

Adopted by the Security Council at its 1747th
Meeting, on 21/22 October 1973
The Security Council,

    1. Calls upon all parties to the present fighting to cease all firing and terminate all military activity immediately, no later than 12 hours after the moment of the adoption of this decision, in the positions they now occupy,

    2. Calls upon the parties concerned to start immediately after the cease-fire the implementation of security council resolution 242 (197) in all of its parts.

    3. Decides that, immediately and concurrently with the cease-fire, negotiations start between the parties concerned under appropriate auspices aimed at establishing a just and durable peace in the Middle East.

THE FRAMEWORK FOR THE CONCLUSION
OF A PEACE TREATY
BETWEEN EGYPT AND ISRAEL

In order to achieve peace between them, Israel and Egypt agree to negotiate in good faith with a goal of concluding within three months of the signing of this framework a peace treaty between them.
It is agreed that:

The site of the negotiations will be under a United Nations flag at a location or locations to be mutually agreed.

All of the principles of UN Resolution 242 will apply in this resolution of the dispute between Israel and Egypt.

Unless otherwise mutually agreed, terms of the peace treaty will be implemented between 2 and 3 years after the peace treaty is signed.

The following matters are agreed between the parties:

(a) The full exercise of Egyptian sovereignty up to the internationally recognized border between Egypt and Mandated Palestine;

(b) The withdrawal of Israeli armed forces from the Sinai;

(c) The use of airfields left by the Israelis near El Arish, Rafah, Rasen-Naqb and Sharm-el-Sheikh for civilian purposes only, including possible commercial use by all nations;

(d) The right of free passage by ships of Israel through the Gulf of Suez and the Suez Canal on the basis of the Constantinople Convention of 1888 applying to all nations; the Strait of Tiran and the Gulf of Aqaba are international waterways to be open to all nations for unimpeded and non-suspendible freedom of navigation and overflight;

(e) The construction of a highway between the Sinai and Jordan near Eilat with guaranteed free and peaceful passage by Egypt and Jordan; and

(f) The stationing of military forces listed below.

STATIONING OF FORCES

A. No more than one division (mechanized or infantry) of Egyptian armed forces will be stationed within an area lying approximately 50 kilometres east of the Gulf of Suez and the Suez Canal.

B. Only UN forces and civil police equipped with light weapons to perform normal police functions will be stationed within an area lying west of the international border and the Gulf of Aqaba, varying in width from 20 km. to 40 km.

C. In the area within three kilometres east of the international border there will be Israeli limited military forces not to exceed 4 infantry battalions and UN observers.

D. Border patrol units, not to exceed 3 battalions, will supplement the civil police in maintaining order in the area not included above.

The exact demarcation of the above areas will be as decided during the peace negotiations. Early warning stations may exist to insure compliance with the terms of the agreement.

UN forces will be stationed:

A. In part of the area in the Sinai lying within about 20 km. of the Mediterranean Sea, and adjacent to the international border, and

B. In the Sharm-el-Sheikh area to insure freedom of passage through the Strait of Tiran; and these forces will not be removed unless such removal is approved by the Security Council of the UN with a unanimous vote of the five permanent members.

After a peace treaty is signed, and after the interim withdrawal is complete, normal relations will be established between Egypt and Israel, including: Full recognition, including diplomatic, economic and cultural relations; termination of economic boycotts and barriers to the free movement of goods and people; and mutual protection of citizens by the due process of law.

INTERIM WITHDRAWAL

Between 3 months and 9 months after the signing of the peace treaty, all Israeli forces will withdraw east of line extending from a point east of El Arish to Ras Mohammed, the exact location of this line to be determined by mutual agreement.

54

Camp David Peace Agreement
1978

In an agreement that most thought was not possible, Menahem Begin and Anwar Sadat came together in order to develop a framework within which Israel and Egypt could live together peacefully in the Middle East.

Mohammed Anwar al-Sadat, President of the Arab Republic of Egypt, and Menahem Begin, Prime Minister of Israel, met with Jimmy Carter, President of the United States of America at Camp David from Sept. 5 to Sept. 17, 1978, and have agreed on the following framework for peace in the Middle East. They invite other parties to the Arab-Israeli conflict to adhere to it:

Preamble:

The search for peace in the Middle East must be guided by the following:

The agreed basis for a peaceful settlement of the conflict between Israel and its neighbors is U.N. Security Council Resolution 242 in all its parts.

After four wars during 30 years, despite intensive humane efforts, the Middle East, which is the cradle of civilization and the birthplace of the three great religions, does not yet enjoy the blessings of peace. The people of the Middle East yearn for peace, so that the vast human and natural resources of the region can be turned to the pursuits of peace and so that this area can become a model for coexistence and cooperation among nations.

The historic initiative by President Sadat in visiting Jerusalem and the reception accorded to him by the parliament, government and people of Israel, and the reciprocal visit of Prime Minister Begin to Ismaailia, the peace proposals made by both leaders, as well as the warm reception of these missions by the peoples of both countries, have created an unprecedented opportunity for peace which must not be lost if this generation and future generations are to be spared the tragedies of war.

The provisions of the Charter of the United Nations and the other accepted norms of international law and legitimacy now provide accepted standards for the conduct of relations between all states.

To achieve a relationship of peace, in the spirit of Article 2 of the U.N. Charter, future negotiations between Israel and any neighbour prepared to negotiate peace and security with it, are necessary for the purpose of carrying out all the provisions and principles of Resolutions 242 and 338.

Peace requires respect for sovereignty, territorial integrity and political independence of every state in the area and their right to live in peace within secure and recognized boundaries free from threats or acts of force. Progress toward that goal can accelerate movement toward a new era of reconciliation in the Middle East marked by cooperation in promoting economic development, in maintaining stability and in assuring security.

Security is enhanced by a relationship of peace and by cooperation between nations which enjoy normal relations. In addition, under the terms of peace treaties, the parties can, on the basis of reciprocity, agree to special security arrangements such as demilitarized zones, limited armament areas, early warning stations, the presence of international forces, liaison, agreed measures for monitoring, and other arrangements that they agree are useful.

Taking these factors into account, the parties are determined to reach a just, comprehensive, and durable settlement of the Middle East conflict through the conclusion of peace treaties based on Security Council Resolutions 242 and 338 in all their parts. Their purpose is to achieve peace and good neighbourly relations. They recognize that, for peace to endure, it must involve all those who have been most deeply affected by the conflict. They therefore agree that this framework as appropriate is intended by them to constitute a basis for peace not only between Egypt and Israel, but also between Israel and each of its other neighbours which is prepared to negotiate peace with Israel on this basis.

With that objective in mind, they have agreed to proceed as follows:

A. WEST BANK AND GAZA

1. Egypt, Israel, Jordan and the representatives of the Palestinian people should participate in negotiations on the resolution of the Palestinian problem in all its aspects. To achieve that objective, negotiations relating to the West Bank and Gaza should proceed in three stages.

(A) Egypt and Israel agree that, in order to ensure a peaceful and orderly transfer of authority, and taking into account the security concerns of all the parties, there should be transitional arrangements for the West Bank and Gaza for a period not exceeding five years. In order to provide full autonomy to the inhabitants, under these arrangements the Israeli military government and its civilian administration will be withdrawn as soon as a self-governing authority has been freely elected by the inhabitants of these areas to replace the existing government.

To negotiate the details of a transitional arrangement, the government of Jordan will be invited to join the negotiations on the basis of this framework. These new arrangements should give due consideration to both the principle of self-government by the inhabitants of these territories and to the legitimate security concerns of the parties involved.

(B) Egypt, Israel and Jordan will agree on the modalities for establishing the elected self-governing authority in the West Bank and Gaza. The delegations of Egypt and Jordan may include Palestinians from the West Bank and Gaza or other Palestinians as mutually agreed. The parties will negotiate an agreement which will define the powers and responsibilities of the self-governing authority to be exercised in the West Bank and Gaza. A withdrawal of Israeli armed forces will take place and there will be a redeployment of the remaining Israeli forces into specified security locations.

The agreement will also include arrangements for assuring internal and external security and public order. A strong local police force will be established, which may include Jordanian citizens. In addition, Israeli and Jordanian forces will participate in joint patrols and in the manning of control posts to assure the security of the borders.

(C) When the self-governing authority (administrative council) in the West Bank and Gaza is established and inaugurated, the transitional period of five years will begin. As soon as possible, but not later than the third year after the beginning of the transitional period, negotiations will take place to determine the final status of the West Bank and Gaza and its relationship with its neighbours, and to conclude a peace treaty between Israel and Jordan by the end of the transitional period.

These negotiations will be conducted among Egypt, Israel and Jordan, and the elected representatives of the inhabitants of the West Bank and Gaza. Two separate but related committees will be convened, one committee, consisting of representatives of the four parties which will negotiate and agree on the final status of the West Bank and Gaza, and its relationship with its neighbours, and the second committee, consisting of representatives of Israel and representatives of Jordan to be joined by the elected representatives of the inhabitants of the West Bank and Gaza, to negotiate the peace treaty between Israel and Jordan, taking into account the agreement reached on the final status of the West Bank and Gaza.

The negotiations shall be based on all the provisions and principles of U.N. Security Council Resolution 242. The negotiations will resolve, among other matters, the location of the boundaries and the nature of the security arrangements.

The solution from the negotiations must also recognize the legitimate rights of the Palestinian people and their just requirements. In this way, the Palestinians will participate in the determination of their own future through:

(1) The negotiations among Egypt, Israel, Jordan and the representatives of the inhabitants of the West Bank and Gaza to agree on the final status of the West Bank and Gaza and other outstanding issues by the end of the transitional period.

(2) Submitting their agreement to a vote by the elected representatives of the inhabitants of the West Bank and Gaza.

(3) Providing for the elected representatives of the inhabitants on the West Bank and Gaza to decide how they shall govern themselves consistent with the provisions of their agreement.

(4) Participating as stated above in the work of the committee negotiating the peace treaty between Israel and Jordan.

2. All necessary measures will be taken and provisions made to assure the security of Israel and its neighbours during the transitional period and beyond. To assist in providing such security, a strong local police force will be constituted by the self-governing authority. It will be composed of inhabitants of the West Bank and Gaza. The police will maintain continuing liaison on internal security matters with the designated Israeli, Jordanian and Egyptian officers.

3. During the transitional period, the representatives of Egypt, Israel, Jordan and the self-governing authority will constitute a continuing committee to decide by agreement on the modalities of admission of persons displaced from the West Bank and Gaza in 1967, together with necessary measures to prevent disruption and disorder. Other matters of common concern may also be dealt with by this committee.

4. Egypt and Israel will work with each other and with other interested parties to establish agreed procedures for a prompt, just and permanent implementation of the resolution of the refugee problem.

B. EGYPT-ISRAEL

1. Egypt and Israel undertake not to resort to the threat or the use of force to settle disputes. Any disputes shall be settled by peaceful means in

accordance with the provisions of Article 33 of the Charter of the United Nations.

2. In order to achieve peace between them, the parties agree to negotiate in good faith with a goal of concluding within three months from the signing of this framework a peace treaty between them, while inviting the other parties to the conflict to proceed simultaneously to negotiate and conclude similar peace treaties with a view to achieving a comprehensive peace in the area. The framework for the conclusion of a peace treaty between Egypt and Israel will govern the peace negotiations between them. The parties will agree on the modalities and the timetable for the implementation of their obligation under the treaty.

C. ASSOCIATED PRINCIPLES

1. Egypt and Israel state that the principles and provisions described below should apply to peace treaties between Israel and each of its neighbours—Egypt, Jordan, Syria and Lebanon.

2. Signatories shall establish among themselves relationships normal to states at peace with one another. To this end, they should undertake to abide by all the provisions of the Charter of the United Nations. Steps to be taken in this respect include:

(A) Full recognition,

(B) Abolishing economic boycotts,

(C) Guaranteeing that under their jurisdiction the citizens of the other parties shall enjoy the protection of the due process of law.

3. Signatories should explore possibilities for economic development in the context of final peace treaties, with the objective of contributing to the atmosphere of peace, cooperation and friendship which is their common goal.

4. Claims commissions may be established for the mutual settlement of all financial claims.

5. The United States shall be invited to participate in the talks on matters related to modalities of the implementation of the agreement and working out the timetable for the carrying out of the obligations of the parties.

6. The United Nations Security Council shall be requested to endorse the peace treaties and ensure that their provisions shall not be violated. The permanent members of the Security Council shall be requested to underwrite the peace treaties and ensure respect for their provisions. They shall also be requested to conform their policies and actions with the undertakings contained in this framework.

55

Treaty of Peace between the State of Israel and the Arab Republic of Egypt 1979

While the construction of this agreement is implied in the Camp David Accords, the details had to be worked out in the form of a formal treaty ratified by the two countries.

Instrument of Ratification
Whereas the Treaty of Peace between the State of Israel and the Arab Republic of Egypt was approved by the Knesset on the 22nd day of March, 1979:
And whereas the said Treaty of Peace was done at Washington D.C. on the 26th day of March 1979, and was signed by Prime Minister Menachem Begin for the Government of Israel and by President Mohamed Anwar El-Sadat for the Government of the Arab Republic of Egypt, and witnessed by Jimmy Carter, President of the United States of America, on the same day:
And whereas Article IX of the said Treaty of Peace provides that it shall enter into force upon exchange of the instruments of ratification:
And whereas on the 1st day of April 1979 the Government of Israel, in accordance with the powers vested in it by law, decided to ratify the Treaty of Peace:
And whereas the text of the said Treaty of Peace is word for word annexed hereto:
Now therefore it is hereby declared that the Government of Israel ratifies the Treaty of Peace between the State of Israel and the Arab Republic of Egypt. In witness whereof I, Yitzhak Navon, President of the State of Israel, have subscribed my signature and have caused the Seal of the State of Israel to be affixed hereunto at Jerusalem, this 23rd day of Nisan, Five Thousand Seven Hundred and Thirty-Nine, which corresponds to the 20th day of April, One Thousand Nine Hundred and Seventy-Nine.

Countersigned:
Moshe Dayan   Y. Navon

Documents Accompanying the Treaty of Peace
between the State of Israel and the Arab Republic of Egypt

Instrument of Ratification

Whereas the following documents accompanying the Treaty of Peace between the State of Israel and the Arab Republic of Egypt were approved by the Knesset on the 22nd day of March 1979:

(1) Agreed minutes to Articles I, IV, V and VI and Annexes I and III of the Treaty of Peace:

(2) A letter from Jimmy Carter, President of the United States of America, to Prime Minister Menachem Begin on the implementation of the Treaty of Peace:

(3) An exchange of letters between President Jimmy Carter and Prime Minister Menachem Begin concerning the exchange of ambassadors between the State of Israel and the Arab Republic of Egypt.

And whereas on the 26th day of March 1979 the said Agreed Minutes were signed at Washington D.C. by Prime Minister Menachem Begin for the Government of Israel and by President Mohamed Anwar El-Sadat for the Government of the Arab Republic of Egypt and witnessed by President Jimmy Carter:

And whereas the said letters were also signed on the 26th day of March 1979:

And whereas on the 1st day of April 1979 the Government of Israel, in accordance with the powers invested in it by law, decided to ratify the said documents:

And whereas the texts of the said documents are word for word annexed hereto:

Now therefore it is hereby declared that the Government of Israel ratifies the said documents accompanying the Treaty of Peace.

In witness whereof I, Yitzhak Navon, President of the State of Israel, have subscribed my signature and have caused the Seal of the State of Israel to be affixed hereunto at Jerusalem, this 23rd day of Nisan, Five Thousand Seven Hundred and Thirty-Nine, which corresponds to the 20th day of April, One Thousand Nine Hundred and Seventy-Nine.

Countersigned:
Moshe Dayan   Y. Navon
Minister of Foreign Affairs

Treaty of Peace between the State of Israel and the Arab Republic of Egypt.
    The Government of the State of Israel and the Government of the Arab
Republic of Egypt:

Preamble
Convinced of the urgent necessity of the establishment of a just, compre-
hensive and lasting peace in the Middle East in accordance with Security
Council Resolutions 242 and 338;
Reaffirming their adherence to the "Framework for Peace in the Middle East
Agreed at Camp David," dated September 17, 1978;
Noting that the aforementioned Framework as appropriate is intended to
constitute a basis for peace not only between Israel and Egypt but also be-
tween Israel and each of its other Arab neighbors which is prepared to nego-
tiate peace with it on this basis;
Desiring to bring to an end the state of war between them and to establish a
peace in which every state in the area can live in security;
Convinced that the conclusion of a Treaty of Peace between Israel and Egypt
is an important step in the search for comprehensive peace in the area and for
the attainment of the settlement of the Arab-Israeli conflict in all its aspects;
Inviting the other Arab parties to this dispute to join the peace process with
Israel guided by and based on the principles of the aforementioned Framework;
Desiring as well to develop friendly relations and cooperation between themselves in accordance with the United Nations Charter and the principles of
international law governing international relations in times of peace;
Agree to the following provisions in the free exercise of their sovereignty, in
order to implement the "Framework for the Conclusion of a Peace Treaty
Between Israel and Egypt":

Article I
    1. The state of war between the Parties will be terminated and peace
will be established between them upon the exchange of instruments of ratification of this Treaty.
    2. Israel will withdraw all its armed forces and civilians from the Sinai
behind the international boundary between Egypt and mandated Palestine,
as provided in the annexed protocol (Annex I), and Egypt will resume the
exercise of its full sovereignty over the Sinai.
    3. Upon completion of the interim withdrawal provided for in Annex I,
the Parties will establish normal and friendly relations, in accordance with
Article III (3).

Article II

The permanent boundary between Egypt and Israel is the recognized international boundary between Egypt and the former mandated territory of Palestine, as shown on the map at Annex II, without prejudice to the issue of the status of the Gaza Strip. The Parties recognize this boundary as inviolable. Each will respect the territorial of the other, including their territorial waters and airspace.

Article III

1. The Parties will apply between them the provisions of the Charter of the United Nations and the principles of international law governing relations among states in times of peace. In particular

a. They recognize and will respect each other's sovereignty, territorial integrity and political independence;

b. They recognize and will respect each other's right to live in peace within their secure and recognized boundaries;

c. They will refrain from the threat or use of force, directly or indirectly, against each other and will settle all disputes between them by peaceful means.

2. Each Party undertakes to ensure that acts or threats of belligerency, hostility, or violence do not originate from and are not committed from within its territory, or by any forces subject to its control or by any other forces stationed on its territory, against the population, citizens or property of the other Party. Each Party also undertakes to refrain from organizing, instigating, inciting, assisting or participating in acts or threats of belligerency, hostility, subversion or violence against the other Party, anywhere, and undertakes to ensure that perpetrators of such acts are brought to justice.

3. The Parties agree that the normal relationship established between them will include full recognition, diplomatic, economic and cultural relations, termination of economic boycotts and discriminatory barriers to the free movement of people and goods, and will guarantee the mutual enjoyment by citizens of the due process of law. The process by which they undertake to achieve such a relationship parallel to the implementation of other provisions of this Treaty is set out in the annexed protocol (Annex III).

Article IV

1. In order to provide maximum security for both Parties on the basis of reciprocity, agreed security arrangements will be established including limited force zones in Egyptian and Israeli territory, and United Nations forces and observers, described in detail as to nature and timing in Annex I, and other security arrangements the Parties may agree upon.

2. The Parties agree to the stationing of United Nations personnel in areas described in Annex I. The Parties agree not to request withdrawal of the United Nations personnel and that these personnel will not be removed unless such removal is approved by the Security Council of the United Nations, with the affirmative vote of the five Permanent Members, unless the Parties otherwise agree.

3. A Joint commission will be established to facilitate the implementation of the Treaty, as provided for in Annex I.

4. The security arrangements provided for in paragraphs 1 and 2 of this Article may at the request of either party be reviewed and amended by mutual agreement of the Parties.

Article V

1. Ships of Israel, and cargoes destined for or coming from Israel, shall enjoy the right of free passage through the Suez Canal and its approaches through the Gulf of Suez and the Mediterranean Sea on the basis of the Constantinople Convention of 1888, applying to all nations. Israel nationals, vessels and cargoes, as well as persons, vessels and cargoes destined for or coming from Israel, shall be accorded non-discriminatory treatment in all matters connected with usage of the canal.

2. The Parties consider the Strait of Tiran and the Gulf of Aqaba to be international waterways open to all nations for unimpeded and non-suspendable freedom of navigation and overflight. The Parties will respect each other's right to navigation and overflight for access to either country.

Article VI

1. This Treaty does not affect and shall not be interpreted as affecting in any way the rights and obligations of the Parties under the Charter of the United Nations.

2. The parties undertake to fulfill in good faith their obligations under this Treaty, without regard or inactions of any other party and independently of any instrument external to this Treaty.

3. They further undertake to take all the necessary measures for the application in their relations of the provisions of the multilateral conventions to which they are parties, including the submission of appropriate notifications to the Secretary General of the United Nations and other depositaries of such conventions.

4. The Parties undertake not to enter into any obligation in conflict with this Treaty.

5. Subject to Article 103 of the United Nations Charter, in the event of a conflict between the obligations of the Parties under the present Treaty and any of their other obligations, the obligations under this Treaty will be binding and implemented.

Done at Washington D.C. this 26th day of March, 1979, in triplicate in the Hebrew, Arabic and English languages, each text being equally authentic. In case of any divergence of interpretation, the English text shall prevail. For the Government of the Arab Republic of Egypt: A. El-Sadat Witnessed by: Jimmy Carter, President of the United States For the Government of Israel: M. Begin

Annex I
Protocol Concerning Israeli Withdrawal and Security Arrangements

Article I
Concept of Withdrawal
1. Israel will complete withdrawal of all its armed forces and civilians from the Sinai not later than three years from the date of exchange of instruments of ratification of this Treaty.
2. To ensure the mutual security of the Parties, the implementation of phased withdrawal will be accompanied by the military measures and establishment of zones set out in this Annex and in Map 1, hereinafter referred to as "the Zones."
3. The withdrawal from the Sinai will be accomplished in two phases:
a. The interim withdrawal behind the line from east of El Arish to Ras Muhammed as delineated on Map 2 within nine months from the date of exchange of instruments of ratification of this Treaty.
b. The final withdrawal from the Sinai behind the international boundary not later than three years from the date of exchange of instruments of ratification of this Treaty.
4. A Joint Commission will be formed immediately after the exchange of instruments of ratification of this Treaty in order to supervise and coordinate movements and schedules during the withdrawal, and to adjust plans and timetables as necessary within the limits established by paragraph 3, above. Details relating to the Joint Commission are set out in Article IV of the attached Appendix. The Joint Commission will be dissolved upon completion of final Israeli withdrawal from the Sinai.

Article II
Determination of Final Lines and Zones
   1. In order to provide maximum security for both Parties after the final withdrawal, the lines and Zones delineated on Map 1 are to be established and organized as follows:
a. Zone A
   1. Zone A is bounded on the east by line A (red line) and on the west by the Suez Canal and the east coast of the Gulf of Suez, as shown on Map 1.
   2. An Egyptian armed force of one mechanized infantry division and its military installations, and field fortifications, will be in this Zone.
   3. The main elements of that division will consist of:
      a. Three mechanized infantry brigades.
      b. One armored brigade.
      c. Seven field artillery battalions including up to 126 artillery pieces.
      d. Seven anti-aircraft artillery battalions including individual surface-to-air missiles and up to 126 anti-aircraft guns of 37mm and above.
      e. Up to 230 tanks.
      f. Up to 480 armored personnel vehicles of all types.
      g. Up to a total of twenty-two thousand personnel.

b. Zone B
   1. Zone B is bounded by line B (green line) on the east and by line A (red line) on the west, as shown on Map 1.
   2. Egyptian border units of four battalions equipped with light weapons and wheeled vehicles will provide security and supplement the civil police in maintaining order in Zone B. The main elements of the four border battalions will consist of up to a total of four thousand personnel.
   3. Land based, short range, low power, coastal warning points of the border patrol units may be established on the coast of this Zone.
   4. There will be in Zone B field fortifications and military installations of the four border battalions.

c. Zone C
   1. Zone C is bounded by line B (green line) on the west and the international boundary and the Gulf of Aqaba on the east, as shown on Map 1.
   2. Only United Nations forces and Egyptian civil police will be stationed in Zone C.

3. The Egyptian civil police armed with light weapons will perform normal police functions within this Zone.

4. The United Nations Force will be deployed within Zone C and perform its functions as defined in Article VI of this Annex.

5. The United Nations Force will be stationed mainly in camps located within the following stationing areas shown on Map 1, and will establish its precise locations after consultations with Egypt:

    a. In that part of the area in the Sinai lying within about 20 km. of the Mediterranean Sea and adjacent to the international boundary.

    b. In the Sharm el Sheikh area.

d. Zone D

1. Zone D is bounded by line D (blue line) on the east and the international boundary on the west, as shown on Map 1.

2. In this Zone there will be an Israeli limited force of four infantry battalions, their military installations, and field fortifications, and United Nations observers.

3. The Israeli forces in Zone D will not include tanks, artillery and anti-aircraft missiles except individual surface-to-air missiles.

4. The main elements of the four Israeli infantry battalions will consist of up to 180 armored personnel vehicles of all types and up to a total of four thousand personnel.

2. Access across the international boundary shall only be permitted through entry check points designated by each party and under its control. Such access shall be in accordance with laws and regulations of each country.

3. Only those field fortifications, military installations, forces and weapons specifically permitted by this Annex shall be in the Zones.

Article III
Aerial Military Regime

1. Flights of combat aircraft and reconnaissance flights of Egypt and Israel shall take place only over Zones A and D respectively.

2. Only unarmed, non-combat aircraft of Egypt and Israel will be stationed in Zones A and D respectively.

3. Only Egyptian unarmed transport aircraft will take off and land in Zone B and up to eight such aircraft may be maintained in Zone B. The Egyptian border units may be equipped with unarmed helicopters to perform their functions in Zone B.

4. The Egyptian civil police may be equipped with unarmed police helicopters to perform normal police functions in Zone C.

5. Only civilian airfields may be built in the Zones.

6. Without prejudice to the provisions of this Treaty, only those military aerial activities specifically permitted by this Annex shall be allowed in the Zones and the airspace above their territorial waters.

Article IV
Naval Regime

1. Egypt and Israel may base and operate naval vessels along the coasts of Zones A and D, respectively.

2. Egyptian coast guard boats, lightly armed, may be stationed and operate in the territorial waters of Zone B to assist the border units in performing their functions in this Zone.

3. Egyptian civil police equipped with light boats, lightly armed, shall perform normal police functions within the territorial waters of Zone C.

4. Nothing in this Annex shall be considered as derogating from the right of innocent passage of the naval vessels of either Party.

5. Only civilian maritime ports and installations may be built in the Zones.

6. Without prejudice to the provisions of this Treaty, only those naval activities specifically permitted by this Annex shall be allowed in the Zones and in their territorial waters.

Article V
Early Warning Systems

Egypt and Israel may establish and operate early warning systems only in Zones A and D, respectively.

Article VI
United Nations Operations

1. The Parties will request the United Nations to provide forces and observers to supervise the implementation of this Annex and employ their best efforts to prevent any violation of its terms.

2. With respect to these United Nations forces and observers, as appropriate, the Parties agree to request the following arrangements:

a. Operation of check points, reconnaissance patrols, and observation posts along the international boundary and line B, and within Zone C.

b. Periodic verification of the implementation of the provisions of this Annex will be carried out not less than twice a month unless otherwise agreed by the Parties.

c. Additional verifications within 48 hours after the receipt of a request from either Party.

d. Enduring the freedom of navigation through the Strait of Tiran in accordance with Article V of the Treaty of Peace.

3. The arrangements described in this article for each zone will be implemented in Zones A, B, and C by the United Nations Force and in Zone D by the United Nations Observers.

4. United Nations verification teams shall be accompanied by liaison officers of the respective Party.

5. The United Nations Force and Observers will report their findings to both parties.

6. The United Nations Force and Observers operating in the Zones will enjoy freedom of movement and other facilities necessary for the performance of their tasks.

7. The United Nations Force and Observers are not empowered to authorize the crossing of the international boundary.

8. The Parties shall agree on the nations from which the United Nations Force and Observers will be drawn. They will be drawn from nations other than those which are Permanent Members of the United Nations Security Council.

9. The Parties agree that the United Nations should make those command arrangements that will best assure the effective implementation of its responsibilities.

Article VII
Liaison System

1. Upon dissolution of the Joint Commission, a liaison system between the Parties will be established. This liaison system is intended to provide an effective method to assess progress in the implementation of obligations under the present Annex and to resolve any problem that may arise in the course of implementation, and refer other unresolved matters to the higher military authorities of the two countries respectively for consideration. It is also intended to prevent situations resulting from errors of misinterpretation on the part of either Party.

2. An Egyptian liaison office will be established in the city of El Arish and an Israeli liaison office will be established in the city of Beer-Sheba. Each office will be headed by an officer of the respective country, and assisted by a number of officers.

3. A direct telephone line, between the two offices, will be set up and also direct telephone lines with the United Nations command will be maintained by both offices.

Article VIII
Respect for War Memorials
Each Party undertakes to preserve in good condition the War Memorials erected in memory of the soldiers of the other Party, namely those erected by Israel in the Sinai and those to be erected by Egypt in Israel, and shall permit access to such monuments.

Article IX
Interim Arrangements
The withdrawal of Israeli armed forces and civilians behind the interim withdrawal line, and the conduct of the forces of the parties and the United Nations prior to the final withdrawal, will be governed by the attached Appendix and Maps 2 and 3.

Appendix to Annex I
Organization of Movements in the Sinai

Article I
Principles of Withdrawal
1. The withdrawal of Israeli armed forces and civilians from the Sinai will be accomplished in two phases as described in Article I of Annex I. The description and timing of the withdrawal are included in this Appendix. The Joint Commission will develop and present to the Chief Coordinator of the United Nations forces in the Middle East the details of these phases not later than one month before the initiation of each phase of withdrawal.

2. Both Parties agree on the following principles for the sequence of military movements.

Notwithstanding the provisions of Article IX, paragraph 2, of this Treaty, until Israeli armed forces complete withdrawal from the current J and M Lines established by the Egyptian-Israeli Agreement of September 1975, hereinafter referred to as the 1975 Agreement, up to the interim withdrawal line, all military arrangements existing under that Agreement will remain in effect, except those military arrangements otherwise provided for in this Appendix.

b. As Israeli armed forces withdraw, United Nations forces will immediately enter the evacuated areas to establish interim and temporary buffer zones as shown on Maps 2 and 3, respectively, for the purpose of maintaining a separation of forces. United Nations forces' deployment will precede the movement of any other personnel into these areas.

c. Within a period of seven days after Israeli armed forces have evacuated any area located in Zone A, units of Egyptian armed forces shall deploy in accordance with the provisions of Article II of this Appendix.

d. Within a period of seven days after Israeli armed forces have evacuated any local area in Zones A or B, Egyptian border units shall deploy in accordance with the provisions of Article II of this Appendix, and will function in accordance with the provisions of Article II of Annex I.

e. Egyptian civil police will enter evacuated areas immediately after the United Nations forces to perform normal police functions.

f. Egyptian naval units shall deploy in the Gulf of Suez in accordance with the provisions of Article II of this Appendix.

g. Except those movements mentioned above, deployments of Egyptian armed forces and the activities covered in Annex I will be effected in the evacuated areas when Israeli armed forces have completed their withdrawal behind the interim withdrawal line.

Article II
Subphases of the Withdrawal to the Interim Withdrawal Line

1. The withdrawal to the interim withdrawal line will be accomplished in subphases as described in this Article and as shown on Map 3. Each subphase will be completed within the indicated number of months from the date of the exchange of instruments of ratification of this Treaty.

a. First subphase: within two months, Israeli armed forces will withdraw from the area of El Arish, including the town of El Arish and its airfield, shown as Area I on Map 3.

b. Second subphase: within three months, Israeli armed forces will withdraw from the area between line M of the 1975 Agreement and line A, shown as Area 2 on Map 3.

c. Third subphase: within five months, Israeli armed forces will withdraw from the areas east and south of Area II, shown as Area III on Map 3.

d. Fourth subphase: within seven months, Israeli armed forces will withdraw from the area of El Tor-Ras El Kenisa, shown as Area IV on Map 3.

e. Fifth subphase: within nine months, Israeli armed forces will withdraw from the remaining areas west of the interim withdrawal line, including the areas of Santa Katrina and the areas east of the Giddi and Mitla passes, shown as Area V on Map 3, thereby completing Israeli withdrawal behind the interim withdrawal line.

2. Egyptian forces will deploy in the areas evacuated by Israeli armed forces as follows:

a. Up to one-third of the Egyptian armed forces in the Sinai in accordance with the 1975 Agreement will deploy in the portions of Zone A lying within Area I, until the completion of interim withdrawal. Thereafter, Egyptian armed forces as described in Article II of Annex I will be deployed in Zone A up to the limits of the interim buffer zone.

b. The Egyptian naval activity in accordance with Article IV of Annex I will commence along the coasts of Areas II, III, and IV, upon completion of the second, third, and fourth subphases, respectively.

c. Of the Egyptian border units described in Article II of Annex I, upon completion of the first subphase one battalion will be deployed in Area I. A second battalion will be deployed in Area II upon completion of the second subphase.

3. United Nations forces in Buffer Zone I of the 1975 Agreement will redeploy to enable the deployment of Egyptian forces described above upon the completion of the first subphase, but will otherwise continue to function in accordance with the provisions of that Agreement in the remainder of that zone until the completion of interim withdrawal, as indicated in Article I of this Appendix.

4. Israeli convoys may use the roads south and east of the main road junction east of El Arish to evacuate Israeli forces and equipment up to the completion of interim withdrawal. These convoys will proceed in daylight upon four hours notice to the Egyptian liaison group and United Nations forces, will be escorted by United Nations forces, and will be in accordance with schedules coordinated by the Joint Committee. An Egyptian liaison officer will accompany convoys to assure uninterrupted movement. The Joint Commission may approve other arrangements for convoys.

Article III
United Nations Forces

1. The Parties shall request that United Nations forces be deployed as necessary to perform the function described in this Appendix up to the time of completion of final Israeli withdrawal. For that purpose, the Parties agree to the redeployment of the United Nations Emergency Force.

2. United Nations forces will supervise the implementation of this Appendix and will employ their best efforts to prevent any violation of its terms.

3. When United Nations forces deploy in accordance with the provisions of Articles I and II of this Appendix, they will perform the functions of verification in limited force zones in accordance with Article VI of Annex I, and will establish check points, reconnaissance patrols, and observation posts in the temporary buffer zones described in Article II above. Other functions

of the United Nations forces which concern the interim buffer zone are described in Article V of this Appendix.

Article IV
Joint Commission and Liaison
1. The Joint Commission referred to in Article IV of this Treaty will function from the date of exchange of instruments of ratification of this Treaty up to the date of completion of final Israeli withdrawal from the Sinai.
2. The Joint Commission will be composed of representatives of each Party headed by senior officers. This Commission shall invite a representative of the United Nations when discussing subjects concerning the United Nations, or when either Party requests United Nations presence. Decisions of the Joint Commission will be reached by agreement of Egypt and Israel.
3. The Joint Commission will supervise the implementation of the arrangements described in Annex I and the Appendix. To this end, and by agreement of both Parties, it will:
a. coordinate military movements described in this Appendix and supervise their implementation;
b. address and seek to resolve any problem arising out of the implementation of Annex I and this Appendix, and discuss any violations reported by the United Nations Force and Observers and refer to the Governments of Egypt and Israel any unresolved problems;
c. assist the United Nations Force and Observers in the execution of their mandates, and deal with the timetables of the periodic verifications when referred to it by the Parties as provided for in Annex I and in this Appendix;
d. organize the demarcation of the international boundary and all lines and zones described in Annex I and this Appendix;
e. supervise the handing over of the main installations in the Sinai from Israel to Egypt;
f. agree on necessary arrangements for finding and returning missing bodies of Egyptian and Israeli soldiers;
g. organize the setting up and operation of entry check points along the El Arish-Ras Muhammed line in accordance with the provisions of Article 4 of Annex III;
h. conduct its operations through the use of joint liaison teams, maintain local coordination and cooperation with the United Nations Force stationed in specific areas or United Nations Observers monitoring specific areas for any assistance as needed;
i. provide liaison and coordination to the United Nations command

implementing provisions of the Treaty, and, through the joint liaison teams, maintain local coordination and cooperation with the United Nations Force stationed in specific areas or United Nations Observers monitoring specific areas for any assistance as needed;

j. discuss any other matters which the Parties by agreement may place before it.

4. Meetings of the Joint Commission shall be held at least once a month. In the event that either Party or the Command of the United Nations Force requests a special meeting, it will be convened within 24 hours.

5. The Joint Commission will meet in the buffer zone until the completion of the interim withdrawal and in El Arish and Beer-Sheba alternately afterwards. The first meeting will be held not later than two weeks after the entry into force of this Treaty.

Article V
Definition of the Interim Buffer Zone and its Activities

1. An interim buffer zone, by which the United Nations Force will effect a separation of Egyptian and Israeli elements, will be established west of and adjacent to the interim withdrawal line as shown on Map 2 after implementation of Israeli withdrawal and deployment behind the interim withdrawal line. Egyptian civil police equipped with light weapons will perform normal police functions within this zone.

2. The United Nations Force will operate check points, reconnaissance patrols and observation posts within the interim buffer zone in order to ensure compliance with the terms of this Article.

3. In accordance with arrangements agreed upon by both Parties and to be coordinated by the Joint Commission, Israeli personnel will operate military technical installations at four specific locations shown on Map 2 and designated as T1 (map central coordinate 57163940), T2 (map central coordinate 59351541), T3 (map central coordinate 593315527), and T4 (map coordinate 611309979) under the following principles:

a. The technical installations shall be manned by technical and administrative personnel equipped with small arms required for their protection (revolvers, rifles, sub-machine-guns, light machine guns, hand grenades, and ammunition), as follows:

T1 — up to 150 personnel
T2 and T3 — up to 350 personnel
T4 — up to 200 personnel.

b. Israeli personnel will not carry weapons outside the sites, except officers who may carry personal weapons.

c. Only a third party agreed to by Egypt and Israel will enter and conduct inspections within the perimeters of technical installations in the buffer zone. The third party will conduct inspections in a random manner at least once a month. The inspections will verify the nature of the operation of the installations and the weapons and personnel therein. The third party will immediately report to the Parties any divergence from an installation's visual and electronic surveillance or communications role.

d. Supply of the installations, visits for technical and administrative purposes, and replacement of personnel and equipment situated in the sites, may occur uninterruptedly from the United Nations check points to the perimeter of the technical installations, after checking and being escorted by only the United Nations forces.

e. Israel will be permitted to introduce into its technical installations items required for the proper functioning of the installations and personnel.

f. As determined by the Joint Commission, Israel will be permitted to:

1. Maintain in its installations fire-fighting and general maintenance equipment as well as wheeled administrative vehicles and mobile engineering equipment necessary for the maintenance of the sites. All vehicles shall be unarmed.

2. Within the sites and in the buffer zone, maintain roads, water lines, and communications cables which serve the sites. At each of the three installation locations (T1, T2, and T3, and T4), this maintenance may be performed with up to two armed wheeled vehicles and by up to twelve unarmed personnel with only necessary equipment, including heavy engineering equipment if needed. This maintenance may be performed three times a week, except for special problems, and only after giving the United Nations four hours notice. The teams will be escorted by the United Nations.

g. Movement to and from the technical installations will take place only during daylight hours. Access to, and exit from, the technical installations shall be as follows:

1. T1: through a United Nations check point, and via the road between Abu Aweigila and the intersection of the Abu Aweigila road and the Gebel Libni road (at Km.161), as shown on Map 2.

2. T2 and T3: through a United Nations check point via the road constructed across the buffer zone to Gebel Katrina, as shown on Map 2.

3. T2, T3 and T4: via helicopter flying within a corridor at the times, and according to a flight profile, agreed to by the Joint

Commission. The helicopters will be checked by the United Nations Force at landing sites outside the perimeter of the installations.

h. Israel will inform the United Nations force at least one hour in advance of each intended movement to and from the installations.

i. Israel shall be entitled to evacuate sick and wounded and summon medical experts and medical teams at any time after giving immediate notice to the United Nations Force.

4. The details of the above principles and all other matters in this Article requiring coordination by the Parties will be handled by the Joint Commission.

5. These technical installations will be withdrawn when Israeli forces withdraw from the interim withdrawal line, or at a time agreed by the Parties.

Article VI
Disposition of Installations and Military Barriers
Disposition of installations and military barriers will be determined by the Parties in accordance with the following guidelines:

1. Up to three weeks before Israeli withdrawal from any area, the Joint Commission will arrange for Israeli and Egyptian liaison and technical teams to conduct a joint inspection of all appropriate installations to agree upon condition of structures and articles which will be transferred to Egyptian control and to arrange for such transfer. Israel will declare, at that time, its plans for disposition of installations and articles within the installations.

2. Israel undertakes to transfer to Egypt all agreed infrastructure, utilities, and installations intact, inter alia, airfield, roads, pumping stations, and ports. Israel will present to Egypt the information necessary for the maintenance and operation of these facilities. Egyptian technical teams will be permitted to observe and familiarize themselves with the operation of these facilities for a period of up to two weeks prior to transfer.

3. When Israel relinquishes Israeli military water points near El Arish and El Tor, Egyptian technical teams will assume control of those installations and ancillary equipment in accordance with an orderly transfer process arranged beforehand by the Joint Commission. Egypt undertakes to continue to make available at all water supply points the normal quantity of currently available water up to the time Israel withdraws behind the international boundary, unless otherwise agreed in the Joint Commission.

4. Israel will make its best effort to remove or destroy all military barriers, including obstacles and minefields, in the areas and adjacent waters from which it withdraws, according to the following concept:

a. Military barriers will be cleared first from areas near populations, roads, and major installations and utilities.

b. For those obstacles and minefields which cannot be removed or destroyed prior to Israeli withdrawal, Israel will provide detailed maps to Egypt and the United Nations through the Joint Commission not later than 15 days before entry of United Nations forces into the affected areas.

c. Egyptian military engineers will enter those areas after United Nations forces enter to conduct barrier clearance operations in accordance with Egyptian plans to be submitted prior to implementation.

Article VII
Surveillance Activities
1. Aerial surveillance activities during the withdrawal will be carried out as follows:

a. Both Parties request the United States to continue airborne surveillance flights in accordance with previous agreements until the completion of final Israeli withdrawal.

b. Flight profiles will cover the Limited Forces Zones to monitor the limitations on forces and armaments, and to determine that Israeli armed forces have withdrawn from the areas described in Article II of Annex I, Article II of this Appendix, and Maps 2 and 3, and that these forces thereafter remain behind their lines. Special inspection flights may be flown at the request of either Party or of the United Nations.

c. Only the main elements in the military organizations of each Party, as described in Annex I and in this Appendix, will be reported.

2. Both Parties request the United States operated Sinai Field Mission to continue its operations in accordance with previous agreements until completion of the Israeli withdrawal from the area east of the Giddi and Mitla Passes. Thereafter, the Mission will be terminated.

Article VIII
Exercise of Egyptian Sovereignty
Egypt will resume the exercise of its full sovereignty over evacuated parts of the Sinai upon Israeli withdrawal as provided for in Article I of this Treaty.

Annex III
Protocol Concerning Relations of the Parties

Article I
Diplomatic and Consular Relations
The Parties agree to establish diplomatic and consular relations and to exchange ambassadors upon completion of the interim withdrawal.

Article II

Economic and Trade Relations

1. The Parties agree to remove all discriminatory barriers to normal economic relations and to terminate economic boycotts of each other upon completion of the interim withdrawal.

2. As soon as possible, and not later than six months after the completion of the interim withdrawal, the Parties will enter negotiations with a view to concluding an agreement on trade and commerce for the purpose of promoting beneficial economic relations.

Article III

Cultural Relations

1. The Parties agree to establish normal cultural relations following completion of the interim withdrawal.

2. They agree on the desirability of cultural exchanges in all fields, and shall, as soon as possible and not later than six months after completion of the interim withdrawal, enter into negotiations with a view to concluding a cultural agreement for this purpose.

Article IV

Freedom of Movement

1. Upon completion of the interim withdrawal, each party will permit the free movement of the nations and vehicles of the other into and within its territory according to the general rules applicable to nationals and vehicles of other states. Neither party will impose discriminatory restrictions on the free movement of persons and vehicles from its territory to the territory of the other.

2. Mutual unimpeded access to places of religious and historical significance will be provided on a nondiscriminatory basis.

Article V

Cooperation for Development and Good Neighborly Relations

1. The Parties recognize a mutuality of interest in good neighborly relations and agree to consider means to promote such relations.

2. The Parties will cooperate in promoting peace, stability and development in their region. Each agrees to consider proposals the other may wish to make to this end.

3. The Parties shall seek to foster mutual understanding and tolerance and will, accordingly, abstain from hostile propaganda against each other.

Article VI
Transportation and Telecommunications

1. The Parties recognize as applicable to each other the rights, privileges and obligations provided for by the aviation agreements to which they are both party, particularly by the Convention on International Civil Aviation, 1944 ("The Chicago Convention") and the International Air Services Transit Agreement, 1944.

2. Upon completion of the interim withdrawal any declaration of national emergency by a party under Article 89 of the Chicago Convention will not be applied to the other party on a discriminatory basis.

3. Egypt agrees that the use of airfields left by Israel near El Arish, Rafah, Ras El Nagb and Sharm el Sheikh shall be for civilian purposes only, including possible commercial use by all nations.

4. As soon as possible and not later than six months after the completion of the interim withdrawal, the Parties shall enter into negotiations for the purpose of concluding a civil aviation agreement.

5. The Parties will reopen and maintain roads and railways between their countries and will consider further road and rail links. The Parties further agree that a highway will be constructed and maintained between Egypt, Israel and Jordan near Eilat with guaranteed free and peaceful passage of persons, vehicles and goods between Egypt and Jordan, without prejudice to their sovereignty over that part of the highway which falls within their respective territory.

6. Upon completion of the interim withdrawal, normal postal, telephone, telex, data facsimile, wireless and cable communications and television relay services by cable, radio and satellite shall be established between the two Parties in accordance with all relevant international conventions and regulations.

7. Upon completion of the interim withdrawal, each party shall grant normal access to its ports for vessels and cargoes of the other, as well as vessels and cargoes destined for or coming from the other. Such access shall be granted on the same conditions generally applicable to vessels and cargoes of other nations. Article 5 of the Treaty of Peace will be implemented upon the exchange of instruments of ratification of the aforementioned Treaty.

Article VII
Enjoyment of Human Rights
The Parties affirm their commitment to respect and observe human rights and fundamental freedoms for all, and they will promote these rights and freedoms in accordance with the United Nations Charter.

Article VIII
Territorial Seas
Without prejudice to the provisions of Article 5 of the Treaty of Peace each
Party recognizes the right of the vessels of the other Party to innocent pas-
sage through its territorial sea in accordance with the rules of international
law.

Agreed Minutes to Articles I, IV, V and VI and Annexes I and III of Treaty of
Peace
Article I
Egypt's resumption of the exercise of full sovereignty over the Sinai provided
for in paragraph 2 of Article I shall occur with regard to each area upon Israel's
withdrawal from that area.

Article IV
It is agreed between the parties that the review provided for in Article IV (4)
will be undertaken when requested by either party, commencing within three
months of such a request, but that any amendment can be made only with
the mutual agreement of both parties.

Article V
The second sentence of paragraph 2 of Article V shall not be construed as
limiting the first sentence of that paragraph. The foregoing is not to be construed as contravening the second sentence of paragraph 2 of Article V, which
reads as follows:
    "The Parties will respect each other's right to navigation and overflight
for access to either country through the Strait of Tiran and the Gulf of Aqaba."

Article VI (2)
The provisions of Article VI shall not be construed in contradiction to the
provisions of the framework for peace in the Middle East agreed at Camp
David. The foregoing is not to be construed as contravening the provisions
of Article VI (2) of the Treaty, which reads as follows:
    "The Parties undertake to fulfill in good faith their obligations under
this Treaty, without regard to action or inaction of any other Party and independently of any instrument external to this Treaty."

Article VI (5)
It is agreed by the Parties that there is no assertion that this Treaty prevails
over other Treaties or agreements or that other Treaties or agreements pre-

vail over this Treaty. The foregoing is not to be construed as contravening the provisions of Article VI (5) of the Treaty, which reads as follows:

"Subject to Article 103 of the United Nations Charter, in the event of a conflict between the obligations of the Parties under the present Treaty and any of their other obligations, the obligations under this Treaty will be binding and implemented."

Annex I

Article VI, Paragraph 8, of Annex I provides as follows:

"The Parties shall agree on the nations from which the United Nations force and observers will be drawn. They will be drawn from nations other than those which are permanent members of the United Nations Security Council." The Parties have agreed as follows:

"With respect to the provisions of paragraph 8, Article VI, of Annex I, if no agreement is reached between the Parties, they will accept or support a U.S. proposal concerning the composition of the United Nations force and observers."

Annex III

The Treaty of Peace and Annex III thereto provide for establishing normal economic relations between the Parties. In accordance therewith, it is agreed that such relations will include normal commercial sales of oil by Egypt to Israel, and that Israel shall be fully entitled to make bids for Egyptian-origin oil not needed for Egyptian domestic oil consumption, and Egypt and its oil concessionaires will entertain bids made by Israel, on the same basis and terms as apply to other bidders for such oil.

For the Government of the Arab Republic of Egypt:
A. El-Sadat
Witnessed by: Jimmy Carter, President of the United States
For the Government of Israel: M. Begin

56

Declaration of Principles on Interim Self-Government Arrangements 1993

In a move many said was not possible, the government of Israel joined together with the Palestine Liberation Organization (P.L.O.) in order to work out an agreement that would lead to the self-government of Palestinians living in the territories administered by Israel, primarily the Gaza Strip and the area of Jericho.

The Government of the State of Israel and the P.L.O. team (in the Jordanian-Palestinian delegation to the Middle East Peace Conference) (the "Palestinian Delegation"), representing the Palestinian people, agree that it is time to put an end to decades of confrontation and conflict, recognize their mutual legitimate and political rights, and strive to live in peaceful coexistence and mutual dignity and security and achieve a just, lasting and comprehensive peace settlement and historic reconciliation through the agreed political process.

Accordingly, the two sides agree to the following principles:

Article I
AIM OF THE NEGOTIATIONS

The aim of the Israeli-Palestinian negotiations within the current Middle East peace process is, among other things, to establish a Palestinian Interim Self-Government Authority, the elected Council (the "Council"), for the Palestinian people in the West Bank and Gaza Strip, for a transitional period not exceeding five years, leading to a permanent settlement based on Security Council Resolutions 242 and 338.

It is understood that the interim arrangements are an integral part of the whole peace process and that the negotiations on the permanent status will lead to the implementation of Security Council Resolutions 242 and 338.

Article II
FRAMEWORK FOR THE INTERIM PERIOD

The agreed framework for the interim period is set forth in the Declaration of Principles.

Article III
ELECTIONS

1. In order that the Palestinian people in the West Bank and Gaza Strip may govern themselves according to democratic principles, direct, free and general political elections will be held for the Council under agreed supervision and international observation, while the Palestinian police will ensure public order.

2. An agreement will be concluded on the exact mode and conditions of the elections in accordance with the protocol as Annex I, with the goal of holding the elections not later than nine months after the entry into force of this Declaration of Principles.

3. These elections will constitute a significant interim preparatory step toward the realization of the legitimate rights of the Palestinian people and their just requirements.

Article IV
JURISDICTION

Jurisdiction of the Council will cover the West Bank and Gaza Strip territory, except for issues that will be negotiated in the permanent status negotiations. These two sides view the West Bank and the Gaza Strip as a single territorial unit, whose integrity will be preserved during the interim period.

Article V
TRANSITIONAL PERIOD AND PERMANENT
STATUS NEGOTIATIONS

1. The five-year transitional period will begin upon the withdrawal from the Gaza Strip and Jericho area.

2. Permanent status negotiations will commence as soon as possible, but not later than the beginning of the third year of the interim period, between the Government of Israel and the Palestinian people representatives.

3. It is understood that these negotiations shall cover remaining issues, including: Jerusalem, refugees, settlements, security arrangements, borders, relations and cooperation with other neighbors, and other issues of common interest.

4. The two parties agree that the outcome of the permanent status negotiations should not be prejudiced or preempted by agreements reached for the interim period.

Article VI
PREPARATORY TRANSFER OF POWERS AND RESPONSIBILITIES

1. Upon the entry into force of this Declaration of Principles and the withdrawal from the Gaza Strip and the Jericho area, a transfer of authority from the Israeli military government and its Civil Administration to the authorised Palestinians for this task, as detailed herein, will commence. This transfer of authority will be of a preparatory nature until the inauguration of the Council.

2. Immediately after the entry into force of this Declaration of Principles and the withdrawal from the Gaza Strip and Jericho area, with the view to promoting economic development in the West Bank and Gaza Strip, authority will be transferred to the Palestinians on the following spheres: education and culture, health, social welfare, direct taxation, and tourism. The Palestinian side will commence in building the Palestinian police force, as agreed upon. Pending the inauguration of the Council, the two parties may negotiate the transfer of additional powers and responsibilities, as agreed upon.

Article VII
INTERIM AGREEMENT

1. The Israeli and Palestinian delegations will negotiate an agreement on the interim period (the "Interim Agreement").

2. The Interim Agreement shall specify, among other things, the structure of the Council, the number of its members, and the transfer of powers and responsibilities from the Israeli military government and its Civil Administration to the Council. The Interim Agreement shall also specify the

Council's executive authority, legislative authority in accordance with Article IX below, and the independent judicial organs.

3. The Interim Agreement shall include arrangements, to be implemented upon the inauguration of the Council, for the assumption by the Council of all of the powers and responsibilities transferred previously in accordance with Article VI above.

4. In order to enable the Council to promote economic growth, upon its inauguration, the Council will establish among other things, a Palestinian Electricity Authority, a Gaza Sea Port Authority, a Palestinian Development Bank, a Palestinian Export Promotion Board, a Palestinian Environmental Authority, a Palestinian Land Authority and a Palestinian Water Administration Authority, and any other Authorities agreed upon, in accordance with the Interim Agreement that will specify their powers and responsibilities.

5. After the inauguration of the Council, the Civil Administration will be dissolved, and the Israeli military government will be withdrawn.

Article VIII
PUBLIC ORDER AND SECURITY

In order to guarantee public order and internal security for the Palestinians of the West Bank and the Gaza Strip, the Council will establish a strong police force, while Israel will continue to carry the responsibility for defending against external threats, as well as the responsibility for overall security of Israelis for the purpose of safeguarding their internal security and public order.

Article IX
LAWS AND MILITARY ORDERS

1. The Council will be empowered to legislate, in accordance with the Interim Agreement, within all authorities transferred to it.

2. Both parties will review jointly laws and military orders presently in force in remaining spheres.

Article X
JOINT ISRAELI-PALESTINIAN LIAISON COMMITTEE

In order to provide for a smooth implementation of this Declaration of Principles and any subsequent agreements pertaining to the interim period, upon the entry into force of this Declaration of Principles, a Joint Israeli-Palestinian Liaison Committee will be established in order to deal with issues requiring coordination, other issues of common interest, and disputes.

Article XI
ISRAELI-PALESTINIAN COOPERATION IN ECONOMIC FIELDS

Recognizing the mutual benefit of cooperation in promoting the development of the West Bank, the Gaza Strip and Israel, upon the entry of this Declaration of Principles, an Israeli-Palestinian Economic Cooperation Committee will be established in order to develop and implement in a cooperative manner the programs identified in the protocols attached as Annex III and Annex IV.

Article XII
LIAISON AND COOPERATION WITH JORDAN AND EGYPT

The two parties will invite the Governments of Jordan and Egypt to participate in establishing further liaison and cooperation arrangements between the Government of Israel and the Palestinian representative, on the one hand, and the Governments of Jordan and Egypt, on the other hand, to promote cooperation between them. These arrangements will include the constitution of a Continuing Committee that will decide by agreement on the modalities of admission of persons displaced from the West Bank and Gaza Strip in 1967, together with necessary measures to prevent disruption and disorder. Other matters of common concern will be dealt with by this Committee.

Article XIII
REDEPLOYMENT OF ISRAELI FORCES

1. After the entry into force of this Declaration of Principles, and not later than the eve of elections for the Council, a redeployment of Israeli military forces in the West Bank and the Gaza Strip will take place, in addition to withdrawal of Israeli forces carried out in accordance with Article XIV.

2. In redeploying its military forces, Israel will be guided by the principle that its military forces should be redeployed outside populated areas.

3. Further redeployments to specified locations will be gradually implemented commensurate with the assumption of responsibility for public order and internal security by the Palestinian police force pursuant to Article VIII above.

Article XIV
ISRAELI WITHDRAWAL FROM THE GAZA STRIP AND JERICHO
AREA

Israel will withdraw from the Gaza Strip and Jericho area, as detailed in the protocol attached as Annex II.

Article XV
RESOLUTION OF DISPUTES

1. Disputes arising out of the application or interpretation of this Declaration of Principles or any subsequent agreements pertaining to the interim period, shall be resolved by negotiations through the Joint Liaison Committee to be established pursuant to Article X above.

2. Disputes which cannot be settled by negotiations may be resolved by a mechanism of conciliation to be agreed upon by the parties.

3. The parties may agree to submit to arbitration disputes relating to the interim period, which cannot be settled through conciliation. To this end, upon agreement of both parties, the parties will establish an Arbitration Committee.

Article XVI
ISRAELI-PALESTINIAN COOPERATION CONCERNING REGIONAL
PROGRAMS

Both parties view the multilateral working groups as an appropriate instrument for promoting a "Marshall Plan," the regional programs and other programs, including special programs for the West Bank and Gaza Strip, as indicated in the protocol attached as Annex IV.

Article XVII
MISCELLANEOUS PROVISIONS

1. This Declaration of Principles will enter into force one month after its signing.

2. All protocols annexed to this Declaration of Principles and Agreed Minutes pertaining thereto shall be regarded as an integral part hereof.

Done at Washington, D.C., this thirteenth of September, 1993.

For the Government of Israel: For the P.L.O.:
Shimon Peres   Mahmoud Abbas
                        Witnessed By:

Warren Christopher   Andrei Kozyrev
The United States of America   The Russian Federation

ANNEX I
PROTOCOL ON THE MODE AND CONDITIONS OF ELECTIONS

1. Palestinians of Jerusalem who live there will have the right to participate in the election process, according to an agreement between the two sides.

2. In addition, the election agreement should cover, among other things,
the following issues:

   a. the system of elections;

   b. the mode of the agreed supervision and international observation and
      their personal composition; and

   c. rules and regulations regarding election campaign, including agreed
      arrangements for the organizing of mass media, and the possibil-
      ity of licensing a broadcasting and TV station.

3. The future status of displaced Palestinians who were registered on
4th June 1967 will not be prejudiced because they are unable to participate
in the election process due to practical reasons.

ANNEX II
PROTOCOL ON WITHDRAWAL OF ISRAELI FORCES
FROM THE GAZA STRIP AND JERICHO AREA

1. The two sides will conclude and sign within two months from the
date of entry into force of this Declaration of Principles, an agreement on
the withdrawal of Israeli military forces from the Gaza Strip and Jericho area.
This agreement will include comprehensive arrangements to apply in the
Gaza Strip and the Jericho area subsequent to the Israeli withdrawal.

2. Israel will implement an accelerated and scheduled withdrawal of
Israeli military forces from the Gaza Strip and Jericho area, beginning immediately with the signing of the agreement on the Gaza Strip and Jericho
area and to be completed within a period not exceeding four months after
the signing of this agreement.

3. The above agreement will include, among other things:

   a. Arrangements for a smooth and peaceful transfer of authority from

the Israel military government and Civil Administration to the Palestinian representatives.
b. Structure, powers and responsibilities of the Palestinian authority in these areas, except: external security, settlements, Israelis, foreign relations, and other mutually agreed matters.
c. Arrangements for the assumption of internal security and public order by the Palestinian police force consisting of police officers recruited locally and from abroad holding Jordanian passports and Palestinian documents issued by Egypt. Those who will participate in the Palestinian police force coming from abroad should be trained as police and police officers.
d. A temporary international or foreign presence, as agreed upon.
e. Establishment of a joint Palestinian-Israeli Coordination and Cooperation Committee for mutual security purposes.
f. An economic development and stabilization program, including the establishment of an Emergency Fund, to encourage foreign investment, and financial and economic support. Both sides will coordinate and cooperate jointly and unilaterally with regional and international parties to support these aims.
g. Arrangements for a safe passage for persons and transportation between the Gaza Strip and Jericho area.

4. The above agreement will include arrangements for coordination between both parties regarding passages:
a. Gaza–Egypt; and
b. Jericho–Jordan.

5. The offices responsible for carrying out the powers and responsibilities of the Palestinian authority under this Annex II and Article VI of the Declaration of Principles will be located in the Gaza Strip and in the Jericho area pending the inauguration of the Council.

6. Other than these agreed arrangements, the status of the Gaza Strip and Jericho area will continue to be an integral part of the West Bank and Gaza Strip, and will not be changed in the interim period.

ANNEX III
PROTOCOL ON ISRAELI-PALESTINIAN COOPERATION IN ECONOMIC AND DEVELOPMENT PROGRAMS

The two sides agree to establish an Israeli-Palestinian continuing Committee for Economic Cooperation, focusing, among other things, on the following:

1. Cooperation in the field of water, including a Water Development Program prepared by experts from both sides, which will also specify the mode of cooperation in the management of water resources in the West Bank and Gaza Strip, and will include proposals for studies and plans on water rights of each party, as well as on the equitable utilization of joint water resources for implementation in and beyond the interim period.

2. Cooperation in the field of electricity, including an Electricity Development Program, which will also specify the mode of cooperation for the production, maintenance, purchase and sale of electricity resources.

3. Cooperation in the field of energy, including an Energy Development Program, which will provide for the exploitation of oil and gas for industrial purposes, particularly in the Gaza Strip and in the Negev, and will encourage further joint exploitation of other energy resources. This Program may also provide for the construction of a Petrochemical industrial complex in the Gaza Strip and the construction of oil and gas pipelines.

4. Cooperation in the field of finance, including a Financial Development and Action Program for the encouragement of international investment in the West Bank and the Gaza Strip, and in Israel, as well as the establishment of a Palestinian Development Bank.

5. Cooperation in the field of transport and communications, including a Program, which will define guidelines for the establishment of a Gaza Sea Port Area, and will provide for the establishing of transport and communications lines to and from the West Bank and the Gaza Strip to Israel and to other countries. In addition, this Program will provide for carrying out the necessary construction of roads, railways, communications lines, etc.

6. Cooperation in the field of trade, including studies, and Trade Promotion Programs, which will encourage local, regional and inter-regional trade, as well as a feasibility study of creating free trade zones in the Gaza strip and in Israel, mutual access to these zones, and cooperation in other areas related to trade and commerce.

7. Cooperation in the field of industry, including Industrial Development Programs, which will provide for the establishment of joint Israeli-Palestinian Industrial Research and Development Centers, will promote Palestinian-Israeli joint ventures, and provide guidelines for cooperation in the textile, food, pharmaceutical, electronics, diamonds, computer and science-based industries.

8. A program for cooperation in, and regulation of, labor relations and cooperation in social welfare issues.

9. A Human Resources Development and Cooperation Plan, providing for joint Israeli-Palestinian workshops and seminars, and for the estab-

lishment of joint vocational training centers, research institutes and data banks.

10. An Environmental Protection Plan, providing for joint and/or coordinated measures in this sphere.

11. A program for developing coordination and cooperation in the field of communication and media.

12. Any other programs of mutual interest.

ANNEX IV
PROTOCOL ON ISRAELI-PALESTINIAN COOPERATION CONCERNING REGIONAL DEVELOPMENT PROGRAMS

1. The two sides will cooperate in the context of the multilateral peace efforts in promoting a Development Program for the region, including the West Bank and the Gaza Strip, to be initiated by the G-7. The parties will request the G-7 to seek the participation in this program of other interested states, such as members of the organisation for Economic Cooperation and Development, regional Arab states and institutions, as well as members of the private sector.

2. The Development Program will consist of two elements:

a. an Economic Development Program for the West Bank and the Gaza Strip,

b. a Regional Economic Development Program.

A. The Economic Development Program for the West Bank and the Gaza Strip will consist of the following elements:

(1) A Social Rehabilitation Program, including a Housing and Construction Program.

(2) A Small and Medium Business Development Plan.

(3) An Infrastructure Development Program (water, electricity, transportation and communications, etc.).

(4) A Human Resources Plan.

(5) Other programs.

B. The Regional Economic Development Program may consist of the following elements:

(1) The establishment of a Middle East Development Fund, as a first step, and a Middle East Development Bank, as a second step.

(2) The development of a joint Israeli-Palestinian-Jordanian Plan for coordinated exploitation of the Dead Sea area.

(3) The Mediterranean Sea (Gaza)-Dead Sea Canal.

(4) Regional Desalinization and other water development projects.

(5) A regional plan for agricultural development, including a co-ordinated regional effort for the prevention of desertification.

(6) Interconnection of electricity grids.

(7) Regional cooperation for the transfer, distribution and industrial exploitation of gas, oil and other energy resources.

(8) A Regional Tourism, Transportation and Telecommunications Development Plan.

(9) Regional cooperation in other spheres.

3. The two sides will encourage the multilateral working groups, and will coordinate towards its success. The two parties will encourage intercessional activities, as well as pre-feasibility and feasibility studies, within the various multilateral working groups.

AGREED MINUTES TO THE DECLARATION OF PRINCIPLES ON INTERIM SELF-GOVERNMENT ARRANGEMENTS

A. GENERAL UNDERSTANDINGS AND AGREEMENTS

Any powers and responsibilities transferred to the Palestinians pursuant to the Declaration of Principles prior to the inauguration of the Council will be subject to the same principles pertaining to Article IV, as set out in these Agreed Minutes below.

B. SPECIFIC UNDERSTANDINGS AND AGREEMENTS

Article IV

It is understood that:

1. Jurisdiction of the Council will cover West Bank and Gaza Strip territory, except for issues that will be negotiated in the permanent status negotiations: Jerusalem, settlements, military locations, and Israelis.

2. The council's jurisdiction will apply with regard to the agreed powers, responsibilities, spheres and authorities transferred to it.

Article VI (2)

It is agreed that the transfer of authority will be as follows:

1. The Palestinian side will inform the Israeli side of the names of the authorised Palestinians who will assume the powers, authorities and responsibilities that will be transferred to the Palestinians according to the declaration of Principles in the following fields: education and culture, health, social welfare, direct taxation, tourism, and any other authorities agreed upon.

2. It is understood that the rights and obligations of these offices will not be affected.

3. Each of the spheres described above will continue to enjoy existing budgetary allocations in accordance with arrangements to be mutually agreed upon. These arrangements also will provide for the necessary adjustments required in order to take into account the taxes collected by the direct taxation office.

4. Upon the execution of the Declaration of Principles, the Israeli and Palestinian delegations will immediately commence negotiations on a detailed plan for the transfer of authority on the above offices in accordance with the above understandings.

Article VII (2)
The Interim Agreement will also include arrangements for coordination and cooperation.

Article VII (5)
The withdrawal of the military government will not prevent Israel from exercising the powers and responsibilities not transferred to the council.

Article VIII
It is understood that the Interim Agreement will include arrangements for cooperation and coordination between the two parties in this regard. It is also agreed that the transfer of powers and responsibilities to the Palestinian police will be accomplished in a phased manner, as agreed in the Interim Agreement.

Article X
It is agreed that, upon the entry into force of the Declaration of Principles, the Israeli and Palestinian delegations will exchange the names of the individuals designated by them as members of the Joint Israeli-Palestinian Liaison Committee.

It is further agreed that each side will have an equal number of members in the Joint Committee. The Joint Committee will reach decisions by agreement. The Joint Committee may add other technicians and experts, as necessary. The Joint Committee will decide on the frequency and place or places of its meetings.

ANNEX II
It is understood that, subsequent to the Israeli withdrawal, Israel will continue to be responsible for external security, and for internal security and public order of settlements and Israelis. Israeli military forces and civilians may continue to use roads freely within the Gaza Strip and the Jericho area.

57

Fundamental Agreement between the Holy See and the State of Israel 1993

Since the modern State of Israel declared its independence in 1948, the Vatican has refused to recognize its sovereignty. Yet it has openly embraced the Palestine Liberation Organization (P.L.O.) and its chairman Yasir Arafat. In the spirit of peace in the 1990s, the Vatican finally agreed to establish diplomatic relations with Israel.

Preamble

The Holy See and the State of Israel,

Mindful of the singular character and universal significance of the Holy Land:

Aware of the unique nature of the relationship between the Catholic Church and the Jewish people, and of the historic process of reconciliation and growth in mutual understanding and friendship between Catholics and Jews;

Having decided on 29 July 1992 to establish a "Bilateral Permanent Working Commission," in order to study and define together issues of common interest, and in view of normalizing their relations;

Recognizing that such Agreement will provide a sound and lasting basis for the continued development of their future relations and for the furtherance of the Commission's task,

Agree upon the following Articles:

Article 1

1. The State of Israel, recalling its Declaration of Independence, affirms its continuing commitment to uphold and observe the human right to freedom of religion and conscience, as set forth in the Universal Declaration of Human Rights and in other international instruments to which it is a party.

2. The Holy See, recalling the Declaration on Religious Freedom of the Second Vatican Ecumenical Council, "Dignitatis humanea," affirms the Catholic Church's commitment to uphold the human right to freedom of religion and conscience, as set forth in the Universal Declaration of Human Rights and in other international instruments to which it is party. The Holy See wishes to affirm as well the Catholic Church's respect for other religions and their followers as solemnly stated by the Second Vatican Ecumenical Council in its Declaration on the Relation of the Church to Non-Christian Religions, "Nostra aetate."

Article 2

1. The Holy See and the State of Israel are committed to appropriate cooperation in combatting all forms of anti-Semitism and all kinds of racism and of religious intolerance, and in promoting mutual understanding among nations, tolerance among communities and respect for human life and dignity.

2. The Holy See takes this occasion to reiterate its condemnation of hatred, persecution and all other manifestations of anti-Semitism directed against the Jewish people and individual Jews anywhere, at any time and by anyone. In particular, the Holy See deplores attacks on Jews and desecration of Jewish synagogues and cemeteries, acts which offend the memory of the victims of the Holocaust, especially when they occur in the same places which witnessed it.

Article 3

1. The Holy See and the State of Israel recognize that both are free in the exercise of their respective rights and powers, and commit themselves to respect this principle in their mutual relations and in their cooperation for the good of the people.

2. The State of Israel recognizes the right of the Catholic Church to carry out its religious, moral, educational and charitable functions, and to have its own institutions, and to train, appoint and deploy its own personnel in the said institutions or for the said functions to these ends. The Church recognizes the right of the State to carry out its functions, such as promoting and protecting the welfare and the safety of the people. Both the State and

the Church recognize the need for dialogue and cooperation in such matters as by their nature call for it.

3. Concerning Catholic legal personality at canon law the Holy See and the State of Israel will negotiate on giving it full effect in Israeli law, following a report from a joint subcommission of experts.

Article 4

1. The State of Israel affirms its continuing commitment to maintain and respect the "Status quo" in the Christian Holy Places to which it applies and the respective rights of the Christian communities thereunder. The Holy See affirms the Catholic Church's continuing commitment to respect the aforementioned "Status quo" and the said rights.

2. The above shall apply notwithstanding an interpretation to the contrary of any Article in this Fundamental Agreement.

3. The State of Israel agrees with the Holy See on the obligation of continuing respect for and protection of the character proper to Catholic sacred places, such as churches, monasteries, convents, cemeteries and their like.

4. The State of Israel agrees with the Holy See on the continuing guarantee on the freedom of Catholic worship.

Article 5

1. The Holy See and the State of Israel recognize that both have an interest in favoring Christian pilgrimages to the Holy Land. Whenever the need for coordination arises, the proper agencies of the Church and of the State will consult and cooperate as required.

2. The State of Israel and the Holy See express the hope that such pilgrimages will provide an occasion for better understanding between the pilgrims and the people and religions in Israel.

Article 6

The Holy See and the State of Israel jointly reaffirm the right of the Catholic Church to establish, maintain and direct schools and institutes of study at all levels; this right being exercised in harmony with the rights of the State in the field of education.

Article 7

The Holy See and the State of Israel recognize a common interest in promoting and encouraging cultural exchanges between Catholic institutions worldwide, and educational, cultural and research institutions in Israel, and in facilitating access to manuscripts, historical documents and similar source materials, in conformity with applicable laws and regulations.

Article 8
The State of Israel recognizes that the right of the Catholic Church to freedom of expression in the carrying out of its functions is exercised also through the Church's own communications media; this right being exercised in harmony with the rights of the State in the field of communications media.

Article 9
The Holy See and the State of Israel jointly reaffirm the right of the Catholic Church to carry out its charitable functions through its health care and social welfare institutions, this right being exercised in harmony with the rights of the State in this field.

Article 10
1. The Holy See and the State of Israel jointly reaffirm the right of the Catholic Church to property.
2. Without prejudice to rights relied upon the Parties:
(a) The Holy See and the State of Israel will negotiate in good faith a comprehensive agreement, containing solutions acceptable to both Parties, on unclear, unsettled and disputed issues, concerning property, economic and fiscal matters relating to the Catholic Church generally, or to specific Catholic Communities or institutions.
(b) For the purpose of the said negotiations, the Permanent Bilateral Working Commission will appoint one or more bilateral subcommissions of experts to study the issues and make proposals.
(c) The Parties intend to commence the aforementioned negotiations within three months of entry into force of the present Agreement, and aim to reach agreement within two years from the beginning of the negotiations.
(d) During the period of these negotiations, actions incompatible with these commitments shall be avoided.

Article 11
1. The Holy See and the State of Israel declare their respective commitment to the promotion of the peaceful resolution of conflicts among States and nations, excluding violence and terror from international life.
2. The Holy See, while maintaining in every case the right to exercise its moral and spiritual teaching-office, deems it opportune to recall that, owing

to its own character, it is solemnly committed to remaining a stranger to all merely temporal conflicts, which principle applies specifically to disputed territories and unsettled borders.

Article 12
The Holy See and the State of Israel will continue to negotiate in good faith in pursuance of the Agenda agreed upon in Jerusalem, on 15 July 1992, and confirmed at the Vatican, on 29 July 1992; likewise on issues arising from the Articles of the present Agreement, as well as on other issues bilaterally agreed upon as objects of negotiation.

Article 13
    1. In this Agreement the Parties use these terms in the following sense:
    (a) The Catholic Church and the Church—including, inter alia, its Communities and institutions,
    (b) Communities of the Catholic Church—meaning the Catholic religious entities considered by the Holy See as Churches sui juris and by the State of Israel as Recognized Religious Communities;
    (c) The State of Israel and the State—including, inter alia, its authorities established by law.
    2. Notwithstanding the validity of this Agreement as between the Parties, and without detracting from this generality of any applicable rule of law with reference to treaties, the Parties agree that this Agreement does not prejudice rights and obligations arising from existing treaties between either Party and a State or States, which are known and in fact available to both Parties at the time of the signature of this Agreement.

Article 14
    1. Upon signature of the present Fundamental Agreement and in preparation for the establishment of full diplomatic relations, the Holy See and the State of Israel exchange Special Representatives, whose rank and privileges are specified in an Additional Protocol.
    2. Following the entry into force and immediately upon the beginning of the implementation of the present Fundamental Agreement, the Holy See and the State of Israel will establish full diplomatic relations at the level of Apostolic Nunciature, on the part of the Holy See, and Embassy, on the part of the State of Israel.

Article 15
This agreement shall enter into force on the date of the latter notification of ratification by a Party.

Done in two original copies in the English and Hebrew languages, both texts being equally authentic. In case of divergency, the English text shall prevail.

Signed in Jerusalem, this thirtieth day of the month of December, in the year 1993, which corresponds to the sixteenth day of the month of Tevet, in the year 5754.

Yossi Beilin,   Monsignor Claudio Celli
Deputy Foreign Minister   Undersecretary of State
FOR THE GOVERNMENT OF   FOR THE HOLY SEE
THE STATE OF ISRAEL

ADDITIONAL PROTOCOL

1. In relation to Art. 14(1) of the Fundamental Agreement, signed by the Holy See and the State of Israel, the "Special Representatives" shall have, respectively, the personal rank of Apostolic Nuncio and Ambassador.

2. These Special Representatives shall enjoy all the rights, privileges and immunities granted the Heads of Diplomatic Missions under international law and common usage, on the basis of reciprocity.

3. The Special Representative of the State of Israel to the Holy See, while residing in Italy, shall enjoy all the rights, privileges and immunities defined by Art. 12 of the Treaty of 1929 between the Holy See and Italy, regarding Envoys of Foreign Governments to the Holy See residing in Italy. The rights, privileges and immunities extended to the personnel of a Diplomatic Mission shall likewise be granted to the personnel of the Israeli Special Representative's Mission. According to an established custom, neither the Special Representative, nor the official members of his Mission, can at the same time be members of Israel's Diplomatic Mission to Italy.

4. The Special Representative of the Holy See to the State of Israel may at the same time exercise other representative functions of the Holy See and be accredited to other States. He and the personnel of his Mission shall enjoy all the rights, privileges and immunities granted by Israel to Diplomatic Agents and Missions.

5. The names, rank and functions of the Special Representatives will appear, in an appropriate way, in the official lists of Foreign Missions to each Party.

Signed in Jerusalem, this thirtieth day of the month of December, in the year 1993, which corresponds to the sixteenth day of the month of Tevet, in the year 5754.

Yossi Beilin,   Monsignor Claudio Celli
Deputy Foreign Minister   Undersecretary of State
FOR THE GOVERNMENT OF   FOR THE HOLY SEE
THE STATE OF ISRAEL

Agreed Minute

Agreed Interpretation of Article 14

With reference to Article 14 of the Fundamental Agreement, signed by the Holy See and the State of Israel it is agreed that "the beginning of the implementation of the recent Fundamental Agreement" means the establishment of two of the Bilateral Subcommission of Experts, but not later than four months after the coming in to force of this Agreement.

Signed in Jerusalem, this thirtieth day of the month of December, in the year 1993, which corresponds to the sixteenth day of the month of Tevet, in the year 5754.

Yossi Beilin   Monsignor Claudio Celli
Deputy Foreign Minister   Undersecretary of State
FOR THE GOVERNMENT OF   FOR THE HOLY SEE
THE STATE OF ISRAEL

VIII

ORTHODOX JUDAISM

While some argue that Orthodoxy represents the traditional mainstream of Judaism throughout its history, others believe that Orthodoxy represents a specifically fixed Judaism, which grew out of the community context that produced the medieval literature of law codes. Whatever the case may be, an indigenous Orthodoxy arose in America. Unlike the movements of Reform, Conservative, and Reconstructionist Judaism—which are generally represented by a core of organizations—there are a variety of institutions and organizations that are all considered central to the Orthodox community. Thus, the documents included in this section can only provide a sampling of these organizations, those we believe offer the individual reader insight into the contemporary, organized, and generally mainstream Orthodox community.

58

Constitution of the Society Machzeki Jeshibath Etz Chaiem 1886

When the traditional Jewish community realized that it needed an educational institution that could combine secular and Jewish learning, Jeshibath Etz Chaiem was founded—the first society of its kind in this country. For the most part, this was European Orthodoxy transplanted to American soil.

ARTICLE I
NAME AND LANGUAGE

Sec. 1. This Academy shall always bear the name of
MACHZEKI JESHIBATH ETZ CHAIEM.

Sec. 2. All business and transactions shall be made in the Jewish language, especially the Minute Book which shall be in the Hebrew Language (Loshon Hakodosh).

Sec. 3. This Academy can never be dissolved and must exist so long as ten creditable members keep themselves together.

ARTICLE II
PURPOSE

Sec. 1. The purpose of this Academy shall be to give free instruction to poor Hebrew Children in the Hebrew language and the Hebrew Law—Talmud, Bible and Sulchon Aurach during the whole day from nine in the morning until four in the afternoon. Also from four in the afternoon, two hours shall be devoted to teach the native language, English, and one hour to teach Hebrew—Loshon Hakodosh and Jargon to read and write.

Sec. 2. This Academy shall be guided according to the strict Orthodox and Talmudical Law and the custom of Poland and Russia.

ARTICLE III
MEMBERSHIP

Sec. 1. Every Hebrew can become a member of this Academy.
Sec. 2. The dues shall be from three dollars a year and upwards.
Sec. 3. When a member gives to this Academy a hundred dollars at one time, he remains a member during his whole life time.

ARTICLE IV
OFFICERS

Sec. 1. This Academy shall be governed by fourteen officers, namely: one President; one Vice-President; one Treasurer ; one Secretary and ten Directors.
Sec. 2. The ten Directors shall be divided into the following committees: One Committee consisting of four Directors, named Trustees, whose duty it is to superintend the house and money affairs, such as to repair the house when it is necessary, to make programmes, to appoint Hebrew and English teachers, to buy books and everything which belongs to it, according to the income of the time.
Sec. 3. Another Committee consisting of six members who shall be called Leaders—Mnahalim, shall superintend the course of study in Talmud, Bible and Shulchon Aurach to appoint Hebrew teachers, and also in some occurrence to be a Hebrew teacher, and to discharge one if they have sufficient reason for it.
Sec. 4. If all the six leaders agree on some point, they can act according to their opinion, if they disagree they must bring the matter before the President and the Board of Trustees.

ARTICLE XII
TEACHERS

Sec. 1. It is the duty of the Teachers to teach according to the Programme of the Board of Leaders.
Sec. 2. They must be found in the Academy every day in the week; in the right time according to the Programme of the Board of Leaders.

ARTICLE XIII
EXAMINATIONS

Sec. I. The principal examination shall take place on the fifteenth day of Shebat and on the fifteenth day of Ab.

Sec. 2. Ordinary examinations shall be made by the Leaders from time to time according to their opinion.

Sec. 3. Excepting the Leaders and the Officers of the Academy, no one has the right to come in the Academy and examine the children without the permission of the Superintendent of the Academy.

ARTICLE XIV
BENEFIT

Sec. 1. When an officer becomes sick and this is reported to the Secretary, a Director shall visit him daily.

Sec. 2. When a Director dies, the Secretary shall send notice to all the Officers that they shall pay the last honor to the deceased.

Sec. 3. The Academy shall send a carriage and also a committee of four, to the cemetery.

Sec. 4. Ten children from every class shall attend the funeral and say Psalms.

Sec. 5. When anyone was a Director or any other officer during the three years following the establishment of the Academy, he shall be entitled to all this during his whole life, provided that he obeys the Jewish Law and is interested in the benefit of the Academy.

Sec. 6. The Directors shall assemble in the Academy every morning to pray jointly. Also a chapter of Mishna shall be learned every day, together with the prayer beginning with "Anna" and "Kadish" . . . "for the rising of his soul."

Sec. 7. "Hazkoras Nshamos" (Memorial Prayer) shall be made every Saturday and Holiday of the first year.

Sec. 8. The same shall be made every "Yahrzeit" day as long as the Academy exists.

Sec. 9. If any man not an officer of the Academy should have given a Hundred dollars at one time to the Academy, "Hazkoras Nshamos" shall be made every Saturday and Holiday of the first year of his death.

Sec. 10. When any one gave $500 at one time or left that sum to the Academy, "Hazkoras Nshamos" shall be made during the first year, and a "Neir Nishmas" (Candle for his soul), shall be lighted on the "Yahrzeit Day" during the first ten years.

Sec. 11. When any man left $1000, "Hazkoras Nshamos" shall be made during the first year, and the twenty years following his death, a candle shall be lighted on the "Yahrzeit" day.

Sec. 12. When any man gives more than a $1000, then all the above things shall be made and as long as the Academy exists the "Yahrzeit" shall be held and a chapter of "Mishna" shall be learned on that day.

Sec. 13. When such donations are given to the Academy, the names of the donators shall be inscribed on a tablet of the Academy, to be remembered forever.

59

Certificate of Incorporation, Chebrah Machsika Ishiwas Etz Chaim 1886

When the Ishiwas Etz Chaim was incorporated, it was founded as a benevolent society whose sole purpose was the improvement of the social, educational, and religious condition of Jewish boys in New York's Orthodox Jewish community.

State of New York
County of New York }   ss:
City of New York

     We the undersigned,

MORRIS BERNSTEIN
SAMUEL WAXMAN
ABRAM RUBENOWITZ
RACHMIEL WITMAN AND
HENRY C. GREENBERG

Citizens of the United States, also Citizens and Residents of the City, County and State of New York being desirous to associate ourselves together for the purpose of forming and organizing a *Benevolent Society, do hereby certify*

     That we have pursuant to the Laws of the State of New York, as prescribed in Article III Title 6, Chapter 18 of the Revised Statutes entitled, "An Act" for the Incorporation of Benevolent, Charitable, Scientific, and Missionary Societies, passed April 12th 1848, and the Acts amendatory thereof, associated ourselves together for the purpose of forming and organizing a *Benevolent Society.*

     That the name by which said society or organization shall be known in law is the:

Chebrah Machrika Ishiwas Etz Chaim

That the objects and business of the society or organization are the improvement of the spiritual, mental and social condition of *Hebrew Boys,* to provide for them Teachers and instructions in *Hebrew,* to foster and encourage the study of the *Sacred Scriptures,* the *Talmud,* and the Hebrew language and literature; to hold religious service in accordance with Orthodox Judaism: also to provide teachers and instruction for said *Hebrew Boys* in reading, writing and speaking the English Language; and to perform such other charitable acts and purposes as may be specified in the Constitution and By-Laws of the Society or Organization.

That the number of Directors or Trustees of the said Society or Organization shall be nine.

That the number of Directors or Trustees, for the first year of the existence of the Society or Organization hereby formed shall be as follows,

JULIUS D. BERNSTEIN	who shall act *as President*
MORRIS BERNSTEIN	who shall act as *First Vice Pres*
MOSES HELLER	who shall act as *Second Vice Pres*
FALK BERMAN	who shall act as *Treasurer*
LOUIS SHAPIRO	who shall act as *Secretary*
ELIAS RATKOWSKY	who shall act as *First Trustee*
LOUIS SIEGELSTEIN	who shall act as *Second Trustee*
RACHMIEL WITMAN	who shall act as *Third Trustee*
BARUCH P. LIBERMAN	who shall act as *Fourth Trustee*

That the said nine members shall hold office as such Directors, Trustees and Officers for one year from the date hereof, and shall constitute the Board of Directors or Trustees.

That the business of the Society or Organization shall be transacted in the City of New York.

In Witness Whereof, we have hereunto set our hands and seals this 15th day of September 1886.

MORRIS BERNSTEIN
S. WAXMAN
ABRAM RUBENOWITZ   [Signed]
RACHMIEL WITMAN
H. C. GREENBERG

State of New York.
City and County of New York. ss.

On this 15th day of September 1886, before me personally came MORRIS BERNSTEIN, SAMUEL WAXMAN, ABRAM RUBENOWTIZ, RACHMIEL WITMAN, and HENRY C. GREENBERG, to me severally known, to be the persons described in and executed the foregoing instrument and they severally acknowledged to me that they executed the same, for the uses and purposes therein mentioned.

ADOLPH COHEN
Notary Public
NYCounty

60

Certificate of Incorporation, Rabbi Isaac Elchanan Theological Seminary Association 1897

As the boys of the Jeshibath Etz Chaiem grew older—among other reasons—it became apparent that the Orthodox Jewish community also needed a rabbinical seminary to preserve and transmit the values of Orthodox Judaism in the United States.

State of New York ⎫ ss:
City of New York ⎭

We, the undersigned, desiring to form a corporation pursuant to the provisions of the membership corporation law, all being of full age and two-thirds being citizens of the United States and at least one a resident of the State of New York, do hereby certify and state:

First: The particular objects for which the corporation is to be formed are to promote the study of the Talmud and to assist in educating and preparing students of the Hebrew faith for the Hebrew Orthodox Ministry.

Second: The name of the proposed corporation is the Rabbi Isaac Elchanan Theological Seminary Association.

Third: The territory in which its operations are to be principally conducted is the City, County and State of New York.

Fourth: The town, village or city in which its principal office is to be located is the City of New York in the County and State of New York.

Fifth: The number of its directors is eleven.

Sixth: The names and places of residence of the persons to be its directors until its first annual meeting are:

Name

SAMUEL SCHATZKIN	1	Canal Street	New York
JEHUDA SOLOMON	134	E. Broadway	" "
ASHER L. GERMANSKY	30	Canal Street	" "
MAX LEWIS	24	Orchard Street	" "
DAVID ABRAMOWITZ	5	Hester Street	" "
MENDEL ZUCKERMAN	162	Henry Street	" "
JULIUS BERNSTEIN	272	E. Broadway	" "
SAMUEL SILBERSTEIN	235	Division Street	" "
MOSES H. BERNSTEIN	89	Division Street	" "
JULIUS [YEHUDA] BERNSTEIN	71	Henry Street	" "
MOSES M. MATLIN	172	Clinton Street	" "

Seventh: The times for holding its annual meeting is the first Sunday in January of each year.

State of New York }
City, County of New York } ss:

On this 26th day of February, 1897, before me personally came Samuel Schatzkin, Jehuda Solomon, Asher L. Germansky, Max Lewis, Jacob H. Selikowitz, Mendel Zuckerman, Julius Bernstein, Samuel Silberstein, David Abramowitz, Simon Selikowitz, M. H. Bernstein, Moses M. Matlin, Joseph Goldenson, Julius D. Bernstein, to me personally known to be the individuals described in and who executed the same.

ABRAHAM ROSENBERG
Commissioner of Deeds
New York County

[Endorsed]
I, the undersigned, Justice of the Supreme Court of the State of New York, do hereby approve of the within certificate

Dated at New York this 8th day of March, 1897.

MILES BEACH
J S C

Certificate of Incorporation
The Rabbi Isaac Elchanan Theological Seminary Association
(A membership corporation)

State of New York

Office of Secretary of State   March 20, 1897

Filed and recorded

ANDREW DAVIDSON

Deputy Secretary of State

61

Founding Resolution, Agudath Israel
1912

A working conference of thousands came to Kattowitz (a Polish city in Silesia) and developed this statement as a way of putting the Orthodox Jewish community on the offensive rather than remaining—as the group considered—subject to the destructive whims of their foes.

The representatives of observant Jews from all parts of the world, having met here in Kattowitz and having listened to various proposals, hereby declare the founding of AGUDATH ISRAEL and commit themselves to work for the growth of Agudath Israel with all their strength. Agudath Israel will take an active part in all matters relating to Jews and Judaism on the basis of Torah, without any political considerations.

62

Psak Din, Prohibiting the Participation of Orthodox Rabbis in Mixed Religious Organization and Local Rabbinical Boards 1956

This classic rabbinic legal decision effectively separated the Orthodox community—and its leadership—from the rest of the Jewish community.

We have been asked by a number of rabbis in the country and by alumni and *musmochim* of yeshivas, if it is permissible to participate with and be a member of The New York Board of Rabbis and similar groups in other communities, which are composed of Reform and Conservative "rabbis."

Having gathered together to clarify this matter, it has been ruled by the undersigned that it is forbidden by the law of our sacred Torah to be a member of and to participate in such an organization.

We have also been asked if it is permissible to participate with and to be a member of the Synagogue Council of America, which is also composed of Reform and Conservative organizations.

We have ruled that it is forbidden by the law of our sacred Torah to participate with them either as an individual or as an organized communal body.

May *Hashem Yisborach* have mercy on His people, and seal the breaches [in Torah life] and may we be worthy of the elevation of the glory of our sacred Torah and our people Israel.

Signed this fifth day, the week of *Parshas Ki Seesah*, the Eighteenth day of Adar, 5716, in the City of New York.

—*Avraham Joffen*
—*Avraham Kalmanowitz*
—*Ahron Kotler*
—*Gedalia Shorr*

—*Dovid Lifshutz*
—*Chaim Mordecai Katz*
—*Yaakov Kaminetsky*
—*Yaakov Yitzchok Halevi Ruderman*
—*Yitzchok Hutner*
—*Menachem Yosef Zachs*
—*Moshe Feinstein*

63

The Founding of Yeshiva College
1925

Bernard Revel

In this classic statement, the *rosh yeshiva* of the Rabbi Isaac Elchanan and founding president of Yeshiva College articulates the founding principles of what
eventually became Yeshiva University, "America's first Jewish College."

The traditional concept of education and its aims are . . . the building of
character and the harmonious development of man's intellectual, religious,
moral and physical faculties. . . . The goal of education, according to Judaism, is the preparation of man for, and his dedication to, his duties as a member or his family, country and Faith. The Yeshiva proposes to establish a College of Liberal Arts and Sciences . . . with the double purpose of educating
both liberally and Jewishly a number of Jewish young men who have been
already imbued with the spirit and the sanctity of Judaism and its teachings,
so that these men may not be lost to us . . .

In existing colleges, Jewish students are led to efface their Jewishness. . . .
Some of our idealistic and talented young men will find in a College of Liberal Arts and Sciences under Jewish auspices a congenial home, unhampered
by real and psychological restrictions, which stifle the spirit; a home where
they will be able to realize their energies and mental endowments for the
enrichment of general and Jewish culture.

Jewish young men who wish to prepare themselves for the rabbinate,
for Jewish social service, for teaching in religious schools, for Jewish scholarship or communal leadership are to be trained in an institution of higher
learning of recognized rank, which is in keeping with the highest educational
standards in this country. . . .

Secondly, Jewish young men who consider Jewish learning an indispensable part of the moral and mental equipment that they wish to attain through
a college education are to have the advantage of such a combined education.

64

The Agudist Programme 1937

In this introductory statement to a small booklet entitled, "The Purpose and Programme of the World Agudist Organization," published in London, Agudath Israel clearly states its operating principles.

None of our contemporaries can possibly remember a world crisis of such gravity, as that in which humanity in general, and the Jewish people in particular, now finds itself.

This crisis is of particular significance to us Agudists.

Instead of feeling themselves as members of the great organism of humanity, and subordinating themselves to God the King, the peoples of the world have immured themselves within their own interests. For that reason chaos has come to our economic and political system, and all the technical achievements which should have served to bring about unification of endeavour, have proved to be useless. This, then, shows that organisation on moral and religious principles is the solution which alone can redeem mankind. Shall we Jews learn nothing from this lesson?

The Jewish nation, still the historic-religious centre of mankind, must first unite and organise on the basis of the Torah, as planned at Sinai. Then, and then alone, can it fulfil its historic mission in the midst of humanity, for its own salvation, and that of mankind.

This—nothing else—is the programme of Agudas Israel.

JACOB ROSENHEIM,
President of the
World Agudist Organisation

65

The Jewish Agency's Pledge
to Agudath Israel
1947

Just prior to the founding of the State of Israel, the Jewish Agency promised four things to Agudath Israel, including the protection of the Sabbath, *kashrut*, personal status, and autonomous education.

The letter concludes with the following key points.

1. Sabbath: It is clear that the legal day of rest in the Jewish State will be the Sabbath, with, of course, rights for Christians and followers of other religions to observe their weekly day of rest.

2. Kashrus: All necessary means should be taken to assure that, in all governmental kitchens intended for Jews, there shall be kosher food.

3. Personal Status: All members of the Administration appreciate the seriousness of this problem and its great difficulties. On behalf of all bodies represented by the Administration of the Jewish Agency, everything possible will be done in this matter to provide for the deep needs of the religious, in order to prevent, G-d forbid, the split of the House of Israel into two peoples.

4. Education: Full autonomy is guaranteed to every educational stream (incidentally, this discipline exists even now in the Zionist Organization and Knesses Yisrael) and there shall be no interference on the part of the government with the religious requirement or conscience of any part of Jewry, . . .

66

Resolution of Agudath Israel
on the Founding of the State of Israel
1947

While wanting to protect itself from what it perceived as the possible secular-ization of Judaism through the establishment of the modern State of Israel, Agudath Israel nonetheless applauded its founding before the United Nations.

A day will come when you will be asked, "Where were you when God's people were murdered?" accused Rabbi Levin.

"I am the eighth generation of Jews who came to Jerusalem in battered ships," proclaimed Rabbi Porush. "This is the best proof that we never gave . . ."

. . . there to establish a Jewish State and to encompass within its borders the banished and scattered members of our people.

This historic event must bring home to every Jew the realization that the Almighty has brought this about in an act of Divine Providence which presents us with a great task and a grave test.

We must face up to this test and establish our life as a people upon the basis of Torah. While we are sorely grieved that the Land has been divided and sections of the Holy Land have been torn asunder, especially Jerusalem, the Holy City, while we still yearn for the aid of our righteous Messiah, who will bring us total redemption, we nevertheless see the Hand of Providence offering us the opportunity to prepare for the complete redemption, if we will walk into the future as God's people.

Rabbi Yitzchok Meir Levin,
Rabbi Moshe Porush

67

Some Comments on Centrist Orthodoxy 1985

Norman Lamm

In what has come to be regarded as a classic statement of centrist Orthodoxy, these comments of Yeshiva University's president (and founding editor of *Tradition*) clearly articulate the position of modern Orthodox Judaism.

Carl Becker, the great American historian, once said: "It is important, every so often, to look at the things that go without saying to be sure that they are still going." I would add the need for intellectual vigilance to this reminder for practical caution by paraphrasing his aphorism: "It is important, every so often, to look at what we are saying about the things that go without saying to make sure we know what we are talking about."

In reflecting on some of the foundations of our *Weltanschauung*, I do not presume to be imparting new information. The task I have set for myself is to summarize and clarify, rather than to innovate. Dr. Johnson once said that it is important not only to instruct people but also to remind them. I shall take his sage advice for this discourse.

We seem to be suffering from a terminological identity crisis. We now call ourselves "Centrist Orthodoxy." There was a time, not too long ago, when we referred to ourselves as "Modern Orthodox." Others tell us that we should call ourselves simply "Orthodox," without any qualifiers, and leave it to the other Orthodox groups to conjure up adjectives for themselves. I agree with the last view in principle, but shall defer to the advocates of "Centrist Orthodoxy" for two reasons: First, it is a waste of intellectual effort and precious time to argue about titles when there are so many truly significant issues that clamor for our attention. In no way should the choice of one adjective over the other be invested with any substantive significance or assumed to be a "signal" of ideological position.

We are what we are, and we should neither brag nor be apologetic about it. These days, we do more of the latter than the former, and I find that reprehensible. Let us be open and forthright about our convictions: They are לכתחילה and not בדיעבד. We must not be intimidated by those who question our legitimacy for whatever reason. Nevertheless—or maybe because of our ideological self-confidence—we must be ready to confront, firmly but respectfully, any challenges to our position.

It is in this spirit that I mention an argument that is often offered to refute our Centrist outlook: that, after all, we have introduced "changes," and that such changes bespeak our lack of fealty to Torah and Halakhah. We are taunted by the old aphorism, חדש אסור מן התורה, that anything new, any change, constitutes an offense against Torah. (It is interesting how a homiletical *bon mot* by the immortal Hatam Sofer has been adopted as an Article of Faith. I wonder how many good Jews really believe that it is an ancient warning against any new ideas and not a halakhic proscription of certain types of grain at certain times of the year . . .)

Have we really introduced "changes"? Yes and No. No, not a single fundamental of Judaism has been disturbed by us. We adhere to the same *ikkarim*, we are loyal to the same Torah, we strive for the same study of Torah and observance of the *mitsvot* that our parents and grandparents before us cherished throughout the generations, from Sinai onward.

But yes, we have introduced innovations, certainly relative to the East European model which is our cherished touchstone, our intellectual and spiritual origin, and the source of our nostalgia. We are Orthodox Jews, most of us of East European descent, who have, however, undergone the modern experience—and survived it; who refuse to accept modernity uncritically, but equally so refuse to reject it unthinkingly; who have lived through the most fateful period of the history of our people and want to derive some invaluable lessons from this experience, truths that may have been latent heretofore. In this sense, we have indeed changed from the idealized, romanticized, and in many ways real picture of the *shtetl*, whether of "lomdisch" Lithuania or the Hasidic courts.

Do these changes delegitimize us as Orthodox Jews, as followers of Halakhah, as *benei Torah*? My answer is a full and unequivocal No.

The "changes" we have introduced into the theory and practice of Orthodox Judaism have resulted not in the diminution of Torah but in its expansion. Some changes are, indeed, for the good. And such positive and welcome changes were introduced at many a critical juncture in Jewish history.

These changes (actually changes in emphasis rather than substance), which we will describe and explain presently, were occasioned by the radically new life experiences of the last several generations. They are genuine Torah responses to unprecedented challenges to our whole way of life and way of thinking. They include modernity—its openness, its critical stance, its historicism; the democratic experience which, most recently, has raised the serious challenge of the new role of women in family and society; the growth of science and technology, and the scientific method applied to so many fields beyond the natural sciences; almost universal higher worldly education amongst Jews—which destroys the common assumption of bygone generations that an *am ha-aretz* in Torah is an unlettered ignoramus in general; the historically wrenching experience of the Holocaust; the miraculous rise of the State of Israel; and the reduction of observant and believing Jews to a small minority of the Jewish people—a condition unknown since the darkest periods of the biblical era.

What are some of our contributions to Torah Judaism? Let us adumbrate several of the more characteristic foundations of our *Weltanschauung*, some of which may appear more innovative and some of which are "different" only because of the emphasis we place upon them relative to other ideas and ideals. They deal with the general areas of education, moderation, and the people of Israel.

The first is Torah Umadda, the "synthesis" of Torah and worldly knowledge. For the latter term, *Madda*, we can just as well substitute the Hirschian *Derekh Eretz*, though I prefer *Hokhmah* to both; it is the term used both in the Midrash and in the writings of Maimonides.

For us, the study of worldly wisdom is not a concession to economic necessity. It is *de jure*, not *de facto*. I have never understood how the excuse of permitting "college" for the sake of "*parnasah*" or earning a living can be advocated by religiously serious people. If all secular learning is regarded as dangerous spiritually and forbidden halakhically, what right does one have to tolerate it at all? Why not restrict careers for Orthodox Jews to the trades and small businesses? Is the difference in wages between a computer programmer and a shoe salesman large enough to dismiss the "halakhic" prohibition of the academic training necessary for the former? The Hasidic communities and part of the Mitnagdic yeshiva world, which indeed proscribe any and all contact with secular academic learning, have at least the virtue of consistency. One cannot say the same for the more moderate or modernist factions of the "yeshiva world" which condone "college" for purposes of a livelihood (while insisting upon rather arbitrary and even bizarre distinctions amongst various courses and disciplines) at the same time that they criticize, usually intemperately, the Centrist Orthodox for their open attitude towards the world of culture.

For us the study of worldly wisdom *enhances* Torah. It reveals not a lowering of the value of Torah in the hierarchy of values, but a symbiotic or synergistic view.

Critics of the *Torah Umadda* school have argued that our view is premised on a flawed appreciation of Torah, namely, that we do not subscribe to the wholeness and self-sufficiency of Torah. *Torah Umadda* implies, they aver, that Torah is not complete, that it is lacking; else, why the need for secular learning?

This critique is usually based upon the Mishnah in *Avot* (5:26) that "הפך בה והפך בה דכולא בה"—delve into Torah intensively, and you will discover that it contains everything. Hence, the Tannaim believed that Torah is the repository of all wisdom, and therefore independent study of other systems of thought and culture is a denial of this authoritative comprehensiveness of Torah.

Truth to tell, this is indeed the interpretation of this particular Mishnah by the Gaon of Vilna in his Commentary: The Torah contains, in hidden as well as revealed form, the totality of knowledge. But does this really imply that there is no independent role for *Madda* or *Hokhmah*?

Not at all. First, the Gaon himself is quoted by one of his students, R. Baruch of Shklov, as saying that ignorance of other forms of wisdom results in a hundredfold ignorance of Torah: כי כפי התורה כי התורה והחכמה נצמדים יחד הקדמה לספר אוקלידוס, האג, תק"ם) מה שיחסר לאדם ידיעות משארי החכמות לעומת זה יחסרו). לו מאה ידות בחכמת. The last clause itself belies the view that all wisdom, including worldly wisdom, is contained within the Torah. While it is true that the Gaon was extremely adept at demonstrating, through various complex and arcane means, that the many aspects of Torah interpenetrate each other so that, for instance, elements of the Oral Torah are discoverable in the text of Scripture, still we may not be correct in assuming that his interpretation of this Mishnah is anything more than its face value. In all probability it does *not* represent the essence of his encompassing view on the nature of Torah. Moreover, even if one insists upon ascribing to the Gaon such a radical view of Torah based upon this comment, he clearly does maintain that the secular disciplines are necessary to unlock the vault of Torah in order to reveal the profane wisdom that lies latent within it.

Second, we find instances where the Sages clearly delineate Torah from Wisdom, *Hokhmah*. Thus, in Midrash Ekhah, 2, we read: אם יאמר לך אדם יש חכמה בגויים האמין ... יש תורה בגויים אל תאמין—if you are told that the Gentiles possess wisdom, believe it; that they possess Torah, do not believe it.

we have here is not a confrontation between sacred and secular wisdom, but an expression of their complementarity: Each is valuable, each has its particular sphere. "Torah" is our particularist corpus of sacred wisdom, confined to the people of Israel, while "Wisdom" is the universal heritage of all mankind in which Jews share equally even though it is not their own exclusive preserve.

Finally, the debate on the meaning of the Gaon's words notwithstanding, his is not the only authoritative interpretation of the passage in the Mishnah. Meiri sees this passage as teaching that any problem within Torah itself is solvable without having recourse to sources outside of Torah. Torah, thus, is self-sufficient as sacred teaching; it makes no claims on being the sole repository of all wisdom, divine and human. This much more modest exegesis is certainly more palatable for us, living in an age of the explosion of knowledge and the incredible advances of science and technology. The view some ascribe to the Gaon, that there is no autonomous wisdom other than Torah, because it is all contained in Torah, would leave us profoundly perplexed. No amount of intellectual legerdemain or midrashic pyrotechnics can convince us that the Torah, somehow, possesses within itself the secrets of quantum mechanics and the synthesis of DNA and the mathematics that underlie the prediction of macroeconomic fluctuations and . . . and . . . No such problems arise if we adopt the simpler explanation of Meiri.

For those of us in the Centrist camp, *Torah Umadda* does not imply the coequality of the two poles. Torah remains the unchallenged and preeminent center of our lives, our community, our value system. But centrality is not the same as exclusivity. It does not imply the rejection of all other forms or sources of knowledge, such that non-sacred learning constitutes a transgression. It does not yield the astounding conclusion that ignorance of Wisdom becomes a virtue. I cannot reconcile myself, or my reading of the whole Torah tradition with the idea that ignorance—any ignorance—should be raised to the level of a transcendental good and a source of ideological pride.

Time does not permit a more extensive analysis, based upon appropriate sources, of the relationship between *Torah* and *Madda* within the context of *Torah Umadda*. But this one note should be added: Granting that Wisdom has autonomous rights, it does not remain outside the purview of Torah as a worldview, even though it may not be absorbed in Torah as a corpus of texts or body of knowledge. Ultimately, as Rav Kook taught, both the sacred and the profane are profoundly interrelated; the קודש הקדשים is the source of both יסוד הקודש ויסוד החול. The Author of the Book of Exodus, the repository of the beginnings of the halakhic portions of the Torah, is the self-same Author of the Book of Genesis, the teachings about God as the universal Creator, and hence the subject matter of all the non-halakhic disciplines. Truly, "both these and these are the words of the living God!" (This may provide an alternative answer to the famous question of Rashi at the beginning of Genesis, as to why the Torah begins with the story of the genesis of the world rather than with the first *mitsvah* as recorded in Exodus.)

The second important principle that distinguishes Centrist Orthodoxy is that of *moderation*. Of course, this should by no means be considered a "change" or "innovation"; moderation is, if anything, more mainstream than extremism. But in today's environment, true moderation appears as an aberration or, worse, a manifestation of spinelessness, a lack of commitment. And that is precisely what moderation is not. It is the result neither of guile nor of indifference nor of prudence; it is a matter of sacred principle. Moderation must not be understood as the mindless application of an arithmetic average or mean to any and all problems. It is the expression of an earnest, sober, and intelligent assessment of each situation, bearing in mind two things: the need to consider the realities of any particular situation as well as general abstract theories or principles; and the awareness of the complexities of life, the "stubborn and irreducible" facts of existence, as William James called them, which refuse to yield to simplistic or single-minded solutions. Moderation issues from a broad *Weltanschauung* or worldview rather than from tunnel vision.

It was, as is well known, Maimonides who established moderation as a principle of Judaism when he elaborated his doctrine of "the middle way" (דרך הבינונית, דרך האמצעית) as the Judaized version of the Aristotelian Golden Mean in his *Hilkhot De'ot* as well as in his earlier "Eight Chapters." The mean is, for Rambam, the right way and the way of the virtuous (הדרך הישרה, דרך הטובים) The mean is not absolute; Maimonides records two standard exceptions and describes certain general situations where the mean does not apply. This alone demonstrates that the principle of moderation is not, as I previously mentioned, a "mindless application of arithmetic averages" to his philosophy of character.

Of course, Maimonides is speaking primarily of moral dispositions and individual personality, not of political or social conduct. Yet, there is good reason to assume that the broad outlines of his doctrine of moderation apply as well to the social and political spheres. First, there is no *prima facie* reason to assume that because Maimonides exemplifies his principle by references to personal or characterological dispositions, that this concept does not apply to collectivities, such as the polis or society or the nation, *mutaris mutandis*. Indeed, there is less justification for mass extremism than for individual imbalance. Second, his own historical record reveals a balanced approach to communal problems which, while often heroic, is not at all extremist. Special mention might be made of his conciliatory attitude towards the Karaites despite his judgment as to their halakhic status. But this is a subject which will take us far afield and must be left for another time.

Third, Maimonides refers to a specific verse which, upon further investigation, reveals significant insights. He identifies the Middle Way with the "way of the Lord," citing Genesis 18:19—כי ידעתיו למען אשר יצוה את בניו ואת ביתו אחריו ושמרו דרך ה' לעשות צדקה ומשפט. The Middle Way is the Divine Way, the Way of the Lord, and the assurance of a just and moral world ("to do righteousness and justice"). It is the essential legacy that one generation must aspire to bequeath to the next: "that he (Abraham) may command his children and his household after him that they may keep the way of the Lord. . . ."

Now consider the context of this verse, which Maimonides sees as the source of the teaching of moderation. It appears just after the very beginning of the story of the evil of Sodom and Gomorrah. Verses 16, 17, and 18, just preceding the passages we have cited, tell of the angels looking upon Sodom as Abraham accompanies them onto their way. "And the Lord said: Shall I hide from Abraham that which I am doing [to Sodom], seeing that Abraham shall surely become a great and mighty nation, and all the nations shall be blessed in him? For I have known him (or, preferably: I love him) to the end that he may command his children and his household after him that they may keep the way of the Lord. . . ." God wants Abraham to exercise his quality of moderation, the Way of the Lord, on the Lord Himself as it were, praying for the Lord to moderate the extreme decree of destruction against Sodom and Gomorrah. And Abraham almost succeeds: What follows is the immortal passage of the Lord informing Abraham of His intention to utterly destroy the two cities of wickedness, and Abraham pleading for their survival if they contain at least ten innocent people.

Surely, the "way of the Lord" refers to more than personal temperance alone; the doctrine of moderation, which the term implies according to Maimonides, is set in the context of Abraham's office of a blessing to all the peoples of the earth, and of his heroic defense of Sodom and Gomorrah—symbols of the very antithesis of all Abraham stands for. A more political or communal example of moderation and temperance, of tolerance and sensitivity, is hard to come by. Yet for Maimonides, this is the Way of the Lord. The Way of the Lord speaks, therefore, not only of personal attributes but of the widest and broadest scopes of human endeavor as well.

Our times are marked by a painful absence of moderation. Extremism is rampant, especially in our religious life. Of course, there are reasons — unhappily, too often they are very good reasons — for the new expressions of zealotry. There is so very much in contemporary life that is reprehensible and ugly, that it is hard to fault those who reject all of it with unconcealed and indiscriminate contempt. Moreover, extremism is psychologically more satisfying and intellectually easier to handle. It requires fewer fine distinctions, it imposes no burden of selection and evaluation, and substitutes passion for subtlety. Simplicism and extremism go hand in hand. Yet one must always bear in mind what Murray Nicholas Butler once said: The extremes are more logical and more consistent — but they are absurd.

It is this moral recoil from absurdity and the penchant for simplistic solutions and intellectual short-cuts, as well as the positive Jewish teaching of moderation as the "way of the Lord," that must inform our public policy in Jewish matters today. The Way of the Lord that was imparted to Abraham at the eve of the great cataclysm of antiquity must remain the guiding principle for Jews of our era who have emerged from an incomparably greater and more evil catastrophe. Moderation, in our times, requires courage and the willingness to risk not only criticism but abuse.

Test the accuracy of this statement by an exercise of the imagination. Speculate on what the reactions would be to Abraham if he were to be alive today, in the 1980's, pleading for Sodom and Gomorrah. Placards would no doubt rise on every wall of Jerusalem: "שומו שמים על זאת . . . ," the scandal of a purportedly Orthodox leader daring to speak out on behalf of the wicked evildoers and defying the opinions of all the "Gedolim" of our times! Emergency meetings of rabbinic organizations in New York would be convened, resulting in a statement to the press that what could one expect of a man who had stooped to a dialogue with the King of Sodom himself. Rumors would fly that the dialogue was occasioned by self-interest — the concern for his nephew Lot. American-born Neturei Karta demonstrators in Israel would parade their signs before the foreign press and TV cameras: "WASTE SODOM . . . NUKE GOMORRAH . . . ABRAHAM DOESN'T SPEAK FOR RELIGIOUS JEWRY." Halakhic periodicals would carry editorials granting that Abraham was indeed a *talmid hakham*, but he has violated the principle of *emunat hakhamim* (assumed to be the warrant for a kind of intellectual authoritarianism) by ignoring the weight of rabbinic opinion that Sodom and Gomorrah, like Amalek, must be exterminated. Indeed, what can one expect other than pernicious results from one who is well known to have flirted with Zionism . . . ? And beyond words and demonstrations,

Abraham would be physically threatened by the Kach strongmen, shaking their fists and shouting accusations of treason at him. And so on and so on.

I cannot leave the subject of moderation without at least some reference to a matter which never fails to irritate me, and that is: bad manners. Some may dismiss this concern as mere etiquette and unworthy of serious consideration. But I beg to differ. The chronic nastiness that characterizes so much of our internal polemics in Jewish life is more than esthetically repugnant; it is both the cause and effect of extremism, insensitivity, and intolerance in our ranks. We savage each other mercilessly, thinking we are scoring points with "our side"—whichever side that is—and are unaware that we are winning naught but scorn from the "outside world." Our debates are measured in decibels, or numbers of media outlets reached, rather than by the ideas propounded and the cogency of our arguments. True, when one takes things seriously it is difficult to observe all the canons of propriety; tolerance comes easier to men of convenience than to men of conviction. But there is a world of difference between a *cri de coeur* that occasionally issues from genuine outrage and the hoarse cry of coarseness for its own sake that infects our public discourse like a foul plague.

Let others do as they wish. We, of our camp, must know and do better. If our encounter with our dissenting fellow Jews of any persuasion is to be conducted out of love and concern rather than enmity and contempt, then moderation must mark the form and style as well as substance of our position.

That is our task as part of our affirmation of moderation as a guiding principle of Centrist Orthodoxy. Our halakhic decisions, whether favorable or unfavorable to the questioner, whether strict or liberal, must never be phrased in a manner designed to repel people and cause Torah to be lowered in their esteem. Unfortunately, that often happens—even in our own circles, especially when we try to outdo others in manifestations of our piety.

The third principle of Centrist Orthodoxy is the centrality of the people of Israel אהבת ישראל, the love of Israel, and the high significance it attains in our lives is the only value that can in any way challenge the preeminence of Torah and its corollary, אהבת התורה, the love of Torah.

The tension between these two values, Torah and Israel, has lain dormant for centuries. Thus, in the High Middle Ages we find divergent approaches by R. Saadia Gaon and by R. Yehuda Halevi. The former asserts the undisputed primacy of Torah. It is that which fashioned Israel and which remains, therefore, axiologically central. Saadia avers: "our people Israel is a people only by virtue of its Torahs" (i.e., the Written and the Oral Torah; Emunot ve-De'ot 3:7). Halevi maintains the reverse position: "If not for the

Children of Israel, there would be no Torah in the world" (Kuzari 2:56). Israel precedes Torah both chronologically and axiologically. Hints of the one position or the other may be found scattered through the literature, both before and after Saadia and Halevi. Perhaps the most explicit is that of Tanna de-Vei Eliahu, which tells of an encounter between a scholar and an incompletely educated Jew. The scholar records the following conversation: אמר לי: רבי, שני דברים יש לי בלבבי, ואני אוהבן אהבה גדולה, תורה וישראל, אבל איני יודע אי זה מהן קודם. אמרתי לו, דרכן של בני אדם שאומרים תורה קדומה לכל, שנאמר ה' קני ראשית דרכו, אבל (אני) הייתי אומר ישראל קדושם [קודמין] שנאמר קדוש ישראל לה' ראשית תבואתו. The sage's interlocutor wishes to know which of his own loves, Torah or Israel, takes precedence. His response is that most people think that Torah precedes Israel, but that is not so: The love of Israel takes precedence over Torah (סדר אליהו רבה, הוצ' מאיר א"ש, [פי"ד] פי"ד, עמ'17).

Now, these two opposing viewpoints have lived peacefully, side by side for centuries, their conflict latent—until our own days when, as a result of the trauma of the Holocaust and the reduction of Orthodoxy to a decided minority, the problem assumes large, poignant, and possibly tragic proportions. The confrontation between the two, if allowed to get out of hand, can have the most cataclysmic effects on the future of the House of Israel as well as the State of Israel. History calls upon us to abandon tired formulas and ossified cliches and make a deliberate, conscious effort to develop policies which, even if choices between the two must be made, will lead us to embrace both and retain the maximum of each. We shall have to undertake a difficult analytic calculus: Which of the two leads to the other and which does not lead to the other?—and give primacy to the preference which inexorably moves us on to the next love, so that in the end we love neither. Ultimately, there can be no Torah without Israel and no Israel without Torah. ישראל ואורייתא חד הוא.

If indeed such a calculus has to be undertaken, then Orthodox Jews will have to rethink their policy. Heretofore, the attitude most prevalent has been that Torah takes precedence—witness the readiness of our fellow Orthodox Jews to turn exclusivist, to the extent that psychologically, though certainly not halakhically, many of our people no longer regard non-Orthodox Jews as part of Kelal Yisrael. But this choice of love of Torah over love of Israel is a dead end: Such a decision is a final one, for it cuts off the rest of the Jewish people permanently. Such love of Torah does not lead to love of Israel; most certainly not. The alternative, the precedence given to love of Israel over love of Torah, is more reasonable, for although we may rue the outrageous violations of Torah and Halakhah and their legitimation by non-Orthodox groups, a more open and tolerant attitude to our deviationist brethren may somehow lead to their rethinking their positions and returning to identification with Torah and its values; לארשי תבהא may well lead to אהבת התורה. A posture of rejection, certainly one of triumphalist arrogance, will most certainly not prove attractive and fruitful.

Moreover, if there ever was a time that a hard choice had to be made to reject Jews, this is not the time to do so. In this post-Holocaust age, when we lost fully one third of our people, and when the combination of negative demography and rampant assimilation and out-marriage threaten our viability as a people, we must seek to hold on to Jews and not repel them. Love of Israel has so often been used as a slogan—and a political one, at that—that it dulls the senses and evokes no reaction. Yet, like cliches, slogans contain nuggets of truth and wisdom, and we ignore them at our own peril.

Included in the rubric of the centrality of the people of Israel as a fundamental distinguishing tenet of Centrist Orthodoxy is the high significance of the State of Israel. If I fail to elaborate on this principle it is not because of its lack of importance but, on the contrary, because it is self-evident. Whether or not we attribute Messianic dimensions to the State of Israel, and I personally do not subscribe to or recite the prayer of ראשית צמיחת גאולתנו, its value to us and all of Jewish history is beyond dispute. Our love of Israel clearly embraces the State of Israel, without which the fate of the people of Israel would have been tragically sealed.

Such, in summary, are some of the major premises of Centrist Orthodoxy. They are not all, of course, but they are important and consequential.

The path we have chosen for ourselves is not an easy one. It requires of us to exercise our Torah responsibility at almost every step, facing new challenges with the courage of constant renewal. It means we must always assess each new situation as it arises and often perform delicate balancing acts as the tension between opposing goods confronts us. But we know that, with confidence in our ultimate convictions, we shall prevail. For our ultimate faith and our greatest love is—the love of God. The great Hasidic thinker, R. Zadok haKohen, taught us in his *Tsidkat ha-Tsaddik* (no. 197) that there are three primary loves—of God and Torah and Israel. The latter two he calls "revealed" loves, and the love of God—the "concealed" love, for even if the religious dimension seems absent, as long as there is genuine love of Torah or love of Israel, we may be sure that it is empowered and energized by the love of God, but that the latter is concealed, and often buried in the unconscious. It is this above all that is the source of our loves, our commitments, our confidence.

Rav Kook used to tell of his school days as a youngster in White Russia. The winters were fierce, the snows massive, the roads impenetrable. He and the others lived on a hill, and the school was at the bottom of that hill. He and his classmates would arrive spotless, safe, and clean. When asked by his charges how he managed this feat, he replied: there is a stake fastened into the hill, and another here at school, and a rope connects them. Hold onto this life-line, and you will be safe: אז מען איז צוגעבונדן אויבן, גליטשט מען נישט אונטן — "if you are firmly anchored up above, you will not slip here below."

68

A New Era in Jewish History
1980

Irving (Yitz) Greenberg

The National Center for Jewish Learning and Leadership (CLAL) grew out of the National Jewish Resource Center. The latter organization was founded in 1974 by Rabbi Irving (Yitz) Greenberg to define the identity of the Jewish community that witnessed the rebirth of modern Israel out of the ashes of the Holocaust. More than any other institution, CLAL has worked—primarily through the network of Jewish federations—to bring together constituencies in the Jewish community regardless of movement affiliation. This paper identifies the one aspect of Jewish community that transcends the status quo of leadership as we formerly knew it. Thus, it represents a watershed understanding of Jewish leadership and the challenges it must confront.

Judaism is a midrash on history. Its fundamental assertion is that human life and history are rooted in the divine, an infinite source of life and goodness. History, therefore, is moving toward a final perfection. At the end, human life will be redeemed and every human will attain his or her fullest expression as a creature created in the image of God. In that age, the infinite value, equality and uniqueness of every human being will be upheld by the socio-economic realities of the world; there will be no oppression or exploitation; there will be adequate resources to take care of every single life appropriately. The physical, emotional and relational aspects of the individual's life will be perfected. Judaism dreams that life will win out so that eventually even sickness and death will be overcome. Judaism affirms that this incredible perfection will be attained in this world, in actual human history. God, the ultimate source of life and energy, has made that promise. In return, the Jews pledged to live their lives in obedience to the divine mandate and as witnesses to the promised final perfection. This mutual pledge constitutes the covenant of the Jewish people.

The meaning of redemption that is central to Jewish tradition grew out of and is validated by an event in Jewish history: the Exodus, the freeing of the Hebrew slaves from bondage in Egypt. The lessons of the Exodus—that there is a redeeming God, that human power is not absolute and will not be permitted to oppress people indefinitely; and that freedom and dignity are the inherent rights of all individuals—will be universalized at the onset of the Messianic Age, which will be the culmination of history. Judaism has been guided by the Exodus as its orienting event since Biblical times. This orientation has set the basic direction, goal and operating methods of Judaism in history.

Since the religion is committed to the proposition that the final realization of the Exodus will take place in actual history and not in some other world or reality, the credibility and persuasive power of the promise of redemption rises and falls under the impact of historical events. History apparently confirms or denies the basic teaching. Jewish triumphs or rescues from evil traditionally have been perceived as confirmations of the promise of history. Occasionally, historical events were of such magnitude that they profoundly affected the understanding of the central model—one could not go on affirming the central message without taking the new event into account. Such events became orienting events themselves and were incorporated into the religion and way of life of the Jewish people.

Why should the vicissitudes of Jewish history affect divine teaching so much? According to the Bible, the Jewish people are the carriers of the message of redemption to the world. This people models moments of perfection, testifies to the future redemption and witnesses to the divine concern and presence which will bring it all about. Because God is infinite and beyond human comprehension, the news of God's presence and promise is communicated through the Jewish people. Therefore, the persuasiveness of the message is directly correlated to Jewish existence and Jewish life. The ultimate message of the infinite has been turned over to a flesh and blood people to deliver to others and to incarnate in its own life. While Jewish sociology and Jewish theology are not identical, they are profoundly inter-related.

The Jews are all too human. Even the heros and great religious figures of Jewish history are flawed, as are all humans. This fallibility is built into the divine assumptions; the sociological dynamics and personal needs of the people which are bound to shape, if not distort, every teaching are allowed for in the divine strategy of redemption. It follows that events which are everyday history in other people's annals become part of the sacred history of the Jewish people. Furthermore, the triumphs and tragedies of the Jews have direct effects on the believability and the understanding of the central message of redemption. For this reason, again, great events in Jewish history do not only affect the sociological or geographical condition of the Jews but directly influence their theological and cultural self-understanding. Consequently such events powerfully affect the legitimacy and credibility of Jewish institutions and that of Jewish leadership groups.

Classical Jewish theology holds that God continually calls into existence the leadership needed to guide the people and replaces or rejects those who do not measure up. But one need not even accept the notion of divine agency to see how powerfully sociology confirms this tendency. Leadership—especially political leadership—is primarily tested by its ability to insure the basic needs of security and livelihood. When the Jews ruled their own land, kings could stay in power by meeting these needs, even if they diverged from the higher purposes and values of the Jewish covenant. But the land of Israel was never insulated from outside cultures. In the final analysis, Jews were a miniscule minority. Only a mission of universal significance made it essential in their eyes that they go on living and testifying as Jews. The price of surrendering meaningful differences between Jewish and non-Jewish culture was the bleeding away of the Jews. Whenever the legitimacy of institutions or the persuasiveness of the content of Jewish testimony was shaken by events, the leadership quickly lost its following unless it could convincingly explain the events and make sense of the Jewish condition. It had to incorporate the event into the Jewish way and harmonize or correlate it with Jewish destiny. If it could not do so, the leadership itself gave up or lost its hold on the people. Leadership passed to any group that could again correlate the Jewish purpose and Jewish condition.

Because of the fragility of Jewish existence and the incredible breadth of Jewish claim to significance, Jewish history has been harsh to Jewish leadership. There is a continuous pressure which sweeps clean and insures the survival of the fittest. In the short run "the fittest" are not necessarily measured by a values standard; given the pressure which must be met, "fittest" is clearly defined by survival itself, not by the highest ideals of Judaism. In the long run, though, leaders who merely ensured survival while ignoring, repudiating or excessively diluting the religion's ultimate redemptive message would typically lose their effectiveness as Jews assimilated or as conditions changed again.

There need not be a fundamental transformation in the understanding of the redemption paradigm after each event. Given the power of inertia, the desire for the familiar and the power of cultural homeostasis, new evidence and developments are assimilated to the existing structures. Important changes may lead to the coexistence of newer institutions and leadership with the old. For example, the growth of prophecy in the monarchical period of Biblical history from the tenth to the sixth century B.C.E. did not overthrow the centrality of king and priest, or of the monarchy and the Temple, as the cultic center. The Temple retained its force because there the same God who spoke through prophets could be contacted and would speak to the masses through the priest. However, sometimes an event is so shattering or so transforms the basic Jewish condition that it cannot be simply assimilated to the central Jewish paradigm. Either the paradigm is changed or new institutions, theology and, consequently, new leadership are needed to make the whole amalgam cohere once again.

In retrospect, we can see that in all of Jewish history, there have been two grand fusions of basic condition, theological message, institutional performance and leadership group. Despite continuing shifts in local situations, institutions, practices and self-understanding, these four elements were so coherent that one may characterize the overall era as a unity. In each case, it took a fundamental change in condition to motivate the kind of transformation which led to a new synthesis. Yet the resolution was seen as a continuation of the previous pattern and the new Jewish equilibrium that emerged was perceived as a station on the way to the final goal. These two historical syntheses correspond to the Biblical and the Rabbinic eras. Each era oriented the Jewish way in the light of a major event. In the Biblical Age, the event was one of great redemption, the Exodus; in the Rabbinic Age, it was an event of great tragedy, the Destruction of the Temple. Remarkably enough, in this age the emergence of a new synthesis is taking place before our very eyes. The third era is beginning under the sign of a great event of destruction, the Holocaust, and a great event of redemption, the rebirth of the State of Israel.

THE BIBLICAL ERA

Historians and scholars, traditionalists and critics argue about the actual historical character of the Exodus and about how and in what sequence Biblical understandings flowed from it. Such arguments are important but they reflect the ideological agenda of modern culture, primarily the concern that the divine authority of the Bible would be challenged by different versions of its origins or by showing outside cultural parallels to its teachings. But, all this is a moot point from the perspective of the overall synthesis of the Biblical era. Whether the monotheism exemplified by the Exodus applies to all people immediately or centuries later; whether freedom from slavery initially applies only to Jews and later is generalized; whether the Exodus is the miraculous departure of more than a million Jewish slaves and families or the flight from Egypt of a small group of tribes and fellow travelers is secondary in light of the overarching unity of the Biblical period. Out of the Exodus, directly and through interpretation, by revelation and by generalization, come the teachings which revolutionized Jewish fate and humanity's history. Central to Biblical thought is the idea that there is an ultimate power that cares about humanity; that there is a fundamental human right to freedom and dignity; that the covenant makes the divine commandments binding on both ruler and ruled; and that there are basic laws by which human behavior should be guided as exemplified in the Ten Commandments.

According to Biblical teaching, whatever happens to Jews to form Jewish values also shapes the destiny of the world. It follows from the Exodus that, sooner or later, the entire world will be perfected. This concept implies that until that perfection is attained, one should not settle for anything less. Telling and retelling the Exodus story and its underlying event has been the Jewish religious vocation. Out of this soil grew the Christian teaching of salvation that passed over to other nations and changed the values of half the world. Centuries later, in secularized form, the redemption paradigm was the seed for Marxism's insistence that the dispossessed must revolt and that all institutions will be overthrown until a final equality is reached. Millenarian movements in earlier centuries and liberation theology in the twentieth century have turned this idea toward the political and economic spheres while preserving its religious ground with explosive effects on the status quo. Alfred North Whitehead, the great British philosopher, has argued that the Biblical idea of an orderly created universe whose laws can be discovered combined with the idea of perfecting the world gave rise to Western culture in which science, treating nature lawfully yet instrumentally, can grow.[1] Hence, Jewish values and culture have shaped political behavior, shaken the local culture of billions of people in the modern period and stimulated some of the great dynamic thrusts of Western culture.

The great internal struggle of the Biblical era lay in coping with the challenge of Jewish sovereignty and statehood while trying to live up to covenantal values. The land of Israel was located at a highly strategic crossroads of the world, along the invasion routes between Europe, Asia and Africa. Thus,

---

1. Alfred North Whitehead, *Science and the Modern World* (New York: Macmillan, 1926).

every world empire sooner or later marched its armies on the road to Jerusalem. The vulnerability and fragility of Jewish existence in the land was exacerbated by the relatively small Jewish population and the continual magnetism of foreign cultures. International pressure made a central ruler an inescapable necessity, so the monarchy was instituted over the opposition of tribal loyalties, religious objections and other centrifugal forces. But the monarchs and ruling classes into whose hands Jewish fate was consigned were continually forced or drawn into active contact with outside powers which only increased the cultural vulnerability of the Hebrew religion. It was difficult to live up to covenantal values of dignity for the weak or freedom for Hebrew slaves when comfort, power and the need for defense conspired to legitimize self-interest and the rule of might makes right. The dialectic of power and covenantal values was fought out in confrontations between prophets and kings, even as the need for legitimacy and religious guidance unified kings, priests and court prophets.

How noble to us, but how naive to their contemporaries, the prophets appeared as, in the name of God, they made their demands for absolute righteousness and immediate freedom for the slaves. I recall how moved I was as a child by *Jeremiah*, Chapter 34, in which the prophet chastises the kings and nobles for their failure to live up to the covenant and free the Hebrew slaves after six years. How powerful the message and how unequivocal! The nobility had not kept the covenant and God would therefore give the people into the hands of the Babylonians as slaves. When I grew up and became an administrator, my perspective changed. I envisioned the king and nobility desperately trying to build defenses as the mighty armies of Babylonia drew near. It was hard enough to build fortresses under the best of conditions. Now they had to use all the labor—both free and slave—they could get. Without adequate defenses, the people of God could well be crushed and destroyed! Yet, at the moment of gravest danger, the prophet—that wild man—walks in and says: "Let the slaves go free!" Obviously, kings cannot depend on the insubstantial words of prophets for national security. Government must defend its people or fail totally. The prophet speaks with all the idealism of a man who never met a payroll in his life!

Of course, the "realist" version is likewise incomplete. If pure political calculation was to win out, the sense of Jewish calling would dissipate, leaving Israel and Judea totally vulnerable to disintegration and assimilation. Fortunately, in Biblical times, periodic phases of religious renewal maintained some balance of values and power. Nevertheless, in the Biblical period, the prophets did not, by and large, succeed with the masses. Their uncompromising demands, coming from a source beyond the people, were too far away from the equivocal realities of everyday life. Later the Rabbis, operating out of the people's reality, compromised and improved matters, step-by-step. They educated the people, and finally uplifted them to the point where they accepted the prophets as normative and saw prophetic ethics as within reach.

During the Biblical era, the covenantal relationship itself was marked by a high degree of divine intervention. God's manifest presence in the Temple was the cultic counterpart of prophecy. Even as God spoke directly to Israel through prophets, so at Jerusalem the divine could be contacted. The awe and power of the place demanded that Israelites go through careful ritual purification before entering. Unauthorized encounters with the divine presence led to instant death.[2]

The same overt divine intervention expressed itself in the events of Biblical history. When Israel obeyed the Lord, it was victorious. When it strayed, it was defeated. Defeat, itself, was the best proof that disobedience had taken place. Thus, the setback to Joshua's invading army at Ai—coming as it did after the great victory at Jericho—was quickly traceable to the sacrilegious taking of booty by a man named Achan.[3] "Stand and see the salvation of the Lord," says Moses. "God will fight for you and you will hold your peace."[4] These words precede the splitting of the Red Sea, the triumphal moment of the Exodus when divine power finally and completely shattered Pharaoh's human might, underscoring the ultimate weakness and relativity of all human power. This overwhelming divine might was the best proof of God's presence and God's existence. Human power denied God's might.[5] At this moment of divine triumph, Israel saw the great hand, feared the Lord and believed.[6] The covenant may be a partnership but it is very clear that God is the initiator, the senior partner, who punishes, rewards and enforces the partnership if the Jews slacken. In the stinging words of Ezekiel, "You say, we will be as the nations. . . . As I live, says the Lord God, with a strong hand and an outstretched arm and with poured out fury . . . I will rule over you."[7]

In sum, during the Biblical period, the way of redemption is marked by a growing sense of mission; both manifest divinity and holiness are expressed in cult and prophecy. The primary institutions of Temple, priests and prophets

2. Cf. Leviticus 10:10; II Samuel 6:6ff.
3. Joshua, Chapter 7.
4. Exodus 14:13–14.
5. Exodus 10:1–2.
6. Exodus 14:31.
7. Ezekiel 20:32–33.

and the Jewish leadership reflect the active intervention of the divine in Jewish life as well as the struggle to live with the tensions between the covenant and realpolitik. This entire complex was first challenged and then transformed in the aftermath of the Temple's destruction and the people of Israel's exile.

THE RABBINIC ERA

The destruction of the Second Temple and the succeedingly crushing defeats of the Jews in 70 and 135 C.E., after wars that bled Judea white, generated a major crisis of faith and meaning in the Jewish people. The massive loss of life, the sale of tens of thousands of Jews into slavery and the triumph of Rome despite the conviction of Jewish Zealots that God alone should rule Israel, deepened the questions. Was there not God? Had God been overpowered by the Roman gods? Had God rejected the covenant with Israel and allowed his people and Holy Temple to be destroyed? Were the traditional channels of divine love, forgiveness and blessing now closed to the Jewish people?

Today it is hard to recapture the monumental importance of those questions in the first century. It is now 1900 years after the Rabbis resolved the crisis of faith that followed the Temple's destruction. We are the beneficiaries of the Rabbis' achievement and of the ways they responded to the questions. Their responses are so entrenched in the tradition as to blur the importance of the questions they answered. In that powerful and undermining crisis of faith, at least one group of Jews concluded that Judaism was finished following the destruction. Christian Jews until then had operated within the covenant of Judaism, praying in synagogues and regarding Jesus as the fulfillment of the Messianic promises within Judaism. The polarizing effect of the Roman wars, the spread of Christianity primarily among Gentiles but not Jews and the destruction of the Temple convinced them that they had misread the signs. The razing of the sanctuary meant that the old channels of atonement and connection with God, which they initially thought were being paralleled in Jesus, were in fact blotted out by the destruction. They concluded that Jesus was not a continuation of the Jewish way but a *new* channel of salvation. The Gospels were a *New* Testament, not a section of the Old; Jesus' life was the occasion of a new covenant, not merely a renewed one. The destruction meant that Jesus' sacrifice must have replaced the Temple and Judaism. This reinterpretation of Jesus' life was to guide them over the next section of the road to final perfection. Paradoxically enough, the Christian Jews were very Jewish in their thinking when they concluded that the Temple's destruction was a great historical event that held a religious message for them.

The Christian analysis was shared by other Jews. The Sadducees, especially the court nobility and the priests, could not envision Judaism without a temple. When they proved unable to rebuild the sanctuary, the Sadducees could not cope with the Jewish people's situation and religious needs and so faded from the scene. Indeed, many Pharisees and Rabbis shared the Sadducees' analysis and poured enormous efforts into trying to rebuild the Temple. Some declared they would have no children and no celebrations — they would allow no normal life — until the Temple was restored. Although Rabbi Akiva reassured the Jews that even without the Temple, it was possible to obtain atonement directly from God, he nonetheless gave all-out support to Bar Kochba's desperate attempt to recapture independence and rebuild the Holy Sanctuary. Akiva went so far as to endorse Bar Kochba as the Messiah. It was all in vain. The Romans were too powerful. Had the Temple-centered view triumphed, the Jews would have put all their effort into regaining Jerusalem, a policy that would have spelled frustration, spiritual exhaustion and, finally, devastation.

Another effect of the destruction and exile was the increased exposure of Jews to the external culture. By destroying the major lodestone of Jewish life and, through geographic dispersion, immersing more Jews in Greek culture, the destruction exposed Jews to the extraordinary magnetism of Hellenism. Hellenism was a cosmopolitan, sophisticated culture led by an affluent and pleasure-seeking elite that had already drawn many followers from the Jewish leadership. The loss of the Jewish land brought Hellenism to the masses, as well. In fact, Jewry could not have maintained itself in the face of this competition but for the Rabbis' development of a more learned and more internalized Jewish practice and value system.

The Rabbis responded with what became the first public education system for adults. If the direct connection to the Temple was lost, then Torah study would enable the Jews to internalize the teachings and values of God's way. This would allow them to confront the challenge of Hellenism and the more open society in which they lived following the Dispersion. Study was glorified as the ultimate mitzvah in the saying "Talmud Torah (Study of Torah) equals them all."[8] The Beit Knesset (House of Assembly/Synagogue) was made into a Beit Midrash (House of Study). Opportunities for study were built into the services and the home liturgies. All aspects of life could be suffused with Jewish values and the meanings taught through actions and words.

8. *Mishnah Peah* 1:1.

The Rabbis' fundamental theological breakthrough was a kind of secularization insight. The manifest divine presence and activity was being reduced but the covenant was actually being renewed. God had not rejected the Jews, but rather had called them to a new stage of relationship and service. From where did the Rabbis draw the authority to take charge of Jewish religion and destiny, to expand required observance in every area of life, to shape new institutions and to legitimize the use of their minds and reason as the key source for deriving knowledge of "what does the Lord require of thee?" The unspoken, oft-used axiom is the unfolding of the covenantal model. The Jewish people, the passive partner in the Biblical covenant, is being urged to assume a new level of responsibility by its divine counterpart. If Israel's phylacteries praise God as the *echad*, the unique one, its God also wears phylacteries which contain the praise of Israel: "Who is like your people, Israel, one unique nation in the earth?" The Divine Partner becomes more restrained, more hidden, more intimate in relationship to the Jews.

In the Biblical period, God's presence was manifest by splitting the Red Sea and drowning the Egyptians. In the Second Temple siege, God did not show up, like the cavalry in the last scene of a Western movie, to save the day. God had, as it were, withdrawn, become more hidden, so as to give humans more freedom and to call the Jews to more responsible partnership in the covenant. Rabbi Joshua ben Levi said that God's might, shown in Biblical times by destroying the wicked, is now manifest in divine self-control. The *Ethics of the Fathers* say: "Who is mighty? He who exercises self-restraint."[9] God allows the wicked to act without being cut off immediately.[10] The great Biblical praise of God as "great, mighty and awesome" found in Deuteronomy[11] is used as the model of divine praise for the opening of the central Rabbinic prayer, the Amidah, the standing, silent prayer, *but the meaning is reversed.* God's might is expressed in allowing human freedom instead of punishing the wicked.

Although the central Biblical idea of covenant implies a treaty between two sides, nowhere in the Bible is the term "partner" or "partnership" used. Divine intervention is so overwhelming that the term partnership is hardly appropriate. One of the Rabbis' most powerful ideas is that the people Israel and the individual Jew become partners of God through religious activity. "He who prays on the eve of Sabbath and chants *Vayechulu* ("And the heavens and the earth were complete," Genesis 2:1) becomes, as it were, *a part-*

9. *Ethics of the Fathers* 4:1.
10. *Yoma* 69b.
11. Deuteronomy 10:17.

ner to the Holy One, blessed be He, in the work of creation" (italics sup-
plied).[12] A judge who gives true judgment[13] and one who observes the holy
days[14] become partners with God.

A world in which God is more hidden is a more secular world. Paradoxically, this secularization makes possible the emergence of the synagogue
as the central place of Jewish worship. In the Temple, God was manifest.
Visible holiness was concentrated in one place. A more hidden God can be
encountered everywhere, but one must look and find. The visible presence
of God in the Temple gave a sacramental quality to the cultic life of the sanctuary. Through the High Priest's ministrations and the scapegoat ceremony,
the national sins were forgiven and a year of rain and prosperity assured. In
the synagogue, the community's prayers are more powerful and elaborate
than the individual's but the primary effect grows out of the individual's own
merits and efforts. One may enter the synagogue at all times without the
elaborate purification required for Temple entrance because sacredness is
more shielded in the synagogue. In the Temple era God spoke directly,
through prophecy or through the *urim* and *tumim* breastplate. In the synagogue, God does not speak. The human-divine dialogue goes on through
human address to God.[15] Prayer, which we view today as a visibly sacred
activity, was, by contrast with Temple worship, a more secular act. Prayer
became the central religious act because of the silence of God.

The classic expression of the broadening and diffusion of holiness is the
Rabbinic application of Temple purity standards to the home and other non-
sacred settings, a process that started before the destruction. Indeed, Jacob
Neusner suggests that the Oral Torah—the Rabbi's primary document—
existed from Sinai as a Torah for the world outside the cult, paralleling and
completing the written Torah which was written for the cult. However, the
"worldly" Torah won out when Rabbinic leadership won out in the aftermath
of the Temple's destruction. The Rabbinic interpretation and intertwining
of the two Torahs shaped the understanding which became dominant for
those who survived as Jews. Temple holiness was metaphysically applied to
everyday acts of life. By washing hands ritually before the meal and by learning Torah at the meal, the table becomes an altar. The Shechinah, the divine
presence, is there when people eat together and exchange words of Torah,

12. *Shabbat* 119b.
13. *Shabbat* 10a.
14. *Pesikta Zutrati Pinchas.*
15. Joseph B. Soloveitchik, "The Lonely Man of Faith," *Tradition* 7:2 (Summer 1965): 37.

or when even one person studies Torah. "The Shechinah is at the head of the bed when one visits the sick."[16] "When husband and wife are loving and worthy, the Divine Presence is between them."[17] Blessings to express gratitude and the awareness of God were articulated for every moment of life from awakening to going to sleep, from feeling or flexing muscles to urination or defecation. In effect, the blessings help the individual discover the divine that is hidden in the everyday secular society.

The Rabbis were a more secular leadership than priests or prophets. Priests were born to holiness and were bound to ritually circumscribed lives. The Rabbis won their status through learning and were not bound to sacramental requirements different from the average Jew. Prophets spoke the unmediated word of God: "Thus, saith the Lord. . . ." By contrast, the Rabbi judged what God asks of us by the best exercise of his judgment, guided by his knowledge of the past record of God's instruction—the Biblical models and the legal precedents. The Rabbis stated that prophecy had ended with the destruction and the exile. In fact, however, Biblical prophets such as Ezekiel had prophesied during the Babylonian exile. What the Rabbis really meant, then, was prescriptive. After the second destruction, there can be no prophecy. If God has withdrawn, then prophecy is inappropriate. Prophecy is the communicative counterpart of splitting the Red Sea! Rabbinic guidance is the theological counterpart of a hidden God.

The prophets gave clear, unambiguous instruction from God. If two prophets disagreed about the divine mandate, one of the two was a false prophet. But if human judgment is the new source of understanding, then two Rabbis can come to different conclusions. The Talmud captures the uneasiness caused by this departure from the old certainty by stating that when the students of Hillel and Shammai did not serve their teachers properly, disagreements as to the law multiplied. People feared that the two schools' opposing views could not coexist and therefore, one school's view must be false. After three years of anxiety, prayer and seeking divine guidance, a heavenly voice told them that "both views are the words of the Living God."[18] Since humans are being given more responsibility for leading Israel on its redemptive way, then it is right that there be more than one path to follow. For practical reasons, the majority decides which of the two paths shall be followed but the views of the minority are *not* wrong. The authority for this

16. *Shabbat* 12b.
17. *Sota* 17a.
18. *Eruvim* 13b.

transition comes from the old source, a heavenly voice, but one which can only speak to confirm the new Rabbinic responsibility.

The famous Rabbinic story of Rabbi Eliezer ben Hyrkenus' refusal to accept a majority vote against his legal ruling takes on new meaning in light of this analysis. Rabbi Eliezer evokes three divine miracles and a heavenly voice to prove that his view of the divine will was correct but he was still overruled.[19] The story is not merely an example of the democratic assertion of human authority. Rather, it shows the Rabbis in action, willing to face the consequences of divine withdrawal. If the human power is to be more responsible, then God cannot intervene in the legal process with miracles and heavenly voices such as Rabbi Eliezer had invoked. The majority of the Rabbis must rule. It is surely no coincidence that Rabbi Eliezer was a part of the first generation of students of Rabbi Yohanan ben Zakkai, the great leader of the Rabbinic response to the Temple destruction. Rabbi Eliezer's excommunication for his refusal to accept the majority opinion also makes sense. It is a harsh penalty but it is asserted in a generation which is struggling to affirm the calling of the Jews to responsibility. The Rabbis' own hesitations and inner divisions about assuming the authority to interpret the divine mandate create the need to punish disobedience.

The Rabbis recognized that God's withdrawal and their own new authority meant that an event such as the Exodus in which God directly intervened would not occur again. This led them to postulate a new central redemptive event for their age. The Rabbis saw Purim as the redemptive paradigm for the post-destruction world. In the Purim story, the Jewish people in exile after the first destruction is threatened with genocide. The nation is saved by the actions of Esther and Mordecai. Operating as fallible and flawed human redeemers, the two manage, by court intrigues and bedroom politics, to save the Jewish people and win permission for the Jews to fight off their enemies. The Rabbis point out that the story of Esther marks the end of redemptive miracles; it is not a miracle, it is a natural event. In justifying the new holiday of Purim, the Rabbis connect Esther's name to the Biblical verse "I (the Lord) will hide (*asteer* in Hebrew, closely resembling the word *Esther*) my face on that day."[20] God's name does not appear in the book of Esther, yet this hidden presence is the redemptive force which the people acknowledge. In an incredibly bold analogy, the Rabbis go one step beyond, comparing Purim to Sinai as a moment of covenant acceptance. They say

19. *Baba Metzia* 59b.
20. Deuteronomy 31:18.

acceptance of the covenant at Sinai was "coerced" by the manifest miracles of God and would not be legally binding today. However, on Purim the Jewish people reaccepted that covenant by recognizing God's presence and salvation in the guise of the secular redemption.[21] This acceptance was binding because it occurred in the context of a world in which God does not split the sea but works in mysterious ways through human redeemers. Thus, the reacceptance of the covenant is legally the equivalent of the Jewish people's maturation and the acknowledgment of their new responsibilities.

Of course there are no neat dividing lines in history. People are too conditioned by their habitual modes of thinking to make total breaks in response to any event. The kernel of the synagogue and of the major Rabbinic theological themes existed before the destruction and were available for development.[22] "God prepares the medicine before the sickness comes," said the Rabbis. And the Rabbis were neither consistent nor total secularizers. They invoked divine intervention through miracles throughout this era. But God's intervention was perceived in more limited forms and without *manifest* participation in major historical events. The shift in Judaism is a percentage shift but the effect—in terms of theological understanding, the perception of the Jewish people's role and the development of new centers—is a new era. Having successfully interpreted and coped with the new Jewish condition, the new cadre of Rabbis replaced the Biblical leadership groups.

This argument is not meant to suggest that the Rabbis won strictly on the theological merits. In all historical situations, sociology and theology interact. Jacob Neusner has pointed to the Rabbis' link-up with the Babylonian ruling authorities. Their role as civil servants undergirded their spiritual role with political power and legitimacy.[23] Still the Rabbis' ability to interpret the meaning of Jewish fate, to give assurance that the covenant was not broken, to broaden holiness and make it available everywhere and to teach their values to disciples and the masses made their victory possible. Indeed, they were most suited to interpret the meaning of the new Jewish condition of powerlessness and exile. Their teaching and halachic developments gave

21. *Shabbat* 88a.

22. See on this, Jacob Neusner, "Emergent Rabbinic Judaism in a time of Crisis: Four Responses to the Destruction of the Second Temple," in *Early Rabbinic Judaism* (Leiden: E. J. Brill, 1975), pp. 34–49. See also, Neusner, A *Life of Yochanan Ben Zakkai*, 1st ed. (Leiden: E. J. Brill, 1962).

23. Jacob Neusner, *There We Sat Down: Talmudic Judaism in the Making* (Nashville: Abingdon Press, 1971).

sustenance to a people that had lost the power of policy-making and of deciding its own fate.

Although the long exile led to many dispersions, persecutions and changing cultural conditions, there was enough flexibility and dynamism in the system to adjust to new conditions. Some of the crises generated major new developments. The Spanish expulsion brought Kabbalah to the fore as a means of interpreting and overcoming the disaster. Kabbalah gave new inner content and theological models to the Rabbinic system. The Sabbetai Zvi false messianic movement in the seventeenth century shook and divided Rabbinic leadership. Later, social estrangement and spiritual isolation in Eastern Europe brought Hasidism into being, replacing Rabbis with Rebbes. Yet all these developments can be seen as articulations or modifications of the Rabbinic synthesis. The basic unity of a condition of relative political powerlessness; of a hidden or more withdrawn God; of synagogues as institutional centers; and of Rabbinic leadership gave coherence to the second era of Jewish history.

The Rabbinic synthesis was continuous with the Biblical. The carrier people of salvation was the same: Israel. The covenantal goal was the same: redemption. The covenantal partner was the same: God. However, the level of Jewish participation was transformed. The Rabbis were aware of their role in transforming Judaism. Yet they insisted that their teachings were derived directly from Sinai. One Rabbinic legend captures this dialectic superbly: Moses, visiting Rabbi Akiva's academy, was totally unable to comprehend the form and details of the Torah study there and he grew faint at the shock of his ignorance. He was revived and reassured when a master told his disciple that the Torah he is teaching was from Moses at Sinai.[24]

Finally, it should be pointed out that the influence of the Rabbinic synthesis did not stop with the Jewish people. Despite the relative isolation and pariah status of the Jews and despite their outsider status in Christian and, often, in Moslem societies, Rabbinic Judaism affected the world. Islam was formed under the influence of Rabbinic Judaism. Medieval Christianity was influenced by Judaism. One might also argue that the tremendous Rabbinic expansion of the law and articulation of the covenant played an important role in shaping the parameters of Western constitutional thought and its focus on the law. Thus did Jewry and Judaism—being truthful to themselves and sharing their story with the outside world—play the role of witness and source of blessing in the second era. Yet, that era too has come to an end in the twentieth century.

24. *Menachot* 29b.

THE THIRD ERA THAT WASN'T

Judaism's first confrontation with modernity can be analyzed as an initial attempt to enter a third era. In the late eighteenth and nineteenth centuries, drawn by the dynamic modern culture, Jews were pulled from rural and pre-modern ghettoes into the cities and the frontiers of the new world aborning. The remarkable flowering of ideals—democracy, liberalism, socialism, revolution, to mention only a few—seemed to many Jews to offer the possibility of a basic transformation of the Jewish condition from outsider to full participant, from pariah to equal citizen of the nation or of the world. To many Jews, fundamental theological transformations were dictated by the new culture. For some, God could be dispensed with as men took charge of human fate. For others, the concepts of God and Judaism were transformed by rational or evolutionary criteria. The result was the (re)casting of Judaism into more universal, rational forms by Reform Judaism; into modern, more folk-oriented criteria by Conservative Judaism and later by Reconstructionism; or by secular standards ranging from Zionism to Ethical Culture.

New leadership emerged in the Jewish community, its authority validated by a superior relationship with the modern culture's authorities. Thus, in the early modern period access to Gentile ruling circles bestowed leadership on people whose life style and involvement had moved them out of the traditional community. Affluence, political links, philanthropy and competence in modern culture became keys to Jewish community leadership. Access to modern culture became a more important power source than access to traditional culture. One can trace the growing modernity in Eastern Europe by a shift in the alliances between riches and learning when rabbinic students were replaced by university educated beaus as preferred matches for daughters of wealthy families.

New organizations arose to represent Jewish interests and care for Jewish redemption. The Zionists felt that a basic change in the Jewish condition could only come about by reestablishment of Jewish sovereignty. For others, the basic change took the form of citizenship in a host country or in some worldwide humanitarian movement. Reform Jews spoke freely of the end of Rabbinic Judaism. Nowhere is the dynamic of the new era captured as well as in American Reform's Pittsburgh Platform of 1886 which speaks of "the modern era" as "the approach of the realization of Israel's great Messianic hope for the establishment of the kingdom of truth, justice and peace among all men." Of course, to the Rabbis in Pittsburgh, the fundamental change in the Jewish condition was the giving up of nationhood and attaining full participation in the world, as a religious community.

In retrospect, we see that this initial attempt to enter a third era of Judaism was stillborn and did not change the fundamental Jewish condition. The Holocaust showed that Jewish powerlessness had not changed in the modern period. As the catastrophe revealed, the real change was that the oppressive power that could be brought to bear on the Jews had been enormously multiplied by the unfolding technology and bureaucracy of modern culture. The theological transformations induced by modernity ultimately came under review and fire. No new leadership cadres and institutions totally won out in Jewish life, although they did begin to develop. Still, modernity had an enormous impact on Jews and Jewish culture, primarily by universalizing Judaism or substituting universalisms for Judaism and Jewish identity. But modernity was an outside force. Using it as the touchstone for the emergence of a third era constitutes the imposition of external categories on Jewish history. In any event, for many Jews this cut-to-measure Judaism has been overturned by the Holocaust and the rebirth of Israel. The Holocaust posed a radical challenge to all the hopes and assertions of modernity as it did to Jewish existence itself. And Israel reborn cast its own spell on Jews, drawing them to the central significance of redemption and the nature of Jewish life in our time. For those Jews who will remain Jewish, these events do impact Jewish history—they neutralize and even shatter the magnet of modernity. Future ages will recognize that in these two events of destruction and redemption the third era of Jewish history was born.

Modernity is not likely to be rejected by the Jews. The Holocaust assured modernity's triumph by killing off 90 percent of the Jewish groups that still actively resisted modern culture. But modern values are likely to be filtered and recast in the Jewish categories of existence. The earlier overwhelming rush to modernity will be seen as a temporary jiggle on the graph of Jewish history and destiny. The question that must be posed is this: If the Biblical era, under the sign of the Exodus, produced a Bible which has been a central values force in Western culture; and if the Rabbinic era, under the sign of the Second Temple's destruction, produced a Talmud and many other treasures that also affected humanity; then what will be the outcome of an era that grows out of both an event of destruction unparalleled in Jewish history and an event of redemption that rivals the Exodus?

THE THIRD ERA

About 6,000,000 Jews were killed in the Holocaust, approximately one third of the world's Jewish population. But the Holocaust cut even deeper. It is estimated that more than 80 percent of the Rabbis, Judaica scholars and full-time Talmud students alive in 1939 were dead by 1945. Ninety percent of Eastern European Jewry—the biological and cultural heartland of Jewry—was decimated.

The Nazis sought to wipe out Judaism, not just Jews. Before they were killed, Jews were denied access to synagogues, mikvehs and kosher food. They were stripped of Jewish learning, opportunities and cultural resources. Parents were forced to choose between their own survival or their children's and children were told to sacrifice elderly parents or face their own deaths. Nazi round-ups and *aktionen* were systematically scheduled for Shabbat and Jewish holidays to poison reverence and depress Jews on those days. In persecution, as in life, Jewish existence and faith were inseparable. Theologically speaking, the decision to kill every last Jew was an attempt to kill God, the covenantal partner known to humanity through the Jewish people's life and history. As the frenzy of mass killing unfolded, the murderers sought to make Jewish life less worthy of care and respect, ever cheaper to eliminate. The total assault on the value and dignity of the Jew—an absolute contradiction of the Jewish belief in the infinite value of human life—reached a stunningly successful climax in the summer of 1944 when thousands of Jewish children were thrown into the burning pits while still alive in order to economize on the two-fifths of a cent worth of Zyklon B it would have taken to gas them first. This triumph of murder and oppression was and still is countertestimony to the Jewish witness that life will triumph over death and that redemption is the fate of humanity. The Nazi assault shattered the covenant of redemption.

Thus, the third era opens with a crisis of faith and meaning that dwarfs the earlier ones. The burning children challenge the faith in a God who cares; the meanness and cruelty of the deaths of 6,000,000 Jews and the apathy and indifference of the world toward their deaths make the dream of perfection appear to be an illusion.

Those who seek to minimize the religious significance of the Holocaust argue that there have been other catastrophes in Jewish life and that there is nothing especially decisive about this one. Actually, the opposite is closer to the truth. Lesser disasters had a profound impact on Judaism. The Kabbalah's spread and triumph in Jewish life was made possible and even necessary by the need for consolation and redemptive hope and meaning after the expulsion from Spain. And both the Shabbetai Zvi false messianic movement and Hasidism's growth owed a great deal to the search for meaning after the Chmelnitsky mass pogroms of the seventeenth century.

The Nazi decision to kill every last Jew and their near success raised the crisis to a whole new level. When Richard Rubenstein wrote that after

Auschwitz "we live in the time of 'the death of God,'" he meant that hope of redemption was destroyed. Rubenstein quotes an Isaac Bashevis Singer character who states that "Death is the Messiah." He concludes that "the world will forever remain a place of pain . . . and ultimate defeat."[25] Rubenstein thus expresses the dimensions of the crisis well, although his response is not representative of the Jewish people and I do not believe that his views will prevail. What is underway is an enormous communal and theological effort by the Jewish people to confront the challenges of the Holocaust and to integrate this unassimilable surd into the Jewish midrash on history. That response is shaping the third era.

At the same time, the redemption inherent in the rebirth of Israel puts it on a par with the Exodus. Three hundred thousand survivors were taken from hunger, psychic wounding and memories of terror, from statelessness and marginality, and given a chance for a renewed and dignified life in the state of Israel. The ascent from the depths of the slavery and genocide of Auschwitz or Sobibor to the heights of Jerusalem reborn surpasses the climb from the slavery and slaying of children in Egypt to Mount Sinai. In addition, 800,000 Jews came to Israel from Arab lands where most had lived as second class citizens, many in a state of pre-modern poverty and illiteracy. While the Sephardim's integration into Israeli society has been less than perfect, the net improvement in their lives has been enormous. The same can be said of Soviet Jewry and other groups of immigrants. The restoration of Jewish sovereignty after 1900 years and the reunification of Jerusalem only confirm Israel's rebirth as a redemptive event of historic magnitude.

The Holocaust and the rebirth of Israel are profoundly linked yet dialectically opposed to each other, deepening the power of these events over Jewish self-understanding. Does the Holocaust disprove the classic Jewish teaching of redemption? Does Israel validate it? Does mass murder overwhelm the divine concern? How should we understand the covenant after such a devastating and isolating experience? Can the Jewish condition be the same after sovereignty is regained? These questions are being answered by the lives of the Jewish people. Already the basic condition of the Jewish people has changed. New institutions have grown up. New leadership is emerging that offers credible visions of Jewish purpose and methods of coping with the challenge of Jewish existence. That this is not clear stems from the fact that, by contrast with the past, today there are no universally accepted interpretations—or interpreters—of Jewish life. The lack of clarity is an his-

25. Richard Rubenstein, *After Auschwitz* (Indianapolis: Bobbs-Merrill Company, 1966).

torical optical illusion. Only in retrospect do the prophets stand out as the authoritative interpreters of the Biblical experience. Only in hindsight, and after their rivals have faded from Jewish history, do the Rabbis clearly appear to give the correct understanding of Jewish life's transformation after the destruction. Yet one cannot sit out history and wait for an official guideline. Most people react to a new situation by trying to act as they did before the orienting event occurred or by using their inherited models as best they can to respond to the new challenge. However, if we study Jewish behavior since 1940, we can discern the outlines of an emerging new synthesis in Jewish life and culture.

THE HIDDENNESS OF GOD: OR, HOLY SECULARITY

The key Rabbinic insight that led to the transformation of the covenant after the destruction was the understanding that God had become more hidden. God's withdrawal respected human freedom and was a call to Jews to assume a more responsible partnership in the covenant. If God was more hidden after the destruction of the Temple, how much more hidden must God be in the world after the Holocaust? Thus, religious activity itself must be profoundly immersed in the secular, where God is hidden. In fact, this has been the primary thrust of Jewish activity since 1945.

There are good theological reasons that there be less talk about God now. Faith is living life in the presence of the Redeemer, even when the world is unredeemed. After Auschwitz, there are moments when the Redeemer and the vision of redemption are present and moments when the flames and smoke of burning children blot out faith.[26] But even when faith reasserts itself, the smoke of Auschwitz obscures the presence of God.

Heinrich Himmler, the man in charge of the final solution, told Felix Kersten that he insisted members of the S.S. believe in God, otherwise "we should be no better than the [atheistic] Marxists." Many of the defense affidavits introduced at the trial of Einsatzgruppen (shooting squads) leaders spoke of their religiosity. In December 1941, the Commander of the German 11th army in the Crimea told the head of the Einsatzkommando in Simferopol to finish killing the Jews *before* Christmas (so killing on the day itself would not spoil the holiday spirit). The Vatican and other churches protested the deportation of Jews converted to Christianity but not of Jews

---

26. Irving Greenberg, "Cloud of Smoke, Pillar of Fire," in *Auschwitz: Beginning of a New Era?* ed. Eva Fleishchner (New York: Ktav, 1977), p. 27.

who were still Jews. In light of such behavior, it is incumbent on religious people to hide the divine presence until the murderers and the indifferent will have forgotten about God and released God's name from the grip of evil.

Elsewhere I have suggested that "no statement, theological or otherwise, should be made that would not be credible in the presence of burning children."[27] This suggests that we are entering a period of silence in theology — a silence that corresponds to profound hiddenness. The fundamental religious act is the reaffirmation of faith, redemption and meaningfulness through acts of love and life giving. Indeed, creating life is only possible out of enormous faith in ultimate redemption and a willingness to risk the worst suffering to keep the covenantal chain going. In an age when one is ashamed or embarrassed to talk about God in the presence of burning children, the creation of an image of God — viz, a human being of infinite value, equality and uniqueness — is an act that speaks even louder than words. This image points beyond itself to transcendence. The human vessel imprinted with the image of God testifies by its very existence to the source of that image. Perhaps this testimony is the only statement about God we can make.

The religious enterprise is an all-out, even desperate attempt to create, save and heal the image of God. Every departure from the standard of human beings' infinite value, equality and uniqueness, becomes a confirmation of the Holocaust's denial of God. Thus, past acceptance of the inequality of the other, and residual denigration of the infinite value of another, become intolerable in an age when the entire religious witness is all but overwhelmed by the mass weight and countertestimony of six million dead. Indeed, creating life is only possible where there is enormous faith in the meaningfulness of ultimate redemption. Yet, the very acts of love and conception, justice and equality, concern and respect of uniqueness are generally viewed as secular activities. Hence, the paradox that in the third era, the primary scene of religious activity must be the secular.

The Talmud asked: If God is profoundly hidden after the destruction, how do we know God's presence? How do we know God is awesome? The answer is: The ongoing existence of the Jewish people testifies to it. How else can the Jewish people, one nation alone in a world of hostile or apathetic nations, like a sheep among seventy wolves, survive? How else but that there is a hidden force field, the Divine, that is with it?![28] Thus the physical presence of the Jewish people — and that existence is made possible by secular Israelis as well as religious Jews — is the best testimony to the Divine.

27. Ibid., p. 23.
28. *Yoma* 69b.

To restore the credibility of redemption, there must be an extraordinary outburst of life and redeeming work in the world. The State of Israel, including its rehabilitation of more than a million survivors and Oriental Jews, is the Jewish people's fundamental act of life and meaning after Auschwitz. The great Biblical sign of the ongoing validity of the covenant—the affirmation of God and hope—is the restoration of Jewry to Israel.[29] Yet, the State shifts the balance of Jewish activity and concern to the secular enterprises of society building, social justice and human politics. The revelation of Israel is a call to secularity; the religious enterprise must focus on the mundane.

This secularism must not be confused with atheism or the celebration of the death of God. The claims of absolute secular humanism have been shattered in the Holocaust. The absence of limits or belief in a judge led directly to the belief that humans can become God and can hold the ultimate power of life and death. Mengele and other selectors at Auschwitz openly joked about this, especially when they scheduled selections for Yom Kippur—the day when, according to Jewish tradition, God decides who shall live and who shall die. A world in which humans are grounded in the infinite is a world in which humans have infinite value. If we have human, finite gods, then the image of God must be reduced proportionately as it was reduced in Auschwitz to "an anonymous mass . . . non-men who march and labor in silence, the divine spark dead with them . . . on whose face and in whose eyes not a trace of thought is to be seen. . . ."[30] At the heart of this new secular effort to recreate the infinite value of the human being is a hidden relationship to God's presence in history and a lovingkindness that, out of faith in redemption, defies death and evil. The old categories of secular and religious are undone. Religion is as religion does; all the rest is talk.

Here we come to the paradox of the Rabbis' insight. After the destruction, God was more hidden but the divine presence could be found in more places. If the divine presence resided on Jerusalem's holy mount, then the hidden God could be found everywhere. So synagogues could be located anywhere. By this logic, the God who, after the Holocaust, is even more profoundly hidden must be found everywhere. The divine is experienced neither as the intervening, commanding One of the Bible, nor the law-giving Partner of the Rabbinic experience but as the everpresent Presence of our era. "I [God] am with him in trouble" (Psalm 91:15) means that where Israel

29. See Isaiah, Chapters 41, 42, 45, 48, 49, 50. Jeremiah 16:9–15 and Chapters 30, 31, 32, 33.
30. Primo Levi, *Survival in Auschwitz* (New York: Collier Books, 1961), p. 82.

suffers, God is present, suffering with God's people.[31] The answer to the question "Where was God at Auschwitz?" is: God was there starving, beaten, humiliated, gassed and burned alive, sharing the infinite pain as only an infinite capacity for pain can share it.

A presence need not formally command. Indeed, it does not command if a command means an order in words from the outside. The fact that I relate to the presence of God means that I sense more clearly the expectations, I feel more obligation and motivation and I am more deeply moved than any words or formalized commands can express. If God did not stop the murder and the torture, then what was the statement made by the infinitely suffering Divine Presence in Auschwitz? It was a cry for action, a call to humans to stop the Holocaust, a call to the people Israel to rise to a new, unprecedented level of covenantal responsibility. It was as if God said: "Enough, stop it, never again, bring redemption!" The world did not heed that call and stop the Holocaust. European Jews were unable to respond. World Jewry did not respond adequately. But the response finally did come with the creation of the State of Israel. The Jews took on enough power and responsibility to act. And this call was answered as much by so-called secular Jews as by the so-called religious. Even as God was in Treblinka, so God went up with Israel to Jerusalem. Says the Talmud: "Wherever Israel was exiled, the Shechinah was with them . . . in Egypt, in Babylon. Even so, when they will be redeemed in the future, the Divine Presence will be with them, as it is said, 'the Loving God, Your Lord shall come back with your captivity.'"[32] It does not say "shall bring back" but rather "shall come back" which teaches that the Holy One, blessed be He, comes back with them from the exile.[33] This is the answer to Richard Rubenstein's argument that God cannot be absolved of the Holocaust yet credited with the rebirth of Israel. God is involved with both events in the same way.

Thus, we are at the opening of a major new transformation of the covenant in which Jewish loyalty and commitment manifests itself by Jews taking action and responsibility for the achievement of its goals. This is not a radical break from the past. In retrospect, this move is intrinsic in the very concept of covenant. Says Rabbi Joseph Soloveitchik, "[God] . . . became a partner in this community. . . . He joins man and shares in his covenantal existence. Finitude and infinity, temporality and eternity, creature and creator become involved in the same community. They bind themselves together and participate in a

31. *Exodus Rabba, Mishpatim* 30:24.
32. Deuteronomy 30:3.
33. *Megillah* 29a.

unitive existence." Soloveitchik explains, "the whole concept of 'I shall be with him in trouble' can only be understood with the perspective of the covenantal community which involves God in the destiny of His fellow members."[34]

To see the divine everywhere, the Jewish people must be attuned to covenant. The people's religious receptors must be developed. The divine is more present than ever, in street and factory, media and stage, but the catch is that one must look and be open to the encounter. One is reminded of the story of Mendel of Kotzk who asked: "Where is God?" And he answered: "Wherever you let God in." If Jewry fails to deepen its insight, it runs the risk that it will continue to cling to existing concepts of ritual and denigrate the new activity instead of relating to it with its halakhic structures. It may mistakenly define the new activity as secular and cut off from the covenant instead of being grounded in it. The incredible effort on behalf of Israel has fallen afoul of both risks. In America, particularly as Jewish observance and the power of the synagogue have declined and that of federations has risen, there has been a growing, almost petulant, dismissal of UJA and the work for Israel as "check book Judaism," "civil Judaism," "vulgarization," and so forth. Israel has been dismissed as a vicarious inauthentic myth, an instrument for the ignorant, non-observant nouveau riche to assert mastery over the community without living Jewishly. Even more dangerously, too many practitioners of philanthropy have accepted the definition of secularity and ruled out Federation involvement in religions or personal Jewish education. Both views are incorrect. The focus on philanthropy, the creation of a society and the restoration of the dignity of Jewish life have been the profoundest religious responses of the Jewish community to the Holocaust. The Nazis said, "Jewish life is not worth one-half a cent to put it out of its misery." Somebody else came along and said, "Have you anything to say that contradicts the Nazi testimony, other than the cheap and easy way of saying a prayer?" And one Jew, and another and then another said, "I say a Jewish life is worth a million dollars!" That became the power and testimony of UJA and Israel!

The focus on life and even materialism in Israel, and elsewhere, is part of the reaffirmation of all of life's sacredness. Biblical Judaism emphasized the unity of body and soul and stressed that the real world is where God's love and man's redemption is realized. Over the course of the exile, the separation of the spiritual from the material deeply penetrated Judaism as it did

34. Soloveitchik, "Lonely Man of Faith," loc. cit. p. 28. See also *Sanhedrin* 46a, Y. *Sukkah* 4:3. N.B. This question is dealt with more fully in "Voluntary Covenant," Chapter II in Irving Greenberg, *The Third Great Cycle of Jewish History* (New York, n.d.), pp. 27–44.

Christianity. Now body and soul will come together again in the sacred significance of the secular.

The synagogue and the tradition have been weakened by their failure to fully grasp this situation. They have clung so strongly to the inherited model of the covenant that they have been unable to respond adequately to its renewal. This failure has encouraged lay people to continue to neglect the tradition and to succumb to modernity's temptations. As long as the present model persists, the synagogue will continue to lose ground. Indeed, the synagogues' dilemma is comparable to that of the Temple and prophecy after the destruction. Even when prophecy spoke it was not listened to after the destruction. The Temple was too sacramental and prophecy too manifest in light of the more hidden Presence of God; the synagogue which functions as if nothing has changed is also too sacramental in light of the even more hidden God of the post-Holocaust era. Today, the most successful synagogues are those that have moved to a more havurah-like approach, a more secular style that reaches out into the home, street, and so forth.

But the greatest danger of misunderstanding may lay in the opposite direction. The religious devotion required to faithfully carry out secular activity—the sacrificial giving work and soldiering—may not develop if the secular Jews fail to see the profound religious context out of which they grow. The rising incidence of emigration from Israel is the first warning of what can happen when religious and cultural deracination goes unchecked and materialistic values triumph. Much of the recent *yeridah* has been among Sephardic Jews cut off from the life of Israeli society in part by the deliberate, politically motivated actions of past Labor governments. Among them are many who still accept the traditional categories. They have now tasted the erosive affluence of modern culture and can neither renounce materialism nor relate it to tradition. The pity is that the exploration of affluence's religious dimensions may well be one of the special aspects of the call to secularity. After rehabilitation and liberation, the next stage is the imbuing of daily life and affluence with meaning and values. Just as the move from powerlessness to power calls on the Jews to stop the suffering, so the move to secularity is a call to explore the religious dimensions of pleasure and the material. A more secular halakhah would go from denial to directed enjoyment. Thus, the religious challenge is not merely to give up work on Shabbat in testimony to creaturehood but to explore work as a sacred means of perfecting creation all week long.[35]

35. Irving Greenberg, *Guide to Shabbat* (New York: National Jewish Resource Center, 1981) Section II.

The religious challenge of sexuality is met not only in disciplining it through relationships and fidelity or occasionally giving it up through the mikveh ritual but in "making one's self holy in the permitted," making sexuality the expression of a loving relationship and discovery of the uniqueness of the body and soul of another. Affluence becomes the experience of leisure to develop one's self; the increased opportunity for sharing; and the giving of direction to pleasure through blessings.[36]

The same issue underlies the continuing conflict over autopsies in Israel. The sacramental notion of the sacredness of the body, which is not to be exploited or instrumentally used after death, has blinded many rabbis to the holiness of using human power to gain medical insight and thereby save lives, giving more holiness and dignity to life. The secular notion of scientific power has blinded many doctors to the importance of not making autopsy a routine procedure. Using dead patients instrumentally can lead to a breakdown of reverence for the human being, a loss of values often expressed in excessive medical use of patients, both living and dead.

Finally, the Rabbis' secularizing insight following the destruction led them to the concept of a renewed covenant based on a further event of redemption. Saying that the covenant of Sinai was coercive and less binding in a world where the Romans triumphed, the Rabbis put forth Purim, with its hidden, human agency and flawed redemption, as *the* new redemptive model to which the Jews gave assent in upholding the covenant. Today we can say that the covenant validated by Purim is also coercive, for then the genocide was foiled, and it is less binding in a world that saw Hitler's murder of six million Jews. The redemptive event which evokes Jewish assent in upholding the covenant after the Holocaust is a new one: the re-creation of the State of Israel. It is more flawed, because Israel has many social problems; more secular in that God's role and presence are even more hidden; and more vulnerable as it is challenged and assaulted by Arabs, Russians, and so forth. Paradoxically enough, Israel's flaws and shortcomings are the best proof that this is the true, appropriate hidden redemption for this era. Anything more manifest would be inappropriate for this age and would not be heard. Note, too, that the religious group that does see Israel in manifestly Messianic terms, Gush Emunim, has, in fact, shaken support for Israel among a wide spectrum of American Jews and non-Jews of a more liberal, secular stripe. Only a hidden Messianism can be fully credible—once it is discerned.

History suggests that even as Purim renewed the covenant of redemp-

36. I will deal with this question in a future essay in this series, "Toward a Holy Secularity."

tion, upholding the Exodus and bringing its traditions into the Rabbinic era, so the rebirth of Israel must uphold the Exodus and Purim, bringing them with it into the third era. The contemporary task, therefore, is to find new meaning in the tradition, a process that has already started with the "Judaization" of Federation and UJA circles and the explosion of Torah study in Israel.

Franz Rosenzweig once suggested that some day, as religious insight broadened, a mother's recipe for gefilte fish would be passed on in the family, bearing with it the same sense of tradition as do formal commandments or customs. Every act of social justice, every humane or productive factory, every sport contest in community centers, every act of human socializing and dignity will become a secularized halakhah as Jewish religious insight deepens and the sacred dimensions of the profane are uncovered. The classic memories and religious models of the Jewish people will have to be brought closer to daily life in order to influence and shape it. Nowhere is this more focused than in the State of Israel and the exercise of Jewish power everywhere. This is, at once, the transformation of the Jewish condition and the test of the ongoing validity of Jewish tradition and culture.

FROM POWERLESSNESS TO POWER: SECULARITY APPLIED

The most decisive change in the Jewish condition and in the shift of focus from the realm of the sacred to the realm of the secular is the move from powerlessness to power. The creation of Israel is an act of restoration and redemption and is the affirmation of the covenant through worldly effort. It is the key application of religion to actuality and as such it is the classic expression of hiddenness and the new holy secularity.

Attaining sovereignty brought a major shift in the allocation of Jewish resources, energy and spirit as it became necessary to create a society and build the infrastructure of power. The bulk of the activity in society and state is secular by pre-Holocaust standards. In itself this assures the relative centrality of secular activity in the third era. But this activity is also central to the defense of Jewish existence and therefore is life affirming and gives religious testimony. The real power of the secular is that it combines natural and spiritual paths in an indissoluble way. Similarly, relating to and backing the state become socially and theologically compelling activities, providing legitimacy and importance to fundraising, political activity and other secular activities while also giving great emotional and spiritual moment to prayer and the synagogue. The secular organizations, however, have been frankly designed to serve this purpose, while the synagogue has been slower and more reluctant to respond, further tilting the balance in Jewish life toward the secular realm.

As the state, or the exercise of Jewish power elsewhere, becomes central to Jewish life, the litmus test of the classic ideas increasingly becomes whether they work in real life and whether a society can be shaped by them. In similar fashion, the ability to generate moral or responsible exercises of power and a sense of purpose and meaning in personal activity becomes critical to the State's ability to hold its own Jews and to attract others. Incompetence in daily functions or loss of moral and ethical standards will quickly be translated into loss of participation. Thus, every act of daily performance takes on transcendent meaning in completing the redemption of the Jewish people. Building the earthly Jerusalem becomes the basis for reestablishing the heavenly Jerusalem. The ability and willingness to perform daily actions faithfully and meticulously will also make or break the State physically and spiritually.

The key to performance and ethical excellence will be the systematic reconciliation of Jewish covenantal ideas and historical memory to the contemporary lives and activities of the Jewish people. Since power is results-oriented, more pragmatic and even more amoral than ideals, the capacity of the tradition to supply power with values and direction will be tested to the limit. Purists will recoil and dream of a purer religious reality or will offer a spiritual critique of the grubby Israeli reality. Yet the assumption of power is inescapable if Jewish existence is to continue. This secularity is a matter of life or death. Thus, the Holocaust and Israel come together, compelling the assumption of full responsibility for Jewish fate through the every day activities of the Jewish state and of the Jewish society. There is a steady flow of Jewish energy, wealth and talent as well as continuing reorganization of the community in Israel and abroad to deal with the exercise of power.

The reasons for this are *historically inescapable*.[37] The Holocaust made it overwhelmingly clear that Jewish powerlessness was no longer compatible with Jewish survival.[38] The Nazis' extraordinary success was made possible by Jewish powerlessness. Had the Jews ruled their own land, millions could have been saved. In the crunch, even decent countries like the United States of America failed to open their doors to Jewish refugees. It is no accident that the PLO continually attacks the Law of Return which guarantees every

37. Yehuda Bauer, *The Jewish Emergence from Powerlessness* (Buffalo: University of Toronto Press, 1971).

38. This idea is expanded in Chapter III, "Power and Politics," in Greenberg, *Great Cycle*.

Jew the automatic right to become a citizen of Israel. The right to unlimited immigration means more than recruitment of the population that Israel needs. At the present time, the immigration rate is insufficient for this purpose. Despite the continuing attack on the law as racist, the Law of Return is staunchly upheld by Israelis because it is the most sensitive indicator that Jews are masters in their own land, that they exist by right and not by sufferance or by tolerant goodwill. Before the Holocaust, Zionism was a mass movement only in countries of Jewish persecution and Western Jewry was neutral or negative toward it. Since the Holocaust, however, Jews have become overwhelmingly Zionist because they have learned the lesson. Dig beneath the surface and you will discover that even Jews who prefer to live in the lands of the Diaspora have learned the lesson of the Holocaust. Even if you believe that it *won't* happen here, you can never again say it *can't* happen here. Only the Jews who reject the significance of the Holocaust and live as if it never happened, such as Neturei Karta or all out assimilationists, now deny this truism.

Jewish powerlessness is also immoral. It tempts anti-Semites into evil behavior.[39] Had there been no Jewish army or air force there would have been another Holocaust or two since 1945 and the singling out of Jews for imprisonment or destruction such as almost happened at Entebbe would have gone unchecked. Since the kind of power needed for self-defense in the modern period is only available to sovereign states, the Jewish consensus has raised the obligation for Jews to assume power to the level of sacred principle. Thus, the experience of the Jews in the Holocaust demands that Jews take power and the re-creation of the Jewish State in Israel responds to this demand. Any principle that is generated by the Holocaust and to which Israel responds, any action which is confirmed by the revelation in both of the two great events of this era, becomes overwhelmingly normative for the Jewish people. The shift from powerlessness to power becomes the necessary change in the fundamental Jewish condition in the third era. This recognition explains Arthur Hertzberg's inspired observation that the only sin for which the organized Jewish community decrees excommunication is the sin of denying Israel.[40] However, arguing about how the power is used is acceptable, especially inside Israel where it is not threatening to the Jewish possession of power. How to use the power is the new halakhah, but denial or endangering the power

39. Manes Sperber, . . . *Than a Tear in the Sea*, intro. Andre Malraux, trans. Constantine Fitzgibbon (New York: Bergen Belsen Memorial Press, 1967).
40. Arthur Hertzberg, *Being Jewish in America* (New York: Schocken Books, 1978).

is considered the unforgivable sin. In this era, which orients by the Holocaust and Israel, such a denial is the equivalent of the excommunicable sins of earlier eras: denying the Exodus and the God who worked it in the Biblical age or denying the Rabbis and separating from Jewish fate in the Rabbinic era. I believe that the community has been too fearful of discussion or criticism in this matter and would benefit by expanding the margins of discussion. However, a famous Yiddish proverb is operating here: "If you burn your tongue once on hot soup, in the future you blow first, even on cold soup." Having tasted the bitter cup of powerlessness to its dregs, the community overreacts to any perceived threat or undermining of the power it has.

Yet, there is a great deal of confusion regarding assumption of power as a basic change in the Jewish condition. Some scholars argue that, far from ending the threat to Jews, Israel itself is threatened and that far from ending Jewish ghetto existence, Israel is a kind of national ghetto in the Middle East. These observations only prove that Jews do not yet have enough power to remove the active threat to their existence. In the world we live in, no nation has enough power totally to insure its safety. In the case of the Jews, the relative balance of strength and threat is still too close for comfort. But there is a fundamental difference between the two situations. A threatened ghetto in Eastern Europe could only wait for its enemies to act, hope to sustain bearable losses and to live on by sufferance. When it was destroyed or expelled, the ghetto's wealth and achievement enriched its enemies. By contrast, Israel has a major voice in its own fate, indeed it has decided its own fate repeatedly in the past decades. And, while Israel's wartime losses have been devastating, with their lives the Jewish soldiers bought dignity, freedom and a measure of security for the Jewish people in Israel. Many times more Jews died in the Crusades, pogroms or the Holocaust, but their deaths made the Jews more vulnerable and more persecuted than before. The difference is noteworthy and in the kind of world we live, no small accomplishment. It is a basic measure of human dignity that my life is not cheap and that I give it for my purposes, values and benefit; that I choose for whom it shall be given; and my family and friends, not my enemies, inherit me. Thus power upholds the covenantal statement of Jewish dignity and the sacredness of life.

It is not just a matter of choices about death. It is the application of life's efforts, as well. Ninety years of building in the land of Israel have created a remarkable Jewish infrastructure containing school systems teaching Judaism and Jewish history; media, art, literature and scholarship in Hebrew; a firm foundation of agricultural and industrial productivity, all taxed and utilized for the benefit of Jewish life and Jewish people everywhere. The priorities of Jewish fate and purpose determine everything from national park preserves and museums to phone systems and garbage dumps. One need not deny Israel's many problems or faults to realize what a treasure of life and human sustenance has been built there. Just as in Biblical times, such activity was perceived as holy, despite its flaws, and was blessed, prayed for and nourished by the sacred cult and system, so will this activity today become suffused with religious symbolism and purpose.

Indeed the model is so impressive and catching that, despite their minority status, American Jewry, French Jewry and others have become increasingly politically active. Partly out of the lessons of the Holocaust and the example of Israel and partly out of desire to prevent another Holocaust and to preserve Israel, they have moved from invisibility in the political system to active involvement in it.[41] These Jewries may stay in Diaspora but psychologically they are coming to the end of exilic Judaism. In exile the Jews' destiny was in the hands of others. As a marginal community the Jews could only take the political order as a given and seek to accommodate to it or serve it. Individuals, especially marginal ones, could revolt but the collective could not. The community did not have the power nor could it afford the moral luxury of judging the system. Of course, one must recognize that Jewish power is still limited. However, the change that has occurred has made all the difference in the world.

In the exilic phase, the great task of religion was to give dignity to the powerless, to show that one also serves by standing and waiting. Martyrdom was the highest sanctification of God's name. Since the condition itself could not be changed, the stress on exile as punishment for Israel's sins was a way of asserting control over the Jews' fate, a way of reclaiming moral dignity. If only Jews would repent enough, they would be delivered so they can perform morally responsible actions. The dignity of suffering, the hope for the world to come, the moral heroism of asceticism, penitential prayer—thousands of religious values and practices were conditioned to heal and uphold powerless Jewry.

The emergence of the State of Israel constituted the taking of power into Jewish hands so that Jews could shape their own destiny and affect or even control the lives of others. It represented a revolutionary, 180 degree moral turn in the religious situation. The dilemmas of power are far different from the temptations and problems of powerlessness. Jews have been fond of contrasting Christian persecution of Jews or Christianity's failure to crusade for social justice in the medieval world with Jewish behavior. It remains to be seen whether Judaism did not act similarly merely because it was power-

41. See Chapter III of Greenberg, *Great Cycle.*

less and whether it will not repeat or do worse in a situation of power. Will Judaism be able to function in a situation of power without becoming an established religion which interferes with the freedom of others, both Jews and non-Jews?

Ideally speaking, both Jewish religion and Jewish values can now actually do what they have always wanted to do. The assumption of power will now force them to put up or shut up. Spinning out ideal values will now be seen as empty blather if those values cannot be realized in daily life. If Israeli society fails, the credibility of Judaism drops. Jewish values will be seen, at best, as glittering generalities that do not work in the real world. Yet, all the ambiguities of power and reality will still operate. The recalcitrance of the real to receive the ideal; the frequent lack of a pure good or pure bad side in the real world; the demonic and ironic elements in human nature and history; the exhausting tension between the ideal and the real; the sheer contrast between what can be realized and what can be dreamt will all test the inner fibre of the Jewish people and Jewish culture.

Work in real power situations is closer to the Rabbinic, halakhic process than to prophetic stances. It involves the capacity to judge specific situations and to reconcile shifting claims and facts. This probably spells the end of the traditional Jewish tilt toward the radical end of the political spectrum, a phenomenon that reflected lack of policy-making responsibility. Policy choices involve compromise and conservation as well as reform and perfection. Ultimate ends and proximate means must be linked in a continual process, something which can only be done through involvement, guilt and partial failures. Power inescapably corrupts yet its assumption is inescapable. The test of morality then is relative reduction of evil and better mechanisms of self-criticism, correction and repentance. There is a danger that those who have not grasped the full significance of the shift in Jewish condition will judge Israel by the ideal standards of the state of powerlessness, thereby not only misjudging but unintentionally collaborating with attempted genocide. Ideal moral stances applied unchanged to real situations often come out with the opposite of the intended result.

Yet how can we utilize power without becoming the unwitting slaves of bloodshed or an exploitative status quo? The National Religious Party and Gush Emunim's largely jingoistic position is a warning both of the unsuitability of older models and the overwhelming pull of the new situation. Exercise of power must be accompanied by strong models and constant evocation of the memory of historic Jewish suffering and powerlessness. It is so easy to forget slavery's lessons once one is given power, but such forgetfulness leads to the unfeeling infliction of pain on others. The memory of the

Holocaust has enabled Israel to be a responsible and restrained conqueror. Memory is the key to morality.

The historical record of every group shows that even subtle participation in the realm of the possible can lead to acceptance of the status quo unless judgment is continually refreshed through exposure to prophetic norms. Jews will have to learn to reconcile prophetic idealism with the compromise of policy-making and to incorporate conserving and healing roles in Judaism to deal with tragedies and defeats which are the inescapable consequences of the human condition. The shock and depression of the Israelis following the Yom Kippur War only prove how human they are and how important religious values are in this era of power. But unless religion develops greater openness to other groups' criticism and greater sensitivity to other groups' needs, it may offer a morally deadening moral rearmament. It may also become guilty of idolatry, if it fails to critique even as it affirms the State.

The use of power also mandates the occasional use of immoral strategies to achieve moral ends. The acceptance of the guilt inherent in such actions calls for people of exceptional emotional range and strong orientation both to absolute norms and relative claims, both to judgment and to mercy.

Many inherited models will have to be reversed to function properly today. After Auschwitz, martyrdom is morally offensive. The command is to live and to testify. Power must be widely distributed to insure that it will not be abused. This sets up a dialectic of power which must be applied to Israel as well as to all power-wielding nations. The ideal would be maximum self-government for Palestinians and Arabs as a check on Jewish abuse. But such self-government can only be accepted if it does not threaten the existence and security of the Jewish people. To yield autonomy without overwhelming proof of Palestinian desire to live in peace is to invite martyrdom and morally reprehensible death by genocide. The Palestinians will have to earn their power by living peacefully and convincing Israel of their beneficence or by acquiescing to a situation in which Israel's strength guarantees that the Arabs cannot use their power to endanger Israel.

The same principle applies to internal Jewish society. One of the ironic and unintended side-effects of Israel's 1967 victory was an economic boom that left many Sephardim behind, trapped in poverty. The morally and religiously erosive effects of ill-distributed affluence must be challenged by the application of covenantal values and the political redistribution of power in Israel. While many American Jews are unhappy with the present Likud government and its perceived conservatism, clericalism and even jingoism, they fail to see how much of its support comes from Sephardic Jewry. The redistribution of power caused by the Likud's victory in 1974 brought new people into government, including many who did not know how to function effectively due to lack of experience. The opposition came to power after thirty years of Labor governments and it must be given time to develop competence. This is all part of the normal back-and-forth shifting in the course of learning to exercise power and, despite the fumbling, it is a healthy development. The exaggerated and even apocalyptic talk of the breakdown of Israel now ripe among American Jews as well as Israelis is a reflection of the relative immaturity of the new Jewish culture of power. People who live by ideal principles believe that everything will crumble once there is failure. Politicians know that there are cycles of victory, defeat, competence and ineffectiveness. But in a democracy, there are mechanisms for correction which will eventually bear fruit. Obviously, it is nerve-wracking to watch this ineffectiveness against the background of the continuing Arab and Soviet bloc hostility toward Israel. As Jews grow used to the exercise of power, however, the apocalyptic tone should modulate to a prodding, patient awareness of an involvement with the State of Israel. The ability of Jews to reconcile realities and covenantal ideals; the ability to generate the human, moral and religious resources to carry on the struggle; and the ability to set about perfecting the world, however modestly, will be the test of Judaism in the third era.

NEW INSTITUTIONS

Contemporary Jews live in an era when a basic change in the Jewish condition coincides with a crisis of faith after destruction and assimilation. In the past, the challenge of coping with new conditions and the search for meaning inexorably led to the rise of new institutions and new leadership. Existing established institutions and leadership are deeply invested in the previous reality and are slower to respond to new needs, tending to repeat what they did before but with words that are less credible and actions that are less suited in light of the change. Yet it is hard to create completely new institutions that can quickly win acceptance. Typically, therefore, institutions that existed but were marginal before the crisis, institutions that can be more suited or more responsive to the new situation, become central after the crisis. In the case of the third era, these institutions will be more secular, corresponding to the increased hiddenness of God and the necessity to solve the problems of power and daily life. However, they must also carry on the way of the covenant so that they can supply competence and meaning to the new historic condition.

The primary third era institution that meets these criteria is the State of Israel. Its shift from marginality to centrality in Jewish life is directly related to the Holocaust and its own rebirth and is, at once, demographic, political and spiritual. In 1939, there were 400,000 Jews in Palestine out of a world-wide Jewish population of 17 to 18 million or about two percent of world Jewry. Within two years of the founding of the State, the population numbered 1.15 million out of 12 million Jews or nine percent. Today, Israel's Jewish population is about 3 million or 21 percent of world Jewry. As the main agent of dealing with the challenge of Jewish power, the State has gained increasing support from world Jewry.

Such secular institutions as the Knesset and the Israeli Defense Forces which existed in embryonic form before the Holocaust now have evolved as central organs of coping with the new Jewish condition. They preside over Jewish priorities and investments in self-defense and they help set the agenda of Jewish power regarding the protection of Jewish communities. Of course, the more Israel plays this role, the more support and participation flows toward Israel from the Diaspora. By now, Jewish scientists, many of them completely assimilated, are barred from French nuclear programs and Russian military research even as American Jewish analysts are reportedly excluded from certain military and diplomatic roles in Washington. If one can factor out the anti-Semitism in these discriminations, they clearly also reflect a perception that Israel has a claim on the talents and knowledge of even the most marginal Jews.

Israeli welfare agencies and private organizations do not only serve Israel's population—thereby reasserting the dignity and preciousness of life which is the central religious testimony in the new era—they are increasingly involved with Diaspora Jews who are concerned with Jewish life or looked to by others seeking to deal with problems. Kibbutzim and other settlements absorb Diaspora Jews seeking Jewish expression; problem children are sent to Israeli institutions and orphans to Youth Aliya villages. Israeli universities and yeshivot have become important centers for foreign Jewish students. Even the proliferation of yeshivot in Israel reflects the new situation. The greater governmental support available in a Jewish society has funded their growth.

Israel has also pioneered in the creation of a new sacred institution of the Third Era, the Holocaust memorial center. Even as the synagogue was a place to commemorate the Temple's destruction and to express the continuing, if more secular, sacred values, so Yad VaShem, the government-sponsored memorial, and similar structures are the focal points for a more secularized religious experience. These are places where the memory is preserved, the story told and the acts of mourning and continuity publicly expressed. In traditional religious institutions, legend and miracle embroider the classic myths, the central organizing stories which guide life. Elaboration is part of the evocative power of such stories. However, the new institutions are officially secular; the stories which are at the heart of these religious institutions must be factual and historically reliable in order to be moving. By pre-Holocaust standards, these are secular criteria but the message must meet these tests to be effective in the third era. In masked fashion, these institutions express such classic religious values as the roles of martyrdom, sacrifice, heroism, Jewish and non-Jewish saintliness and continuity.

In America, the institutions which have been thrust into centrality by the after-effects of the third era's two revelatory events are those of the Federation/United Jewish Appeal complex. Their message is: You can respond to the worthlessness of Jewish life in the Holocaust by testifying through giving money to rehabilitate Jewish lives. You are purchasing an indirect share in Jewish power because UJA money frees up Israel's money for defense purposes. The local welfare agencies are also perceived as affirmations of the dignity and value of Jewish lives. Furthermore, support for Israel has naturally led to political representation of Jewish interests. The power center has shifted from the general defense agencies, such as the American Jewish Committee and American Jewish Congress to local Community Relations Councils. In part, CRCs' increased importance is a function of the councils' stronger funding; in part the new religious and spiritual fundamentals bestow an extra measure of status on them. The Community Relations Councils are perceived as representing the entire community, the unity of Jewish fate and purpose which transcends the pre-Holocaust divisions. The organizations and synagogues are tarred by the burst of denominational divisiveness.

Many have argued that the Federations' power is a function of their superior access to money. However, they are able to attract money only because they transmit meaning and values and can bestow status. One of UJA's most magnetic tools has been its ability to offer its givers and workers access to Israeli officials. While this factor was more important to the older generation, it is too simple to dismiss the process as mere celebrity-seeking or simple ego-stroking. Israeli officials are on the front line of Jewish self-defense. It is the combination of social appeal and theological and historical relevance that makes this kind of involvement so magnetic. Similarly, one of the Federations' great recruiting mechanisms has been the mission to Israel and Eastern Europe which bears vivid witness to the role of the Holocaust and of Israel in validating the functions of philanthropy and Jewish political self-defense. I would argue that behind these overt levels of historical consciousness is a sense that the covenant and destiny of the Jewish people is being continued through this vehicle. The continual media attention to Israel, even the obsessive focus on condemning Israel in the United Nations, is often seen by givers as the secularized version of the Jews' role as a "light unto the nations" or as the chosen people, singled out and standing alone, testifying to a world mired in the status quo of power politics and oppression.

Federations also have been pushed toward greater political involvement. The historical maelstrom has pulled them and many individual philanthropists into political areas which decades ago they shunned as the plague for fear of undermining Jewish acceptance in modern society. The main weakness of the Federations as perceived by the community has been that they are not designed to overtly articulate the values which undergird continued Jewish existence. Some of this weakness has been offset by the unarticulated messages implied by their work for Israel and their efforts to commemorate the Holocaust. However, the perceived weakness has led to increasing communal demands to intensify Federations' efforts to transmit Jewish values. Thus the Federations have been pushed toward greater investments in Jewish education, Hillel and college work as well as support for a variety of Jewish cultural and religious concerns. In this way again, the demands of a new reality have led to a strengthening and broadening of their functions. Why were synagogues and schools not the exclusive vehicles for dealing with such concerns? I submit it is because they are not secular enough to be fully credible or fully effective in the emerging third era. They operate with the handicap of being too sacramental, hence their message is not fully heard, too divided because their dividing lines are perceived as pre-Holocaust, pre-Israel; and too detached from the power and defense issues of Jewish life.

Synagogues, schools and yeshivot are treasured by Jews who seek Jewish survival. However, there is a shift of focus in Jewish life toward those institutions that deal with the new Jewish condition in more appropriate, secular settings. Secularity enables them to speak more effectively in the post-Holocaust atmosphere and to deal better with the reality of the open society. A message that is too sacramental or too internal will not be picked up by the media and other disseminating agencies of American culture. Of course, the danger is that this very secularity makes the people trained in the new institutions more subject to the pull of the general society.

New institutions are characteristically *pluralist*. This quality is often attacked as leading to an overemphasis on consensus in all decision-making. However, pluralism is the expression of a powerful theological value statement in Jewish unity and is yet another proof that the Holocaust and Israel are the guiding events of this era. Religious, political, or even financial lines that divide Jews are secondary when it comes to these two events. In the Holocaust, the fact of Jewishness was decisive; the type of Jew one was made no difference. And Israel was built by Jews of every religious, political and financial stripe. The statement of pluralism is the statement that the group is no longer primarily defined by guidelines such as Reform, Orthodox or secular which characterize modern culture, but by the overriding unity of Jewish fate in the new era. This is not to say that the earlier divisions are meaningless. After all, they do reflect the variety of Jewish life conditions and observances. However, most Jews see these elements as secondary characteristics. Those who treat these issues as primary lose some plausibility.

Pluralism is also the theological consequence of the reformulation of the covenant into a voluntary covenant.[42] The unprecedented openness of American society combines with the risk and suffering of Jewish fate to insure that those who are Jewish are those who choose to be so. There can hardly be any punishment, divine or human, that can force Jews into the covenantal role when it is obviously far more risky to choose to be Jewish. Given the voluntary nature of Jewish commitment, there cannot be one imposed standard of Jewish loyalty or excellence. Organizations which respect this fact are successful, for they tap the full moral and historical force of the new condition.

Since the new institutions operate in a secular setting, they and their leadership cannot claim any born authority. They have an earned, not traditional, respect. After the second destruction, the Rabbis were in a similar situation vis-à-vis the prophets and priests who had bestowed status and sacramental powers. By contrast, today's rabbis and synagogues claim ascribed status based on traditional authority and standing. The lay groups have no inherited authority and cannot present themselves as masters of the tradition. They must appeal, rather, on the grounds that they are competent to deal with the Jewish situation, have a relationship to the Holocaust and Israel, and offer participatory roles to all. This approach gives them an advantage over groups that appeal to tradition. In an open society all the voices in the culture are heard and the self-evident nature of authority is eroded. One must be able to get out the message and be heard amidst the claims of other voices and to persuade and move people. The claim of sole authority weakens the message's credibility because it is heard as "parochial," "intolerant" or "withdrawn" in contrast to the multiple voices of an open society.

The open society has also "decultured" many Jews. They are less in

42. See Chapter II, "Voluntary Covenant," in Greenberg, *Great Cycle*, for fuller explanation.

touch with tradition and classic Jewish terms and values because they have been stripped of Jewish culture and its memories. Those Jews who are not inside the community are more likely to respond to agencies or institutions able to send their messages out through general channels such as the media or public schools. The net effect is that those institutions which go to where the Jews are do better and become stronger than those which do not. Typically, the established, pre-Holocaust institutions whose constituency still comes to them are less outgoing and their messages are less able to circulate through the open media.

Finally, the need for legitimacy coupled with society's openness leads to a participatory style. Process, discussion and the right of participants to take part in decision-making become the keys to acceptance of policies. Participants are presumed to have sufficient knowledge and judgment to make the decisions, even if this is not necessarily so. In the competitive situation of the open society such styles constantly win out over authority-centered structures.

In addition to the State of Israel and the Federations, other new institutions are developing. One example is retreat centers such as Brandeis-Bardin Camp Institute near Los Angeles. Unlike the synagogues, the retreat center is secular ground. Its religious components must be carved out and set up by the group. Characteristically, a retreat center is pluralist, bringing together people with a wide variety of backgrounds and using faculty of varying persuasions. The retreat center's ability to transmit values is enhanced because it is a total environment in which a Jewish mini-society is established that envelops the individual. In fact, the retreat experience is an excellent tool to strengthen the synagogue.

In recent years, the Holocaust memorial center has also emerged as a new post-Holocaust institution. Such centers have developed locally and each community has responded to its own set of forces. Typically, the center is secular, although some space for meditation or prayer is often set aside. But since all types of Jews endured the Holocaust, most center's presentations are pluralist in tone, frequently using such secular tools as films and focusing on teaching and participation.

Jacob Neusner, in decrying excessive emphasis on the Holocaust, has argued that the story should be told through the synagogue as one of many messages about Judaism. Neusner asks why the Holocaust should have a place dedicated just to it?[43] The answer again is that the Holocaust is increasingly

43. Jacob Neusner, "Toward A Jewish Renewal . . . After the Flood, After the Rainbow," *Moment* 3:6 (May 1978): 11–16.

viewed as an orienting event in Jewish history, one of a handful of events that we recognize as so decisive that the Jewish way through history and the individual's way of life is guided or shaped by its implications. Just as the Exodus and Divine Presence were made manifest in the Temple and just as the synagogue brought together community, new covenantal values and liturgical expression after the destruction of the Temple, so the Holocaust center makes visible this new revelatory event. The lesson is pluralist and "secular" in guise and in tone; the synagogue is not. While the synagogue can and should incorporate this event and the rebirth of Israel into its liturgy and life, incorporating the Holocaust into the synagogue liturgy is a challenge, for the countertestimony to faith in this event must not be evaded in the service. Holocaust centers are typically set up as citywide or regional institutions. The memorial center is the natural channel to externally symbolize and to vividly communicate the reenactment dimension of Jewish liturgy using films, documents and actual materials. In effect, the center becomes the place where the event that shapes the new era and the lessons and value implications of the third era are represented.

The growth of such centers in the United States has been slow and halting. There has been significant opposition from those who argue that the Holocaust should not be overstressed, as well as from some rabbis and synagogues which have feared theological "distortion" — or institutional rivalry. Although there is no framework in which to understand the significance of the issue or of the fledgling institutions, there is evidence that this pattern of development is very much like that of post-Biblical holidays. Many scholars believe that Purim developed at the grass roots, with significant resistance to its content and form evinced by rabbis and others. Only after the holiday had spread was it adopted and fully integrated into Jewish religious and communal life. This pattern is even more appropriate in this era given the masked nature of the holiness and sacredness of Yom HaShoah and the revelatory nature of the Holocaust and of Israel's rebirth.

In recent decades, Jewish studies in universities have undergone significant growth. The official culture of the university denies that such courses can or should be a vehicle that transmits religion or values. Furthermore, the pluralist, secular style of the university is perceived as non-theological and non-sacred. Nevertheless, there are hundreds of students of Jewish studies who make clear that such courses have profoundly affected their Jewish commitments and identities. Many students openly state that they take such courses as expressions of or in search of deepening their Jewish identities. While Jewish studies professors are not chaplains, it is precisely because their style is secular and pluralist that they have such impact within the framework of third era credibility. Many students who would not enter a synagogue or a more overtly sacred place, will encounter Jewish destiny and memory in the academic setting because it makes no official claims or demands. Yet once students experience the reality of Jewish experience or past values, they often are touched or stimulated to new levels of commitment. Of course, the pluralistic nature of the setting makes the outcome unpredictable, but, more often than not, the result is positive.

The media, too, have become a major source of Jewish experience and values. For many Jews, especially those who will not come to a synagogue or other overtly Jewish setting, the secular character and the hiddenness of the values messages presented by the media makes them acceptable. Such films as "Holocaust" and "Masada" have had enormous impact on Jews and on the Jewish community. There is, of course, a danger that the values transmitted may be based on ignorance or shaped by commercial considerations, but such programs seem destined for even greater influence. The way the community gathers to watch such programs makes them important transmitters of values.

The creation of Beit Hatefutsot, the Diaspora Museum, in Israel is another example of a third era institution. Beit Hatefutsot is not really a museum. It is a liturgical recounting and reenacting of the Jewish experience in the Diaspora presented in a secular, pluralist, hidden religious fashion. Since Israel and the Holocaust are events of major magnitude and Jewish life is filled with ferment and response, such new and creative institutions will continue to emerge and to attract Jews. The visitors, often family groups, come from a wide variety of religious backgrounds and Jewish communities. Their visits are often "holy days" on the family calendar in which the family or other groups come to witness the Jewish experience and proclaim or confirm their own Jewishness. On the surface, such institutions have no claim to authority or sacredness. Yet the behavior of the Jews involved has many of the characteristics of religious behavior. Often the visit is a repetitive ritual, done in family units, and includes moments of reminiscence, meditation, devotion or even tears. Thus, the religious dimensions are hidden below the surface of the experience. The institution claims no intrinsic sacred effect or authority and any such impact is earned by the sheer power of the program. Its sacred impact is greater for being hidden and pluralistic, which is to say it is broadcasting on the right wave-length, the one with the most resonance in the third era.

As the Jewish way and the channels of its communication turn toward a more secular setting, the question of the role of the synagogue becomes more acute. By continuing to proclaim the evident sacredness of God and of its own place as it did before the Holocaust and rebirth, the synagogue comes across as too sacramental. Even as the Sadducees and priests proclaimed the unbroken authority of the Temple but were not persuasive in the more secularized Rabbinic era, so today's rabbis and synagogues risk a similar loss of credibility. The continuing division of synagogues by denomination also hurts because it represents a tacit claim that the divisions generated by the Emancipation are as salient as ever. Such divisiveness also contradicts the unity of Jewish fate which more and more Jews feel follows inevitably from the events of the Holocaust and the rebirth of Israel. The synagogue leadership has reacted to its loss of credibility with defensiveness and insistence that the synagogue must remain the center of Jewish life. Not infrequently, they oppose the new institutions. There is a danger that the synagogue leadership will become the B'nai Bateira of the post-Holocaust period. The B'nai Bateira were members of a group that opposed Rabbi Yohanan ben Zakkai's symbolic transfer of the legal, religious authority of the Temple to the court and academy of Yavneh where new institutions were emerging following the Temple's destruction. In that case, faithfulness and the desire to give the familiar response led to a rear-guard opposition that was essentially obstructionist. Eventually, the synagogue and academy won and those who staked their fate on reconstituting the Temple died out. In our time, the danger is compounded in that the Temple was visibly destroyed, encouraging the search for alternative ways of religious expression, whereas the synagogue remains physically intact although its theological and cultural substrata have been fundamentally transformed.

The loss of the synagogue would be a cultural and religious catastrophe of disastrous magnitude for Jewry. The alternative is to renew the synagogue, and to help it develop communicative powers appropriate for the new era. The synagogue can learn to speak and operate in a secular world, a tendency already seen when community center, sports and other secular activities were added to the synagogue program. While such activities have added vitality to temple life, there is the danger that they will remain separate from the sacred and liturgical functions of the synagogue which continue to contract and may be overwhelmed by the new activities. Too many synagogues have become captive to the catering or health and recreation uses of the building. Such activities must be positively related to the sacred strands of synagogue life, but not allowed to substitute for them. Turning the synagogue into a vehicle for the United Jewish Appeal and Israel Bonds, for activities and rallies for Soviet Jewry, Israel and other Jewish concerns, allows the synagogue to reach out from sacred space into the secular reality and to connect with the vital shaping events which nourish Jewish spiritual life. Many synagogues have begun to incorporate the Holocaust and Israel into their liturgical life with special prayers, commemoration of Yom HaShoah and Yom HaAtzmaut and other special occasions. Thus the religious force of the synagogue is stepped up by the power of these events.

Still other tactics promise to strengthen the religious core of temple life. The development of synagogue havurot is another way of moving into secular space. Havurah members frequently share life cycle events, using the rabbi as a resource. Much of the learning and teaching is done by group members and the teacher, in effect a secular "rabbi," speaks with less sacramental authority. Despite the synagogue's official membership in a denomination, havurot are de facto pluralistic because of the range of participants' background and the eclectic nature of their sources of information. Thus, they pick up both the strength of pluralism and of Jewish unity. The National Havurah Coordinating Committee (of which CLAL, then the NJRC, was a founding partner) has sponsored national study institutes which offered a remarkable round of learning opportunities taught by a wide variety of teachers and spiritual figures. The Coalition for Alternatives in Jewish Education conferences follow a similar model and by all accounts the effects of the programs are extraordinary.

Some synagogues have encouraged their rabbis to move out into the community as teachers and models of Jewish values. Sometimes the rabbi must trade in the automatic authority he has in his own bailiwick in return for access and a chance to be heard. Those rabbis who accept and meet the challenge often find their impact multiplied. Frequently the ground rules provide that they cannot demand or offer traditional values as the only legitimate option as they can back on home ground. Yet both the audience *and the effect* is often *expanded*. In an open society and in an era when the sacred is hidden, less is often more; the tentativeness and modesty of the claims enormously increase their impact and acceptance.

This is not to say that the synagogue should surrender its character and completely adapt to a more secular society. Indeed a good strategy might be to offer a more sharply defined alternative to the new society. Mysticism and deeper religious experience offer a religious option for those who are dissatisfied with the dominant secular tone or for those who seek an encounter with the hidden divine for themselves. A synagogue that enriches its religious offerings and creates specialized, selected groups to explore spirituality in more disciplined and taxing ways can reach the seekers. Currently, it is difficult to explore spirituality in the synagogue. The general membership is too mixed and unselected; those uninterested in spirituality hold back the more able or adventurous people. The possibility of plural offerings—for seekers, learners, for conventional prayers—may be more promising than the present, denominationally defined variety of offerings. Plural religious activities can go hand-in-hand with secular outreach and community activity programs.

The synagogue can also offer itself as a consciously articulated alternative community. Such a synagogue can make special ethical or religious norms obligatory for all members. In effect, such a synagogue becomes a "guerrilla base." It recognizes that it is in opposition to the established moral and religious regime. People come to it for consciousness raising, ideological training and for support, venturing forth to confront and offer alternative values to the society. In the guerilla handbook, the key to victory lies in the dialectic of swimming in the sea of the people. One must share the values and lives of the people even as one seeks to channel them, generate other visions, and radicalize them by creating enough perception of conflict so that the masses withdraw assent to the legitimacy of the existing system. This guerrilla analogy may sound exaggerated, but Judaism and the synagogue are, in fact, in significant opposition to the assimilating (and many of the other) values of society. By the light of this model, the synagogue building and service become the rest and recreation area for guerrillas, the place where the peer group is renewed; and where the commitment to persist and challenge the prevailing values is revived.

A policy of opposition would lead to the loss of many conventional members but it offers the hope of creating a committed, persistent minority alternative. The present policy runs the risk of death by inanition. Services that are conventional, denominational and sacramental continually lose out to the competing religious or secular authority. Adaptation in either direction is more promising for the synagogue than a stand pat philosophy or a reactionary attitude toward new institutions. The growth of a militant right-wing Orthodoxy in the decades of the '60s and '70s at the expense of modern Orthodoxy shows some of the promise in this alternative strategy. The growth of havurot and other experimental communities is another straw in the wind. Thus far there has been little help given by the national level for the local synagogues which are developing these models.

The synagogue is too important to be left only to synagogue members, or even rabbis. Helping the synagogue adapt should be high on the agenda of American Jewry. This generation has already sustained a too crushing physical loss of thousands of synagogues by enemy action. A further equivalent loss to spiritual erosion would be intolerable. By contrast, successfully bringing the synagogue into the third era will insure that the riches of the past will be available as resources for Jewish life in the new setting.

NEW LEADERSHIP

Each era of Jewish history has generated its own characteristic leadership cadre. Leadership has gravitated toward those who could cope with the problems of living while addressing, overtly or through their work, the meaning and purpose of being a Jew. Jewish minority status and exposure to countervailing civilizations has made dealing with problems of meaning as essential for continuity, and therefore for leadership, as the more prosaic challenges of daily life. The unfolding new era is characterized by a change in condition, from powerlessness to power; a change in the theological and religious paradigm, toward greater secularity and divine hiddenness; and the rise of new institutions. Therefore, these forces are generating a change in the type of leadership the Jewish people requires.

The Biblical era was an age of split leadership. Kings, judges and nobles dealt with issues of sovereignty; priests and prophets managed the Temple and direct revelation, two channels of access to the God who intervened. The Rabbinic era also had two leadership groups: the lay or political element and the Rabbis who discerned the will of the more hidden God. However, the lines between them blurred somewhat. Political power weakened and the Rabbis often played legal or political roles within the internally autonomous Jewish community.

The laypeople are emerging as the dominant group of the third era. In Israel, politicians—who could be more secular in image than politicians?—decide the priorities and mechanisms for pursuing the Jewish mission. Ironically, the official status of religion in Israel has only intensified the policy-making influence of secularists on the rabbinic leadership by allowing them significant influence in the selection of Chief Rabbis. In America, lay leadership is most obviously expressed in the institutions which have been the main beneficiaries of the third era. However, Jews in media, government, unions and other secular settings have gained important weight in Jewish community decisions. Even within the synagogue and other traditional institutions, much power has passed to lay leadership. The secularization process shows up another way as well. Some academics, workers and activists have become spiritual or charismatic leaders who play many of the classic roles of rebbe/rabbi. They offer access to God, give spiritual direction, incarnate norms and values, and offer policy guidance.

Coping with the issues of power is, in itself, a great stimulus toward secularization of leadership. Power is exercised in everyday, mundane realities. Religious or idealistic norms are often perceived as unworldly and, therefore, religious involvement is often seen as inappropriate both by religious people steeped in the old values and by the secular politicians themselves. In fact, invoking religious authority for political decisions runs the risk of investing partial, temporary actions with claims of absolute authority. These claims can endanger both the freedom of others and the pluralism which the democratic system needs to function well. Therefore, through tacit agreements, the religious types tend to withdraw and allow secular people to represent all interests including their own. A parallel situation is the case of Father Robert Drinan who, in 1980, was instructed by the Pope to end his career as a congressman on the grounds that he should return to religious vocation and service. It is true that this concept of separating religion from political life was challenged by the rise of the Moral Majority and other political evangelical groups. However, the new political involvement was a reaction reflecting the feeling that the secular representatives had betrayed or failed to represent the concerns of the religious sector.

Lay leaders are particularly suited for effectiveness in the third era. They earn their authority, be it from money, knowledge, or competence in directing people. Rabbis also earn their wisdom or standing but once they receive the title or role of rabbi, they are automatically vested with all the associations of authority and tradition. There is a short-run advantage in getting such extra authority. On balance, however, the rabbinic aura weakens the effectiveness of rabbis, serving as a "protective tariff" which insulates them from the competition of an open society. Worst of all, the overtones give a sacramental halo to Rabbinic communications and to the synagogue which *reduces* credibility in the age of the deepest hiddenness of God.

For many people, the same sacramental quality puts the rabbi and synagogue out of their range of hearing and reduces the desire for contact. For such people, the Jewish lay leadership who meet them in secular settings are the only possible connecting links between themselves and the Jewish past and traditions. For such people, the lay leader is their only rabbi. Lay leaders appear as normal, everyday people. Their claims are seen thereby as more tentative and more likely to acknowledge other's claims. Their guise of secularity naturally makes the activities they offer a part of the new era. Therefore, if the deeper levels of religion and spirituality in these activities are perceived or articulated by the lay leadership, then the effect can be extraordinary. The danger is that the laypeople, lacking the spiritual insight, may be unable to see this significance. Thus, the secularity of the age does not mean the end of rabbinic influence. Rabbis can become educators, teachers and insight givers to laypeople who in turn can communicate them in the secular reality. In an age when laypeople are rabbis, rabbis can become rabbis' rabbis and may actually increase their influence in the process.

One more factor increases the stature of lay leadership. The changed Jewish condition has moved the larger issues into the realm of the lay leaders and moved the overtly religious issues away from the center of life. People grow to fullest stature when they deal with the largest issues. Some years ago, Arthur Hertzberg bemoaned the disappearance of great Rabbinic leaders, such as Abba Hillel Silver, who once led the Jewish community. Such leaders attained their stature in the secular or power areas of life, but even so, the shift in the equilibrium means either that greater leaders go where the action is or that, despite their talents, rabbis are reduced in size by the smallness of the concerns with which they deal. The synagogues' smaller concerns often attract smaller lay leaders which further shrinks the growth of the rabbis.

Yet the blame does not rest entirely on the rabbis. Many rabbis feel that synagogues offer a poor environment for their own personal and spiritual growth. Pettiness, overuse of the rabbi, and excessively formal roles often deny rabbis the opportunity to form friendships or even let their hair down and are frequently mentioned as factors that erode rabbis' personal and spiritual resources. The entire community should be concerned. Investments in retreats, sabbaticals and rabbinic fellowship groups would enrich the entire Jewish people. In the interim, the entire process steadily moves leadership and power toward laypeople.

The emerging lay leadership, however, does have some serious weaknesses. It is shaped all too much by the assimilationist forces of modern culture and does not know enough of the Jewish past or traditional resources.

When the second era of Jewish history emerged, the Rabbis were able to bring the riches of the Biblical era with them. They were masters of the Biblical text, models, and experience. While they modified, translated and even transformed the Biblical message, they fundamentally linked their own teaching to the Biblical text. Their teachings grew out of a creative hermeneutic on Jewish text and Jewish history and thus the Rabbis enriched the vocabulary and instruments of Jewish culture rather than reduced them. Despite the loss of direct revelation and the sacramental cult, the tradition emerged with a greater variety of methods, models and teachings.

There is a real danger that due to ignorance, the lay leadership could seriously impoverish Jewish life. By default, they may cast away major elements in Judaism's vast arsenal of communication, value-shaping teachings and observances. A Judaism cut off from its first and second era elements would be a tragically weakened and impoverished way of life. It may be that we are witnessing the emergence of an internalized, secularized Judaism that can maintain itself with little outward, traditional symbolism, concrete observances or memories of the past. Maybe voluntary Judaism will be relatively indistinguishable from the American way of life. But it is more likely that as-similation and dissolution will follow. Even if it doesn't collapse, such a Juda-ism would probably become not holy secularism but wholly secularist.

An obvious crisis of continuity has struck the Jewish community over the past two centuries and the crisis has deepened with the impact of the open society. This supports the notion that a modern bowdlerized Jewish culture and way of life won't do. Past Jewish history suggests that the better way to proceed is to educate the laypeople and help them recover the viable past.

A second weakness of the new lay leadership is that it is more equipped for action than for the transmission of values and of the will to go on being Jewish. Here we can invoke the principle that the new secular institutions are too important to be left to lay leaders exclusively. By taking up the chal-lenge of working in the third era, rabbis and synagogues, as well as new insti-tutions such as retreat centers, Holocaust memorial centers and Jewish Stud-ies departments, can help the lay leadership overcome the crisis of continuity. This could insure that a rich Jewish culture deeply steeped in the past can be the medium of Jewish survival.

The key to achieving these goals is the re-creation of Jewish commu-nity. Within the community, values, identities and knowledge can be com-municated. Lay leaders and others who are properly trained and educated can provide personal models of Judaism, Jewish living and Jewish values in action. Their witness is the key to encouraging other Jews to identify as Jews and with the community. An important dimension, the dimension of cele-bration and joy, must be recaptured for Jewish living. To be a Jew is not just to feel compelled to help other Jews in trouble, or to be scarred by the Holo-caust or to be attacked by anti-Semitism. To be a Jew is to taste the flavor of Jewish history every day whether through eating food or through the mind. It is to experience a special sort of family life or to be regularly exposed to models of wisdom, compassion, sacrifice and heroism. It is to dance on a Shabbat evening, on Simhat Torah, at a Purim masquerade, at a wedding, in front of a Russian consulate or the Western Wall. When these experiences are recovered, then people will choose to be Jewish not by the definition of a hostile world but by the deeply human choices of destiny, memory and meaning and of fulfillment in family and self.

To achieve these goals, the synagogue will have to reshape itself as a community and function as an agency of learning and transmission both for its own membership and for the rest of the community. The Federations and Jewish community centers will have to make themselves over into vehicles of tradition, transmission and educational growth. This does not mean that each agency will lose its distinctive character and function. It does mean that there will be an exchange of agendas and a willingness to work together to strengthen one another. The joint goal is to recover a sense of the overall destiny and mission of the people of Israel so that the institutions can make a contribution to the common cause.

NEW SCRIPTURES, NEW REVELATIONS

Each great era of Jewish history has spawned a sacred literature of its own. The revelations and teachings of the Jewish way have been entered into that literature and each literature has been centrally shaped by the dominant historical event of the period. Moreover, each has reflected the method of revelation of the era.

The Bible is the classic distillation of the first cycle of Jewish history. It is shaped by the Exodus and its central message is that of redemption. The struggle of the people of Israel to cope with historical experience and the mission of the Jews is recorded in these books. The manifest God thunders forth the revelation in the Bible and the prophets bring the direct word of God to the people.

The Talmud is the authoritative work of the Rabbinic era. Its content and emphasis is profoundly affected by the destruction of the Temple and the exile of Israel. While redemption is the ultimate goal, the method and way to that goal is reshaped by historical experience and a new understanding of the human-divine partnership. Although heavenly voices and messengers appear throughout the Talmud, it is the Rabbis' reflections on the Scriptures and their deductions, applications and analogies from the Biblical texts and models that make clear what God wants of Israel. Of course, there is a great deal of further development beyond the Talmud but the legal models and precedents of those books remained dominant until almost the end of the Rabbinic era.

In order to deny Christian claims that further revelations had superceded Judaism, and because the model of the more hidden God suggests that the age of manifest revelation was over, the Rabbis did not apply the term of revelation to their own work. They officially subordinated the authority of the Oral Law to that of Scripture. Yet, in fact, the Rabbis and their interpretations and rulings attain the level of revelation *in effect* as well as *de facto* authority. Revelation is not merely command or specific instructions. Revelation is the orienting direction which guides the covenantal people on its way to the goal of redemption. Only in the initial phase is Revelation experienced as direct command from the Divine. Even in Biblical times, the events such as the Exodus are as much revelation as are God's words of instruction. Indeed, one might say that the revelation at Sinai is only putting into words, commandments and actions the implications of the Exodus event. When an event reaches the magnitude of the destruction of the Temple and leads to the reorientation of the understanding of the covenant and of the direction, methods and obligations of Israel in the march to redemption, it is, in fact, revelation. The revelation in the Rabbinic period, however, is more indirect and hidden as is appropriate to the theological environment.

The same principle applies to the emerging third cycle of Jewish history. If the thesis of this paper is correct, then the covenantal way is undergoing a major reorientation in light of the Holocaust and the rebirth of Israel. We are living in an age of renewed revelation. In retrospect, this should have been anticipated because it is implicit in the Jewish model of a way to redemption in which later events illuminate and shed new light on the original redemption patterns and commandments.[44] The original goal always remains the same but the content of the goal emerges in history. The best proof that this is recognized as revelation is that the later events carry as much theological weight as the initial events. Most remarkably, Jeremiah articulated this model in his prophecy that "behold the days will come, says the Lord, when they shall not say again, 'As the Lord lives, Who brought up the children of Israel from the land of Egypt' but rather: 'As the Lord lives Who uplifted and brought the children of Israel up from the land of the north, and from all the countries where I had driven them' and they shall dwell in their land."[45] In other words, God will be turned to more as the God of the return than as the God of the Exodus.

When these days come and people are oriented by new revelations, such as the restoration of Israel and the Holocaust, then there will be new "Scriptures" to express the event. In classic style, the Scriptures tell and retell the event until the Jew is caught up and says, "This is my story. I was there." The Scriptures also draw lessons and models from the event and give over commandments that respond to the event so that it can be applied to the further path of Israel toward its final, covenantal goal.

Such Scriptures are being written in our time, too. The reason that both the revelation and the Scriptures are not already recognized is that in accor-

44. Irving Greenberg, "New Revelations and New Patterns in the Relationship of Judaism and Christianity," *Journal of Ecumenical Studies* 16:2 (Spring 1979): 249–267.
45. Jeremiah 23:7–8; Jeremiah 14:14–15.

dance with the nature of the third era, they are, by definition, hidden. The destructive event and the redemptive one are so obscured, flawed and ambiguous that it is easy to miss their religious significance altogether. Yet any other kind of claim for these Scriptures, such as self-evident authority, would be, like prophecy in the Rabbinic era, inappropriate. The Scriptures of the new era are hidden. They do not present themselves as Scripture but as history, fact and, sometimes, as anti-Scripture. Revelation has been successfully obscured thanks to the deep hiddenness of the events and the continuing grip of modern ideas which seemingly cut off human culture from revelation channels. The inherited traditions in Judaism and Christianity that there will be no further revelation, which are defensive and designed to protect them from supercession, also serve to block consciousness of revelation by dismissing it in advance. Yet the Scriptures are being written. They are the accounts that tell and retell the event, draw its conclusions and orient the living. In the Warsaw Ghetto, Chaim Kaplan wrote in his journal: "I will write a scroll of agony in order to remember the past in the future."[46] When the Germans finally abandoned Auschwitz, Primo Levi wrote, despite his secularism and assimilationist background: "in that hour the memory of biblical salvation in times of extreme adversity passed like a wind through our minds."[47]

Nor are the Scriptures restricted to writing alone. One cannot view Chaim Guri's The Last Sea with its incredible films of the exodus from Poland to Palestine—of journeys over rocks and mountains, through endless seas and detention camps, to the beaches and cities of Palestine—without feeling that here is an account, no less grand than Biblical accounts, of the Exodus of our time. And do the lives of survivors who have lived through hell, whose families and loved ones passed through the fires of death, yet who renewed their hopes, their lives and families, fall short of the account of Jacob's struggle or Ruth's odyssey from the despair of death to the redemption of renewed life? It is too early to say which accounts will enter the canon which will become the permanent common possession of the Jewish people. There may be no official establishment of literature this time, in keeping with the more hidden character of the Scriptures. However, we must be open to hear the story, to enter into it until it becomes part of our lives as well. Those that understand and respond can become part of this revelation movement with its enormous significance for the covenant and for the hope of the world.

46. Chaim Kaplan, The Warsaw Diary of Chaim Kaplan, rev. ed., trans. and ed. Abraham I. Katsh (New York: Collier Books, 1973), p. 30.

47. Levi, Survival in Auschwitz, p. 43.

One more implication flows from the pattern of the previous cycles. In the past, what happened to the Jews influenced the rest of the world. Through the Bible, the experiences of Isaac and Moses, of David and Ruth, became part of the human story and through Christianity and Western culture formed the values of humanity. The Talmud impressed Islam, Christianity and Western legal procedures and affected the destiny of the world. We should expect no less than that in the third era. Jewish experience will remold the world.

Intimations of this fact have already appeared in contemporary history. Israel's anti-colonial revolt in 1946—a response to the bitter lessons of power-lessness in the Holocaust—helped set off a world-wide chain-reaction which ended Western political control and brought the Third World into being. Although the oil power of the Arabs has temporarily blocked its role, Israel has been a model of agricultural liberation and the transformation of population from pre-modern passivity to modern productivity without total loss of self or past values. Israel's model is full of flaws but that is inescapably part of real-life, secular redemption.

Another example of the paradigmatic role of Jewish events is the United States' recent encounter with the Holocaust. The appointment of the President's Commission on the Holocaust, the acceptance of its recommendations by congressional legislation and the establishment of the United States Holocaust Memorial Council constitute a commitment by the Federal Government that the Holocaust become part of the sacred culture and memory of the entire American people. In 1979, when the flight of Vietnamese boat people was at its height, the United States government convened an international conference, took in 250,000 refugees and persuaded the nations of the world to absorb hundreds of thousands more to give them dignity and new life. The United States made clear that it did so to avoid repeating the tragic apathy and indifference of which it was guilty in 1938, when dealing with Jewish refugees at Evian. Thus, again, when the Jewish people shared its own most deeply felt suffering and struggle for life with the rest of the world, it reshaped values and brought a touch of redemption.

Many of the issues the Jewish people are wrestling with in the third era are paradigmatic challenges for the world. The tension of creating the new world without losing the memory of the past; how to self-fulfill yet avoid slipping into narcissism and the dissolution of family and community; the challenge of reconciling dignity through nationalism with the needs of other people; and the need to reconcile patriotism with multiple loyalties lest nationalism metastasize into imperialism and aggression are the issues being confronted by the Jewish people every day. The Jewish people has the opportunity to draw strength from its past, from its balance of family and self and from its ongoing covenant to create a model nation and a model Diaspora community. Since this will take place in real life, even if it is successful it will not be perfect. Other nations will undoubtedly explore the same issues and educate the Jews as well as the rest of the world. Still, an effective response to these challenges would mark this as a great creative period of Jewish history, the third great cycle of rebirth of the Jewish people and of its covenant. The model would be studied and imitated everywhere. Again, the ancient covenantal blessing would be fulfilled: "Through you—in you—will the nation-families of the earth be blessed" (Genesis 12:3).

Index

ABOUT THE EDITORS

Rabbi Ronald H. Isaacs has been the spiritual leader of Temple Sholom in Bridgewater since 1975. He received his doctorate in instructional technology from Columbia University's Teacher's College. He is the author of numerous books, including *Jewish Family Matters: A Leader's Guide* and *Loving Companions: Our Jewish Wedding Album*, coauthored with Leora Isaacs; *The How To Handbook for Jewish Living*, coauthored with Kerry M. Olitzky; and *Becoming Jewish*. Rabbi Isaacs is currently on the editorial board of *Shofar* magazine and serves as first vice president of the New Jersey Rabbinical Assembly. He resides in New Jersey with his wife, Leora, and their children, Keren and Zachary.

Rabbi Kerry M. Olitzky, D. H. L., is director of the School of Education at Hebrew Union College–Jewish Institute of Religion, New York, where he also directs its graduate studies program. He writes and lectures widely on topics related to innovative religious education and spiritual renewal. In addition, he is a scholar in the field of American Jewish history and the author or editor of 25 books and over 100 articles. Rabbi Olitzky's recent works include *Will the Real Hero of Purim Please Stand Up?* and *Sacred Moments: Tales from the Jewish Life Cycle* (with Ronald H. Isaacs). He is the editor for Reform Judaism of the *Oxford Dictionary of the Jewish Religion* and is currently completing a reference book on the history of the American synagogue. Rabbi Olitzky and his wife, Sheryl, live in suburban New Jersey with their children, Avi and Jesse.